SEBASTIANO SERLIO
ON
DOMESTIC
ARCHITECTURE

THE ARCHITECTURAL HISTORY FOUNDATION/
MIT PRESS SERIES

————

NUMBER ONE

On Domestic Architecture, Sebastiano Serlio's Sixth Book

————

The Foundation gratefully acknowledges the support of the Ford and
Kaufmann Foundations, Skidmore, Owings & Merrill, Phyllis Lambert,
Samuel I. Newhouse, Jr., and Mrs. Barnett Newman.

SEBASTIANO SERLIO ON DOMESTIC ARCHITECTURE

Different Dwellings From the Meanest Hovel to the Most Ornate Palace

*The Sixteenth-Century Manuscript of Book VI
in the Avery Library of Columbia University*

Foreword by Adolf K. Placzek

Introduction by James S. Ackerman

Text by Myra Nan Rosenfeld

THE ARCHITECTURAL HISTORY FOUNDATION, NEW YORK

THE MIT PRESS, CAMBRIDGE, MASSACHUSETTS AND LONDON, ENGLAND

Library of Congress Cataloging in Publication Data

Serlio, Sebastiano, 1475–1554.
    On domestic architecture, the sixth book.

    (The Architectural History Foundation/MIT
Press series ; 1)
    Italian text with English commentary.
    Reproduced from a ms. in Avery Library, Columbia
University.
    1. Architecture, Domestic. 2. Architecture—
Early works to 1800. I. Rosenfeld, Myra Nan.
II. Title.
NA7109.S47 1978   728   78–16112
ISBN 0–262–19174–1

THIS BOOK was set in Caledonia by Fuller Typesetting of Lancaster
printed on Mohawk Superfine by the Meriden Gravure Company
and bound by Publishers Bindery in the United States of America.

Designed by Mike Firpo

CONTENTS

Dedicated to the Memory of

Rudolf Wittkower (1901–1971)

and

William Bell Dinsmoor (1886–1973)

Foreword ✾

It is with profound satisfaction that this work is presented to the public. The nature, importance and history of this great Renaissance volume—the first compendium on domestic architecture—will be thoroughly explored by Myra Nan Rosenfeld and commented upon by James Ackerman in the following pages. Briefly, the manuscript, published here for the first time in its entirety, consists of Sebastiano Serlio's preparatory drawings and textual notes for his projected Sixth Book of Architecture. Sebastiano Serlio (1475–1554)—Bolognese painter, architect, writer and teacher—was the first of the great Cinquecento theoreticians to formulate the architectural canon of the Italian High Renaissance; he continued where Leon Battista Alberti had begun a century before and in turn ushered in the generation of Palladio and Vignola. He intended his work to encompass the entire range of architectural thought, knowledge and application, but published it in separate "books" over the years. The earliest to appear was Book IV (Venice, 1537), on the five orders. It was the first systematic guide to the rules of Doric, Ionic, Corinthian, Tuscan and Composite design, which were so all-important to his classic-minded contemporaries. Book IV also contained the prospectus for Serlio's other books. There was to be a Book I on geometry, a Book II on perspective (to include his splendid stage scenes, the ancestors of Palladio's Teatro Olimpico), a Book III on classic antiquities, a Book V on church architecture and, remarkably, a Book VI on domestic architecture. Indeed, Serlio did publish all the books he had announced—except Book VI. In 1541 Serlio moved to France. There he played an important role at the court of François I at Fontainebleau, not only as architect to the King, but as a transmitter of the Italian Renaissance to the French. Several of the buildings he built in France are still standing—parts of Fontainebleau and the great château, Ancy-le-Franc in Burgundy (drawings of which are contained in the following pages). Also, toward the end of his life, he published a little potboiler (as we would call it now), the *Extraordinario libro,* on doors and archways (Lyons, 1551). A Book VII, on "accidents" (i.e., miscellanea), was brought out after Serlio's death by the publisher Jacobo Strada, to whom the aging and impoverished architect had sold his manuscripts. But there still was no Book VI on that most intriguing of subjects—domestic architecture, although Serlio had repeatedly, with considerable pride, referred in his writings to his labors on it. In the collected works *(Tutte l'opere)* which came out some thirty years after his death, the *Extraordinario libro* was included as Book VI—which it clearly was not.

In 1920 a manuscript was deposited in the Avery Architectural Library of Columbia University. In 1924 it was formally acquired from the London bookdealer Bernard Quaritch by the then Avery Librarian William Bell Dinsmoor. It was he who, combining a great librarian's memory with a great scholar's eye, identified the manuscript (labeled Book VIII by an eighteenth-century hand) as the long-lost Book VI. It had been in England and Scotland for about one hundred and fifty years; and the watermarks on the paper mounts point to the fact that during the seventeenth and eigtheenth centuries it had been in France. In the same year, 1924, in which Dinsmoor identified the Avery

Book VI, Ernst Cassirer identified a manuscript in the Bavarian State Library in Munich as another copy of Book VI, albeit one significantly different. The differences—which enhance the interest of *both* manuscripts—will be discussed in detail in the following pages. The Munich manuscript (drawn on vellum, whereas Avery's is on paper) is a presentation copy. It was produced several years later than the Avery manuscript—after the death of François I (1547), to whom the Avery—but not the Munich—manuscript refers several times. The Avery manuscript is of particular interest because it reflects Serlio at work—as an architect of various projects in progress, as a thinker and as book producer. Pentimenti, pencil lines and pricking marks are clearly visible in many places. Personal remarks—omitted in the Munich manuscript—abound. The latter was published in facsimile by Marco Rosci (Milan, 1967).

The intention to publish the Avery version in its entirety was announced as far back as 1942 by Dinsmoor in his pioneering articles (*Art Bulletin,* March–June, 1942). But—as if to repeat Serlio's own experience—endless obstacles to the ambitious project intervened. Dinsmoor, having completed his researches, did not live to see his labors rewarded: he died in 1973. A young scholar, Myra Nan Rosenfeld, took up where he left off. As will be evident in the chapters that follow, she turned to many new aspects of Serlio's role, especially his connections with Northern art (including Dürer), and also reached some new conclusions about the internal order of the manuscript. But to publish the masterly drawings and Serlio's textual notes, as well as the essential scholarly commentary, without compromises in quality or scope seemed beyond reach. Rudolf Wittkower, as chairman of the Department of Art History and Archaeology at Columbia University, never tired of pressing for publication and searching for funds. Nor did Myra Nan Rosenfeld ever falter in her resolve and her work. It is due to the energy, resourcefulness and faith of the directors of the Architectural History Foundation that the long-desired publication of this famous manuscript has been finally realized. To the Foundation, to Myra Nan Rosenfeld, to Rudolf Wittkower and to William Bell Dinsmoor, homage and gratitude must be rendered.

Thanks to them, not only the scholars, but also the less specialized reader can now enjoy and admire a work which may be called the first typology of domestic architecture in the Western world. It ranges from thatched-roofed houses for the very poor (a concern heretofore unheard-of) to a grandiose palace for the King, the Louvre. Between lie middle-class town houses, row houses, palaces, and châteaux in the country—in fact, all manner of dwellings. All are conceived by a protagonist of the new spirit who had received his training in the Rome of Peruzzi and Bramante and produced his work in the France of François I. Thus, not only for anyone interested in French architecture and in the Italian Renaissance, but also for all students of social organization, and the history of living spaces, this book will be a unique visual source.

May, 1978   ADOLF K. PLACZEK

Introduction ✺

Sebastiano Serlio projected seven books for his architectural treatise. Six of these were published, and one, Book VI on domestic dwellings, remained in two autograph manuscript versions, the one presented for the first time to the public in this facsimile edition and a later one in the Munich Staatsbibliothek. Book VI is in some ways the most important of Serlio's works—I do not call them "writings," because they are conceived essentially as illustrations with explanatory texts. Like the preceding book on churches, Book VI consists entirely of proposals for contemporary buildings, but readers of the time would have been far more likely to turn to Serlio's plans of dwellings than to his designs of churches. Then, as now, most housing was built without architects, and there was a vast potential market for standardized models in the latest style such as Book VI would have provided had it been available in print. Builders long after Serlio's death would surely have continued to rely on this book for inspiration as they did on Palladio's publication of twenty-five years later. For today's students of the Renaissance it offers an insight into the full spectrum of domestic building problems of that age and the social and political structure that shaped them.

Serlio's architectural career was blocked, for reasons that are not clear. In his early years in Rome, he was an assistant to Baldassare Peruzzi and had no independent commissions. He moved to Venice following the Sack of Rome in 1527, at the same time as two great contemporary architects, Jacopo Sansovino and Michele Sanmicheli, who were given official positions and captured most of the important public commissions while native architects were assigned the remainder. But it is odd that a designer with the fertile imagination displayed by Serlio's published and manuscript works was almost totally rejected at a time when building in the Venetian republic was undergoing a great spurt after a generation of inactivity. Certainly his expertise was recognized: in 1534 he was appointed to a commission including Sanmicheli and Titian to advise on a proposal, based on a system of harmonic proportions, by the monk Francesco Giorgi to alter Sansovino's design for the church of San Francesco della Vigna. In 1539 he was summoned to Vicenza to consult on the project to envelop the civic "Basilica" there with a new portico; other experts in the "arte architectoria e fabricandi usu praestantes" called there for advice were the most celebrated of their generation: Sansovino, Sanmicheli, Giulio Romano, Spavento and later Palladio, who was awarded the commission for the building. Apparently some trait of Serlio's character repelled, or at least failed to attract, prospective clients. To this fact we well may owe his literary career, and the ample time permitted him to gather his thoughts, to measure ancient and modern monuments and to draw the buildings and architectural details that became a resource to generations of followers.

The Urban Revolution

Serlio's manuscript is a contribution to and evidence of one of the great social and political revolutions of Western history: the rise to power and influence of a new class—the bourgeoisie. The city was the theater of this revolution. Cities as we know them today, as dense concentrations of people governed by a more or less representative local body that provides services, water, markets, protection from external and internal coercion, public streets and gathering places, began to appear only in the later Middle Ages after a millennium of virtual disuse. This flowering was stimulated by different needs in different places; some cities grew out of markets and fairs, some were launched by grants of political and economic freedoms by kings and lords in exchange for taxes and other revenues, some were strengthened and even newly founded to guard frontiers. In the nascent city of Italy, where Serlio's social and political concepts were formed, the urban trader and artisan struggled for rights and for autonomy against the traditional aristocracy of the feudal period, whose power and wealth were based on the yield of the land. On the eve of the urban revolution the few towns that had survived the Dark Ages may have been concentrations of towered, fortress-like enclaves of extended aristocratic families, each enclave containing its own servants, soldiers, artisans, chaplains, notaries and physicians, and each claiming sovereignty over a portion of the area within the walls. San Gimigniano in Tuscany, with its forest of tall, thin family towers, is one of the few towns that still evokes its feudal origins because it failed to grow in the subsequent capitalist era, though the private enclaves were broken through to create public streets and a civic area was carved out at the center.

The documents of the self-governing cities from the twelfth to the fourteenth centuries record incessant battles by communal governments to assert public rights over private privilege in access to urban space. At the same time, the urban dweller gained increasing freedom from the obligations and protections of a feudal relationship; the artisan or the merchant could set up shop and sell his product or his labor to the public; being no longer a member of the nobleman's extended family, his residence and workshop no longer had to be attached to the family enclave. In many cities, such as Florence, Venice and the towns of the Hanseatic League, the rise of the bourgeoisie was so decisive that the richer merchants and bankers became themselves the ruling class and virtually an urban aristocracy; they built accessible palaces rather than fortified precincts, palaces designed for use by a single family and domestics, not for a mini-community representing a cross section of the whole of society. Other, lesser towns of the later Middle Ages, such as the one illustrated in fig. 38, had no individuals sufficiently eminent in either birth or wealth to distinguish themselves from other citizens by the size and elegance of their dwellings.

The dissolution of traditional bonds and the realignment of class structures in the late Middle Ages and Early Renaissance cut urban dwellers of all levels loose from their habitual locales within the city and brought about totally new spatial distributions of the population. In the older large cities, the change came about slowly, because housing, work space and institutions of earlier eras continued to serve traditional functions. But in newly built structures and districts, and in the ideal projects of the theorists, the urban configuration was altered radically. Grand squares were carved out in town centers. They were bordered by imposing structures of the municipality and the church. Rich and powerful citizens sought to build either on the major squares or along major arteries leading from them. The spatial configuration, once a cluster of separate enclaves or cells, now became one of concentric rings, with the more privileged citizens located at or near the center, and others in circumferences of shorter or longer radii according to their degree of eminence and wealth. The poor were forced to the outer periphery: Serlio places them even outside the city gates, a position traditionally indicative of disenfranchisement and denial of rights.

The city of Serlio, like that of the earlier theorists Filarete and Francesco di Giorgio, would thus have had a conical profile, with the tallest and most imposing structures at the center and the lowest and simplest in the immediate suburbs—the poorest artisans' huts are arranged in row housing one story in height (Pl. XLVIII). Likewise cleanliness and the freshness of air would have declined from an apex at the center to the foul odors and refuse produced by tanneries and slaughterhouses in the poor areas, compounded, no doubt, by the filth of unpaved streets.

Segregation of the population by trade is another innovative feature of the Renaissance theorists' city: districts would be assigned to each industry and craft, which had the effect of accelerating the separation of work space from living space. Very few of Serlio's working-class houses has a workshop area. Presumably even the merchants who tended the shops provided in his Palace for the *Podestà* (Justice of the Peace; Pl. LXII) lived elsewhere.

Serlio does not fully articulate his new conception of urban form in Book VI—he is too much a participant in an evolving social structure to see it quite in perspective. In his view, contemporary society has a highly differentiated number of socioeconomic strata which he accepts without consciousness of potential alternatives, and which he attempts to accommodate in suitable dwellings. He wants an individual's status to be exactly reflected in the height and decorative detailing of the façade and in the number, size and degree of privacy of interior spaces.

We would assume, from what Serlio tells us, that each person builds for himself the dwelling suited to his income. But that would not have been any more plausible in his time than it would be today. A dual class division must be superimposed on Serlio's multiple strata, differentiating those who own and build their own living space from those who depend on housing built by others, for which they pay in rent or services. But apparently Serlio's "artisan" housing is distinguished not only in being owned by others but, more significantly, in being built for the specific purpose of rental by developers with disposable capital. It reflects one of the revolutionary innovations of the age of capitalism. The semi-detached and duplex artisans' dwellings in Pls. XLVIII and XLIX—the first of their kind in architectural literature—were obviously designed for mass production and not as individual undertakings, along streets newly laid out for the purpose. The few developments of this kind that survive from the Renaissance are discussed by Myra Rosenfeld (pp. 44–45 below). Serlio's urban situation, in short, is that of modern Western bourgeois society, except that the tenements are designed as row housing rather than as multistoried high-rise or walk-up housing. This fact reveals what a major leap Renaissance planning as represented in Book VI has made away from the medieval city. Whether that leap can be called progress is uncertain, partly because of the absence of adequate data, and partly because the answer depends on one's system of values.

Though Serlio identified many economic strata in Book VI, they are assigned to only four classes: 1) artisan (including unskilled laborers), 2) citizen (roughly equivalent to "professional") and merchant (the notes in French translate either of these two as "bourgeois"), 3) nobility and high officers of the state, and 4) royalty. Serlio does not refer to the hierarchy of the church, though its upper strata abounded in patrons of architecture, and though one of his two château commissions came from the Ferrarese Cardinal-Legate at Fontainebleau. Apparently he believed that clerical patrons were the exact equivalents of laymen of comparable means; nothing about their dwellings was intended to symbolize or even to reveal their spiritual calling; worldly rank was what mattered. This conformed to Renaissance practice and was probably an unconsciously acquired attitude.

Serlio assumes equivalence of social and economic level as a general rule, though he recognizes that the barriers are so vague that on occasion a merchant may be able to "live more sumptuously than some gentlemen by reason of the great earnings brought by commerce" (Pl. L). At one point he implies even that there is an ethical-spiritual hierarchy of class that may raise people above—or drag them below—their economic level:

> I do not want to dedicate a house rather to a merchant than to a citizen or rich gentleman because minds are not always at the level of rank. Sometimes a very rich citizen will have a spirit so low and vile that, overcome by avarice, he will live in an old, smoky, and even ruinous house, and another citizen of modest means living with difficulty on current income will be liberal and generous, and will sell property to build a beautiful house. [Munich ms., fol. 49v.]

Serlio's suggestion that virtue may be measured in terms of one's degree of willingness to build a new house is not just the special pleading of an underemployed architect. It reflects the conviction of Renaissance intellectuals, and specifically of the French King, that to replace medieval buildings with new ones in the *all'antica* style was to participate with others of lofty purpose in a great spiritual-cultural renewal. Similar moralistic implications were imputed by Ruskin in the last century to patrons who reversed that process and replaced classical buildings with neo-medieval ones, and by the pioneers of twentieth-century architecture who sought to put an end to revivals of any sort.

The Villa

In the Sixth Book, Serlio, like Palladio a quarter of a century later, presents his domestic designs in two categories: buildings for the country and buildings for the city. But unlike Palladio, he seeks to accommodate in each case the entire social spectrum, ranging from rustic huts to grand villas and from minimal urban housing units to royal palaces. This evenhanded distribution of urban and rural projects was not typical of an Italian Renaissance architectural practice, but was a particularly Venetian phenomenon. While wealthy patrons in Rome, Florence, Milan or in the smaller states occasionally commissioned grand suburban villas, Venetians of Serlio's generation were moving onto the mainland—called the *terraferma*—in unprecedented numbers. Writing shortly after 1500, the Venetian patrician Girolamo Priuli mourned the abandonment by his compatriots of their glorious, virile and enriching seafaring tradition in favor of the debilitating pursuit of agriculture or simply of leisure:

> There is no citizen, nobleman or working man who, having the means, has not bought at least a piece of land and a house in the terraferma, and particularly in the provinces of Padua and Treviso, since these places are nearby, in order to go there to relax and to return in a day or two. . . . Nowadays, to tell the truth, the young Venetian nobles and citizens, who earlier in this epoch used to attend to navigation and to earning, pursue relaxation, pleasure, falconing, the making of houses and aviaries at enormous expense and, having once been merchants, are now farmers without the slightest experience of the things of the world.

The country buildings of the Veneto were thus quite unlike those of the rest of Italy, which were typically palatial retreats for lavish entertainment set in formal gardens, designed for powerful dignitaries of the church or the state and, more rarely, persons of private wealth like the banker Agostino Chigi, for whom Serlio's mentor Baldassare Peruzzi built the Farnesina Villa in Rome. Serlio had included three examples of this kind in his Third Book, published in Venice in 1540: the Belvedere Court in the Vatican, Villa Madama in Rome and Poggioreale in Naples, all of which he must have illustrated from drawings made before his departure for Venice in 1527. The demand for villas of this sort continued throughout the Renaissance in many parts of Italy, the Palazzo del Te in Mantua and the Villa d'Este in Tivoli being characteristic examples built contemporaneously with the earlier and later years of Serlio's career.

What distinguished the Venetian *terraferma* phenomenon from that of the other states of Italy was not just that, on Priuli's evidence, the patronage represented almost the entire economic and social spectrum; it was the fact that the villas, though they provided delightful environments for relaxation, were virtually all working farms. They represented a revival of the villas described by ancient Roman writers such as Pliny, Virgil, Cato and Varro, and their owners, despite Priuli's polemic appeals to the contrary, typically interested themselves deeply in agriculture and land reclamation—sufficiently, in the case of large landholders, to counterbalance the decline of income from maritime commerce. This explains why Serlio was concerned in the designs and accompanying texts to provide a majority of the villa schemes with working areas, and why a number of the designs have, in addition to the main dwelling, outbuildings for the accommodation of tenant farmers and their equipment (the more elaborate villas would have isolated such accommodations in more distant places).

Thus the middle-sized projects in the Sixth Book correspond closely with Venetian *terraferma* practice of the mid-sixteenth century. For obvious reasons, the more modest huts proposed by Serlio were not destined to be and never had been architect-designed: the impoverished *contadini* lived in round mud hovels with floors of earth and thatched roofs; and, at the other end of the spectrum, there were in the Venetian Republic no viceroys, princes or kings to build on the scale of the more elegant projects proposed to Serlio's royal patron.

How applicable the Venetian villa type would have been to conditions elsewhere in Europe is uncertain. In France, where Serlio sought to get support for the publication of his book, the countryside remained in the hands of the landed aristocracy and was cultivated by peasants in a virtually feudal condition. There could not have been a body of lower- and middle-class city dwellers seeking to invest capital in modest rural estates for the pursuit of pleasure and gain through agriculture. Thus, the numerous designs for "citizens or merchants" appearing on plates II–VI of the manuscript would probably not have been of interest to that social stratum. Even Serlio's term "citizen" is peculiarly Venetian: it was the designation for a legally distinct category of the population which might be designated today as the "professional" class—the doctors, lawyers and civil servants who enjoyed a considerable degree of rights and privileges, not, however, including direct participation in the legislative activities of the Republic, which was reserved to a limited number of the patrician class. Serlio's modest villas, however, might have attracted the interest of an occasional French aristocrat of moderate means whose hereditary castle needed replacement as opposed to the traditional custom of piecemeal extension. But, judging from the relatively few small châteaux newly constructed in Renaissance style in mid-sixteenth-century France, there must have been economic constraints coupled with a reluctance on the part of aristocrats outside court circles to assimilate the Italian Renaissance style.

City Houses and Palaces

The city dwellings presented in Book VI range from the meanest one-story, two-room structure outside the city walls to a royal palace. There is a significant division at the level of the first habitation devised for a "gentleman," which is to say aristocrat (Pl. LII): that palace and those which follow, for military and civic chiefs, princes and kings, are inventions that for the most part recall in some way the grander palaces of Rome and Venice. Frequently they are rich in imaginative variations on their Italian forerunners, but for two reasons they are less informative than the simple houses and mansions. First, little of the less pretentious architecture of the sixteenth century has survived to the present day unchanged; the more modest the structure, the more likely it is to have been destroyed or remodeled. Second, for each of the simpler designs Serlio matched his Italian models with French, particularly Parisian, counterparts, which he does not do for the more grand, assuming, no doubt, that his richer clients would want to adopt the Italian style, with perhaps minor accommodations to French tradition. Thus he gives a unique insight into what vernacular architecture may have been like in his time, and what differences there were from country to country, though the information has to be taken cautiously. The designs are ideal rather than actual schemes: the houses may have been no more like real dwellings than were Le Corbusier's Domino or Citrohan projects of the 1920s. Also, in his simplest buildings, Serlio seems to have been interested in the French tradition only insofar as it affected the façades.

Italy and France

Serlio's role in France was that of a purveyor of Italian Renaissance taste. François I, in inviting him to the court in 1540, may or may not have had grand building projects in mind for him; as it turned out, he commissioned no more than a relatively minor work at Fontainebleau, and Serlio had a chance to build only one villa-château for a French patron, Ancy-le-Franc, and one for an Italian, Le Grand Ferrare. Serlio, and perhaps François I himself, must have wanted this modest contribution to the great shift that ultimately interrupted the tradition of French fifteenth-century building and replaced it with Italian norms (as Myra Rosenfeld has shown in earlier studies), to be reinforced and consolidated by the power of the printed word. His Sixth Book, unlike those which preceded it, was specifically addressed to the situation in France, though its Italianate versions of many designs were calculated to attract the attention of Venetians and other Italians.

The fact that Serlio's effort to lead the French out of what some progressive arbiters of taste regarded as medieval darkness into the light of the *maniera antica* did not blind him to the virtues of the French tradition is extraordinary in a culture as ethnocentric as that of Renaissance Italy. I do not believe that his decision to present the projects of his more modest dwellings in a French version as well as an Italian one is to be attributed simply to his hope of attracting French patronage for his publication. He confesses, indeed, to have learned something from the French medieval tradition: "Although the French articulate their buildings," he says, "in a way that is different from ours, nonetheless they have the same comfort" (Pl. IV). From today's perspective, in fact, they may have been more comfortable, particularly with respect to personal privacy: the French frequently provided corridors that skirted bedrooms, while the Italians invariably made all but the end rooms in a file so that private chambers doubled as public passages (Pls. IV, VI–VII). The other significant aspects of French tradition apparent in the projects of Book VI are the high pitched roofs with dormer windows (or, in the case of some urban designs, windows within the gables), tall, thin windows to admit greater light, and the avoidance of ground-floor porticoes, all traceable to climatic differences between the Mediterranean and central France.

Serlio's Achievement

It would not be quite just to compare Serlio's unexecuted designs with the villas and palaces of his contemporaries who executed many buildings. Ideal schemes unavoidably are conceived without the constraints and stimuli provided by clients, by the need to accommodate specific functions and ideals or by the character of a particular site. Serlio's one surviving residence, Ancy-le-Franc, shows how different an actual building can be from the architect's initial preparatory designs (compare figs. 11, 12 and Pls. XVI–XVIII), even in a situation where the client was at hand and, presumably, a site was established. Still, the

verdict of later criticism has been that Serlio was not as original or as gifted an architect as his contemporaries who succeeded in getting the major commissions in Italy. He had, however, an exceptionally fertile imagination in conceiving variations and enrichments—*invenzioni,* in the professional language of the time—of the ideas he had absorbed in Rome, Bologna, Venice and France. He demonstrates this gift in his published *Extraordinary Book on Doors,* a collection of lavish, mannered fantasies that stimulated the imagination of generations of later designers of garden portals—a genre that has always invited whimsy. He was a veritable sponge for the innovative designs of his time, and this was a great virtue in one who was to become the pioneer of the architectural pattern book, the first in a succession that continued up to the present day, of architects whose published drawings and commentaries served both to stimulate the art and to record its evolution.

Palladio was an early beneficiary of this achievement; no doubt he was inspired by Serlio to publish in 1570 a volume that capitalized on the essential innovation of a text made subordinate to illustration, a book the success and influence of which would depend almost entirely on the woodcuts, and which could survive essentially untarnished through many editions with newly copied plates, often adjusted to suit the taste of later ages. In illustrating his own inventions for country and city dwellings (that division follows Serlio's), Palladio could, unlike Serlio, turn to an abundance of drawings that had been commissioned by the wealthy patrons of Venice and the *terraferma.* And, since these patrons were all in more or less the same economic condition, the *Quattro Libri* differs from its forerunner by not undertaking to offer models for a wide spectrum of clients: there is nothing for those of low or modest income, and nothing for princes and kings. But a number of Palladio's solutions are similar to Serlio's middle range; Dr. Rosenfeld illustrates an instance in comparing Plates V and VII to figures 78 and 81 (early drawings for villas in the *Quattro Libri*). Palladio's book was incalculably influential—more so than any architectural book ever published. His villas and palaces, conceived for the Veneto, proved to accommodate the social and aesthetic aspirations and the economic condition of centuries of European and American middle- and upper-class patrons. Serlio would undoubtedly have shared some of that fame if Book VI had been printed: because it remained in manuscript, Palladio got all the glory.

But one factor in Palladio's success was absent from Serlio's projects: the harmonic system of proportions that underlies the measurements indicated on the plans, sections and elevations. Serlio did not concern himself much with measurements, beyond indicating occasionally an approximate scale in feet, and this was not due just to the fact that the majority of his projects were ideal schemes. Nor was he particularly sensitive to proportions, as is evident from his postscript to the Munich manuscript (fol. 74r), in which he discusses the question of how to determine the heights of rooms (apparently to give the reader a key to interpreting many of the preceding drawings in which only plan measurements are provided). He criticizes Vitruvius's rule of thumb (height = ½ length + width) because it results in rooms that are too high, and suggests rather that the height of entrances and loggias be twice their width and that of rooms

Preface ✸

be equal to their width. This oversimplified system would reduce flexibility and produce exceptionally monotonous sequences of spaces; it is the antithesis of Palladio's carefully orchestrated ensembles. Weaknesses in Serlio's proportioning are especially noticeable in the treatment of elevations in which he employed superimposed orders: the columns and pilasters often look squat or inert (Pls. X, XXV, XXVII). And the grand, multistoried palace schemes tend to have an excess of small elements that draw attention away from the overall form. For this reason, the projects for small villas and houses in which the classical orders are not employed, or appear sparingly, are the most appealing; the simple forms are treated with a straightforwardness rare in Serlio's time. The minimal plans are also better conceived than those for royal monuments, some of which appear to be grandiose assemblages of abstract and functionless forms (Pl. XLVI).

But enough of criticism: Book VI is a unique treasure because in the great variety of needs it seeks to accommodate it gives us, as no other book of its age has done, an insight into Renaissance society and customs. The insight is not, of course, that of a judicious and enlightened critic of society, or analyst of the real needs of clients in the several classes. Like all artists of his time, Serlio saw the path to success in terms of accepting as his own the attitudes of the rich and powerful who might employ him to build a mansion, or at least assist him to publish a book.

Finally, the book is important for its form as well as its content, for the fact that the manuscript was prepared to exploit creatively to the full the technology of printing with illustrations, initiating a great tradition of books that communicate through their pictures, a tradition that has had untold impact on the history of architecture.

In the following pages, Myra Nan Rosenfeld distills the fruit of her many years of study on Serlio, on French Renaissance domestic architecture, and on this manuscript in particular in a text illuminating the essential issues raised by Book VI. Her work has made possible the restoration of the manuscript to its original sequence of folios, which were scrambled in the process of binding in 1919, and has facilitated our grasp of the structure of the text. I have written this introduction as an expression of the gratitude of our scholarly profession to her and to the Architectural History Foundation for making this long-anticipated volume a reality.

May, 1978   JAMES S. ACKERMAN

I have been interested in Book VI since 1967, when I was studying for an M.A. at Columbia University. In my first course on Renaissance architecture, Rudolf Wittkower encouraged the students to look at the manuscript. I am deeply indebted to Professor Wittkower for introducing me to this extraordinary document which provides the impetus for so many years of rewarding scholarship. I would like also to express my gratitude to Adolf K. Placzek, Director of the Avery Library. Without his constant support of my research over the past ten years, this project never would have come to fruition. I would also like to thank Professor James S. Ackerman, who encouraged me to look at Serlio's unorthodox side in the research we undertook in fulfillment of my studies for a Ph.D. at Harvard University; I am extremely grateful to Professor Ackerman for reading the first draft of my manuscript, in particular for his comments on the development of scientific manuals in the Renaissance. I have also benefited from Fritz Grossmann's encouragement and his knowledge of the careers of Pieter Coecke, Dürer and Brueghel. I had the opportunity of discussing with Sylvie Béguin Serlio's relationship with painters in France, and I appreciate the kind generosity of Martin Kubelik. My father, Howard Rosenfeld, unraveled some of the mathematical mysteries of Serlio's proportions and measurements in Book VI. Thanks must also go to Konrad Oberhuber, who gave me his photographs and notes on the printer's proofs of Book VI in the Nationalbibliothek in Vienna. I am grateful to the Princesse de Mérode for permitting me to study her Château of Ancy-le-Franc, and to Pierre Michel, custodian of the château. André Corboz helped me in procuring articles from libraries in Italy. The late Franco Simone aided me in understanding the literary and historical background of Renaissance France. Sir Anthony Blunt, André Chastel, Spiro Kostof, Kurt W. Forster, Stanislaw Wilinski and Lucile Golson have all given me invaluable assistance.

The staff of the Avery Library at Columbia University, in particular Herbert Mitchell and Mrs. Neville Thompson, helped me immeasurably. The research for this book would not have been possible without access to the outstanding collection of Renaissance architectural treatises in the Avery Library. I am also indebted to the staffs of the following libraries for their help: London: The Courtauld Institute, The Conway Library; The Library and Drawing Collection of the Royal British Institute of Architects, John Harris. Vienna: The Nationalbibliothek, Dr. Otto Mazal, Dr. Magda Ströbl. Munich: The Bayerische Staatsbibliothek, Dr. Hans Haucke. Paris: Bibliothèque Nationale, Département des Imprimés, Cabinet des Estampes, Jean Adhémar; Bibliothèque Historique de la Ville de Paris. Ghent: Rijksuniversiteit, Centrale Bibliotheek, Dr. K. G. Acker. New York: Pierpont Morgan Library, Dr. John Plummer; New York Public Library. Montreal: McGill University, Blackaeder Library, Mrs. Eva Doelle; McLennan Graduate Library.

I was aided in my research by the staffs of the following museums: London: The British Museum, Print and Drawing Department, Edward Croft-Murray, former Keeper; The Manuscript Department. Vienna: Kunsthistorisches Museum, Dr. Erwin Auer. Paris: Musée du Louvre, Cabinet des Dessins, Roseline Bacou; Archives des Monuments Historiques, Francine

Bercé. New York: Metropolitan Museum of Art, Department of Prints, Janet Byrne.

The initial financial support for my research and photographs was provided by a generous grant from the Canada Council in the summer of 1972. I also received aid from the McGill University Graduate Faculties in 1973, and The American Council of Learned Societies in 1975. My parents gave me both financial and moral support. I am extremely grateful to Robert Little for his understanding, support and encouragement. The Architectural History Foundation has made this publication possible.

April, 1978   M.N.R.
                                               Montreal

SEBASTIANO SERLIO
ON
DOMESTIC
ARCHITECTURE

CHAPTER I

Biographical Background: Serlio's Publications and Buildings

Sebastiano Serlio (fig. 1) wrote one of the first illustrated architectural treatises in a modern language that was printed in Europe.[1] Because he had trouble finding patronage, Serlio was obliged to publish his treatise piecemeal, book by book. The initial installment, Book IV, was published in Venice in 1537 (fig. 2). It was dedicated to the Roman orders and entitled *Regole generale di architetura sopra le cinque maniere de gli edifici, cioe Thoscano, Dorico, Ionico, Corinthio, et Composito.* In the introduction to this book, Serlio outlined his future treatise, which was to consist of seven books. The first would be devoted to geometry, the second to perspective, the third to Roman antiquity, the fifth to churches, the sixth to houses and the seventh to accidents.[2] Serlio's books were published with woodcut illustrations and letterpress text except for the *Extraordinary Book on Doors* (not one of the numbered books of the treatise), which was engraved. All the books were published eventually except for the present Sixth Book, *On Domestic Architecture.*[3]

There are two preparatory manuscripts for Book VI, one on parchment in the Bayerische Staatsbibliothek in Munich (Codex Icon. 189) and a second on French paper in the Avery Architectural Library of Columbia University. Parts of the Avery Library version were published in 1942 in a scholarly, pioneering study by William B. Dinsmoor. We are indebted to Dinsmoor for much of our basic information about Serlio's life and profession.[4] The present publication of the complete manuscript for Book VI makes accessible new information about his career as an architect and the character of his treatise. Because the Avery manuscript is a preparatory manuscript for the Munich version, it reveals the genesis of the architect's ideas. The Munich version is quite different and appears to have been edited and revised for publication, as we shall see in Chapter VI.

Serlio's *On Domestic Architecture* was one of the most influential of his writings. The projects provided subsequent generations of architects with a selection of the different types of European domestic buildings prevalent in the middle of the sixteenth century. Serlio also gave his readers a great deal of information about the relationship between patron and architect at this time. Although never published, Book VI was known to later architects from Palladio to Ledoux, who must have had access to manuscript copies. One of Serlio's most important contributions to European architecture was the standardization of the urban "row house," proposed in Book VI.

In spite of several recent discoveries, documentation of our author's life is fragmentary. A woodcut portrait found by Stanislaw Wilinski in 1971 gives us an idea of the architect's heavyset appearance. According to the letters of Guillaume Pellicier, French ambassador to Venice, Serlio was married to Francesca Palladia, a lady-in-waiting to Bona Sforza, Queen of Poland. Wilinski suggests that Serlio married late in life—in his fifties—since he was accompanied by several children when he went to France in 1540, one of whom was considered too young for the trip. The architect's constant references in Book VI to disputes with his patrons suggest a difficult personality, and the bitter tone of the treatise is probably the result of the many years he worked without success—until the age of sixty-five, when he was appointed Royal Architect to François I.[5]

According to the parish register of the church of San Tommaso della Brania, Sebastiano Serlio was born on September 6, 1475, in Bologna. He was the son of a painter, Bartolomeo Serlio.[6] Sebastiano was also trained as a painter; he was listed as such in Beatrice da Manfredi da Reggio's will

1. Giovanni Caroto: Portrait of Sebastiano Serlio. From Torello Sarayna, *De origine et amplitudine civitatis Veronae,* Verona (1540), folio Aiv, woodcut, Avery Library, AA 327 V5 Sa7.

of September 17, 1514, in Pesaro, where he had worked since 1511.[7] We do not know when Serlio went to Rome, where he became an assistant to Baldassare Peruzzi (1481–1536). He rendered Peruzzi a particularly moving homage in Book VI:

> I have not found any other important personality who has shown the brilliance and knowledge in our time of my most understanding teacher, Baldassare Peruzzi from Siena, to whom there is no one equal or superior. . . . I am only his humble disciple and heir to a small part of his knowledge.[8]

There are indications in Books III and V that Serlio was in the Vatican workshop sometime during the tenures of Bramante (1505–1514), Raphael (1514–1520) and Peruzzi (1520–1527, 1535).[9]

There is more information about Serlio's activity in Venice, where he went to live after the Sack of Rome in 1527. The first notice of his presence in Venice occurs in a will that Serlio drew up there on April 1, 1528. Lorenzo Lotto, the painter, was listed as his witness, and Giulio Camillo, an historian, was designated as his heir.[10] Venice played a leading role in Italy in the publication of illustrated books. Before Serlio's arrival, a number of such books had been published there.[11]

Between 1528 and 1536, Serlio published a series of details of the Roman orders which were engraved by Agostino Veneziano de' Musi after the architect's drawings.[12] In a letter of September 18, 1528, Serlio asked the Venetian Senate for copyright privileges for ten years for these engravings as well as for several views of Roman ruins he had drawn. In this letter he refers to himself as an "expert in architecture," *Professor di Architettura* [13] —perhaps an indication of his wish to pursue the career of an architectural consultant and writer of manuals rather than that of a practicing architect.

Sixteenth-century Italy offered no direct route to becoming a professional architect. There were no architects' guilds, and most of the important central Italian architects such as Michelangelo, Raphael, Leonardo, Giulio Romano and Peruzzi were trained as painters, as was Serlio. An exception to this rule was Antonio da Sangallo, the Younger, who worked as a carpenter in the workshop of his uncles Giuliano and Antonio, the Elder. Only in the second half of the century, after Serlio's death, did the architectural profession become more specialized. Then education became available through the reading of treatises and attendance at academies in addition to apprenticeship in an architectural workshop.[14]

In Venice, Serlio seems to have worked as a free-lance painter, sculptor and architect. Between 1528 and 1531, he produced a design for a wood soffit for the ceiling of the library of the Ducal Palace which is illustrated at the end of Book IV.[15] In 1532, Marcantonio Michiel described a painting in the house of Andrea di Oddoni that had an architectural background, designed by Serlio.[16] On April 10, 1534, he participated with Titian, Fortunio Spira and Jacopo Sansovino in a debate on the proportions of the church of San Francesco della Vigna.[17] Two years later, our architect was paid for consultation on the design of a new wood ceiling of the Scuola di San Rocco.[18] Rosci traces to this period a drawing in the Uffizi in which Serlio represented the Scuola di San Rocco and the church of San Marco.[19]

Two villas near Venice have been convincingly attributed to Serlio. Carolyn Kolb Lewis discovered that Serlio had contacts with Federico Priuli, who built a villa at Treville near Vicenza before 1533. Because of its similarity to Serlio's villas in Books VI and VII, she suggests that he

2. Sebastiano Serlio: Doric Order. Book IV, Venice (1537), folio XXI, woodcut, Avery Library, AA 520 Se621.

may have provided Priuli with designs after his arrival in Venice. The resemblance of the façade of Villa Trissino at Cricoli and Serlio's illustration of the Villa Madama loggia in Book III (folio CXLVIII) prompted Lionello Puppi's idea that the architect may also have given drawings to Giangiorgio Trissino in 1537–1538 for the renovation of his villa at Cricoli near Vicenza, since Serlio was in contact with Trissino then.[20]

While in Venice, Serio worked and traveled elsewhere in the vicinity. Between July 6, 1538, and September 25, 1539, he corresponded about the design of a sculptured altarpiece with the overseers of the church of the Madonna di Galliera in Bologna.[21] On February 15, 1539, Serlio went to Vicenza where he presented a wood model for the renovation of the Basilica. It has been suggested that his project is illustrated in Book IV.[22] It was probably at this time that Serlio constructed a wood stage in the courtyard of the Palazzo Porto in Vicenza, which he describes in Book II.[23]

By the third decade of the sixteenth century Serlio was in Verona. Torello Sarayna's book on the ancient monuments of Verona, *De origine et amplitudine civitatis Veronae*, was published in 1540 with a dedication to Serlio, whose portrait was used for the frontispiece. Although the illustrations (fig. 3) were executed by the Veronese painter Giovanni Caroto (1488–1566), Serlio may well have played a role in the production of the book.[24] At this time, the architect must also have visited the Palazzo del Te by Giulio Romano in Mantua, the Villa Imperiale by Girolamo Genga in Pesaro and the Odeon built for Alvise Cornaro by Giovanni Maria Falconetto in Padua—all monuments mentioned by Serlio in his books.[25]

Serlio had great difficulty in finding a patron in Venice who would publish his treatise on architecture. In fact, the securing of a steady job was one of the major problems of his career. In his introduction to the parchment version of *On Roman Fortifications According to Polybius (Della castramentatione di Polibio)*, Serlio lamented the lack of financial support for his undertaking:

> Here, kind reader, is the camp of Polybius often praised by literary and refined men which I have represented as a walled citadel . . . not that I think that in this century which represents the summit of avarice any one will pay to print it. . . . No great patron has decided to print it because of the brutal, rapacious avarice of everyone.[26]

Dinsmoor and Marconi have suggested that this book was written in France, but the above comments, with no mention of any other published works, would place its composition sometime before 1537, the date Book IV appeared. Only the last twelve folios are French paper, and they can be traced to Lyons between 1545 and 1549. The first twenty-three folios described above are on parchment; they must have been executed in Italy [27] because in the introduction, Serlio refers to his work on Book III, *On Antiquity*, published in Venice in 1540. There is nothing French in the building designs to indicate the book was written in France. On the contrary, the architect mentions that his reconstruction of Polybius's camp is based on the copy of a drawing of a Roman city in Dacia or Hungary that had been given to him by Marco Grimani, the Patriarch of Aquilea:

> I remember that on several occasions some years ago, the Patriarch of Aquilea, Monsignor Marco Grimani, held discussions with me about having seen in Dacia the remains of a city which was not very large but which was well organized and was a perfect square. He decided to measure it and to make a drawing of it in an even better state. He gave

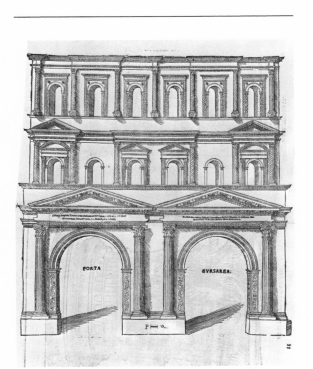

3. Giovanni Caroto: Verona, Porta dei Borsari. From Torello Sarayna, *De origine*, Verona (1540), folio 25r, woodcut.

me a copy. . . . At that time I was completely occupied with my Third Book on Antiquity. Since I had not seen the beauty and order of the above-mentioned camp and having not studied the antiquities of Dacia, I was content to rely on the gentleman who gave me the copy of the drawing.[28]

A member of the illustrious Venetian family, Marco Grimani (1494–1544) was the grand nephew of Doge Antonio Grimani and the nephew of Cardinal Domenico Grimani. He became Patriarch of Aquilea in 1529 when the seat was vacated by his brother Marino. On several occasions, Marco served as ambassador for Popes Clement VII and Paul III: in 1529, Clement VII sent him to Bologna, and between 1543 and 1544 he was in Paris for Paul III. In 1527, just before the Sack, he was in Rome and may have first met Serlio at this time. The drawing of the Roman city he gave to the architect could have been executed on one of his two trips to Jerusalem via Constantinople in 1531 and 1534. Marco's interest in classical antiquity was probably encouraged by his uncle, Domenico, who left him his collection of Roman sculpture at his death in 1523. This was the famous Grimani collection at the Palazzo di Venezia.[29]

Serlio finally found a patron in Ercole II d'Este, Duke of Ferrara (1508–1589), to whom the first edition of Book IV was dedicated on September 20, 1537. This volume was published by one of the most important Venetian publishers of the sixteenth century, Francesco Marcolini da Forlì, who was also the publisher of Aretino, Daniele Barbaro and Anton Francesco Doni. In his own preface to Book IV Serlio lists the citizens of Venice who had encouraged him in his work: Doge Andrea Gritti, Jacopo Sansovino, Michele Sanmicheli, Titian, Gabriele Vendramin, Marcantonio Michiel and Alvise Cornaro. Although this book had been prepared in Rome, Serlio must have continued to work on it in Venice, since many of the illustrations show the influence of Bolognese and Venetian architecture.[30] On October 5, just two weeks after Book IV was published, Serlio again wrote to the Venetian Senate to request copyright privileges, this time for fifteen years, and to publish his treatise on architecture in Latin so that it could be read in the rest of Europe.[31] A series of drawings in the Avery Library by an anonymous artist (fig. 4) indicate that this first book was copied in Venice immediately after it was published. Executed on sheets of fifteenth-century Venetian paper, these drawings are versions of portals in Book IV; they are more complete than the illustrations in the final edition.[32]

Ercole II unfortunately limited his help to Book IV, and Serlio was forced to look for another patron in order to continue the publication of his treatise. On November 15, 1539, Aretino wrote to Lazare de Baïf, the French ambassador to Venice, and asked for his help in obtaining the support of François I. That same year, Serlio himself wrote to Henry VIII of England. By December of 1540, temporary help arrived from Alfonso d'Avalos, Charles V's ambassador to Venice; d'Avalos supported the publication of the second edition of Book IV.[33]

In March, 1540, Book III, *On Antiquity (Il terzo libro nel quale si figurano e descrivano le antiquita di Roma e le altre che sono in Italia e fuori di Italia)*, was published in Venice, dedicated to François I. In the introduction, Serlio states that he had accepted a gift of three hundred crowns from the French King for the publication. The King's sister, Marguerite de Navarre, had already provided an annual retainer of one hundred gold crowns for Serlio, beginning January 1 of that year.[34] Ercole II, together with Aretino, may have played a role in securing François I's patronage.

4. Unknown Venetian artist: Doric Archway, after Serlio, Book IV. Venice (1537), folio Xr, brown ink and wash on paper, Avery Library, J5527, folio 7r.

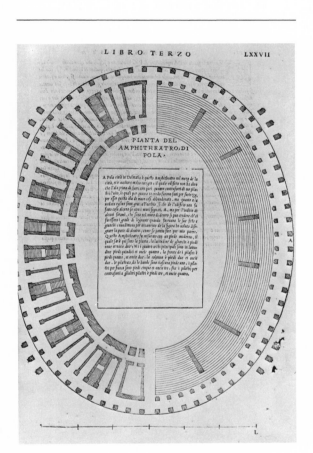

5. Sebastiano Serlio: Pola, Amphitheater. Book III, Venice (1540), folio LXXVII, woodcut, Avery Library, AA 520 Se16.

Ercole had strong ties to France: his brother, Cardinal Ippolito d'Este (1509–1572), was Archbishop of Lyons and Papal Legate to France, and his wife, Renée, was the daughter of King Louis XII. Serlio himself was following the precedent of his onetime legal heir, Giulio Camillo, who in 1535 had sought help from François I for the publication of his *World History*.[35]

On Antiquity is especially important because of the information it provides on Serlio's years in Rome—documentation of the architect's activity in Italy is sparse, with no buildings known to have been executed by him before he left for France. Book III contains Serlio's illustrations of many projects by the Vatican workshop and by Bramante: his Dome of Saint Peter's, Belvedere Courtyard and Tempietto. Illustrations such as the Villa Poggioreale at Naples were executed after drawings by Peruzzi. Serlio also illustrated the loggia of Raphael's Villa Madama. In addition to using earlier drawings he and Peruzzi had executed in Rome, Serlio must have visited the Roman monuments of northern Italy, such as the Amphitheater at Pola (fig. 5), while he was in Venice.[36]

Only at the age of sixty-five did Serlio find a stable position—as architectural adviser to François I. The last evidence of his presence in Venice is the will of the painter Francesco Zeri, to which he was a witness on July 16, 1539.[37] According to a letter of Guillaume Pellicier, French ambassador to Venice, Serlio left sometime after December 12, 1540. He had arrived at Fontainebleau by December 6, 1541, when he received the second installment of his annual stipend from Marguerite de Navarre.[38] Two weeks later, on December 27, our author received his commission from François I as a consultant for the architecture and decoration of the Château at Fontainebleau (fig. 6). Serlio was one of the first to enjoy the title of architect in France; he was called "nostre paintre et architecteur au fait de nosdits bastiments audit Fontainebleau." François I followed a precedent established by Charles VIII, who had appointed Fra Giocondo his royal architect in 1495. Serlio was paid four hundred gold crowns annually for his duties at Fontainebleau and an extra daily stipend for his visits to the other buildings of the King.[39]

François I generally prompted an Italian influence on the arts and literature. In 1530 he founded the Collège de France in Paris under the direction of Guillaume Budé to encourage the teaching of humanist philosophy.[40] With the appointments of the painters Rosso, in 1530, and Primaticcio, in 1532, François I instituted an enclave of Italian artists at Fontainebleau. Vignola and Benvenuto Cellini arrived from Italy the same year as Serlio.[41]

6. Jacques Androuet du Cerceau: Fontainebleau, château. From *Les plus excellents bâtiments de France*, Paris (1579), Vol. II, folios 10–11, Bibliothèque Nationale, Cabinet des Estampes.

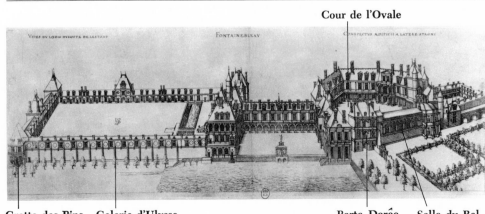

Cour de l'Ovale

Grotte des Pins   Galerie d'Ulysse   Porte Dorée   Salle du Bal

The French King was interested in printing and had named Geoffroy Tory royal printer in 1530. Several architectural treatises had been published in France before Serlio's arrival: Latin editions of Alberti's treatise, *De re aedificatoria* (Florence, 1485), were published in Strasbourg (1511) and in Paris (1512). Diego de Sagredo's *Medidas del Romano* (Toledo, 1526) was translated into French and brought out in Paris in 1539 as *Raison d'architecture*. Dürer's treatise on fortification, *Zu Befestigung der Stett, Schloss und Flecken* (Nuremberg, 1527), was published in Latin in Paris in 1535 as *De urbibus arcibus castellisque*.[42]

Italian influence was common in buildings commissioned by François I even before Serlio came to France. The centralized, Greek cross plan of the keep of Chambord (1519) was inspired by Leonardo da Vinci's drawings. The Porte Dorée, the entrance to the Château of Fontainebleau (1528–1540), resembles the entrance of the Palazzo Ducale in Urbino. The galleries facing the town of Blois in the château that François I built there between 1514 and 1524 were modeled on Raphael's Vatican Loggie.[43] François I had also commissioned Leonardo during his years in France (1517–1519) to build a new town at Romorantin in the Loire Valley; although the project was abandoned, it is known through Leonardo's drawings.[44]

Serlio's main purpose in coming to Fontainebleau was to publish the rest of his treatise, but he was also interested in studying Roman buildings in France. In the dedication of Book III, *On Antiquity*, he states:

> I shall not speak here of all the other monuments which are located in the kingdom of your majesty because I shall reserve the right to treat them when I please and when I will have seen and measured these marvels. I shall make drawings of all these monuments as I have done for the other buildings and I shall publish them with my other works.[45]

7. Sebastiano Serlio: Fontainebleau, château, Grotte des Pins (1541–1546). (Robert Little)*

While at Fontainebleau, Serlio published Books I and II, *On Geometry and Perspective (Il primo [secondo] libro d'architettura;* Paris, 1545). Both volumes were dedicated to François I and included a French translation by Jean Martin. Book II, with its projects for different types of stage sets, tells us something about the architect's earlier career.[46] These two works were followed by Book V, *On Churches (Quinto libro d'architettura nel quale se tratta de diverse forme de tempii),* published in French and Italian in Paris in 1547 and dedicated to Marguerite de Navarre. Although begun in Italy, Book V must have been completed in France, since Serlio includes an example of a French church design; it provides a great deal of information about Serlio's training in the Vatican workshop and his use of Peruzzi's church plans.[47]

The numerous allusions to François I in the text of Book VI indicate that Serlio probably began work on it, also, while he was at Fontainebleau. At the same time, the architect was working on an initial parchment manuscript for Book VII, *On Accidents (Il settimo libro d'architettura nel qual si tratta di molti accidenti;* now in the Nationalbibliothek in Vienna, Codex S.N. 2649). One of this manuscript's folios bears the date 1542. By 1547, Serlio states in his introduction to Book V that most of Book VII was already finished: "And the book on accidents (that has never been written about) which is in large part already finished. . . ."[48] Most of Book VII, like Book VI, is devoted to domestic architecture, although at the end Serlio also discusses the erection of buildings on irregular sites and the restoration of old houses.[49] The introduction to the *Extraordinary Book on Doors*

* Where the name of a photographic source is not indicated in parentheses, the print has been supplied by the institution owning the work.

8. Francesco Primaticcio: Minerva, Drawing for Ceiling Decoration of the Grotte des Pins. Red chalk on beige paper, Louvre, Cabinet des Dessins, Inv. no. 8552. (Réunion des musées nationaux)

9. Sebastiano Serlio: Fontainebleau, château, Salle du Bal (1541–1550). (Archives des Monuments Historiques)

(*Extraordinario libro di architettura*) indicates this book, too, was composed at Fontainebleau although it was published in Lyons in 1551:

> Finding myself continually in the solitude of Fontainebleau where for the present time I am to be seen rather in the company of wild beasts than men, and having brought my long task to an end . . .[50]

Finally, Serlio began, at Fontainebleau, to copy his earlier parchment version of Polybius's *On Roman Fortifications* for publication in France; this second version is lost. At this time he was living at the house of Ippolito d'Este. According to a letter of May 5, 1546, from Giulio Alvarotti to Ercole II d'Este, Serlio began to copy the earlier parchment drawings he had executed in Venice. Alvarotti wrote:

> Piero Strozzi is reading the Encampment of Polybius which Cesano has had illustrated by a certain Sebastiano of Bologna who is living in the house of Monsignor, the brother of your excellency. He is the architect of your brother's house at Fontainebleau. . . .[51]

Piero Strozzi, Chamberlain of François I, was the nephew of Lorenzo Strozzi to whom Machiavelli dedicated *The Art of War*. Gabriele Cesano was Ippolito d'Este's secretary. In 1543, Marco Grimani came to France, on his way to Scotland and England, to see Ippolito d'Este. Serlio may have consulted with him about his second interpretation of Polybius.[52]

François I died on March 31, 1547. With the advent of Henri II, Serlio lost his position at Fontainebleau and was replaced by Philibert Delorme on April 3, 1548. When Marguerite de Navarre died the next year Serlio also lost her retainer, and again found himself without work. Sometime before 1550, when he met Jacopo Strada, Serlio went to live in Lyons.

Serlio may have gone to Lyons with his patron, Ippolito d'Este, who had been Archbishop of Lyons since 1540. In any event, Ippolito was in Lyons on September 23, 1548, for Henri II's Triumphal Entry for which the Archbishop had commissioned three of the decorations, and he left France definitively for Italy on May 26, 1549, at the end of his term as Papal Legate. The year Serlio arrived in Lyons is difficult to establish. He was not listed in the preparations for the Triumphal Entry of 1548, but it is possible, in fact, that he was in the city as early as 1547 when there were payments (discussed below) for the construction of a merchants' square which he designed. Lyons was a book-printing center and Serlio must have gone there to try to get support for the completion of the publication of his treatise.[53] He must have continued to receive some royal subsidization, since the Lyons edition of his *Extraordinary Book on Doors* was dedicated to Henri II in 1551.[54] Serlio completed the second, Munich version of Book VI between the time he arrived in Lyons and 1550; it is dedicated to Henri II and most of the references to François I that appear in the first, Avery version have been eliminated.[55] As we shall see in the next chapter, Serlio probably continued to work on the Avery manuscript in Lyons.

During the reign of François I, Serlio was active as a practicing architect. However, only five of the structures discussed in Books VI and VII are known to have been built while he was in France. According to Boris Lossky, Serlio was hired to submit ideas to Gilles le Breton, master mason for the Château of Fontainebleau from 1528 to 1548. Indeed there is no record of any payment to Serlio for the actual buildings at Fontainebleau; we possess only the document of his appointment.[56] Two parts of the château can definitely be attributed to Serlio: the Grotte des Pins and the

Salle du Bal. The Grotte des Pins was built between 1541 and 1543, at the end of the Galerie d'Ulysse, now destroyed except for part of its rusticated loggia (fig. 7), located under the gallery. Its original state is represented in the engraving by Jacques Androuet du Cerceau (fig. 6) and in an etching by the L.D. Master. Louis Hautecoeur discovered that Serlio had discussed his original project commissioned by François I in both manuscripts for Book VI. A version of the project as it is presented in our plate XXXIII is an independent round building with a rusticated loggia on the ground floor and an open pavilion above crowned by a dome.[57] There is also evidence that Serlio played a role in the interior decoration of the Grotte des Pins. Two drawings by Primaticcio survive for the fresco decoration of the ceiling of the ground-floor loggia. One shows Juno, the other, Minerva (fig. 8) seated in a pergola and represented in *di sotto in sù* perspective. Primaticcio's use of an architectural backdrop for his ceiling decoration in the adjacent Galerie d'Ulysse is extremely rare. On only one occasion, in the scene of *Minerva Visiting Jupiter and Juno*, did he use such a backdrop.[58] Serlio, on the other hand, suggested the use of illusionistic architecture at the end of Book IV in a discourse on vault decoration:

> If you wish to decorate vaulted ceilings in other ways, you will be wise to imitate the remains of Roman monuments. You can depict figures from cameos or other similar things; even a tempietto, or other architecture can be added with the above so that everything can be painted on ceilings. . . .[59]

The Salle du Bal (fig. 9) is located at the south side of the Cour de l'Ovale. Serlio illustrated his original project in the Vienna manuscript for Book VII (fig. 10). In the text, he stated that the exterior of the final building was transformed by a French master mason (who must have been Gilles le Breton):

> Note dear reader that a similar building is found in the splendid castle of Fontainebleau. However, the orders are different since they were changed by a French mason. . . .[60]

According to payments made to masons in 1541, the Salle du Bal was begun that year, after Serlio's arrival. When he left Fontainebleau, the masonry barrel vault he had planned for the second story was changed to a wood ceiling that was executed by Scibec de Carpi. Serlio has outlined these changes in Book VII; they were directed by Philibert Delorme.[61]

There is reason to believe that plates XLV–XLVII illustrate a project for the modernization of Gilles le Breton's Cour de l'Ovale at Fontainebleau. A portico in the interior of the court may be part of this unfinished project.[62]

Serlio also built a house for Ippolito d'Este at Fontainebleau. Although only the portal of the entry wall to the courtyard remains, its original state is represented in Book VI (Pl. XI). The house was begun in 1542, when there was a payment to two French masons, Jean and Toussaint Richer, and finished by 1546, when Giulio Alvarotti described the building and its interior decoration in a letter to Ercole II on May 5. On October 16, the Cardinal mentioned that the house was completed in a letter to his brother.[63] A recent attempt by François-Charles James to take the authorship of this building away from Serlio should be discounted since Serlio himself states in Book VI:

10. Sebastiano Serlio: Preparatory Drawing for Salle du Bal. Vienna, Nationalbibliothek, Codex S.N. 2649, folios 80v–81r, ink on parchment.

11. Sebastiano Serlio: Ancy-le-Franc, château, North Façade (1541–1546). (Archives des Monuments Historiques)

While I am speaking of villas for gentlemen, it is not out of order for me to discuss the present project which the Cardinal of Ferrara commissioned me to build in Fontainebleau several years ago. . . .[64]

While at Fontainebleau, Serlio designed the Château of Ancy-le-Franc in Burgundy for Count Antoine de Clermont-Tonnerre, the brother-in-law of Diane de Poitiers (figs. 11, 12).[65] The château still stands, but considerably altered from the initial project illustrated here (Pls. XVI–XVIII). Antoine de Clermont-Tonnerre demanded changes in the original design which Serlio discusses in both versions of Book VI. In the present volume he states:

Although this building is in France, the Patron wanted a completely Italian building. . . .[66]

12. Sebastiano Serlio: Ancy-le-Franc, château, Interior Courtyard (1541–1546). (Author)

Rustication was removed from the exterior, Doric pilasters were added and the elevation of the interior courtyard was changed to include a paraphrase of the Belvedere Courtyard. The material in Book VI contradicts Jean Guillaume's hypothesis that Ancy-le-Franc was designed and built by a French architect.[67] Ancy can be dated between 1541, the year of Serlio's arrival in France, and 1550, when he completed the Munich manuscript. In our book, Serlio already speaks of the château in the past tense and mentions that the exterior walls were partly constructed. The folios of French paper on which he drew his original plan can be dated by the watermarks between 1545 and 1546; and in the Munich manuscript, Serlio mentions that the interior was not yet finished.[68] The interior painted decoration was executed mostly after Serlio's death and does not appear to have been planned by him. The Chambre des Arts, which served as a library, was begun in the 1560s and has been attributed to both Primaticcio and the Master of Flora (fig. 13). The other painted decorative ensembles were executed in the seventeenth, eighteenth and nineteenth centuries.[69]

Serlio apparently also worked for François I as a military engineer. Two lost projects for military camps, drawn for François I in Piedmont and Flanders, are listed in a 1576 inventory of Jacopo Strada's library in Vienna:

Two illustrations nine feet square . . . which were executed by Sebastiano Serlio for the King of France showing two military encampments, one in Piedmont, the other in Flanders. These two illustrations I received in France from the author himself, from his very hands.[70]

13. Sebastiano Serlio: Ancy-le-Franc, château, Chambre des Arts (ca. 1565). (Flammarion, Paris)

We also know that Serlio designed three other major projects in and around Lyons, all of which were probably built, but none of which have survived. One was a château at Rosmarino in the south of France, similar to Ancy-le-Franc (fig. 14). The second was a stock exchange (Bourse) in Lyons (fig. 15), and the third was a square for merchants' shops (Place des Marchands) in Lyons. Since the Stock Exchange appears in the Vienna manuscript for Book VII, begun in 1542, we can assume that Serlio initiated these projects while he was still at Fontainebleau.[71] Léon Charvet discovered the documents for the construction of the merchants' square, which are dated from May 6 to July 14 of 1547. The square was located on the rue de Flandres near the church of Sainte Eloi and the Place de la Douane.[72]

The last evidence we have of Serlio's presence in Lyons dates from 1552, when he participated in the entry of the Cardinal of Tournon on November 28. The year of his death is unknown. Charvet suggested that Serlio was dead by 1553, when mention is made of his wife in a document in Lyons without reference to Serlio himself. In the introduction to Book VII,

14. Sebastiano Serlio: Rosmarino, château. Book VII, Frankfurt (1575), folio 215, woodcut, Avery Library, AA 520 Se65.

15. Sebastiano Serlio: Preparatory Drawing for the Bourse, Lyons. Vienna, Nationalbibliothek, Codex S.N. 2649, folio 122r, ink on parchment.

Jacopo Strada claims that Serlio died at Fontainebleau.[73] At the end of his life, the architect's entire treatise had not yet been published. Books VI, VII and the edition of Polybius were in manuscript form. Serlio never regained the important position of architectural adviser to the King that he held under François I; his years at Fontainebleau had been the high point of his career.

After Serlio's death, Jacopo Strada published Books VII and VIII in Frankfurt. Strada was born in Mantua of Dutch parents between 1507 and 1515. He died in Vienna in 1588. In the 1550s he began his career as a goldsmith and art dealer for the Fugger family in Nuremberg. In 1556 he established his residence in Vienna and became the antiquarian and architect of Duke Albert V of Bavaria and Ferdinand I and Maximilian II of Austria.[74] In the introduction to Book VII, Strada states that he had bought the manuscript from Serlio in Lyons in 1550:

> I had many times the intention to publish this seventh book on architecture of Sebastiano Serlio, formerly architect of the most Christian king Francis I, which I received from the author in Lyons in 1550. . . . Since the above-mentioned author was old and affected by gout and worn down with fatigue, he decided to sell me everything that remained of his drawings that he had executed during his life as well as several drawings by others. All of this material he had intended to print and he had divided into many volumes. But since he did not have many years before him, and since money was not readily available, he decided to give me everything.[75]

Book VII was published in Frankfurt in 1575 in Italian and Latin with a dedication to Wilhelm Ursin, Prince of Rosenberg. According to a letter from Ottavio Strada to his father, dated September 5, 1574, the preparatory manuscript in Vienna was not used for the actual printing of the book.[76]

Jacopo Strada claimed to have published a second book by Serlio in Frankfurt, *On Roman Fortifications According to Polybius.* In the introduction to Book VII it was described as Book VIII and was ready to be printed in 1575, according to Strada:

> From the same author I obtained as well his eighth book which is concerned with war . . . and the blocks have been cut in the same way as this book and are ready to be printed.[77]

Book VIII was in fact not printed until the following year, when it was mentioned in an inventory Jacopo Strada made of his library in Vienna on September 11:

> A book of encampments of the ancient Romans which was composed at my expense in Lyons, France, by Sebastiano Serlio, a famous and brilliant man, formerly architect of the king of France. . . . The printed version has the same form as the seventh book and was printed at my expense at Frankfurt.[78]

From both descriptions of this book we can be sure that it corresponds to the edition of Polybius, now in Munich, which Serlio began in Venice and continued to work on at Fontainebleau. The folios of paper that Serlio added in France are of two types: one was used in Lyons in 1545, the other in Lyons after 1549. Thus we know that the architect must have continued to work on this manuscript after he went to Lyons in 1547–1548. Since the second version Serlio worked on at Fontainebleau is lost, and he could not have bought this paper until he returned to Lyons in 1547, he must have started a third version of his Polybius manuscript at this time. It was probably Jacopo Strada who called it Book VIII, since Serlio had not mentioned it in the outline of his treatise.[79] Strada must have sold the Munich manuscript of *On Roman Fortifications According to Polybius* to the Fugger family, since their name is inscribed on the flyleaf. The actual printed book had not yet come to light.[80]

There is also a possibility that Jacopo Strada had started to publish Book VI in Frankfurt at the same time that he was publishing Books VII and VIII. The fact that he continued a consecutive numbering of Books VII and VIII supports this hypothesis.

Konrad Oberhuber recently discovered sixty-two proofs of unfinished wood blocks which resemble both the Avery and Munich versions of Book VI. These proofs are printed on late sixteenth- and seventeenth-century paper from Troyes and Paris. The handwritten title page seems to date from the eighteenth century. The book is called: *Plusieurs dessins d'architecture de Sebastien Serlio Bolognais lesquels il avait promis au commencement de son quatrième livre qui devait faire son sixième.* According to Oberhuber, there must have been a third manuscript for Book VI by Serlio, begun after he had completed the Munich version and used as a basis for these proofs. They are now in the Nationalbibliothek in Vienna.[81] These proofs may have been made from wood blocks which Strada had had cut before his death. Strada did leave some unfinished publishing projects, as proofs he left in Frankfurt are listed in the will he drew up in Vienna in 1584: "So ins zu Franckfurt im Druck lassen ausgaben." [82]

CHAPTER II

The History and Evolution of *On Domestic Architecture:* Serlio's Working Method

On Domestic Architecture was acquired by William B. Dinsmoor for Columbia University in 1920 from Bernard Quaritch Limited in London; however, the manuscript was not officially accessioned by the university until 1924. We do not know how it came into the possession of Quaritch in 1917.[1] At that time, the pages had already been mounted on sheets of paper from Auvergne, dated anywhere between 1660 and 1760, and bound in an eighteenth-century leather binding. A title page, of the same paper as the mounts, was written in French and Italian in script of the same period: *VIII Livre D VIII libro di Serlio m:s: Architettura.* The mounting paper proves that the manuscript was in France in the seventeenth century. It made its way to England sometime before 1724, when the bookplate of the Bird family from Cheshire was pasted on the back of the eighteenth-century title page. By the nineteenth century, a clipping and pencil notations above the Bird family bookplate indicate that the manuscript was in the collection of Dr. David Laing of Edinburgh. It was sold there at the auction of Dr. Laing's library on December 23, 1880.[2] In 1919 Bernard Quaritch Limited had the manuscript rebound in a new leather binding. At this time the backs of the mounts were cut out to make them into frames, and the folios were assembled incorrectly. The text pages were also erroneously matched with the drawings and mounted with hinges onto the illustration folios. A new title page was added identifying this manuscript as Book VIII, together with a page copying the quotation about Peruzzi (Pl. XXXVI), and a table of contents. These additions have been eliminated from the present publication.[3]

At the same time that Dinsmoor acquired the Avery manuscript, Ernst

Cassirer, Julius Schlosser and Annemarie Cetto rediscovered two other manuscripts by Serlio in the Bayerische Staatsbibliothek in Munich. These were the second version of Book VI, and the manuscript of *On Roman Fortifications According to Polybius*. Schlosser and Dinsmoor thus finally corrected the error that had occurred when the *Extraordinary Book on Doors* was called the Sixth Book in the editions of Serlio's Seven Books on Architecture, *Tutte l'opere d'architettura, et prospetiva di Sebastiano Serlio, Bolognese,* that were published in one volume in Venice in 1600, 1618 and 1619.[4]

There is disagreement about the whereabouts of the Avery and Munich versions of Book VI in the sixteenth century. Julius Schlosser's argument that Jacopo Strada bought the two versions of Book VI directly from Serlio is more convincing than Rosci's and Dinsmoor's insistence that the manuscripts did not pass through Strada's hands.[5] As we saw in Chapter I, Strada stated in the introduction to Book VII that he had bought from Serlio all the drawings the architect had in his possession in Lyons in 1550.[6] The fact that he continued the successive numbering of Books VII and VIII indicates that he had some material for Book VI in his possession. Strada probably sold the Munich manuscript of Book VI to Duke Albert V of Bavaria, since it bears two bookplates—of 1618 and 1623—from the Library of the Dukes of Bavaria on the recto and verso of a sheet of paper inserted at the beginning of the manuscript; however, the Dukes of Bavaria did not begin to use bookplates until 1618, and therefore the plates would not have been affixed until many years after the purchase.[7] Jacopo Strada sold manuscripts to Albert V between 1565 and 1571 while he was an antiquarian for Maximilian II of Austria.[8] The preparatory manuscript for Book VIII, *On Roman Fortifications According to Polybius*, was apparently sold by Strada first to the Fugger family in the 1550s and then to Albert V in 1571 when he acquired the Fugger library. It was recorded as being in the Fugger library as early as 1558.[9] It is quite possible that Strada either sold the Munich version of Book VI first to the Fugger family and later to Albert V or directly to the Duke. Strada undoubtedly sold the Avery version of Book VI to someone living in France, since we know that it was in France in the seventeenth century. Both manuscripts must have been sold by Jacopo Strada before September 11, 1576, when they are missing from the inventory he made of his library.[10] The sale would have been logical if Strada indeed had had the intention of printing Book VI from a third manuscript.[11] In this perspective, the Munich and Avery versions of Book VI are both preliminary manuscripts that Jacopo Strada would have been free to sell, like the one for Book VII in Vienna and the one for Book VIII in Munich.[12]

The manuscript reproduced here is composed of seventy-three folios with ink drawings which vary in size between 38.5 centimeters and 83.5 centimeters in height, and 36.5 and 66.7 centimeters in width. There are also sixty-three sheets of text. Since these sheets were probably originally kept unbound by Serlio, they all differ in size. There are eight drawings which are composed of different sheets of paper which Serlio glued together himself (Pls. XIII, XV, XVII, XVIII, XXIX, XLI, LXXI and LXXIII). Several illustrations have flaps which may have been glued onto the main sheets: the upper floor on plate XXXIV, the detail of the portal on plate LXVIa, the cross section of the façade and plan of the vestibule on plates LXXIIIa and b. The flaps on plate LXXI do not seem to correspond to the rest of the palace on the folio. Although they were placed in their present position in the 1919 binding, they may be related to a lost folio. Three of the illustrations (Pls. LV, LVI, LXVII) have unfinished ground plans drawn on their versos; two of these were used by Serlio as a guide to the drawing of the elevations on the recto of the folios. Eleven of the pages of the original text are missing (Pls. I, VII, XXVIII, XXX, XXXV, XLV, LI, LXIII, LXX, LXXII and LXXIII). In addition, there is no introduction or conclusion, and the flaps have no explanatory text either. There are possibly other folios of text and illustration still to be discovered.[13]

Until they were bound for the first time in the eighteenth century, the sheets went through many changes in order. The last reshuffling occurred when the manuscript was rebound in 1919. For the publication of this book, we have restored the original order as it was reconstructed by William B. Dinsmoor. The erroneously placed text pages, as well as the variant texts, have been repositioned with their corresponding illustrations. A concordance between the present order and that of 1919 is included. Dinsmoor reconstructed the original order of the folios of Book VI by following notations Serlio placed on the illustrations and text.[14] On the recto of each illustration are a series of letters in alphabetical order with consecutive numbers, such as A 1, B 2 and C 3. There is one alphabetical series for the villas and one for the town houses. On the verso of each drawing is the number of the illustration to follow; each text page also bears the number of the corresponding drawing. Dinsmoor discovered that Serlio made one mistake and had erroneously attached the text of plate XXV, project V 20, to plate XXIII, project T 19. One drawing, the House of the Cardinal of Ferrara, has no notation on it at all; Dinsmoor placed this project between N 13 and O 14, and called it N 13a.[15] Marco Rosci has contested this order on the grounds that the House of the Cardinal of Ferrara occurs in a different place in the Munich manuscript. In our manuscript, however, it logically follows two other Houses for Gentlemen, M 12 and N 13. In the text to project O 14, Serlio states that this project was "similar to the past one," which could only be the House of the Cardinal of Ferrara, since projects M 12 and N 13 are different in plan from O 14.[16]

After the manuscript left Serlio's possession, several subsequent owners made notations on the folios. One added comments in Latin and Italian, as well as ciphers, on the verso of the drawings. Another added titles in French to the rectos of plates I–VI, VIII, XIII and XIV. A third owner affixed extra Italian titles to the recto of plates LXIX, LXXI and LXXII. A fourth added to the rectos of the drawings the letter "C," a symbol for the Italian word "carta," and a consecutive series of numbers.[17]

Serlio executed his drawings first in pencil and then went over them in ink. In almost all of the folios of Book VI, these under-drawings and guide lines are visible to the naked eye. There are also pricking marks (Pls. X, XXV, XL, XLVI, LII, LVI and LVIII); Serlio may subsequently have transferred these projects onto other sheets during his revisions. *Pentimenti* are also visible (Pls. XI, XIV, XXVI, XXXII, XLIX, L, LI and LVIII). The architect often used a compass to construct his plans: radii are visible on plates XX, XXII, XXIV, XXVIII, XXXI, XXXVI, XLII, XLV, XLVI and LXXI. In these drawings (particularly Pl. XLV, the plan of an oval château for François I), Serlio established a series of radii from a central point in order to determine the median lines of the auxiliary spaces in the same manner as Peruzzi.[18]

Serlio used ground plans, elevations and cross sections to illustrate his projects in the present work. On only six occasions did he use a perspective view to depict part of a building: the façade and forecourt of O 14 (Pl. XIII); the courtyard of Villa S 18 (Pl. XXI); the courtyard of 31 (Pl. XLVII); the ground floor of Ro 26 (Pl. XXXV) and the courtyards of O (Pl. LI) and of V (Pl. LXIX).

Since our manuscript is a preparatory work, the information is not standardized. In some cases, such as in the Château Et 25 (Pl. XXX), the ground plan, cross section and elevation of the main façade are shown on one page; in another instance, the variants of Palace P (Pls. LIV–LVI), the ground plan, cross section and elevation of the façade are on separate sheets. Usually the ground plan precedes cross sections and elevations, but not every project has a cross section. The provisional character of the manuscript is also evident in the architect's failure to space the drawings uniformly on the page. In some folios (Pl. XLI), there is too much space between the drawings; in others (Pl. XXXVII), the drawings are too crowded on the page. One of Serlio's innovations in terms of book illustration is the enlarged details of individual elements that resemble "blow-up" details in modern photographs, such as the main portal of the Governor's Palace (Pl. LXVIa) and the central portions of the façades of the Prince's and King's Palaces (Pls. LXX, LXXIII).

As Rosci has stated, in his use of ground plans, cross sections and elevations, Serlio was influenced by Raphael's famous letter to Pope Leo X on the antiquities of Rome. In this communication, written in 1519, Raphael expressed his desire to use three types of drawings to illustrate the city's ancient monuments: ground plans, elevations and cross sections. Serlio had already tried out this formula in his illustrations for Book III, *On Antiquity*, and in the preparatory manuscript for *On Roman Fortifications According to Polybius*.[19] Serlio's avoidance of the perspective view also reveals the influence of Alberti's warnings against its use in his *Ten Books on Architecture* (Book 2, chapter 1). Alberti believed that perspective did not permit the exact representation of dimensions; he preferred the use of wood models for accuracy. Referring to the cross section of Palace P (Pl. LIII), Serlio states in accordance with Alberti: ". . . there are some things which are badly represented without the material model. . . ." Indeed, this drawing is inaccurate and could not have been used to construct the interior of Palace P.[20] It was for greater accuracy that Leonardo also began to use ground plans, elevations and cross sections without perspective views in his drawings of human anatomy. Antonio da Sangallo, the Younger, who first consistently used the above scheme for architectural drawings, wanted to provide his assistants with accurate working drawings so that he would not have to be present constantly on the site of construction. However, Sangallo must still have relied on wood models, as his measured drawings are not of entire sections of the buildings but mostly details of window frames and entablatures.[21]

The drawings reproduced here have the character of Renaissance presentation drawings. They are often inexact and could not have been used by the practicing architect for actual construction. Serlio's drawings were meant as proposals that could be changed by the patron or master mason; in the text for Town House G, he states: "I have drawn the upper portico with six columns, but it will be up to the patron to choose what he wants. . . ."[22] This characteristic of the drawings corresponds to architectural practice in France at the time. As we saw in the cases of the Salle du Bal and the Château of Ancy-le-Franc discussed in Chapter I, Serlio's buildings were constructed by master masons who changed both his methods of construction and his decorative elements, often at the request of the patron. In some cases, such as that of project G (Pl. XLIX), the architect gives the heights of the first two floors but leaves out that of the attic. Serlio often omits the dimensions of wall thicknesses, saying that these can vary between two and five feet according to the wishes of the patron. As noted earlier, measurements are in many cases indicated only by the scale of the drawing, but since the author never states exactly what scale he used, it is difficult to relate the dimensions of texts and plans. For example, the measurements in the text do not seem to correspond to those on the plan for the cross sections and main façade of project P (Pls. LIII, LV, LVI), in which Serlio appears to have exaggerated the heights of rooms and roofs as a result of the influence of his French environment.

The provisional character of our manuscript is also related to the fact that it was executed on paper. It is important to realize that in the production of printed books by woodcut, the final version was executed on parchment. The parchment sheets were then glued to wood blocks and cut through. Thus the Avery manuscript was never intended to be used in the actual printing process.[23] Serlio probably planned to make changes and to add missing information in his final version.

Our manuscript can be dated by references to Book VI in Serlio's other writings, by two letters written to Ercole II d'Este and by the papers' watermarks. Many of the text pages contain references to François I, such as the description of a château for the King:

> Christian monarchs observe the worship of the divine and in particular the great King François whom I wish always to praise as the greatest of the Christian kings since he is my only patron and supporter. . . .[24]

We can assume that Serlio began *On Domestic Architecture* immediately after his arrival at Fontainebleau in 1541. He referred first to his work on Book VI in Books I and II, which were issued together on August 22, 1545:

> With the grace of God, the other three books will be finished soon, that is, the one on temples which is ready to be printed, and that on the dwellings of men of all stations in life, which above all others will be useful and pleasing to everyone. This latter book is two thirds completed, and that on accidents (which has never been published before) is already for the most part finished.[25]

Books VI and VII were still not ready to be published when Book V was printed in 1547.[26]

There are several references to a book on domestic architecture in two letters written to Ercole II in 1546. These letters, however, are difficult to interpret. Dinsmoor failed to notice that the book mentioned in both letters could also be Book VII, which was almost complete by 1545 as Serlio had mentioned above. The first letter was written from Fontainebleau on May 5, 1546, by Giulio Alvarotti, Ambassador of the Duke of Ferrara:

> A certain Sebastiano . . . has made an illustration of his house at Fontainebleau and he has executed it well. He has also executed a book on architecture with many plans of houses and palaces and he will have it printed in a few days.[27]

The second letter was written by Ippolito d'Este himself on October 16, 1546, from Fontainebleau:

> A Mr. Bastiano Serlio, who is my architect, has placed [the drawing of my house] in his book on architecture which he has just finished and

wished to have printed. And I had him take it out, judging that to see it in an illustration would not be prudent, since it would create criticism. . . .[28]

Obviously Ippolito d'Este wasn't enthusiastic about his house. Here again, the book he is speaking of could be Book VII, since the house of the Cardinal of Ferrara was also illustrated in it on folio 57.

The manuscript itself provides somewhat more precise dates. Dinsmoor identified the approximate dates of nine types of French paper by their watermarks. Although this method is not exact and is based on the supposition that the paper was bought soon after it was manufactured, it does give an indication of the time span of the manuscript. Dinsmoor discovered that Serlio used three types of paper manufactured in southern France for the drawings (I–III) and six types of paper primarily for the text (IV–IX). Two varieties of text paper were manufactured in Paris (IV, VI), a third in St. Germain-en-Laye (V), a fourth in Orléans (VII) and a fifth and sixth in southwestern France near Bordeaux (VIII, IX). A tenth type of paper was not identified, as it carried no watermarks. A diagram of the composition of the folios according to paper type is found at the end of this book.[29] Dinsmoor also noted that Serlio made a differentiation in size between the paper to be used for the text and for the drawings. The three varieties used for the drawings were manufactured in large sheets measuring on the average 50 centimeters in height and 40 centimeters in width. The paper used primarily for the text was manufactured in smaller sheets measuring on the average 40 centimeters in height and 25 centimeters in width. Several folios of drawings also use sections of paper of types IV–IX.[30]

Dinsmoor established a detailed chronology for the manuscript consisting of seven stages from 1541 to 1551; he believed that the text was written at the same time as the illustrations.[31] In contrast to Dinsmoor, only four general phases seem evident to me: three for the execution of the drawings and one for the writing of the text, with the text being written only after all the illustrations had been completed. I also believe it is impossible to determine exactly when Serlio left the Avery manuscript unfinished and turned to work on the Munich version.

During the first stage, from 1541 to 1545, Serlio must have executed forty-six illustrations on paper of type I as Dinsmoor has suggested (Pls. I–VI, VIII, XIV, XVI, XIX–XXI, XXII–XXVIII, XXX–XXXI, XXXIV–XL, XLII–XLVII, LIII–LIX, LXII–LXIV and LXVII–LXIX). Serlio probably bought these sheets in Lyons on his way to Fontainebleau. This paper is very early in date; it is found only in documents of the church of Saint Jean in Lyons between 1530 and 1533. These forty-six illustrations correspond to the two-thirds of the book which was completed by August 22, 1545, the date when Books I and II were printed.[32] The eighteen illustrations executed on paper of type II and the one illustration executed on paper of type III represent the second stage (Pls. VII, IX, X, XII, XXII, XXXII, XXXIII, XLVIII–LII, LX–LXI, LXV–LXVI, LXX and LXXII; and Pl. XI on type III). Serlio must have bought the type II paper when he returned to Lyons between 1547–1548 and 1549; it was used in documents in Lyons between 1545 and 1549 and later in Narbonne in 1551, and in Nîmes from 1553 to 1557.[33] At this time Serlio completed unfinished projects he had begun earlier. The façade and elevation of the garden loggia of Villa M 12 (Pl. VIII) were first executed on a sheet of paper of type I, whereas the plan (Pl. VII) was executed later on paper of type II. Serlio also added completely new projects such as the series of town houses from

A to O on paper of type II (Pls. XLVIII–LI).

The illustration of the House of the Cardinal of Ferrara, N 13a, on paper of type III also fits into the second phase (Pl. XI). Paper of this type was used in Lyons from 1545 to 1574. In fact it was used for Serlio's *Extraordinary Book on Doors,* which was printed in Lyons in 1551. Dinsmoor suggested that Serlio executed this drawing in 1545 at Fontainebleau and included it in his book in 1549 after the Cardinal left Lyons for Italy.[34] The fact that Serlio did not give this project a letter and number would indicate, however, that he waited until the end of the second phase of his project. I would agree with Rosci that Serlio continued this phase of his manuscript in Lyons and may even have made this drawing, a copy of an earlier one, in Lyons.[35] This chronology is supported by the fact that Serlio used paper of types II and III for the revision of his Polybius manuscript which we know he began at Fontainebleau around 1546 and continued in Lyons until 1550, when it was bought by Jacopo Strada.[36]

The third and fourth stages in the manuscript's execution were the completion of the illustrations and the writing of the text on paper of types IV–X. Four varieties of paper from northern France (IV, V, VI, VII) must have been acquired by Serlio, as Dinsmoor suggested, while Serlio was still living at Fontainebleau. Paper of type IV occurs in documents in Paris between 1547 and 1550, of type V in documents at St. Germain-en-Laye as late as 1561, of type VI in documents in Pontoise as early as 1543 and of type VII in documents in Orléans in 1543. Two types of paper which were manufactured in southwestern France (VIII, IX) are the latest in date. I would suggest that Serlio bought these late sheets in Lyons after he returned there between 1547 and 1549. Type VIII paper occurred in documents in Valladolid up to 1550, and type IX was used in Milanese documents as late as 1555.[37] In the third stage, Serlio probably finished the missing illustrations by making eight drawings on a series of composite sheets for which different types of paper were glued together (Pls. XIII, XV, XVII, XVIII, XXIX, XLI, LXXI and LXXIII). Then the author must have added the flaps which he glued to the pertinent drawings: plate XXXIV on paper of type V, LXVIa on type X and LXXIIIa and b on a composite sheet of paper of types I, II and IV.

The fourth and final stage was the writing of the text, which Serlio must have begun sometime before the death of François I, in 1547, and continued in Lyons after 1549 during the reign of Henri II (1547–1559). The commentary follows the final order of the drawings regardless of the time at which they were completed. For example, the plan for Villa M 12 (Pl. VII) was executed on paper of type II later than the façade of the same project which was drawn on paper of type I (Pl. VIII). In spite of this, Serlio refers back to the plan in the text for the façade:

> The drawing you see in front of you shows in the upper portion the interior loggia of the garden of the *preceding plan.*[38]

The description of the illustrations for project P, a Town House for a Venetian Gentleman, is instructive as well. Serlio presents us with two ground plans (Pls. LII, LIV), two cross sections (Pls. LIII, LV) and a front and garden façade for both plans and cross sections (Pls. LVI, LVII). The first ground plan (Pl. LII) was executed on paper of type II, later than the other illustrations which were executed on paper of type I. Despite the later date of the first plan, Serlio in his description of the final façade (Pl. LVII) refers back to the plan on plate LII:

The present figure which you see in front of you will serve for both plans of the house of the Venetian gentleman.[39]

Another indication of a relatively late date for the text is the fact that Serlio talks about buildings he designed at Fontainebleau in the past tense. In the description of the Grotte des Pins, project Y 25, Serlio describes the models and drawings:

> In the beautiful and rich castle of Fontainebleau besides the splendid courtyards and beautiful fountains . . . there is a bridge which has been well built, of good construction. I *made* many drawings and models to erect a building on the top of this bridge. One could call this a pavilion. I have built several for his most Christian majesty who commissioned them. . . .[40]

Dinsmoor noticed one page on which Serlio apparently began a revision of his text on both the recto and verso. These two texts are the variant descriptions for projects L 11 and M 12 (Pls. VI, VII). They have titles, in contrast to all but one of the other text pages, the description of town houses A to F (Pl. XLVIII). Dinsmoor suggested that Serlio began this revision of the text just before he initiated the Munich manuscript, as all of the descriptions in it have titles. Because these two variant descriptions in the Avery manuscript do not correspond exactly to the illustrations, they may be related to the lost manuscript for the third version of Book VI that is reflected in the proofs in Vienna.[41]

When we compare drawings of the first two phases for the Avery manuscript, we detect a change in Serlio's style of architecture. French influences appear earlier in the country villas. In the first series of drawings executed on paper of type I, there is an adaption of the plan of the French manor in projects G 7, I 9 and L 11 (Pls. II, IV and VI). Serlio also modeled projects 30 and 31 (Pls. XLIII, XLIV, XLV–XLVII) on the Châteaux of Chambord and Fontainebleau. French influences do not appear in the series of town houses until the second phase of drawings, on paper of type II. Serlio adapted the gabled, glazed façade of the northern French town house in projects H, K, M and O (Pls. XLIX, L and LI). The first series of town houses on paper of type I follow Italian prototypes much more closely. The two interchangeable façades of project P (Pls. LVI, LVII), on paper of type I, are close to Mauro Codussi's Palazzo Vendramin-Calerghi in Venice and to Serlio's Venetian façade designs in Book IV. Another project, Q (Pls. LVIII, LIX), also an early town house executed on type I paper, resembles Michelangelo's Palazzo Farnese in Rome.[42]

Thus, Serlio probably first designed most of the French and Italian villas, secondly the Italian town houses and finally the French town houses along with missing elements of the first projects. This progression indicates that the architect traveled first in the more rural areas of France in connection with his job as commissioner of royal châteaux for François I. It was probably only after 1547, when he was occupied with more free-lance work, that he gained a knowledge of French cities.

Serlio indeed may have left the Avery manuscript incomplete when he turned to the Munich manuscript. When he began the third version is unknown. As we shall see in Chapter VI, Serlio had great difficulty finding a publisher for his book on domestic architecture because of his unorthodox attitude toward traditional architectural theory.

CHAPTER III

On Domestic Architecture and the Development of the Printed Book in the Renaissance: Serlio, Dürer and Pieter Coecke

❁

Serlio's illustrated treatise on architecture is part of the phenomenal development of the printed illustrated scientific treatise in Europe in the sixteenth century. He presented the practicing architect with building types that would be copied and adapted. Serlio's publisher, Jacopo Strada, aptly summarized the revolutionary quality of Serlio's treatise in his introduction to Book VII:

> He has restored architecture and made it easy [to comprehend] for everyone; and his books have been much more widely read than that of Vitruvius, since Vitruvius was much too difficult to be easily understood by everyone.[1]

The moveable printing press was introduced in Italy by two Germans, Conrad Sweynham of Mainz and A. Pannartz of Prague. In 1465, at Subiaco, they published the first printed book in Italy, an edition of the writings of the Roman author Lactantius. Their book was published under the patronage of Cardinal Torrecremata, of the Saint Scholastica Monastery. This was followed, in 1467, by the first illustrated book printed in Italy, Torrecremata's *Meditationes*, published by another German, Ulrich Han.[2] The first printed herbal, the *Herbarius* of Lucius Apuleius, was published between 1483 and 1484 by J. P. de Lignamine in Rome.[3]

French and German printers had also established themselves in Venice during the third quarter of the fifteenth century. One of the first books

16. Albrecht Dürer: Plan of a Fortified City. *Etliche Underricht zu Befestigung der Stett, Schloss und Flecken,* Nuremberg (1527), folio Ei v, woodcut, New York, Metropolitan Museum of Art, Gift of Felix M. Warburg, 18.58.3.

A, church; *B*, arsenals, graneries, timber warehouses, baths; *C*, goldsmiths, coppersmiths, foundries, tanneries; *D*, food depots and purveyors; *X*, town hall; *2*, religious center, sacristy, vicarage; *12*, market.

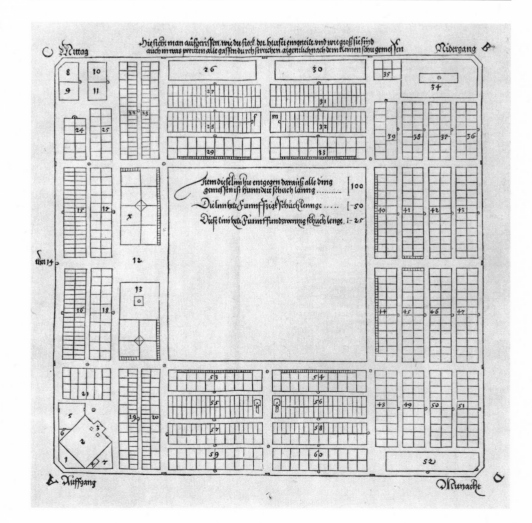

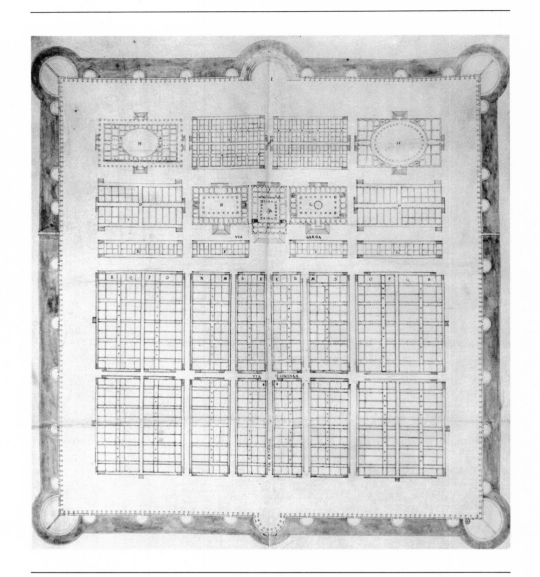

17. Sebastiano Serlio: Plan. *On Roman Fortifications According to Polybius.* Munich, Bayerische Staatsbibliothek, Codex Icon. 190, folio lr, ink on parchment.

A, the general; *B,* the magistrate; *C,* the forum; *D,* regular cavalry; *E,* overseers; *F,* judges; *G,* outstanding cavalry; *H: left,* baths and *right,* amphitheater; *K,* Roman cavalry; *L,* third ranks; *M and N,* first and second ranks.

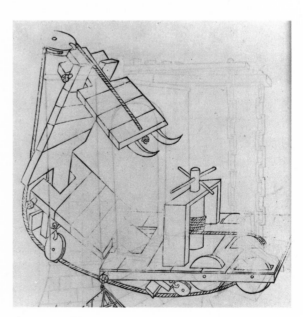

18. Roberto Valturio: Woodcut. *De re militari,* Verona (1472), Chapter III, Book X, Paris, Bibliothèque Nationale, Imprimés, Rés. 606.

printed there, an edition of Cicero's letters, *Epistolae Familiares,* was published in 1469 by the German, John of Speyer. The most important of these German printers in Venice was Erhard Ratdolt of Augsburg, who was active between 1476 and 1486. Ratdolt specialized in astronomical and mathematical books; he is known in particular for his 1482 illustrated edition of Euclid's *Opus elementum in artem geometriae.* Jacopo da Barbari's huge woodcut perspective view of Venice was published in 1500 by Anton Kolb of Nuremberg.[4] An edition of one of the first herbals printed in Germany, Peter Schoeffer's *Herbarius Latinus* (Mainz, 1484), was published in Venice by Bevilacqua (1499).[5] By the end of the fifteenth century, Venice had become one of the most important international printing centers in Europe and the most prominent in Italy.

Before Serlio's arrival in Venice, Dürer's graphic work had been a major influence on the development of new printing techniques. The German artist had made two trips to Venice: the first in 1494–1495, the second in 1505–1507. Titian's first woodcut, the *Triumph of Christ,* published in 1510–1511, shows the influence of Dürer's unification of descriptive and optical lines.[6] In the *Sacrifice of Abraham* of 1515, Titian borrowed motifs from the *Visitation* and *Flight into Egypt* in Dürer's *Life of the Virgin* which had been published in Nuremberg in 1511.[7] In addition, Dürer's illustrated version of the *Apocalypse* of 1498 was republished in a Venetian

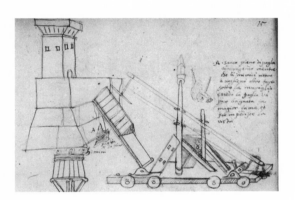

19. Baldassare Peruzzi: Drawings of Military Machines. Vienna, Nationalbibliothek, Codex, 10935, folio 15r, ink on paper.

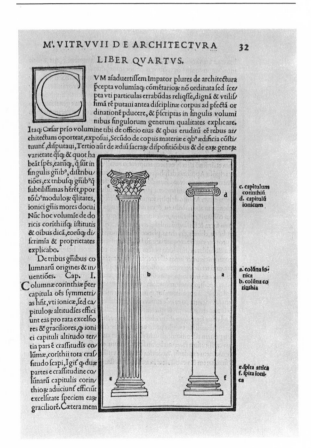

20. Vitruvius: Woodcut. *De architectura*, Venice (1511), illustrated by Fra Giocondo, folio 32, Avery Library, AA2515 V82 1511.

edition in 1515–1516 by Alessandro Paganini with woodcuts by Zoan Andrea. Four of the woodcut illustrations for this Venetian edition have been attributed to Titian. Another aspect of Dürer's original 1498 edition, also adopted in the Venetian edition of 1515–1516, was the separation of the text from the illustrations. Dürer's *Apocalypse* was the first book printed in Europe in the fifteenth century with illustrations opposite the text.[8]

It is Dürer rather than Serlio who should be credited with writing the first original architectural treatise in a modern language to be published with illustrations in the sixteenth century.[9] In Nuremberg, ten years before the publication of Serlio's Book IV in 1537, Dürer published an illustrated treatise on fortifications in German. It was entitled *Etliche Underricht zu Befestigung der Stett, Schloss und Flecken* and included the Plan of a Fortified City (fig. 16). The treatise was dedicated to King Ferdinand of Hungary and Bohemia, the grandson of Maximilian I of Austria. Dürer wrote it as a response to the threat of the Turks who were moving through Hungary toward western Europe. Serlio may have known of Dürer's treatise, since the grid plan, organization and round bastions of his *On Roman Fortifications According to Polybius* (fig. 17) bear a resemblance to Dürer's Plan of a Fortified City. Dürer had also published two other illustrated manuals in Nuremberg—one on perspective, *Underweysung der Messung*, in 1525, and a second on human proportions, *Von menschlicher Proportion*, in 1528.[10] Serlio could have seen the books of Albrecht Dürer in the Grimani library in Venice. We know that when the Croatian painter Giulio Clovio came to Venice from Hungary in 1516 to work for Domenico Grimani, his first task was to execute a manuscript copy of Dürer's *Life of the Virgin* that was in the Grimani library. Marco Grimani, who had helped Serlio with his Polybius manuscript, could have given Serlio access to the library and may even have introduced him to Clovio.[11]

Like Dürer's publications, Serlio's books on architecture were illustrated technical manuals. The first such manual printed in Italy was Roberto Valturio's *De re militari*, a book on war machinery published in Verona in 1472 (fig. 18). Interest in Valturio's book in the sixteenth century is indicated by several drawings, now in the Vienna Nationalbibliothek, by Baldassare Peruzzi of similar machines (fig. 19). Since Serlio was a pupil of Peruzzi's, he, too, must have known of Valturio's treatise.[12]

During the first four decades of the sixteenth century, before the publication of Serlio's Book IV, there is not one example of a modern treatise on architecture printed in Italy with illustrations. All that was available in print was Alberti's *De re aedificatoria* which had been published first in Florence in Latin in 1485 without illustrations. The illustrated treatises of Filarete (1460–1464) and of Francesco di Giorgio (1477–1501) in Italian were never published, but were known through manuscript copies. Francesco di Giorgio had stated in the conclusion to the second version of his treatise how essential illustrations were for him to convey his ideas: ". . . without drawings one cannot show the composition and parts of architecture."[13]

During the first part of the century only the illustrated versions of Vitruvius's *Ten Books on Architecture* were published in Italy. The first edition of this treatise in Latin had been printed in Rome in 1486. Fra Giocondo's illustrated Latin edition was published in Venice in 1511, dedicated to Pope Julius II (fig. 20). Cesare Cesariano printed the illustrated Italian edition in 1521 in Como and dedicated it to François I. In 1536 Gianbattista Caporali printed another partial Italian translation in Pesaro

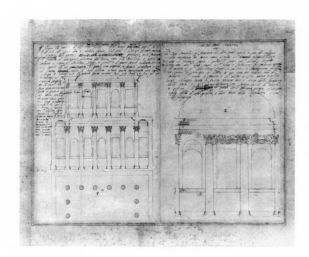

21. Pietro Crescenzi: *Livre des prouffitzs champestres et ruraulx.* Manuscript illuminated by Philippe de Mazerolles (1470), folio 11, ink and tempera on parchment, New York, Morgan Library, M 223.

22. Andrea Palladio: Drawing for the *Quattro libri.* London (ca. 1570), Royal Institute of British Architects, XIII, folio 20r, ink on paper.

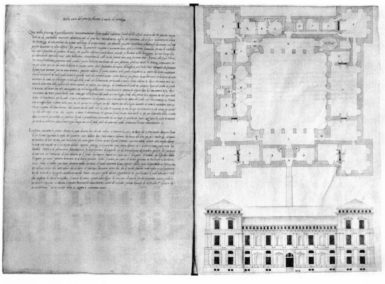

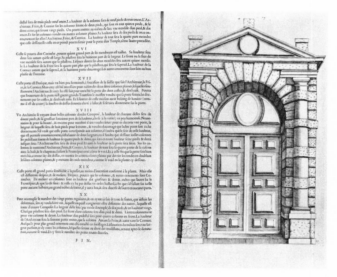

23. Sebastiano Serlio: Ancy-le-Franc, château. Book VI, Munich, Bayerische Staatsbibliothek, Codex Icon. 189, folios 16v–17r, ink on parchment.

24. Sebastiano Serlio: Fontainebleau, Entrance Gate to the House of the Cardinal of Ferrara. *Extraordinary Book on Doors*, Lyons (1551), last folio of text and first illustration, engraving, Avery Library, AA 520 Se 641.

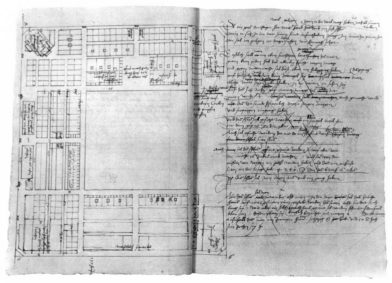

25. Albrecht Dürer: Preparatory Drawing for Plan of a Fortified City. London, British Museum, Manuscript Department, Add. 5229, folios 8v–9r, ink on paper.

with illustrations drawn from the two earlier editions.[14]

During the fifteenth century, printed versions of manuals were often contemporary with illuminated ones. Most printed books adopted the layout of the manuscript and had the text and illustration on the same page.[15] A case in point is Pietro Crescenzi's book on farming, *Liber ruralum commodorum,* written between 1305 and 1309. A manuscript of the French translation, *Livre des prouffitzs champestres et ruraulx,* illuminated by Philippe de Mazerolles in 1470, antedates by only sixteen years the first printed French translation.[16] In the printed version, the text and illustration are on the same folio as they are in the manuscript (fig. 21) and in Fra Giocondo's earlier edition of Vitruvius's *Ten Books.* Even in Palladio's *Four Books on Architecture,* which was not published until 1570 in Venice, there are pages where text and illustration are combined. Palladio wrote the text over the illustration in a study for his treatise (fig. 22).[17]

Both Dinsmoor and Rosci have noted that Serlio placed each full-page illustration directly opposite the corresponding text page in the Munich manuscript for Book VI (fig. 23).[18] This must have been his intention also when he was working on the Avery manuscript, since the explanatory text is on separate sheets and is not incorporated with the illustrations. Serlio also separated text from illustration in the *Extraordinary Book on Doors* (fig. 24) and in the preparatory drawings for Book VII in Vienna (figs. 10, 15). In these last two books, the author intended to place the text pages together at the front of the book with the full-page illustrations at the end; this was carried out in the engraved edition of the *Extraordinary Book on Doors.* The change in layout occurred in France, since in Books III and IV, and in the Polybius manuscript, the text is usually on the same page as the illustrations (figs. 2, 5).

Dürer separated text from illustration and placed them on opposite pages for the first time in the *Apocalypse* of 1498. Serlio must have been influenced in the layout of Book VI both by the design of Dürer's 1498 *Apocalypse* and by his *Zu Befestigung der Stett, Schloss und Flecken.* In addition, about half the illustrations for Dürer's treatise on fortifications are on large fold-out sheets that are bound opposite the text pages. These illustration pages measure on the average 41 by 30.5 centimeters, 2.75 centimeters wider than the text pages. The Plan of a Fortified City is an example of this type of large independent illustration (fig. 16). In the study for this folio (fig. 25), Dürer planned the text to be distinct from the illustrations as they appear in the final printed book.[19] Serlio adopted Dürer's use of the large fold-out illustration in the plans of the Palaces of the Prince and King in both the Munich and Avery versions of Book VI (Avery, Pls. LXVII, LXXI; Munich, folios 63av–64ar, 66v–68r). Finally, both Serlio's manuscripts for Book VI share with Dürer's treatise on fortifications the consistent use of ground plans, elevations and cross sections; on several occasions, Dürer included the three on the same page (fig. 26).[20]

In the cosmopolitan environment of Venice, Serlio could have had access to Dürer's books, not only through the Grimani library, but perhaps through an intermediary, Pieter Coecke van Aelst (1502–1550). Coecke, the teacher of Pieter Brueghel, was a painter, architect and publisher of books, who probably began his career in the workshop of Bernaert van Orley in Brussels and was admitted to the painters' guild in Antwerp in 1527. By 1534, he was listed as a painter for Emperor Charles V.[21] Pieter Coecke made at least two trips to Italy, one before 1527, when he went as

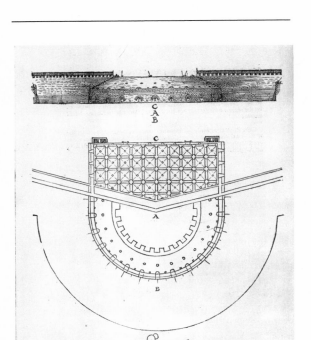

26. Albrecht Dürer: Design of a Bastion. *Etliche Underricht zu Befestigung der Stett, Schloss und Flecken,* Nuremberg (1527), folio ciiiiv, woodcut. (Metropolitan Museum of Art)

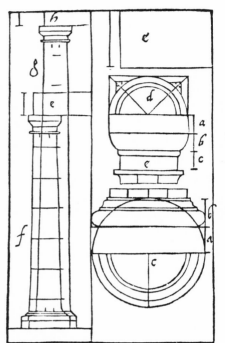

der Columme, de Phrise, denticuli, corona &c.
alfo voer vander Ionica ghefeit is. Aldus is de
Thuf.

27. Pieter Coecke: Doric Column. *Die Inventie der Colomnen,* Antwerp (1539), folio 6r, woodcut, Ghent, Rijksuniversiteit, Centrale Bibliotheek, R 1448.

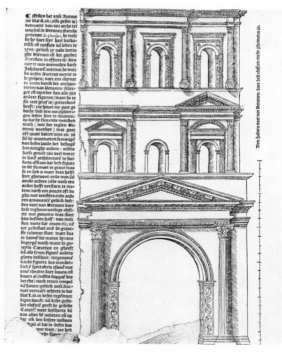

28. Pieter Coecke: Verona, Porta dei Borsari. *Die Aldervermaerste Antique Edificen,* Antwerp (1546), last folio before colophon, woodcut, Avery Library, AA520 Se63.

far as Rome according to Fritz Grossmann, and a second one in 1533, when he probably went to Constantinople via Venice as a member of a delegation sent by Charles V to the Sultan.[22] From 1539 to 1550 he published translations of Serlio's books on architecture in Flemish, German and French. The first publication—in Antwerp in 1539—was a Flemish translation of Book IV, *Generale Regeln der Architecturen op die Viyve Manieren van Edificen.*[23] How Coecke gained access to Serlio's books remains a mystery. According to Lodovico Guicciardini, in his *Descrittione di tutte i paesi bassi* (1567), the Fleming bought editions of Serlio's books during one of his trips to Italy.[24] It is tempting to propose that he may have met Serlio on his second trip to Italy. It has also been suggested that Jacob Seisenegger, court painter to King Ferdinand I of Austria, bought Serlio's books for Coecke on one of his own trips to Italy between 1535 and 1542.[25] In the introduction to the German-language edition of Book IV, *Die Gemaynen Regeln von der Architectur über die fünf Manieren der Gebau* (Antwerp, 1542), Pieter Coecke in fact states that he decided to publish Serlio's books on architecture as a sequel to Dürer's treatise on fortifications at the suggestion of Seisenegger.[26] It would seem that it was indeed Coecke who showed Serlio Dürer's treatise, encouraging Serlio to publish his books in translation as the architect himself had tried to do in 1537.[27]

Pieter Coecke's publishing activities encompassed more than the translations of Serlio.[28] In 1539, he produced in Antwerp his own abbreviated version of Diego de Sagredo's *Medidas del Romano* which had been published first in Toledo in 1526. Coecke's book was called *Die Inventie der Colomnen met haren Coronementen Ende Maten* (fig. 27).[29] In 1546, when Coecke published Flemish translations of Serlio's Third Book, *Die Aldervermaerste Antique Edificen,* he added an illustration that Serlio had left out, the Porta dei Borsari, a Roman triumphal arch in Verona (fig. 28). Serlio had stated in Book III that he considered this arch too licentious with regard to the teachings of Vitruvius to include it in the book. Coecke claimed that he, as the publisher, borrowed the illustration from Torello Sarayna's book on Verona (fig. 3).[30] There are several indications that Coecke did not merely know the Porta dei Borsari second-hand through Sarayna's book. In 1550, he wrote and published in Antwerp an account of Prince Philip of Spain's triumphal entry into that city the preceding year: *Le trioumphe d'Anvers faict en la susception du Prince Philips Prince d'Espaign.* The triumphal arches, also designed by Coecke, reflect the Porta San Zeno (fig. 29), the Porta Nuova, the Palazzo Pompei, and the Cappella Pellegrini in the church of San Bernardino in Verona—all by Michele Sanmicheli. The dates of these buildings suggest that Pieter Coecke made a third trip to Italy in the late 1530s, perhaps after 1537, when he is known to have been in Antwerp.[31]

Serlio's books on architecture can also be related to three other categories of books published in the Renaissance: travel, herbals and anatomy.[32] Some of the earliest accurate illustrations ever printed were those in Bernard Von Breydenbach's account of his travels to Jerusalem, *Sanctae Peregrinationes,* published and illustrated by Ehard Reuwich (Mainz, 1486). Its view of Venice undoubtedly influenced Jacopo Barbari.[33] Great strides were also made in accuracy of image in herbals of the fifteenth and sixteenth centuries, among them, Otto Brunfel's *Herbarum vivae eicones* (Strasbourg, 1530–1536), Leonhart Fuchs's *De historia stirpium* (Basle, 1542) and Pierandrea Mattioli's *Commentarii* (Venice, 1544).[34]

Serlio's first books, III and IV, are contemporary with two of the most

29. Pieter Coecke: Barrière hors de la ville. *Le Triomphe d'Anvers*, Antwerp (1550), folio avi v, woodcut, Ghent, Rijksuniversiteit, Centrale Bibliotheek, R1190.

important illustrated books on anatomy printed in the sixteenth century in Europe: Andreas Vesalius's short *Tabulae sex* (Venice, 1538) and his *De humani corporis fabrica* (Basle, 1543; fig. 30). Serlio shared a common concern with Vesalius: both men wished to represent in accurate illustrations their instructions to the reader and student, so that their treatise could be used as a pedagogical tool. Serlio may have known Vesalius personally, since the latter was Professor of Anatomy at the University of Padua from 1537 until 1542, just at the time when Serlio was in Venice. Vesalius's first book was published by Domenico Bernardi with plates executed by the Flemish artist Jan Stephan van Calcar.[35] There is reason to believe that Titian and members of his workshop contributed to the design and cutting of the illustrations of the second treatise, *De humani corporis fabrica*. The blocks for this book were cut in Venice and were sent to the publisher Johannes Oporinus in Basle in 1542 in the same manner as, subsequently, Serlio's Seventh Book in 1575.[36] Serlio can therefore be considered, together with Albrecht Dürer and Andreas Vesalius, one of the major contributors to the evolution of the printed illustrated scientific manual in the sixteenth century.

CHAPTER IV

Social Structure in Book VI: The Historic and Economic Background

Serlio organized both versions of *On Domestic Architecture* according to a hierarchical structure of society. This had been his intention from his first mention of the book:

> In the Sixth Book I shall discuss all the different dwellings which are used today, beginning with the worst hovel or barrack that one could speak of, then following from level to level, arriving at the most ornate palace for a Prince, in the country and in the city.[1]

In the present manuscript, there are nine house types for the country and eleven for the city:

Country Dwellings

1. Farmhouses of the poor and middle-class citizen for three levels of poverty: Projects A 1–B 2 (Pl. I).
2. Farmhouse of the rich citizen for two levels of wealth: Project C 3 (Pl. I).
3. House of the poor artisan for three levels of poverty: Projects D 4–E 5 (Pl. II).
4. Houses for the citizen or merchant: Project F 6–G 7 (Pl. II).
5. Houses for the richer citizen or merchant: Project H 8 (Pl. III).
6. Houses for the rich citizen or merchant: Projects I 9–L 11 (Pls. IV–VI).
7. Houses for noble gentlemen: Projects M 12–R 17 (Pls. VII–XIX).
8. Houses for Princes: Projects S 18–Et 24 (Pls. XX–XXXI).
9. Houses for the King: Projects Y 25–31 (Pls. XXXII–XLVII).

City Dwellings

1. Houses for the poor artisan: Projects A–D (Pl. XLVIII).
2. Houses for the better-off artisan: Projects E–H (Pls. XLVIII–XLIX).
3. Houses for the rich artisan: Projects I–K (Pl. XLIX).
4. Houses for the citizen or merchant: Projects L–M (Pl. L).
5. Houses for the rich citizen or merchant: Projects N–O (Pl. LI).
6. Houses for noble gentlemen: Projects P–Q (Pls. LII–LIX).
7. Palace of the *Capitano*: Project R (Pls. LX–LXI).

8. Palace of the *Podestà*: Project S (Pls. LXII–LXIV).
9. Palace of the Governor: Project T (Pls. LXV–LXVIa).
10. House of the Prince: Project V (Pls. LXVII–LXX).
11. House of the King: Project W (Pls. LXXI–LXXIIIa,b).

There are six dwellings with fortifications in the series of country houses: three for gentlemen, P 15, Q 16 and R 17 (Pls. XIV–XIX) and three for princes, 22, Et 23 and Et 24 (Pls. XXVIII–XXXI). Serlio includes two such houses in his series of city dwellings, one for the *Capitano*, R (Pls. LX–LXI), and a second for the Governor, T (Pls. LXV–LXVIa).

Marco Rosci has made the interesting suggestion that the social structure of Book VI was based on the example of the French state, which, during the reigns of François I (1515–1547) and Henri II (1547–1559), had developed into an autocratic monarchy.[2] This issue is, in fact, quite complex, as Serlio based his society on an amalgamation of Venice and France; he imposed the French monarchical system on a combined mercantile and rural society that is basically Venetian but not unsimilar to the mixed economy of France.

The basic structure of Book VI can be traced back to the earlier treatises of Leon Battista Alberti, Filarete and Francesco di Giorgio, all of whom combined republican and monarchical systems of government. Alberti began his *Ten Books on Architecture* in 1443 for Leonello d'Este, Duke of Ferrara, and completed it in 1450 for Pope Nicholas V. He established a hierarchy of urban dwellings for artisans and gentlemen, with a fortress for a tyrant and a palace for the elected mayor and for the Prince or King. He also included dwellings for priests in cloisters and soldiers in military camps. In the country, Alberti divided his houses into three categories: farms, villas for the very rich and villas for gentlemen.[3]

Filarete's plan for the ideal city of Sforzinda was written a little later—between 1460 and 1464—while he was working for Federico Sforza, Duke of Milan. The version that has come down to us was dedicated to Piero de Medici in 1464. Filarete's structure of society follows the model of the Duchy of Milan and resembles that of Alberti's *Ten Books*. In Sforzinda, there are houses for artisans, merchants and gentlemen, a palace for the duke or King, for the elected mayor and for the commander of the militia, and a fortress for the duke. In the country, Filarete included a hunting lodge, a gentleman's villa and houses for artisans in the suburbs.[4]

Francesco di Giorgio composed the first version of his treatise in Urbino between 1477 and 1484 while he was working for Duke Federico da Montefeltro. The second version was written between 1480 and 1501 when he was in the employ of the Duke of Calabria and the King of Naples. In this second version, Francesco di Giorgio divided his houses into several categories. Those in the city were for artisans, merchants, students (lawyers and doctors), noblemen, the mayor and the Prince; in the country, he included only one type of villa besides his numerous fortresses.[5]

Like Filarete, Alberti and Francesco di Giorgio, Serlio included a palace for the mayor (Palazzo del Podestà) and for the commander of the militia (Palazzo del Capitano). We can equate Serlio's and Filarete's Palazzo del Capitano since Serlio's commander, in addition, would be responsible for the protection of the inhabitants of the city in case of war. Although Venice did not have such officials, they were a part of the government in cities of the *terraferma* controlled by Venice such as Vicenza and Padua.[6] Venice itself, like the city in Serlio's treatise, had a mixed aristocratic and republi-

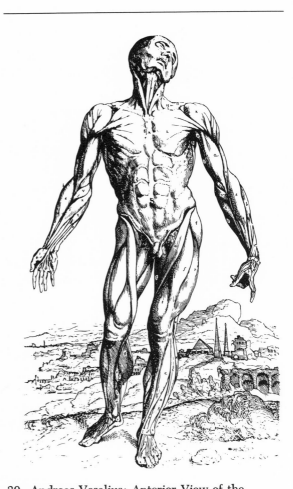

30. Andreas Vesalius: Anterior View of the Skeleton. *De humani corporis fabrica*, Basle (1543), woodcut, New York, New York Academy of Medicine. (Lynton Gardiner)

can type of government. The Doge, elected for life from the noble families who made up the Senate, the Great Council, the Collegio and the Council of Ten, provided the monarchical element in an otherwise republican system of elective government.[7]

There are, however, several important differences between Serlio's conception of domestic architecture and that of his predecessors. In contrast to Alberti, Filarete and Francesco di Giorgio, Serlio chooses to speak of houses for the poor. Filarete had specified that he would not speak of domestic architecture for the poor: "We shall make small mention of the latter because they require little expertise or art. . . ."[8] And although he had illustrated shops for artisans in Sforzinda along a canal,[9] these shops are quite different from the standardized housing proposed by Serlio in Book VI for the poor and middle classes. One of Serlio's major contributions is the standardization of the "row house." A second contribution is the secular character of the society he depicts. The house Serlio illustrates for Ippolito d'Este, Archbishop of Lyons and Cardinal of Ferrara—project N 13a (Pl. XI)—is not placed in a special category, but is included among the houses for gentlemen. This departs from Filarete's house for the bishop, and Alberti's houses for priests in cloisters.[10] Finally, Serlio's treatise differs from those of his predecessors in the large number of different categories of villas that he illustrates.

Serlio's decision to devote an entire book to domestic architecture is symptomatic of the economic conditions in Europe during the first four decades of the sixteenth century. As Ferdinand Braudel points out, there was a general increase in population in the first part of the century in the Mediterranean basin that caused a housing shortage and subsequent increase in building. Because of war and a series of famines and economic depressions between 1500 and 1540, many poor people flocked to cities in search of lodging, food and work.[11] The situation was particularly acute in Venice when Serlio arrived there from Rome. He reflects the Venetian response to this problem by including housing for the poor in Book VI, particularly projects A 1–B 2, D 4–E 5 and projects A–D (Pls. I–II, XLVIII).

Between 1527 and 1529, a famine in northern Italy brought residents of the Polesine, Padua, Vicenza, the Trento area and Friuli to Venice in addition to the refugees from Charles V's invasion of northern Italy, who, in 1527 and 1528, introduced an epidemic of the bubonic plague there.[12] On March 13, 1528, the ducal counselors Alvise Mocenigo and Giovanni Francesco Emiliani introduced a poor law, passed by the Senate on August 12, that provided for the erection of temporary shelters, a poor tax to be levied on all citizens, the prohibition of begging and the acceptance by the Senate of the responsibility for six months to find jobs for those who could work.[13]

Pullan considers this poor law evidence of the influence of the Reformation in Venice, since Martin Luther regarded the elimination of the parasitic classes as a major remedy for the ills of contemporary society. In 1522, the Lutheran city of Nuremberg was the first city in Europe to introduce such a law. Of all the Italian cities, Venice was the most open to the new ideas of the Reformation because of the large number of Germans and Netherlanders living there. Erasmus had come to Venice in 1507 and had stayed there a year. In its emphasis on good deeds rather than on institutional piety, his *Handbook of the Christian Soldier (Enchiridion militis christiani;* published in Augsburg in 1504, in Venice, 1531) was an influence on several Venetian advocates of church reform, the most important of whom was Gaspare Contarini. In 1516, Contarini wrote his treatise, *On the*

31. Venice, the Marinarezza (1335–1450). From Jacopo da Barbari's Map of Venice, woodcut, reproduced by T. Pignatti and G. Mazzariol, *La pianta prospettiva di Venezia del 1500 disegnata da Jacopo da Barbari*, Venice, 1963. (Lynton Gardiner)

Duties of Bishops (De officio episcopi), which placed responsibility for the poor in the hands of the bishops.[14] Serlio must have known Contarini, as the latter was a friend of Marco Grimani who had given Serlio the plan of the Roman city in Hungary for his edition of Polybius. Erasmus himself had had connections with the Grimani family, having stayed in the house of Domenico Grimani, Marco's uncle, in Rome in 1508.[15]

This climate of social reform in Venice is also reflected in the writings of Alvise Cornaro (1475–1566), a proponent of land reform and urban renewal. Cornaro wrote a treatise on urban architecture which has come down to us in two fragmentary versions, the second of which was written in 1550. The date of the first version is unknown; it may have been written in the 1520s.[16] Marco Rosci has suggested that Serlio knew of Cornaro's initial treatise, as his Sixth Book shares a common concern with it for housing the poor and middle classes and Serlio had listed Alvise Cornaro as one of his friends in the introduction to Book IV.[17] In the first version of his treatise, Cornaro stated:

> But above all, the beauty and comfort of houses, dwellings, and abodes of citizens are important, because these are of an infinite number and they make up the city. For without them, there would be no city. However, architects have written so little of these [dwellings]. That is why I shall write about these [dwellings] in order to inform citizens, not architects. I am not writing about theaters, amphitheaters, and how to make a new city, because this never happens and because these other types of buildings cannot be useful [to the ordinary citizen]. The divine Vitruvius and the great Leon Battista Alberti have not written sufficiently about these [dwellings].[18]

Already in the fourteenth and fifteenth centuries, there were several complexes consisting of standardized houses that were built for specific trades in Venice. The Marinarezza was one, built between about 1335 and 1450 for sick members of the ship-building industry in the area of the Corte Colonna (fig. 31). Another was a group of houses built between 1350 and 1400 for the Grain Brokers (fig. 32) on a site adjacent to Jacopo Sansovino's Zecca (Mint). Both complexes are depicted in Jacopo da Barbari's 1500 woodcut map of Venice.[19]

The development of a sense of social consciousness in northern Europe during the sixteenth century is also evident in a complex of standardized houses—the Fuggerei—built by the Fugger family for their workers in Augsburg. Jakob (1459–1525) and Anton Fugger (1493–1560) began buying houses in the area of the Jakobverstrasse as early as 1519; work continued on this complex until 1543.[20] It consisted of an administrative center, a hospital, a chapel and rows of identical gabled houses lining the streets. Although Jakob Fugger may have been influenced by the earlier examples cited in Venice, where he had had factories since 1480, this type of standardized middle-class housing was common as well in fifteenth-century northern Europe, in France, Germany and the Netherlands.[21] Given the international nature of Venice, it is quite possible that both Serlio and Alvise Cornaro knew about the construction of the Fuggerei in Augsburg.

As noted above, Serlio's Sixth Book is characterized by a secular social order; he did not include a specific category of houses for the ecclesiastic hierarchy. The architect's anticlerical attitude may have been nurtured in Venice, which became increasingly antipapal after its defeat by the League of Cambrai, organized in 1509 by Julius II, Maximilian I, Louis XII of

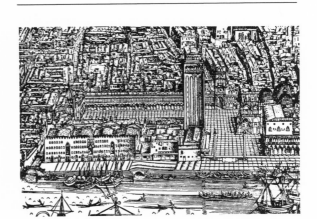

32. Venice, Houses of the Grain Brokers (ca. 1350–1400). From Jacopo da Barbari's Map of Venice. (Lynton Gardiner)

France and Alfonso of Aragon to regain for themselves Bologna and the Romagna, Friuli, the Veneto and Lombardy. The War of the League of Cambrai lasted until 1516, when Venice won back Padua and other parts of the Veneto it had lost in 1509.[22] Serlio seems to reflect sentiments raised by the War of the League of Cambrai and the invasion of Rome by Charles V when he mentions the destruction wrought by civil war in the description of the fortified Palace of the *Capitano:*

> Speaking of houses of gentlemen, I cannot omit speaking of the horrors of war which have divided Italy. In many cities, I have seen discord and civil war and mainly in cities under the control of the Pope. . . . There discord and war result in the most cruel sight: fires, the destruction of houses, and the flight of families.[23]

In Venice in particular, the reformist, anticlerical bias came to the fore in the writings of Gaspare Contarini. In his *Letter to Leo X (Libellus ad Leonem X)* of 1513, and later in his *On the Improvement of the Council of the Church (Consilium de emendanda ecclesia)* of 1536, Contarini made suggestions on the reform of the Catholic Church in Rome.[24] In the sixteenth century, the church in Venice became increasingly secularized: many members of the nobility held the important ecclesiastical positions. Marco Grimani, for example, had been a Prior of San Marco's before his brother, Cardinal Marino Grimani, gave him the Patriarchate of Aquilea in 1529 after the death of his wife in 1526.[25] Increasingly, many functions of the church were taken over by lay organizations such as the guilds or the *Scuole Grandi.* The poor laws of 1528 are one result of this development. In addition, the power of the bishops was also tempered at this time by the communes of the Venetian *terraferma.*[26]

Finally Serlio's Sixth Book differs from the earlier treatises in its detailed discussion of different types of rural domestic buildings. There is evidence of collective housing for farm workers in Lombardy and in the Veneto that goes back to the fourteenth and fifteenth centuries. Earlier, Filarete described, but did not illustrate, houses for artisans outside the city.[27] Neither Filarete nor Francesco di Giorgio had discussed the ordinary farmhouse. As Rosci has noted, Serlio's combination of a mercantile and rural economy reflects a major change that occurred in the Venetian economy in the 1520s.[28] Between 1500 and 1530 according to Ackerman new trade routes opened by the Portuguese and French caused a depression in the Venetian spice trade and a decline in profits from the textile and ship-building industries. After the end of the War of the League of Cambrai, new laws were passed (in 1527 and 1529) to encourage the acquisition of land in the *terraferma* for the production of grain, a trend that reached its peak in the 1550s under the direction of Alvise Cornaro.[29] The exodus from the cities of the lower and middle classes as well as the rich is reflected in Serlio's inclusion of country houses for poor and modest artisans and merchants in projects D 4–G 7 (Pl. II).

It is not a utopian society on which Serlio bases the organization of his book. Although he wished to reorder and improve the material environment, the architect accepted the existing societal structure. Marco Rosci has noted that Serlio was influenced by Machiavelli's *The Prince* rather than Thomas More's *Utopia.*[30] The latter was published in 1516 in Antwerp; *The Prince* was written the same year, but was not published until 1531, in Rome. Both treatises are basically criticisms of contemporary society. More chose a republican system to correct the poverty, corruption and

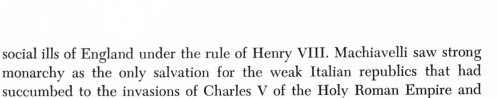

social ills of England under the rule of Henry VIII. Machiavelli saw strong monarchy as the only salvation for the weak Italian republics that had succumbed to the invasions of Charles V of the Holy Roman Empire and Louis XII, Charles VIII and François I.[31] More's *Utopia* was published in Venice by Anton Francesco Doni only in 1548, and did not influence political theory in Italy until the second half of the sixteenth century, when it became the basis of the publisher's communistic society in *The Worlds (I Mondi;* Venice, 1552). In any case, Serlio had left Venice before Doni arrived there from Florence in 1548.[32]

The architect's espousal of a monarchical system of government may indeed have been motivated, like Machiavelli's, by the contemporary situation in Italy. Serlio's dismay about civil war in his description of the Palace of the *Capitano* (Pl. LX) is similar to Machiavelli's view in *The Prince,* "Exhortation to Liberate Italy from the Barbarians":

> Having now considered all the things we have spoken of and thought within myself whether at present, the time was not propitious in Italy for a new Prince, and if there was not a state of things which offered an opportunity to a prudent and capable man to introduce a new system that would do honor to himself and good to the mass of the people.[33]

Furthermore, Serlio may have learned about the advantages of the monarchical government of France through Machiavelli's book, in which the author praised that government:

> Among the Kingdoms that are well ordered and governed in our time is France, and there we find numerous good institutions on which depend the liberty and security of the King. . . .[34]

Machiavelli's influence on Serlio was not limited to Book VI. Paolo Marconi has suggested that Serlio's *On Roman Fortifications According to Polybius* was based on Machiavelli's paraphrase of the Roman author's original text in his *Art of War* (published in Florence in 1521), the earliest Italian interpretation of Polybius. Serlio may have read Machiavelli's *Art of War* in Venice while he was composing his edition of Polybius. It is also possible that Serlio, like Machiavelli, had seen the first translation of Polybius's *Sixth Book on Roman History* from Greek into Latin: *De militia romanorum et castrorum metatione liber.* This translation by the Greek scholar, Janus Lascarus, was published in Venice in 1529. An Italian translation of Polybius's Sixth Book was completed by Filippo Strozzi before his death in 1538, and published in Florence in 1552. It is interesting to note that Filippo's son, Pietro, served as Chamberlain to François I and worked with Serlio at Fontainebleau on the revision of his earlier version of Polybius.[35]

Serlio's illustrated edition of Polybius is important as the background for *On Domestic Architecture,* which may have been influenced by the Roman author's advocacy of a mixed monarchical and republican form of government.[36] In the ideal city plan (fig. 17), dwellings are organized according to the secular, social hierarchy of army ranks.[37] This rectangular city with its grid pattern of streets is modeled on Vitruvius's description of the Roman city as it was illustrated in the edition published by Fra Giocondo in 1511.[38] In his version of Polybius's *On Roman Fortifications,* Serlio organizes the domestic buildings in a pyramid-like configuration with the most important house, that of the General (*Pretorio* [sic], fig. 33), at the apex of the pyramid, at the top of the main street, the via Pretorio. In front

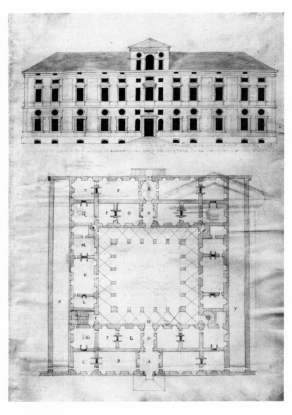

33. Sebastiano Serlio: House of the General. *On Roman Fortifications According to Polybius,* Munich, Bayerische Staatsbibliothek, Codex Icon. 190, folio 2r, ink on parchment (before 1537).

34. Sebastiano Serlio: Houses of the Judges. *On Roman Fortifications According to Polybius,* Munich, Bayerische Staatsbibliothek, Codex Icon. 190, folio 11r, ink on parchment (before 1537).

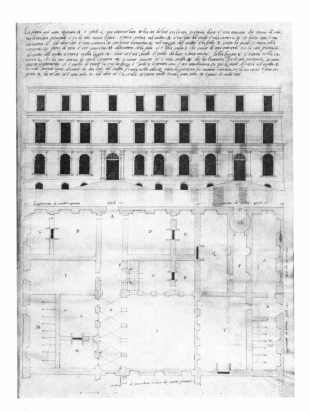

35. Sebastiano Serlio: House of the Roman Cavalry. *On Roman Fortifications According to Polybius,* Munich, Bayerische Staatsbibliothek, Codex Icon. 190, folio 15r, ink on parchment (before 1537).

of and behind this dwelling, Serlio places houses of varying sizes in *insulae* for the members of the army, and houses for the Judges (*Tribuni* [*sic*], fig. 34), Overseers (*Prefetti*) and Roman Cavalry (*Cavalieri Romani,* fig. 35). Next to the General's house are the Forum and the offices of the Magistrate (*Questorio* [*sic*], fig. 17). If one transfers Serlio's conception of this fortified camp to Book VI, one can imagine his domestic buildings ordered in a similar way, with the King's city palace taking the place of the General's house, and the houses of the merchants, gentlemen and artisans replacing those of the soldiers. One could also substitute the palace of the *Podestà* for that of the Magistrate, and that of the Governor for the Forum. The houses in Serlio's Polybius (figs. 34, 35) are similar to the urban dwellings in Book VI (Projects G–O, Pls. XLIX–LI).[39] Typically Venetian in plan, with their central hallways, they resemble the earlier housing complexes such as the Marinarezza (fig. 31) and the dwellings of the Grain Brokers (fig. 32).[40] The simple ornament and lack of orders of their façades show as well the influence of the modest Venetian houses described by Alvise Cornaro in his treatise on housing.

The combination of military planning with elements of contemporary urban architecture is a major characteristic of Dürer's fortified city (fig. 16). Dürer integrated the daily activities of an urban mercantile economy into the plan of a military camp.[41] It is possible that Dürer's project gave Serlio an idea of how to integrate houses of artisans and merchants into an ordered city plan based on a monarchical type of government. He may also, like Serlio, have read the paraphrase of Polybius in Machiavelli's *Art of War.* Dürer placed a square in the center of his town with the King's house in the middle of the square. The dwelling of the Prince was located in the lower right corner of the town, at D.[42] Dürer enlarged the quarters Filarete had given to the artisans and guilds in his plan for Sforzinda.[43] He separated the working quarters according to the different trades. Dürer placed soldiers' barracks along the sides of the city. Artisans were housed in the places where they worked.[44] Although he did not include any illustrations of actual dwellings in his fortified city plan, these houses may have resembled his drawing of a Venetian house in the British Museum (fig. 36).[45] Dürer was also influenced by the concept of the Fuggerei, as he was present at the meeting of the Augsburg Diet in 1518 when the Fuggerei was discussed.[46]

Having analyzed the various influences on Serlio in Venice, we should now turn to the ways in which he was affected by the society and economy of France. When the architect came to France in 1540, he adapted the basic Italian social structure to that of the French monarchy. France was then experiencing a period of peace between the end of the Hundred Years' War and the outbreak of the Wars of Religion. François I had followed the lead of Louis XI (1461–1483) in gradually dismantling the feudal system in order to establish a strong monarchy. By appointing two-thirds of the Parliament, most of the nobles and the clergy, the King created a system of government patronage that enforced his own authority.[47] In Paris, there were three organs of government. The *Syndics,* or *Echevins,* were the elected representatives of the city bourgeoisie; they, in turn, elected the mayor, the *Prévot des marchands.* The King was represented by the Privy Council and Parliament; he also appointed the Governor of Paris, a post created by Louis XI and reinforced by François I with the appointment of a Lieutenant Governor.[48] Serlio's Palaces for the Governor (project T, Pls. LXV–LXVIa) and for the *Podestà* (project S, Pls.

LXII–LXIV) reflect the French system of government: the office of the *Podestà* was the Italian equivalent of the *Prévot* in France. The architect also added to his earlier, urban social structure dwellings for the King in the country and the city (projects Y 25 to 31, Pls. XXXII–XLVII, and project W, Pls. LXXI–LXXIIIb).

An important precedent for the monarchical structure of society in Book VI came from Leonardo's plan for the city of Romorantin in the Loire Valley. This town was based on a rectangular grid pattern, dominated by the royal château in the center. In the *insulae*, Leonardo had planned for palaces of nobles and simple, prefabricated wood, gabled houses for artisans and merchants. Serlio probably did not know of Leonardo's project until he came to France.[49] In addition, Serlio probably had access in France to an important treatise on the French system of government, *La grant monarchie de France*, written by the Savoyard, Claude Seyssel, for Louis XII and published in Paris in 1519, in the first years of François I's reign. Seyssel, a friend of Janus Lascarus, the Polybius scholar, praised the government of France because the monarchy was balanced by the church, the police and parliament. His comparison of the French and Venetian states might have suggested to Serlio a way of adapting his earlier Italian social system to that of the French state.[50]

Several aspects of the social and economic structure of France resembled Venice. The merchant class, or bourgeoisie, had gained in power and grown larger: in 1462, in imitation of the Republic of Venice, Louis XI had allowed the nobles to become involved in commerce. He also began to elevate members of the urban merchant class to titles of nobility; consequently, members of the Briçonnet and Bohier families began to acquire châteaux in the area of Tours and Blois.[51] This may be the reason why Serlio included houses for rich merchants outside the city (in projects I 9 to L 11, Pls. IV–VI). Also in imitation of Venice and Genoa Louis XI and François I had encouraged the development of the spice trade with Brazil and Turkey, and international ports began to develop at Bordeaux, La Rochelle, Rouen, Nantes and Marseilles. The printing and silk industries made Paris and Lyons major international trading centers; both cities had cosmopolitan populations. Other important mercantile centers grew at Amiens, Beauvais, Nîmes and Montpellier for the manufacture of textiles, porcelain, tapestries and glass.[52] The rise of a flourishing merchant class in France is reflected in the urban dwellings for rich merchants (projects N and O, Pl. LI).

With the breakdown of the feudal system in France during the fifteenth and sixteenth centuries, there was, as in Venice, investment in rural land by the urban middle and upper classes. By 1560, 80 percent of France was still rural farm land. For twenty-five miles around both Paris and Lyons, this land was owned by members of the middle and upper merchant class, not by members of the nobility. Land became an investment for these urban owners, who often loaned their land to laborers for an annual fee.[53]

During the reigns of François I and Henri II, the population of France increased by 10 percent every ten years. This produced an exodus of poor artisans and laborers from the cities to the rural areas, which is reflected in Serlio's houses for poor artisans in the country (projects D 4 and E 5, Pl. II).[54] As in Venice, a new social consciousness developed in France during the second and third decades of the sixteenth century. In 1534, Lyons, like Venice, took the problem of the poor away from the church and established the *Aumône Générale*. Under the leadership of two humani-

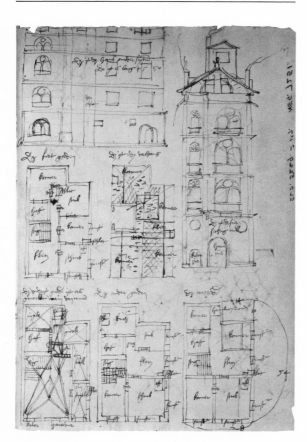

36. Albrecht Dürer: Venetian Artisan's House. British Museum, Manuscript Department, Add. 5229, folio 167, ink on paper (ca. 1505–1507).

tarians, Jean de Vauzelles and Santo Pagnini, and a businessman, Etienne Turquet, the *Aumône* dispensed charity and developed new silk and cotton industries to employ orphan children. Like Venice, Lyons had a large population of German merchants and the influence of the Reformation was prevalent. A sympathizer of the Reformation, Johann Kleberger of Nuremberg, was one of the most generous contributors to the *Aumône* in 1536.[55] Serlio's patroness, Queen Marguerite de Navarre, was an important protagonist of religious reform in France. She had given refuge to Lefèvre d'Etaples, an important humanist who had translated the Bible from Latin into French under the influence of Erasmus. With Guillaume Briçonnet, he had attempted to reform the corrupt Abbey of Saint Germain des Prés before his death in 1536.[56]

France had also witnessed the secularization of the clergy at this time: François I's Concordat of 1516 with Leo X gave the French King the right to appoint bishops and archbishops. He used clerical patronage to obtain the allegiance of the nobility: out of 129 bishops appointed by François I, ninety-three were nobles. Cardinal de Tournon of Lyons, for instance, was also Finance Minister for Henri II, Provincial Governor, and Archbishop of Bourges and Auch. Antoine Duprat, named Chancellor for François I in 1515, was the Archbishop of Sens and Cardinal Legate to the Pope in 1530. The general secularization of life is evident in the Edict of Villers-Cotterêts (1539) which gave lay courts jurisdiction over clerics.[57] The nature of the relationship between the ecclesiastical and the secular segments of society explains why Serlio placed the house of Ippolito d'Este, Cardinal of Ferrara and brother of Duke Ercole II d'Este, in the section with villas for gentlemen in Book VI.

The Reformation brought about increasing tension which led to the outbreak of civil war in France during the second half of the sixteenth century. The fortified château and town house of the *Capitano* that Serlio included in Book VI testify to his awareness of this state of instability. Open hostilities had broken out between the Catholics and Protestants just before the architect's arrival in France. In 1529, Louis de Berguin, who had been a friend of Erasmus and Luther, was executed. In 1533, Calvin espoused Lutheranism and left Paris for Strasbourg, Ferrara and Bologna. A year later, after "the Affair of the Placards," François I began to persecute the Protestants openly.[58] This violence in France parallels the resistance with which Italy met the invasions of Louis XII, François I and Charles V.

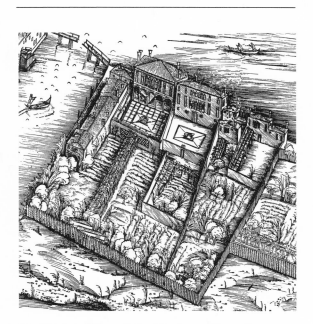

37. Venice: View of the Giudecca. From Jacopo da Barbari's Map of Venice. (Lynton Gardiner)

CHAPTER V

Building Types

The text that accompanies the illustrations in Book VI is an important aid to understanding the different functions of European domestic buildings in the sixteenth century. Serlio was definitely addressing himself to an international audience. In the description of a country house for a poor artisan he states:

> I am going to discuss what appears to me to be necessary in the houses of citizens so that the prudent architect can proceed with the small understanding he will have obtained: and I intend that in this way it can be used for all countries. . . .[1]

To present project E 5, Serlio adds:

> In my procedure, I intend to accompany French comfort with Italian style and ornament.[2]

He cautions the reader not to make value judgments:

> Although the French articulate their buildings in a way which is different from ours, nonetheless they have the same comfort.[3]

The architect chose building types that were common in European countries because of their sources in the Roman tradition. In addition, he was able to adapt certain Italian building types to the French environment, since they had already been introduced into France before his time.

Serlio divided his country dwellings into four basic types:

1. The farm and manor house.
2. Fortresses and villas derived from châteaux.
3. Small pavilions.
4. Villas which represent the revival of the large Roman *villa suburbana*.

The city dwellings were divided into five different types:

1. Houses derived from the Roman *insula* house.
2. The Venetian palace.
3. Central Italian palaces and fortresses.
4. The civic palace.
5. Palaces which represent the revival of the large Roman *villa suburbana*.[4]

There are many interrelationships between both rural and urban building types. The typology of Serlio's houses confirms recent suggestions that the Renaissance villa and town house were composites and variations of many different types.[5] One can observe in Renaissance depictions of cities how often rural building types were adapted to the city, as in the manors found on the Giudecca in Jacopo da Barbari's map of Venice (fig. 37) or the town houses outside the walls of Feurs in Auvergne (fig. 38).[6]

In Book VI Serlio tries to develop a rational system of domestic planning with a high regard for privacy that reflects changes in the structure of the family during the second half of the fifteenth century. Richard Goldthwaite observes the splitting up, in the course of the Quattrocento in Florence, of the extended family which had lived together during the Middle Ages. The single family began to live as a separate unit, especially among the middle and upper classes. The greater demand for privacy resulted in a clearer differentiation in the function of rooms in urban palaces. Goldthwaite also finds a new attitude toward worldly possessions in the Renaissance, with a more conspicuous display of wealth in the home during the second half of the fifteenth century.[7] Serlio seems to reflect these changes in his description of Town House I.

> I have seen rich merchants . . . who live miserably and I also have often seen a middle-class person who is generous in spirit and who spends most of his money on a house: And in truth, two transitory things make a man happy: that is a beautiful and comfortable house, and better, one which is beautiful and follows his wishes. . . .[8]

Country Dwellings

The first type of building that Serlio includes in Book VI is the European farm and manor house. The villas for a rich citizen or merchant (projects H 8, I 9, Pls. III–IV) have a forecourt for farm buildings. The court of H 8 is described as follows:

> The large court in front of the villa serves as an area, specifically, at each side, for the dwellings of the workers.[9]

38. Guillaume de Revel: The Town of Feurs. Paris, Bibliothèque Nationale, Ms. fr. 22297, folio 449, ink on parchment (ca. 1456).

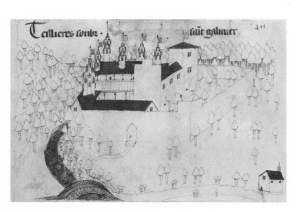

39. Guillaume de Revel: Teillers-sous-Saint Galmier. Paris, Bibliothèque Nationale, Ms. fr. 22297, folio 456, ink on parchment (ca. 1456).

In Serlio's social structure, merchants and rich artisans are sufficiently well-off to have two houses, one in the city and one in the country. Project I 9 is called a French variant of Project H 8:

> In these countries outside the city and especially in places near Fontaine-bleau, they plan a series of rooms in a row the width of which does not pass twenty-four [Venetian] feet between the walls.[10]

Serlio makes a distinction between the massed plan of Italian buildings with central hallways and the *enfilade* plan of French buildings. In this house (I 9), in contrast to the Italian one (H 8), there is no loggia on the garden and no classical orders on the façade, but there are dormer windows which the architect also classifies as French.

Rosci related these villa projects to the development of the trecento and quattrocento villa in northern Italy and in the Veneto, characterized by a forecourt for farm buildings. Both Rosci and Kubelik compared Serlio's villas to the farm illustrated in the frontispiece of the 1495 Venetian edition of Pietro Crescenzi's book on farming, *De agricultura vulgare*.[11] The general configuration of these farms and villas, with their forecourts with lateral wings for stables and storage rooms, recalls in particular the Villa Giustinian at Roncade (1509–1534).[12]

There were the same Roman sources for the survival of the portico villa in England, France, Italy, Germany and North Africa.[13] In fact the Roman villas on the periphery of the Empire had the same economic function as those fifteenth- and sixteenth-century villas in the Veneto: that of farming.[14] The survival of the Roman portico villa in northern Europe would account for similarities in plan and function between French and English manors and Italian farms. It is for this reason that villa projects H 8 and I 9 have the same forecourt. Numerous Roman portico villas have been excavated in France. One important example is the Gallo-Roman Villa at Montmaurin in the southern region of France.[15] A typical early fifteenth-century French manor which is very similar to the Venetian farm is the Manor of Teillers-sous-Saint Galmier which was illustrated in the *Armorial d'Auvergne* by Guillaume Revel (fig. 39). We can see the walled court-yard for farm buildings, the towers and porticoes connecting the farm buildings to the main *corps de logis*.[16] Serlio himself made a mistake when he characterized the centralized plan as Italian and the *enfilade* plan as French. There are examples of Venetian villas with a series of rooms *enfilade*: the Palazzo Bertoldi Negrar near Verona (1450) and the Loggia dei Valmarana near Vicenza (1433–1475), which inherited their plans from the original state of the Fondaco dei Turchi in Venice (twelfth-century), and the Villa of Theodoric at Galatea near Ravenna (sixth-century).[17]

The most imposing and luxurious of these manorial dwellings is a Villa for a Noble Gentleman (project N 13a, Pl. XI), the house which Serlio designed for Ippolito d'Este at Fontainebleau (destroyed except for the entry gate).[18] Here the architect eliminates the farming function of the building to create a country retreat for his patron which could be used for entertaining. The combination of a villa retreat and farm was the norm only for Venice; in other parts of Italy, the simple villa retreat was more common.

There is another Villa for a Noble Gentleman in the farm and manor series which stands out from the others (M 12; Pls. VII, VIII). It is also a retreat for pleasure rather than a working farm. In the description of

40. Sebastiano Serlio: Ancy-le-Franc, château, Northeast Tower (1545–1546). (Author)

41. Sebastiano Serlio: Ancy-le-Franc, château, detail of vaulting, East Loggia in Courtyard (1545–1546). (Author)

42. Sebastiano Serlio: Ancy-le-Franc, château, Galerie de la Pharsale, North Wing, Second Floor. (Author)

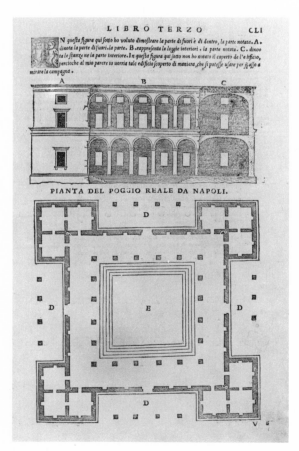

43. Sebastiano Serlio: Naples, View of Poggioreale (1476–1477). Book III, Venice (1540), folio CLI, Avery Library, AA 520 Se16.

the façade, Serlio adds some interesting information:

> Because most of the houses of this type in Italy are decorated with beautiful paintings, of both fables and history, I have left spaces free in this façade for paintings.[19]

The Barco Della Regina at Altivole near Venice (1491) was apparently decorated originally with frescoes, since these are still visible on the one remaining wing of the forecourt.[20] Serlio has given his manor house additional components of the Roman villa, revived from literary sources from Petrarch and Alberti to Pliny the Younger.[21] In addition to the frescoes, which probably would have shown mythological scenes, Serlio provides in Villa M 12 for baths in the loggia at the back of the garden.

Fortresses and villas influenced by château plans constitute the second type of villa in Book VI. Their interior courtyards are reminiscent of the castles of Frederick II (ca. 1250). These projects reveal Serlio's awareness of new methods of fortification that had been proposed by his predecessors, Francesco di Giorgio, Giuliano da Sangallo, Peruzzi and Antonio da Sangallo, the Younger. Gunpowder, invented around 1330, revolutionized the methods of warfare and rendered obsolete medieval types of fortifications such as large round towers, the *chemin de ronde* and stone machicolation. It was not until the middle of the fifteenth century that architects responded to this change. The first designs for triangular bastions and low earth walls were illustrated in Francesco di Giorgio's treatise on architecture. The first actual triangular bastions built were those of the Fortress of Poggio Imperiale near Florence, designed by Giuliano da Sangallo (1487–1488). In the sixteenth century triangular bastions were used by Michele Sanmicheli in his fortifications for the city of Verona (1530s) and by Antonio da Sangallo, the Younger, in the Fortezza da Basso in Florence (1531).[22]

With their earth ditches, moats and keyholes, projects P 15 and Q 16 (Pls. XIV, XV, XVI–XVIII) could have protected their owners against handgun fire. Projects R 17 and 22 have primitive triangular bastions and primitive bastioned towers that would also have been protection against handgun fire (Pls. XIX, XXVIII, XXIX). Et 23 (Pl. XXX) and Et 24 (Pl. XXXI) have fully developed triangular bastions with earth walls and ditches that could have protected their inhabitants against cannon fire. Dürer, in contrast to Serlio, had used the old-fashioned type of round towers in the walls of his fortified city (fig. 26).

Two of the Villas for Noble Gentlemen (P 15, Q 16) are particularly important because they shed light on the construction of the Château of Ancy-le-Franc, discussed in Chapter I. P 15 is the villa outside the city of the *Capitano* responsible for the protection of the populace in case of attack (Chapter IV). Serlio has not placed triangular bastions on this villa perhaps because Machiavelli, in *The Prince*, had warned against a fortified castle that was too forbidding and so could incite the populace to rebellion.[23] In writing about this villa, Serlio reveals his knowledge of the new methods of fortification:

> The house here of the Capitano outside of the city will have to be strong, but only on its flanks: towers and large ditches and raised bridges on the top will not be good. . . . However what will be effective would be to build a house on a piece of land with strong walls well suited for hand battles for defense against enemies. . . .[24]

In his description of the exterior of this villa, Serlio states:

> The windows will be so high from the ground that the enemy will not be able to reach them easily. They will have iron bars, but not frames, because windows with frames can be used as steps by the enemy.[25]

Thus we see here a practical reason for Serlio's elimination of ornament on the exterior of this villa. He also explains that the small windows in the basement can be used as keyholes for guns to protect the house against the enemy.[26]

These comments also show why Serlio was opposed to the changes which Antoine de Clermont-Tonnerre asked for in his Château of Ancy-le-Franc (Q 16, Pls. XVI–XVIII), namely the addition of classical pilasters on the exterior façades, and the elimination of rustication (fig. 11).[27] In the actual elevation proposed by Serlio (Pl. XVIII), the windows near the ground have no frames and the basement is rusticated. However, Serlio did retain in the final building the keyholes (fig. 40) mentioned in the text of project P 15. He is very clear in his description of the purpose of the villa:

> Nonetheless these [noble gentlemen] wish their houses to be fortresses and surrounded by water if it is available so that they can at least survive a hand battle.[28]

The ditch he suggests be filled with water is still visible on the terrain of the Château of Ancy-le-Franc. The other provisions Serlio made for durable construction—the vaulting strong enough not to need iron supports in the basement, courtyard and ground floor, and the wood ceilings in the rooms and loggias of the second floor—were carried out (figs. 41, 42).[29] The basement was also placed above ground as Serlio had suggested, and the courtyard was raised as well (fig. 12).

Projects P 15 and Q 16 are based partly on the prototype of the Villa of Poggioreale in Naples, built by Giuliano da Maiano for Alfonso of Aragon and illustrated by Serlio in Book III (fig. 43).[30] However, since Serlio considered the basic plan of Ancy-le-Franc to be applicable to France, we should consider whether there were French as well as Italian sources for this rectangular château with corner towers. In her discussion of the *villa-castello*, Carolyn Kolb Lewis calls Ancy-le-Franc a universal European type, since its origins lie in the Roman *castro-praetorio* as exemplified in Diocletian's Palace at Split (305–306 A.D.). Lewis notes that the castles of Frederick II in Italy, such as the Palazzo Imperiale at Prato (1250) with its central rectangular courtyard and corner towers, are analogous to contemporary French châteaux, such as the one at Dourdan or the Louvre built by Phillip Augustus (1180–1220).[31] This type was continued in the manor built by Cardinal Pierre de Thury at Villeneuve-les-Avignon (fig. 44)[32] and, close to Ancy-le-Franc in Burgundy, in the château at Posanges near Flavigny, built about 1450 on the foundations of a fourteenth-century château (fig. 45).[33]

Another château found both in France and Italy that is illustrated in Book VI is the type with *donjon* or keep and surrounding *enceinte* or curtain wall.[34] Project 30 (Pls. XLIII, XLIV) bears a striking resemblance to Chambord (figs. 46, 47), not only in the centralized planning of the main villa,[35] but also in the existence of the *enceinte* which Serlio states would be used for apartments for officials (Pl. XLIV).[36] He may have had access to drawings by Leonardo da Vinci which influenced the plan of Chambord

44. Villeneuve-les-Avignon, Manor of Pierre de Thury (1385–1410), now town hall. (Archives Photographiques)

45. Posanges, near Flavigny, château (ca. 1450). (Archives Photographiques)

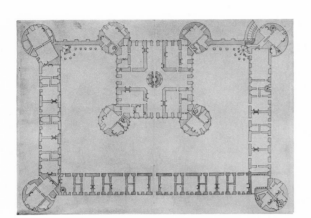

46. Jacques Androuet du Cerceau: Chambord, château (1517–1537), plan. Ink on parchment (ca. 1575), Paris, Bibliothèque Nationale, Cabinet des Estampes.

47. Chambord, aerial view. (Archives Photographiques)

48. Martianville, Hunting Lodge (1485). (Archives Photographiques)

(1517–1537).[37] Serlio reveals his ingenuity in the design of the vault of the central room (K) by providing a solution that would cost much less than a masonry construction:

> As you see in the drawing, the upper room will have a vault, but it will be [made of] wood covered with molten lead. The dome will be one hundred feet high up to the springing of the lantern.[38]

As discussed in Chapter I, the Royal Villa 31 (Pls. XLV–XLVII) may be a project for the remodeling of the Cour de l'Ovale at Fontainebleau (fig. 6). Serlio explains that he chose the oval form for this villa so that it would resemble a Roman amphitheater.[39] As in the preceding project the officials will be lodged in apartments in the *enceinte* (Pl. XLV), while the King will live in the central building (Pl. XLVII). The formal program of Serlio's villa-theater can be traced back not only to Poggioreale (fig. 43), but also to Giuliano da Sangallo's project for the Palace for Ferdinand of Naples which was presented in 1488 at the request of Lorenzo de' Medici, and to the Belvedere Courtyard at the Vatican by Bramante (1504–1505).[40]

The third group of villas can be classified as small houses or pavilions,[41] two of which (T 19 and V 20) are variations of Alvise Cornaro's Odeon which Serlio illustrated in Book VII.[42] Villa T 19 was designed to be a *belvedere:*

> I do not advise that walls of the courtyard limit the views from this house, or even a garden. I would prefer running fountains, and bridges, and that this house would be on a hill and surrounded by walls that are not too high.[43]

This description resembles the one made by Palladio in 1570 of the Villa Rotonda:

> The site is as pleasant and as delightful as can be found; because it is upon a small hill, of very easy access, and is watered on one side by the Bacchiglione, a navigable river; and on the other it is encompassed with most pleasant risings, which look like a very great theatre, and are all cultivated, and abound with most excellent fruits, and most exquisite vines: and therefore, as it enjoys from every part most beautiful views, some of which are limited, some more extended, and others that terminate with the horizon; there are loggias made in all the four fronts.[44]

Serlio mentioned in Chapter I that project Y 25 (Pls. XXXII, XXXIII) is a cleverly planned version of the project he submitted to François I for the design of the Grotte des Pins at Fontainebleau. Project 27 (Pls. XXXVI, XXXVII) is a variant of the above plan for the grotto. These are the two most innovative plans of the pavilion series: both are inspired by the grotto which Giulio Romano built in the garden of the Palazzo del Te and an octagonal pavilion which Leonardo planned for Romorantin.[45] Both also reveal Serlio's study of Nero's Domus Aurea (64–68 A.D.) and the Domus Flavia (81–92 A.D.) in Rome.[46] The plan of the second royal pavilion (27) is based on a church design of Serlio's on folios 17v and 18v of Book V. The two pavilion projects and villa project (Pl. XLIV) are among the earliest domed secular buildings in the Renaissance.[47] They reveal Palladio's debt to Serlio in the design of the Villa Rotonda.

There were, however, French precedents for these small pavilions with centralized plans. One is the hunting lodge at Martianville in Normandy which was built in 1485 (fig. 48) and a second is the original pavilion of

COUNTRY DWELLINGS 55

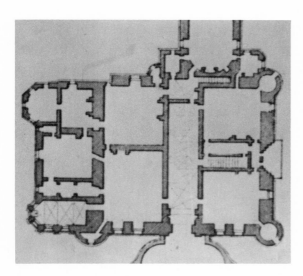

49. Chenonceaux, château (1513–1521), plan. Paris, Archives des Monuments Historiques. (Archives Photographiques)

50. Chenonceaux, château. (Archives Photographiques)

51. Blois, château, François I Wing (1515–1524). (Archives Photographiques)

the Château of Chenonceaux (figs. 49, 50), erected between 1513 and 1521 by Thomas Bohier. It has been suggested that these plans with their long central hallways need not necessarily depend on Italian precedents, but may derive from centrally planned medieval château keeps. Two country pavilions with centralized plans built for François I between 1540 and 1542 (thus contemporaneous with Serlio's designs for pavilions Y 25 and 27) are the Château at Challuau and La Muette at Saint Germain-en-Laye, both the work of Pierre Ier de Chambiges.[48]

The final villa type included by Serlio in Book VI is the large villa with multiple courtyards which represents an attempt to revive the Roman *villa suburbana*. This type was known in the Renaissance primarily through the letters of Pliny the Younger. We have seen how Serlio may have studied the three most important examples of this type, the Domus Aurea, the Domus Flavia and Domus Augustana which were built on the Esquiline and Palatine hills overlooking the city of Rome. Since the Romans situated this kind of building on the outskirts of cities, it can be considered rural as well as urban. Serlio was following a long tradition that began with Giuliano da Sangallo's attempts to revive the Roman *villa suburbana* at Poggio a Caiano (1485) and was magnificently exemplified by Bramante's Belvedere Courtyard.[49]

Rosci and Pagliara noticed that Serlio used a tetrastyle atrium in project X 21 (Pl. XXVI). They felt he must have studied the Roman and Greek peristyle house as it was described by Vitruvius in Book VI of his *Ten Books on Architecture*. He also must have used Fra Giocondo's (1511) and Cesare Cesariano's (1521) illustrated versions of Vitruvius and may even have had access to the illustrations which Battista da Sangallo added to a printed 1486 edition of the latter. Our architect, himself, made a reconstruction in Book III (folio LXXX) of what he thought was a Roman *villa suburbana* on Monte Cavallo in Rome, and which Palladio later discovered to be the remains of the Temple of Aurelian.[50]

As we mentioned earlier, a tradition also existed for the survival of the Roman *villa suburbana* in France. There had been a late Roman villa on the hill of Montmartre overlooking Paris. During the sixteenth century, we know from Gilles Corrozet's *Les antiquitez, histoires, et singularitez de la ville de Paris* (1532) that the frigidarium of the Roman baths next to the Hôtel de Cluny was believed to have been part of a Roman villa.[51] Serlio incorporates French galleries into his two examples of the revival of the Roman *villa suburbana*. In the Villa for the King, 29 (Pl. XL), a chapel is connected to the main apartments of the villa by galleries which divide the area into four octagonal courtyards. Here Serlio uses the words *galeria* and *ambulatione* as opposed to *loggia*.[52] The function of these galleries can be compared to that of the galleries of the Hôtel St. Pol, a manor built by Charles V on the edge of Paris between 1365 and 1380. We know from a fifteenth-century inventory of the manor, and from a description by Henri Sauval, that the gardens of the manor were surrounded by a series of double-leveled galleries; one of these connected the apartment of the Queen to a chapel in the Church Saint Pol which was adjacent to the manor.[53]

French influences are found also in the façade of this royal villa (Pl. XLI). Its irregularly spaced columns, which are recessed behind the protruding window strips, recall the pilasters of the inner court façade of the wing François I added to the Château at Blois between 1515 and 1524 (fig. 51).[54]

City Dwellings

The first type of urban dwellings—which range from houses for the poor artisan to those of the rich merchant (Pls. XLVIII–LI)—is placed on a long narrow plot, sometimes at the edge of the city:

> First of all, the dwellings of the poorest men are located in the suburbs close to the city near the gates.[55]

These houses place the poor artisans next to the markets and fairs; the houses of the rich, on the other hand, are closer to the seat of government—the Palaces of the *Podestà*, of the Prince and King—in the center of the town. Serlio identifies the first type as European:

> I have seen in different countries houses for artisans who exercise menial trades, and these houses are built on narrow sites which are quite long. . . .[56]

52. Unknown French artist: Illumination. From Livy, *History of Rome* (1472), Paris, Bibliothèque Nationale, Ms. fr. 20071, folio 5.

Whereas the poor and middle-class artisans (A–H, Pls. XLVIII–XLIX) are housed in two-family dwellings to be constructed in rows like the Marinarezza and Houses for the Grain Brokers in Venice discussed in Chapter IV, the dwellings of the well-to-do artisans and rich merchants are single-family houses (I–O, Pls. XLIX–LI). Houses I and K (Pl. XLIX), for the rich artisan or merchant, have identical plans, although Serlio meant project K to be French. This difference is shown in the façades. Our architect states that the façade of house I was typical of Bologna and had a loggia in order to protect the rooms from the intense sun; it is similar to that of a Bolognese house he illustrated in Book IV (folio XXXIII). Serlio describes the façade of the second house, K:

> I have placed many windows in the façade of this house, since I have seen similar ones in many parts of France and particularly in Paris. But these are of wood. If you will have to construct this façade of stone, the first three rows of windows will be open and the fourth will be closed.[57]

Serlio later on mentions the use of this type of façade in other countries, relating his designs to environmental conditions, as the quality of the light in Italy is more intense and requires screening such as the loggia would provide, whereas the daylight in northern Europe is more diffuse and requires greater window surface for light:

53. Venice, Artisans' Houses. From Jacopo da Barbari's Map of Venice. (Lynton Gardiner)

> This [type of façade] can also be used in other countries, and especially in England where they will delight in the large amount of light. . . .[58]

This type of house, on a narrow plot with a suite of rooms one behind the other and a shop on the street, can be traced to the Roman *insulae* houses like those in Rome and Ostia, which range in date from Republican times to the Imperial era. The type is exemplified by the House of Diana in Ostia of the second century A.D. This common Roman heritage accounts for the similarity of such houses in northern and southern Europe.[59] If we compare, for instance, a view of a city street in the background of a manuscript illumination for a French translation of Livy's *History of Rome* (fig. 52) to a detail from Jacopo da Barbari's map of Venice (fig. 53), we find an almost identical type of building with a simple colonnade along the street.[60] Examples of these houses can be found from the twelfth to the sixteenth centuries in France, England, Italy and Germany.[61] A French example is the Maison de Nicolas Flanel in Paris in which two families

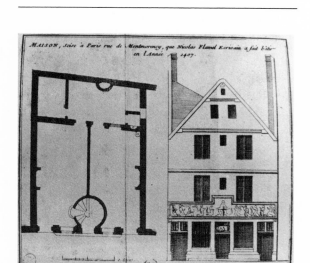

54. Unknown French artist: Maison de Nicolas Flanel (1406–1407). Paris (18th century), ink on paper. Bibliothèque Nationale, Cabinet des Estampes. (Author)

55. Angers, Maison d'Adam (ca. 1450). (Archives Photographiques)

lived and shared a kitchen at the back (fig. 54). The placement of the staircases at the front of the house and the type of gabled façade both relate to project F (Pl. XLVIII).[62] The façade of project K is also typical of fifteenth-century town houses in both northern and southern France, from the wood Maison d'Adam at Angers to the stone Maison Thomassin in Lyons (figs. 55, 56).[63] A Venetian example of this type of house with shop on the street was drawn by Albrecht Dürer (fig. 36).[64] Scholars have often wondered why on plate XLIX Serlio showed the same plan for French and Italian buildings. Although side hallways are more common in French, and central hallways in Venetian houses, there are examples of houses with side hallways in Venice, such as the twelfth-century house on the Salizzada S. Lio, and houses with central hallways in northern Europe, such as the Jew's House at Lincoln (1170–1180).[65]

The second urban dwelling that Serlio illustrates in Book VI is a typical Venetian palace, project P for a noble gentleman (Pls. LII–LVII). This type of house is characterized by a central hallway or room that runs through the building from the street to the garden at the back, usually with loggias along each façade. It can be traced back to the Middle Ages in Venice. Earlier examples still extant are the Palazzi Loredan (1100–1200), Cà d'Oro (1427) and Foscari (1450).[66] This type of plan is found in both Venetian villas and town houses; the plan of Palace P is similar to those of Villas H 8 and M 12.[67] Project P is extremely complex. First of all, Serlio includes two alternate ground plans and elevations (Pls. LII–LV) that could be built on the same foundations. There are a street façade (Pl. LVI) and a garden façade (Pl. LVII) that can be used for both variant plans. The first plan and elevation (Pls. LII, LIII) are for the Venetian type of palace; the second plan and variation (Pls. LIV, LV) are for a central-Italian type of palace.

Serlio began his description of the Venetian palace by stating that it should be isolated from the other dwellings, either on a square or noble street, in contrast to the houses for poor and middle-class citizens, which were to be in rows.[68] The façade of the house on plate LVI reminds us of the Venetian house that Serlio had illustrated earlier in Book IV (folio XXXV), and of the houses we can see in the view of the canal in Jacopo da Barbari's map of Venice (fig. 57). Serlio describes this Venetian palace type as follows:

> Since this city is on the water where land is very expensive, most of the houses have neither gardens nor courtyards, but the houses get their light from the front, and if they are long, they also get light from the back. For this reason there is a common practice to have in the middle of the house a portico as long as the house which will take in the light. But if the house is very long, you can have a small courtyard on one side to give light to the portico in the middle as well as to the other parts. . . .[69]

Serlio includes rooms on either side of the central hallway in the two basements to be used for the storage of wine and food, as was the custom in Venice. Because of the inundation of water from the canal, these rooms were not suitable for living quarters. However, in contrast to the usual Venetian wooden piles and beams, Serlio suggests the use of a primitive type of concrete for these vaulted chambers:

> When the water is low, you can build a basement in the following way: first make a thick floor and walls. Then have a layer of cement of large pieces of terrazzo and above another layer of small well beaten pieces of

terrazzo, and inside the walls, make a bank of sand and another wall of cut stone surfaced with two or three layers of terrazzo. . . . It will be impossible for the salty water to penetrate.[70]

He adds, "Thus it will not be difficult for a gentleman to have cool wine in the summer, a rare thing in this city. . . ."[71]

The third type of urban dwelling that Serlio includes in Book VI is the central-Italian fortress and palace. Each of these palaces has a rectangular plan with an interior, enclosed courtyard completely surrounded by loggias, except for project R, a fortress for the *Capitano* (Pl. LX). Serlio states that he has eliminated the loggias around the courtyard in order to provide the soldiers with more room to practice.[72] R is, in fact, almost an exact copy of the plan for the *Capitano*'s country fortress project P 15 (Pl. XIV). Serlio states that this fortress should be located in the area of the city where the poor live so that the *Capitano* can gain the trust of the people through his generosity and protection of them in case of attack by foreigners.[73] As in the villa for the *Capitano* (P 15), Serlio cautions that the palace should not be forbidding.[74]

The other urban fortress, the palace of the French governor, project T (Pls. LXV–LXVIa), shows Serlio's understanding of the autocratic power of the French monarchy:

> Besides the palace for the *podestà*, it is necessary to have one for the governor or president . . . who imposes justice in a much more violent way. He is not elected by the *syndics* as the *podestà* is. . . . This palace must have strong walls and defenses so that it can be surely protected against popular uprisings. . . .[75]

This palace could also be used for a tyrannical prince. Serlio's governor's palace bears a resemblance to the palace planned by Leonardo at Romorantin. Leonardo chose a similar type of plan with interior courtyard and corner towers; and, like Serlio, he provided stables behind the palace.[76]

This type of palace is a reflection of the central-Italian palace type with central courtyard exemplified in the Palazzo Farnese in Rome (begun by Antonio da Sangallo, the Younger, in 1535), the Palazzo Strozzi (ca. 1495) and the Palazzo Medici in Florence (1443).[77] The typology of Serlio's palaces Q, R and T confirms Jürgen Paul's thesis that the Florentine palace such as the Palazzo Medici is a descendant of the Hohenstaufen castles of Frederick II (1250) and town halls such as the Palazzo Vecchio (1300).[78] There was also a tradition in France for the urban palace with rectangular, enclosed interior courtyard surrounded by porticoes. This type appears in particular in the south of France in Avignon. One of the earliest of these palaces which was clearly influenced by the Château of Villandraut built by Pope Clement V (1305–1314) is the Palais Archiépiscopal in Avignon, erected by Cardinal Arnauld de Via (fig. 58).[79] A few years later, Benedict XII chose a similar type of plan for the first part of the Palais des Papes (1334–1342; figs. 59, 60).[80] In the middle of the fifteenth century in central France, Jacques Coeur also chose a château—Mehun-sur-Yèvre (fig. 61) which had been built by the Duc de Berry between 1367 and 1392 outside of Bourges—as a prototype for his palace in Bourges. Jacques Coeur's house has a series of large towers which enclose an inner courtyard surrounded by porticoes (figs. 62, 63).[81]

The fourth palace type included in Book VI is the Civic Palace, represented by the Palazzo del Podestà, project S (Pls. LXII–LXIV). The exterior loggias (Pl. LXIV) are quite different from Serlio's project for the

56. Lyons, Maison Thomassin (ca. 1450). (Author)

57. Venice, Houses along Canal. From Jacopo da Barbari's Map of Venice. (Lynton Gardiner)

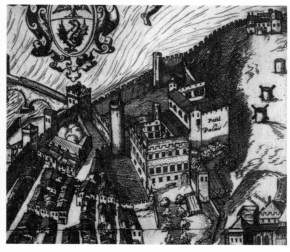

59. Avignon, Palais des Papes (1333–1356).
(Giraudon)

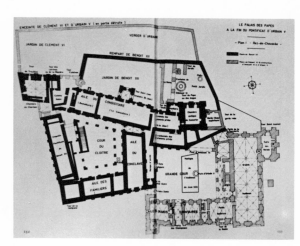

58. Avignon, Palais Archiépiscopal (1317–1335).
From a 17th-century map of Avignon, Paris,
Bibliothèque Nationale, Cabinet des Estampes.

60. Avignon, Palais des Papes, plan. From
Sylvain Gaignière, *Le Palais des Papes d'Avignon*,
p. 152.

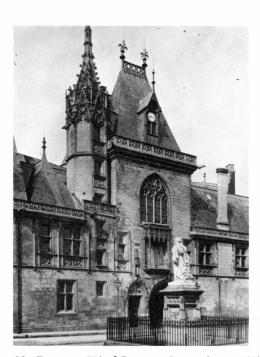

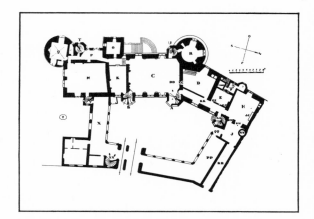

63. Bourges, Hôtel Jacques Coeur, Plan of
the Ground Floor. *Congrès archéologique*,
1931, p. 61.

61. Limbourg Brothers: Mehun-sur-Yèvre,
château. *Les Très Riches Heures du Duc de
Berry* (ca. 1416), Musée Condé Chantilly.
(Archives Photographiques)

62. Bourges, Hôtel Jacques Coeur (ca. 1456),
Entrance. (Archives Photographiques)

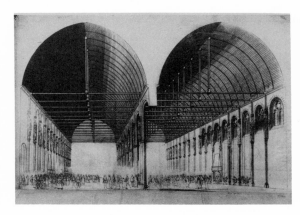

65. Jacques Androuet du Cerceau: Paris, Ile
de la Cité, Palais Royal, Grande Salle (1285–
1316). Engraving 1575, Paris, Bibliothèque
Nationale, Cabinet des Estampes. (Archives
Photographiques)

64. Sebastiano Serlio: Forum, Interior of
Loggia, *On Roman Fortifications According
to Polybius*, Munich, Bayerische
Staatsbibliothek, Codex Icon.
190, folio 10v.

Basilica at Vicenza (Book IV, folio XXIIII). Here they follow rather the elevation of the interior courtyard of the Roman Forum in Serlio's version of Polybius (fig. 64). Although Serlio's plan is similar to Bramante's project for the Palazzo dei Tribunali in Rome (begun in 1508), it seems to depend more directly on a drawing for a civic palace by Francesco di Giorgio in his treatise on architecture. In contrast to Bramante, Francesco di Giorgio placed his meeting room parallel to the front façade of the building. He also included a double staircase leading to the meeting room that is similar to the one planned by Serlio.[82] The civic palaces of all three architects derived from northern Italian town halls of the twelfth century such as those at Novara and Brescia.[83]

The Italian Palazzo del Podestà and the French Palais Royal on the Ile de la Cité, which had been used for meetings of the *Syndics* or *Echevins* of the city of Paris since the fourteenth century, have a common source in the Carolingian Imperial Palaces at Aachen and Goslar. In both medieval palaces, the meeting rooms for the city council derive from Carolingian Imperial audience halls. There is a certain similarity between the ways in which Serlio's wing for the law courts (Pl. LXII) divides the courtyard into two, and Philippe le Bel's Grande Salle (fig. 65) [84] divides the courtyard of the Palais de l'Ile de la Cité (fig. 66).[85]

The final type of palace that Serlio includes in Book VI represents the revival of the Roman *villa suburbana*. The Palaces for a Prince (Pls. LXVII–LXX) and for a King (Pls. LXXI–LXXIIIb) are similar in concept to Villas X 21 and 29. Both include classical atria: that of the Prince a hexastyle, that of the King a tetrastyle atrium. Serlio seems to have misunderstood the Vitruvian text since on plate LXVII he calls the entrance hall (B) the atrium and the actual atrium (A) the vestibule.[86]

Both palaces contain a combination of French and Italian elements in planning and decoration. The configuration of the three courtyards in the Palace of the Prince (Pl. LXVII) recalls the division of courtyards in the Belvedere Courtyard,[87] a reference that reinforces the allusions in these palaces to the Roman *villa suburbana*. However, the function of the galleries along the garden in the Prince's palace is definitely French in inspiration. There were similar galleries in the Hôtel de Nesle, a manor built by the Duc de Berry on the edge of Paris, on the flanks of its fortified wall (1411). Serlio must have been familiar with this house, since Benvenuto Cellini lived there while he was in Paris. The Hôtel de Nesle contained a series of gardens, tennis courts and courtyards surrounded by galleries (fig. 67).[88] The plan of the King's palace (Pl. LXXI) is clearly an adaption of Francesco di Giorgio's attempt to reconstruct the Domus Augustana in the first version of his architectural treatise.[89] Again a reference to the Belvedere Courtyard is found in the "theater" at the end of the garden which is closely related to the hemicycle at the end of the Belvedere Courtyard. Both hemicycles had the same function, since Bramante's was also used for the display of classical sculpture.[90] French references in the King's palace (W) are found in the dormer windows incorporated in an otherwise Italian façade (Pl. LXXIII), influenced by the Palazzo Nobili Tarugi in Montepulciano (ca. 1530).[91] This palace has been identified as a project for the Louvre which Serlio may have presented to François I.[92]

66. Paris, Ile de la Cité, Palais Royal (1100–1375). From Map of Saint Victor (1550), Bibliothèque Nationale, Cabinet des Estampes.

67. Paris, Hôtel de Nesle (1411). Map of Saint Victor (1550), Bibliothèque Nationale, Cabinet des Estampes.

CHAPTER VI

The Theoretical Significance of *On Domestic Architecture:* A Comparison of the Avery and Munich Manuscripts

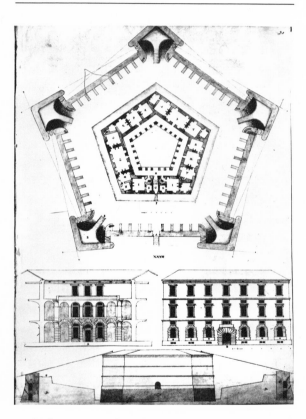

68. Sebastiano Serlio: Fortress for a Tyrant Prince. Project XXVIII, Book VI, Munich, Bayerische Staatsbibliothek, Codex Icon. 189, folio 30v.

To analyze the theoretical content of Book VI, we must consider the Avery and Munich versions together. Sometime in 1547, after the death of François I and before Serlio's subsequent loss of his position as royal architect, he went to Lyons, where he had submitted designs for the new Bourse. While in Lyons, he completed the Avery manuscript and began, also in 1547, a second version of Book VI, now in Munich. Serlio completed this second version by 1550, when it was sold to Jacopo Strada. In the introduction to the Munich manuscript, Serlio eliminated most of the references to François I that were in the Avery manuscript but indicated that he was still in the service of the King of France:

> I shall speak of royal houses since I find myself in the service of his most Christian King, Henri.[1]

The Munich manuscript was a copy on parchment of Book VI, meant for final publication, as opposed to the Avery manuscript on paper which we should consider as a preparatory sketchbook. Serlio added an introduction and a conclusion to the Munich version; he used a standard size of parchment sheet, numbered the pages successively, using both recto and verso of each sheet as in a book, and added titles to the text pages. This manuscript must have been a presentation copy. It could not have been used for the actual printing process as Dinsmoor and Rosci believed,[2] because it has text and drawings on the versos of the folios and if the sheets had been pasted on wood blocks the versos would have been ruined.

The Munich version was thus similar in purpose to the parchment manuscript for Book VII, now in Vienna. We know from a letter of Ottavio Strada to his father, Jacopo, in 1574, that additional drawings were used for the production of the final book. Ottavio indicates that the Vienna manuscript was probably used as a guide when the printer's proofs were being made.[3] In this context, the printer's proofs of Book VI, also in Vienna, were probably made from the third and final drawings of Book VI that were actually pasted onto the blocks. Ottavio Strada's letter suggests that the drawings used for the third stage of the printing process of Book VII may not have been by the artist, but were perhaps traced from a second parchment version.[4]

Serlio was much freer with his text and ideas for the buildings in the Avery manuscript, since it was not intended to be a book. The Munich manuscript was a version that was edited for publication, and therefore the more controversial elements in the Avery version were eliminated. Serlio's tone in the Munich manuscript is much more guarded, and we gain less insight into his personality. For instance, the homage Serlio gave Peruzzi in the Avery manuscript (Pl. XXXVI) has been eliminated in the Munich version. Serlio seems also to have eliminated in the Munich manuscript some of the more unorthodox elements of French architecture: this is why his buildings in this second version seem more Italian and more standardized.[5] Serlio did this to please his French patrons, as he explains in the discussion of Ancy-le-Franc in the Avery manuscript:

> Although this building is in France, the Patron wanted a completely Italian building.[6]

Thus the French wanted from Serlio a more orthodox treatment of architecture than he himself wanted. In terms of theory, they believed in principles that were much closer to Vitruvius.

Serlio made several changes in the social order of his dwellings in the

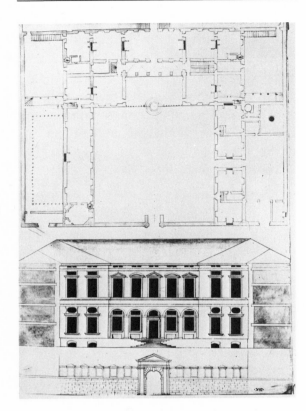

69. Sebastiano Serlio: House for an Illustrious Prince. Project XVI, Book VI, Munich, Bayerische Staatsbibliothek, Codex Icon. 189, folio 16r.

70. Sebastiano Serlio: Villa for a King. Project XL, Book VI, Munich, Bayerische Staatsbibliothek, Codex Icon. 189, folio 44v.

Munich manuscript: he increased the number of villas for princes to ten (projects XV–XIX), as opposed to the seven villas in the Avery manuscript (projects S 18–Et 24, Pls. XX–XXXI); he reduced the number of gentlemen's villas to three (projects XII–XIV) from the six in the Avery manuscript (projects M 12–P 15, Pls. VII–XV). Serlio also increased the number of fortified dwellings for princes to five in the Munich manuscript (projects XVII–XIX, XXVI–XXVIII) from three in the Avery (projects 22, Et 23, Et 24, Pls. XXVIII–XXXI). He changed the Villa of Ippolito d'Este (N 13a, Pl. XI), the Château of Antoine de Clermont-Tonnerre (Q 16, Pls. XVI–XVIII), and their variants (O 14, Pls. XII, XIII; P 17, Pl. XIX) from villas for gentlemen in the Avery version to villas for princes in the Munich; and he transferred the position of the Villa of Ippolito d'Este from before to after the House for the *Capitano*.[7]

It is difficult to explain why Serlio elevated the status of the Este and Clermont-Tonnerre villas; it may have been because he wished to flatter his two major patrons. However, both had the right to the title of prince. Ippolito d'Este's brother, Ercole II, was the ruling Duke of Ferrara and Ippolito himself was Archbishop of Lyons, and thus a prince of the church. Antoine de Clermont-Tonnerre was connected to Henri II through his wife, Françoise de Poitiers, who was the sister of Diane de Poitiers, Henri's mistress; and Antoine may have risen in social position at the beginning of Henri's reign, as he served him as Ministre des Eaux et Forêts and Governor of the Dauphiné. In addition, the family of Clermont-Tonnerre had been ennobled by Pope Calixtus II in 1120, and was permitted to use the Papal arms, the tiara and crossed keys, which appear on the Château of Ancy-le-Franc.[8]

A reason for the increase in the number of fortified dwellings for princes could have been the increase of hostilities which were to lead to the Wars of Religion toward the end of Henri II's reign. From the late 1540s through the 1560s, the Calvinists in Geneva became more militant in their attempts to make converts in France. The adoption of Protestantism was increasingly common in all levels of society, creating a constant threat to royal authority. Serlio perhaps understood that greater violence was to occur in France after the death of Henri II. In 1560, Reneé de France, Duchess of Ferrara, returned to France. She had been an active supporter of Calvin ever since she had protected him at her court in Ferrara during the 1540s.[9] In the 1560s Ippolito d'Este also returned to France to act as Papal Inquisitor.[10]

When we look initially at the Munich manuscript, it is evident that Serlio tried to give the pages a more graphic and organized look, by standardizing their size and paying more attention to the positioning of the drawings on the page. If we compare project XXVIII in the Munich manuscript (fig. 68) to project Et 24 (Pl. XXXI) of the Avery manuscript, we find that Serlio has reorganized the page by placing all the drawings along a central axis. He also added the elevation of a triangular bastion at the bottom, and eliminated the illustration of a rusticated gate which made the design of the Avery page asymmetrical. He deleted all the old-fashioned perspective views that appear in the Avery manuscript (Pls. XIII, XLVII—compare with figs. 69, 70). For greater clarity, the architect added or subtracted pages from certain projects in the Munich manuscript.

Most of the changes in the Munich manuscript occur in the ornament of the façades and in the text; there are very few changes in the ground plans. The only exception to this is in the Palace of the Prince (fig. 71). If we

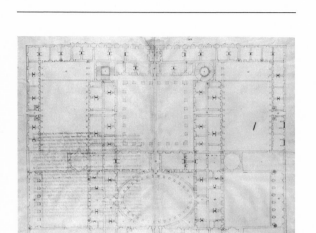

71. Sebastiano Serlio: Palace for a Prince. Project XXI, Book VI, Munich, Bayerische Staatsbibliothek, Codex Icon. 189, folio 64av.

72. Sebastiano Serlio: Villa for an Illustrious Prince. Project XV, Book VI, Munich, Bayerische Staatsbibliothek, Codex Icon. 189, folio 15r.

compare this plan to the one in the Avery manuscript (Pl. LXVII), we find that Serlio has abandoned the three-partite plan for one with nine courtyards, which is closer to the plan of the Palace for a King in both manuscripts (folios 66v–68r in the Munich, Pl. LXXI in the Avery). Serlio has enlarged the number of courtyards in the plan of the King's Palace in the Munich manuscript from nine to fifteen. This may indicate that the flaps on the sides of the Avery plan were originally parts of a larger plan which has been cut down.

The most significant changes in the Munich manuscript are concerned with decorative elements. There are a number of projects from which Serlio has eliminated components which, in the Avery version, he calls unorthodox according to the teachings of Vitruvius. First of all, as we saw in Chapter II, Ippolito d'Este wrote to his brother in Ferrara that he was not happy with his villa and said that it could provoke criticism.[11] When we turn to the illustration of this villa in the Munich manuscript, Serlio has added several quotations from Bramante's Belvedere Courtyard: a loggia along the front façade, and the concave-convex staircase of the hemicycle (fig. 72). In Serlio's words: "I have taken the plan and comfort of this house, but I have added some beauty. . . ."[12] Part of this loggia was also incorporated into the illustration of Ippolito d'Este's house in Book VII (fig. 73).

The articulation of the façade of villa XXXIV for the King in the Munich manuscript reveals the significance of the elements that Serlio eliminated (fig. 74). In the corresponding façade in the Avery manuscript, he states:

> The organization of the windows will seem to some to be discordant, but you have to consider the comfort of the interior rooms, and that the windows will serve a need that I have discussed elsewhere. Nonetheless, you will see a harmony which will be rather concordant disharmony. . . .[13]

It was considered strange that the columns did not enframe the windows as they do in the standard sixteenth-century *aedicula* window of the type we find on the façade of the Palazzo Farnese in Rome. In the Munich version, Serlio has eliminated the columns and spaced the windows more evenly. The architect must have initially considered function more important than what others thought was beautiful, since the spacing of the windows and columns reflected the inner division of space. Changes in the façade for the Munich manuscript take away the reference to the Château at Blois (fig. 51) and therefore make the palace seem more Italian.

A final comparison gives us an indication of Serlio's attitude toward Vitruvius and why he had so much trouble in France with his patrons. A series of applied Doric and Ionic columns articulate the façade of the Venetian Palace for a Noble Gentleman in the Avery manuscript (Pl. LVI). The architect states that there had been criticism of the organization of these orders:

> And because most of the ornaments of the houses of this city are licentious and disorganized as well, I have decided to use orders which many competent architects do not praise too much in order to obey the need for a large number of windows. . . .[14]

Here again the function of the windows was more important to Serlio than what others thought were correct aesthetic principles. The façade was also criticized because it did not follow the precepts of Vitruvius:

> . . . the second order which you see is doric and the ornaments of the windows are ionic, but the triglyphs are not distributed according to Vitruvius.[15]

When we turn to the illustration of this façade in the Munich manuscript, we find that the columns and triglyphs have been eliminated and the windows are spaced more evenly (fig. 75).

Serlio's frustration in France because of this doctrinaire attitude on the part of the French is apparent throughout the Avery manuscript. The conflict with the French, who were much more conventional in their taste than the Italians, was the most likely reason Serlio lost his job as royal architect in 1548, and was unable to publish the Sixth Book during his lifetime.

In addition to the above comparisons, the introduction and conclusion Serlio added to the Munich manuscript are fundamental to an understanding of his approach to architecture. According to Rudolf Wittkower:

> Serlio's work is pedestrian and pragmatic, consisting of a collection of models rather than expressions of principle, and we cannot expect to find here any of Alberti's philosophical concepts.[16]

Yet at the same time, Wittkower modified his statement in view of Serlio's interest in the centralized church plan, the use of which implies an awareness of Alberti's most important theories.[17] Wilinski, on the other hand, felt that Serlio simply adapted the teachings of Alberti and Vitruvius to the circumstances and to the needs of the building at hand.[18] Both Rosci and Wilinski had noticed that Serlio's attitude toward Vitruvius was extremely ambiguous in Books III and IV. The title of Book IV, *On the Roman Orders*, ended with the phrase, "with examples of antiquity which for the most part are in accord with the doctrines of Vitruvius." Serlio actually used the Roman orders as a point of departure to show the architect how to design modern building façades. At the end of Book III Serlio called himself "a good imitator of Vitruvius," but, in fact, he illustrated many classical monuments, such as the Arch of Titus, the Theater of Marcellus and an example of a Doric order, which do not follow the descriptions of Vitruvius (fig. 76).[19]

In France, Serlio became much more decisive, and in the conclusion to the Munich manuscript he forthrightly justified his departure from Vitruvius. In the introduction to the Munich version of Book VI, the architect returned to two sections of Vitruvius's *Ten Books:* Chapter I, Book II, about the origins of architecture, and Chapter IV, Book I, on how to construct basements.[20] Serlio was not interested in merely paraphrasing Alberti and Vitruvius, to whom he rendered homage, but rather encouraged his readers to consult their works themselves.[21] Serlio's basic aim, to design buildings in the city which were "full of proportion and correspondence of the parts of the whole," is based on the teachings of Alberti and Vitruvius.[22] However, his attempt to combine good design with comfort presented him with problems in following their theories closely. Serlio's aims were slightly different from theirs:

> In my sixth book, I will present writing with corresponding drawings comfort and harmonious decoration, using in particular French comfort which I find good.[23]

In the conclusion, Serlio explained his reasons for departing from several of the theories of Vitruvius. He could not follow his rule on room heights since these had to vary according to the different climates:

> The Prince of architects Vitruvius gave a rule about the heights of the rooms . . . [which] in our time, appears too high. I have found my own rule from experience.[24]

73. Sebastiano Serlio: Villa of Ippolito d'Este. Book VII, Frankfurt (1575), folio 57, Avery Library, AA 520 Se65.

74. Sebastiano Serlio: Villa for a King. Project XXXIV, Book VI, Munich, Bayerische Staatsbibliothek, Codex Icon. 189, folio 40r.

Serlio's empiricism also caused him difficulty in following Vitruvius's standards for good ornament:

> I have taken license in some things because I am in countries where by chance people like licentious things more than regular things. . . . I also have given my trust to ancient monuments in diverse parts of Europe which I have found more licentious than regular, according to the teachings of Vitruvius.[25]

For Serlio, practice was as important as theory in the training of the architect. In our manuscript he states that it was very difficult for rich and powerful people to find architects competent in both theory and practice. And it was equally difficult for the architect to find a professor or mentor with the same qualifications.[26] One of the problems Serlio encountered was the many patrons who had read books on architecture and considered themselves competent in the field. In fact, since the main printed treatises were available primarily in Latin, they were more accessible to the patron than to the professional. Alberti himself seems to have been writing more for the patron than for the practicing architect. It is interesting that Serlio praised Antoine de Clermont-Tonnerre for not following this pattern:

> He had sought and wanted the advice of someone who had studied and practiced architecture for a long time. He did not want to rely on his own intelligence and knowledge the way many others have done who have [read] four letters or have [heard] two lectures on architecture and who think they are architects. . . .[27]

In the Avery manuscript Serlio tells the architect to please the patron primarily; comfort is more important than decoration.[28] This is why Serlio often leaves such details as the design of a portal, the height of an attic or the use of a room to the judgment of the patron.[29] In other cases Serlio relies on the "good judgment of the prudent architect" for such things as the height of a vestibule or the placement of the baths according to the source of water on the site.[30] Serlio seems to have left these decisions up to the architect because he expected him to have learned principles in his discussion of other projects that he could apply in specific cases.

Serlio states in the Avery and Munich manuscripts that he planned his buildings so that there would be a proportionate relationship between the parts and the whole.[31] As noted in Chapter I, Serlio participated in the discussion of the Pythagorean harmonic proportions devised by Francesco Giorgi for the church of San Francesco della Vigna in Venice in 1534. Thus we can be sure that Serlio knew Alberti's system of harmonic proportions.[32] Rosci discovered in the Munich manuscript that Serlio applied the same simple arithmetic ratios to the proportions of the building as a whole as he used for the length and width of each room. Villa II is based on a ratio of 4:1; Villa III on a ratio of 3:2; Villa V on the ratio of 2:1. However, Rosci found that Serlio nowhere used the Pythagorean ratios that Palladio employed to relate the height, width and length of his rooms to the dimensions of the building as a whole.[33] In the conclusion to the Munich manuscript, Serlio described his rather simple method of calculating the height of rooms:

> . . . the entrance and the loggias will be twice as high as they are wide, and the reception rooms, small rooms, and bedrooms will be the same height [as width] so that there will be a correspondence of the parts to the whole. . . .[34]

In both versions, however, Serlio states that he had to abandon his rule

75. Sebastiano Serlio: Venetian Palace. Project XVI, Book VI, Munich, Bayerische Staatsbibliothek, Codex Icon. 189, folio 55r.

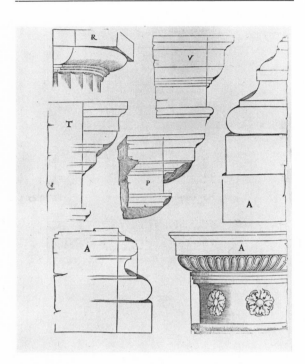

76. Sebastiano Serlio: Doric Order. Book III,
Venice (1540), folio XXIV, Avery Library,
AA 520 Se16.

if the climatic conditions were different. In a cold climate one would have low rooms, in a hot climate, high rooms, and in a temperate climate, rooms of a moderate height.[35] The heights of the rooms could also vary according to their functions: bedrooms would be lower than public rooms.[36]

In an analysis of several projects in the Avery version, none was found to have been planned according to harmonic or arithmetic ratios.[37] When one adds the thicknesses of the walls, in many cases adjustable by the architect, and the heights of the attics, any existing proportions are thrown off. Furthermore, the fact that Serlio did not even always give dimensions for wall thickness or roof height makes it impossible to come to a definite conclusion about his system of measurements. The proportions of the façade of project Ro 26 (Pl. XXXV) confirm Wittkower's statement that the architect continued to use a medieval system of proportions. The measurements of the façade are based on a series of equilateral triangles the sides of which are the diagonals of a square, based on the square root of 2, an irrational number.[38] Carunchio compared a sampling of villa measurements in the Avery and Munich manuscripts, and came to the conclusion that Serlio changed the dimensions in the latter, in order to have more projects based on arithmetic ratios.[39] In conclusion, it is fair to say that Serlio knew Alberti's system of harmonic ratios, but had difficulty in applying them to his architecture because it incorporated French elements such as pitched roofs, dormer windows and narrow rooms.

Serlio's departure from the theories of Vitruvius was not unusual for his time. Most fifteenth- and sixteenth-century writers on architecture in Italy began their treatises by attempting either a translation or a revision of Vitruvius's *Ten Books.* According to Richard Krautheimer, Alberti had started to translate the *Ten Books* for the Duke of Ferrara but abandoned the project. However, he retained Vitruvius's division of ten books for his own treatise.[40] Between 1478 and 1481 Francesco di Giorgio also tried to translate Vitruvius into Italian in several autograph folios attached to the second version of his treatise in the Biblioteca Nazionale in Florence. He explained in the introduction to this second version that he abandoned his plan because he could not understand Vitruvius's vocabulary in Greek and Latin, and because most of the buildings the Roman wrote about were in ruins.[41] In the sixteenth century Fabio Calvo prepared an Italian translation of Vitruvius's *Ten Books* for Raphael, and Battista da Sangallo annotated with sketches a copy of the 1486 printed Latin edition. This interest in Vitruvius led to the foundation of the Vitruvian Academy in Rome in 1540 by Claudio Tolomei.[42] However, Raphael, like Serlio, had stated that he found Vitruvius of little help, in a letter he wrote to Baldassare Castiglione in 1514, when he was studying Roman antiquity for ideas in the planning of the church of Saint Peter's.[43]

One of the most interesting aspects of the Sixth Book is the acceptance of the local idiom of medieval French domestic architecture on the same level as Italian and Roman architecture. Serlio was undoubtedly influenced by the French environment, since an amalgamation similar to his own existed there. In French domestic architecture of the first half of the sixteenth century, Lombard decoration was grafted onto late-Gothic structure and flamboyant ornament.[44] In his pioneering study of the first page of Giorgio Vasari's *Libro di disegno,* Erwin Panofsky provided insights into the Italian sixteenth-century attitude toward Gothic architecture. One would expect Serlio, like Vasari in the preface to his *Lives* (1550, 1568), to condemn Gothic architecture as "barbarous," "monstrous" and "devoid of order," or as the Germanic style that represented a decline of civilization after the grandeur of Rome.[45] However, unlike Vasari Serlio did not condemn Gothic architecture.

The Avery manuscript provides two instances where we gain insight into Serlio's concept of history. Like Vasari, Serlio considered three historical periods: classical antiquity, the Middle Ages and the modern age, his own time. In speaking of the basement of Villa I 9 (Pl. IV), Serlio divides history into two periods: antiquity *(le cose antiche)* and the modern age *(le moderne di CCC anni)*.[46] If we subtract three hundred years from 1541–1542, the date when this drawing was executed, we arrive at a date of 1240 for the beginning of the modern age. This date coincides with Vasari's idea that art began to recover from the decline of the Middle Ages in Tuscany toward 1250.[47] However, later, in a description of an architrave on the façade of Palace P (Pl. LVII), Serlio divides the past into two periods which seem to approximate classical antiquity and the Middle Ages. He distinguishes between ancient *(antichà)* and very old *(vecchissima)*. The architrave, which is very old, is from the Middle Ages. It was probably Byzantine, and Serlio, rather than condemn it, accepts it as a prototype for the one on his façade:

> I have seen a few architraves like this one in several places on ancient buildings, and mostly in this city of Venice, behind the Church of San Eustachio, in a ruin which is not *ancient,* but which is *very old.* And there are several architraves in pieces above the columns. Although this is a barbarous work, the architraves were well done in the work as it was. . . .[48]

Serlio's north Italian background was a major factor in his acceptance of certain aspects of Gothic architecture. The Milanese architect, Cesare Cesariano, apparently felt that Gothic and Roman architecture were equally valid, since he used an elevation of Milan Cathedral to illustrate Vitruvius's description of the methods of architectural drawing in his 1521 edition of the *Ten Books.* When Leonardo and Bramante submitted designs for the tower over the crossing of Milan Cathedral, they also used the local Gothic idiom. The survival of Gothic architecture in sixteenth-century Italy is best illustrated in the competition for the façade design of San Petronio in Bologna.[49] The Bolognese resistance to Renaissance architecture was the cause of both Peruzzi's (fig. 77) and Vignola's attempts in 1523 and 1546, to compose façades in the Gothic style, and of the rejection of Palladio's more Classical solution. Panofsky saw in the outcome of this controversy the development of a new historical attitude toward style, particularly in Pellegrino de' Pellegrini's statement (1582) that the façade of San Petronio should be either completely Gothic or completely Classical, an attitude Panofsky connected to Vasari's choice of a Gothic frame for a Cimabue drawing. The separation of styles was thus based on the notion of their purity.[50]

Serlio's attitude is in contrast to these notions, since he rejects value judgments based on a comparison of Renaissance and Gothic architecture while combining the two in his buildings.[51] Serlio departs from the humanist theory of art, although he paid lip service to it in his introduction to the Munich version of Book VI. Because he does not use Alberti's harmonic proportions and because he combines Gothic, Roman and Italian Renaissance architectural elements, Serlio has clearly rejected the Vitruvian notion of *concinnitas*, the harmony of the parts, which was the basis of Alberti's anthropomorphic theory of architecture.[52] The architecture of

77. Baldassare Peruzzi: Project for the Façade of San Petronio, Bologna. Ink on parchment (1523), London, British Museum, no. 15432.

Book VI, particularly the façades inspired from French models and those which do not have classical orders, show a reversal of Alberti's theory which requires the proportions of the columns and subsequently of the building to be based on those of the human body. Vasari himself distinguished architecture from sculpture and painting because it did not imitate the human body.[53] Serlio also departs from Alberti's revival of Roman building types in using modern sources more frequently than classical.[54] Unlike Palladio, Serlio disguises his antique sources, perhaps as a result of the French environment.

The Avery and Munich versions of Serlio's Sixth Book are indispensable for an evaluation of his architectural theory. Comparison of the two manuscripts illustrates how the French environment caused Serlio to re-evaluate his ideas and rules out Rosci's recent categorization of the architect within the tradition of the Vitruvian academies of the mid-sixteenth century.[55] Serlio developed a theoretical approach, characterized by its freedom from the principles of Alberti and Vitruvius.

CHAPTER VII

Serlio's Legacy

Serlio's Sixth Book, *On Domestic Architecture*, is an important document for an understanding of trends in art and architecture in Cinquecento Europe. First of all, Serlio's book reveals how interrelated northern and southern European developments were at this time. The influence of Albrecht Dürer and of Pieter Coecke on the genesis of Serlio's ideas for his Sixth Book and for his version of Polybius is paralleled by the influence of Dürer's prints on the art of Pontormo, Rosso and Andrea del Sarto in Florence, and Titian and Giorgione in Venice.[1] During the sixteenth century Europe was extremely cosmopolitan: writers, artists, architects, members of the church, politicians, princes, kings and businessmen traveled back and forth between Italy and the North. The French environment was a positive stimulus for Serlio and caused him to come to terms with problems he had grappled with in Italy, and to complete projects he had started earlier in Venice. As Franco Simone has convincingly argued, we often tend to overemphasize the debt of France to Italy when considering the French Renaissance.[2] Serlio's Sixth Book is a good example of France's contribution to the Renaissance in Europe.

Book VI presents us with a realistic and sober view of the problems of the architectural profession at this time. There were no schools of architecture and no sure and direct way for the architect to find patronage. As defined by Serlio, Alberti and Vitruvius, the role of the architect was being undercut by enlightened patrons who had read humanistic treatises, and by the master masons who had a practical knowledge without much theory. Unstable political conditions in both France and Italy made it difficult for architects to gain steady work. In his treatise, and especially in Book VI, Serlio attempts to provide some standards of education and of practice for the architect to enable him to deal with both patron and master mason. *On Domestic Architecture* had considerable influence in Europe in spite of the fact that it was never published. Like the treatises of Filarete and Francesco di Giorgio, it was known through copies that circulated among interested readers. One of the most exciting aspects of Book VI is the influence it must have had on Palladio. Rosci and Chastel have noted how

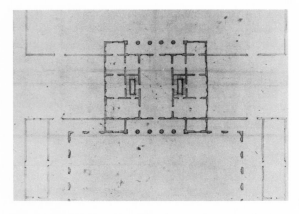

78. Andrea Palladio: Villa (ca. 1545). London, Royal Institute of British Architects, XVI, folio 2v, pen on paper.

the two royal pavilions, Villas Y 25 and 27 (Pls. XXXIII, XXXVII) and the Royal Villa 30 (Pl. XLIV) precede Palladio's Villa Rotonda, a house based on an ecclesiastical building type crowned by a dome. In fact, in the Munich version Serlio states:

> This house has more the form of a temple than a house in order to distinguish it from what people are accustomed to everyday.[3]

By drawing on similar vernacular traditions, Serlio's villa and farm complexes set important precedents for Palladio's villas. Rosci suggested that Book VI probably influenced some of Palladio's early villa designs, such as the drawing of the villa with central hall (fig. 78) which harks back to the Avery manuscript (C 3, Pl. I; H 8, Pl. III; M 12, Pl. VII).[4] The other books which Serlio worked on in France may also have been known through manuscript copies. His version of Polybius could have influenced Palladio's early urban projects such as the plan of the Port at Pesaro for Girolamo Genga, with its standardized row houses (figs. 79, 80).[5] Projects in Book VII such as Villa VI may have influenced the drawing Palladio made for the Villa Pisani at Bagnolo in 1544 (fig. 81).[6]

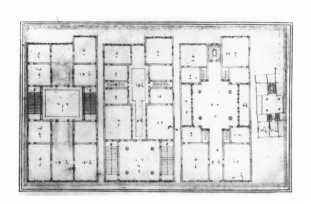

79. Andrea Palladio: Port at Pesaro (1548–1555). London, Royal Institute of British Architects, XVI, folio 16r, ink on paper.

The projects in Serlio's Sixth Book have many elements in common with the later buildings of Jacopo Sansovino and Michele Sanmicheli; however, it is difficult to assume a direct influence of Book VI on these architects. Rather, they must have shared common influences. The Zecca, the Palazzo Dolfin, the Library and the Villa Garzoni by Jacopo Sansovino were begun only at the time that Serlio left Venice in 1540.[7] Buildings such as Sansovino's Palazzo Corner at San Maurizio and Sanmicheli's Villa La Soranza, both begun in the 1550s, resemble projects in the Avery manuscript.[8]

The presence of the Avery manuscript in France until the eighteenth century explains why Serlio's Sixth Book had such an impact on architects like Philibert Delorme, Nicolas Bachelier and Jacques Androuet du Cerceau. Delorme's cryptoporticus at Anet (1547–1552), with its convex-concave Belvedere staircase, shows the influence of Villas O 14 and X 21 (Pls. XIII, XXVI–XXVII).[9] Du Cerceau's Château at Maulne (1566) was based on the pentagonal Fortress for a Prince, Et 24 (Pl. XXXI).[10]

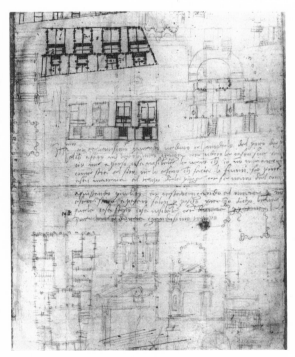

80. Andrea Palladio: Port at Pesaro (1548–1555). London, Royal Institute of British Architects, XVI, folio 16v, ink on paper.

Our Italian architect also influenced the publication of architectural treatises in France. In his *Premier tome de l'architecture* (Paris, 1567), Philibert Delorme took his cue from Serlio in mixing practical information and theory, and went beyond him in defining the relationship between patron, architect and master mason.[11] Serlio's palace and villa designs influenced the projects in Jacques Androuet du Cerceau's *Livre d'architecture* (Paris, 1582) and Pierre Le Muet's *Manière de bastir pour toutes sortes de personnes* (1623).[12]

The presence of the Vienna proofs for Book VI in France in the seventeenth and eighteenth centuries would explain the mention of Serlio's project for a new Louvre for François I during the deliberations on the East Wing of the Louvre for Louis XIV in 1666–1667. Chastel claims that a seventeenth-century engraving in the Institut de France, which includes a copy of the plan of the Palace for a Prince in the Munich manuscript (folios 63av–64r), is evidence of knowledge of Book VI in France at this time.[13] In fact the French attitude to Serlio's unorthodox theoretical ideas was part of the origins for their call for classicism in the deliberations on the East Colonnade of the Louvre between 1663 and 1671. The French criticized the unorthodoxy of Bernini's project, submitted in 1665, and it is significant that Claude Perrault was consulted in the middle of the competition, in 1666, because he was an authority on Vitruvius.[14] French criticism of Serlio parallels their objection to Borromini's architecture that was voiced during Bernini's visit to Paris, on the ground that it incorporated Gothic elements.[15] In the eighteenth century, both Serlio's version of Polybius and his Sixth Book may have affected Ledoux's revolutionary plan for the town of Chaux (1773–1779) in eastern France, which included a hierarchical succession of houses from those for workers to that of the director of the salt works.[16]

In Italy, Serlio's espousal of Gothic architecture was caused by the same factors that resulted in its acceptance by architects in the next century, such as Vicenzo Scamozzi, Francesco Borromini and Guarino Guarini. Like Serlio, Scamozzi, a Venetian who had been to Paris in 1600, attempted to unite French and Italian architecture in his treatise, *Idea dell' architettura universale* (1615). In his book on temples he placed French cathedrals side by side with Roman temples.[17] Borromini, brought up in Milan, used the Gothic method of triangulation for his design for the church of San Carlo alle Quattro Fontane (1635–1641) and a Gothic type of skeletal structure for the vault of the Collegio di Propaganda Fide (1660s), both in Rome. Guarino Guarini, from Modena, praised Gothic architecture in his treatise *Architettura civile*, which was completed by his death in 1683 and published posthumously by Vittone in 1737. Wittkower suggested that these architects were bound by their common north Italian heritage.[18]

An outstanding quality of *On Domestic Architecture* is the way in which the author adapts his design concepts to practical concerns: the needs of the owner represented in the program, the local traditions and the climatic conditions. Serlio's interest in buildings for poor and middle class citizens—neglected by his contemporaries—initiated a concern among architects that persists to this day. Of all his work, Serlio's designs for this kind of housing had the most influence on future generations. Thus, in spite of the difficulties Serlio incurred during his lifetime, his progressive ideas influenced subsequent architects and became part of our architectural heritage.

For many years Serlio's reputation has been overshadowed by those of Palladio, Sansovino and Sanmicheli. Perhaps his difficult personality or the fact that he left Italy for France encouraged some of his contemporaries and successors, like Vasari, to consider him outside the mainstream. Now, with the publication of Book VI, we can appreciate Serlio's true contribution and give him the place he merits in the history of architecture.

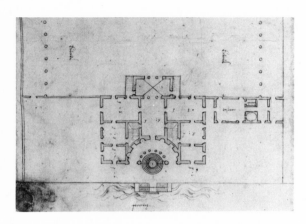

81. Andrea Palladio: Bagnolo, Villa Pisani (1544), London, Royal Institute of British Architects, XVI, folio 7v.

Appendix ✸

I. VILLA TYPE I. EUROPEAN FARM AND VILLA

A. Projects

A 1, B 2, C 3 (Pl. I), D 4, E 5, F 6, G 7 (Pl. II), H 8 (Pl. III), I 9 (Pl. IV), K 10 (Pl. V), L 11 (Pl. VI), M 12 (Pls. VII, VIII), N 13a (Pl. XI) and O 14 (Pls. XII, XIII).

B. Description

Open plan with loggias or galleries; most have a forecourt for farm buildings and a rear garden.

C. Examples

1) D 4–F 6. D 4 has only a bedroom (B: *camera*) and kitchen (C: *cucina*), both with fireplaces. An upper story could be added for a richer artisan. F 6 adds a basement (*cavando*) with the kitchen and a storeroom for food (*cantina*); and another first-floor bedroom. The house should be cleaner than a poor artisan's since the kitchen is away from the living and sleeping areas. C and D in F 6 serve both as bedroom and living room.

2) H 8. A central hallway (A: *andito*) makes two apartments, each with a bedroom (C) and a reception room (B: *anticamera*). In the basement are the kitchen, a storeroom for food, a servants' dining room (*tinello*) and a general storeroom (*salvarobe*) for the storage of grain (*granaro*).

3) I 9. The forecourt has stables. The long entrance hall (A) provides privacy for rooms B, C, F and D. C is the bedroom and B a storeroom for clothes (*guardaroba*). F (*camerino*) may have been a study. The kitchen is in the basement. Basements are built above ground, since the land usually dried and sank over the years.[1]

4) N 13a. There are two courtyards (*corte*), the main one (A) and a sunken court (O) to the right for the kitchens, stables, and a dwelling for the gardener and watchman. On the left are a tennis court (H: *giuco di palla*) and a gallery (I: *galeria*), a small court, the owner's apartment (F, D and C) and the chapel (K). Below the small court are baths (*stuffi*). Below the gallery (I) are a dining room, workshops (*offici*) and a cold storage for food (*cantina freschissima*); above it is a storage room for furniture (*salvaroba da mobili*). L (*sala*) is a reception room. There are several kitchens (R: *cucarezza*; V: *cucina*) and a small court for baking bread (*corticella*). S is a pantry (*dispensa*) and T a wine cellar. A guest dining room is over the kitchen wing (*tinello per gentilhuomini*).

5) M 12. (Description according to variant text.) Two small, enclosed, uncovered courts (I: *cortiletto*) bring light into the central hallway (H: *vestibulo*). Four apartments, one in each corner of the building (e.g., rooms C, D, E, F and G; and L, M, N and O), have privacy. At the back of the court are the baths (T, V, X and Y: *stuffi e bagni*).

D. Additional Sources

1) A 1–C 3 are related to the thatched-roof farms in the province of Rovigo and the Villa Dal Zotto in Venagazzu (1405–1409) in the Treviso with a trabeated wood loggia.[2] Francesco di Giorgio had illustrated the porticoed forecourt of these Italian farms.[3] Similar porticoes and roofs are found in French farmhouses of the Jura.[4]

2) D 4–F 6. The loggia in F 6 refers to the Villa Dall'Aglio in Lughignano in the Treviso (1492) and the Villa Ca'Brusa in Lovolo, in Vicenza (1409–1475).[5] The plan with a central, narrow hallway (F 6) is related to the Villa Porto Colleoni at Thiene in Vicenza (1476)[6] and to the remodeled Villa Trissino at Cricoli (1537–1538).[7] The plan with wide central room (H 8 and C 3) is similar to the Villa

Cappello at Pramaggiore (1464), the Villa Giustinian at Roncade (1509–1534) and the Villa Priuli at Treville (1528–1533).[8] Palladio used this plan in the Villa Cornaro (1565) at Piombino Dese.[9]

3) N 13a. The Manors of Clos-Lucé (1477–1490; fig. A 1)[10] and of Bury (1514–1524) near Blois (figs. A 2–A 3).[11] The Hôtel de Cluny (1456–1485; figs. A 4–A 5) and the destroyed Hôtel de Bourbon (1390–1418) in Paris (fig. A 6), also manors, are similar.[12] At Cluny the kitchen is in the right wing; the owner's apartment is in the left part of the *corps de logis*; the single gallery along the courtyard and the owner's room[13] were joined to the lower *frigidarium* of the Roman Baths of Paris;[14] there was a garden above the *frigidarium*[15] similar to the private court above the baths of N 13a. A gallery in the Hôtel de Bourbon led from the main *corps de logis* to a large chapel; on the second floor was a dining room.[16]

4) M 12 is related to Serlio's variant of Poggioreale (fig. A 7),[17] to Leonardo's plan for a villa for Charles d'Amboise, French governor of Milan (1507–1508),[18] the Villa of Poggio a Caiano (1485),[19] the Château de Madrid (1528) in the Bois de Boulogne[20] and the Villa Priuli at Treville.[21]

The bath wing (T, V, X and Y) relates to the Ninfeo at Genazzano near Palestrina (1511)[22] and to the back wing of the sunken courtyard of the Palazzo Imperiale in Pesaro (1534) by Gerolamo Genga.[23]

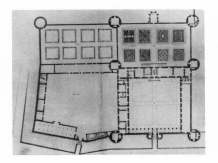

A1. Amboise: Manoir de Clos-Lucé (1477–1490). (Author)

A2. Jacques Androuet du Cerceau: Bury, château (1514–1524), Plan. Ink on parchment (ca. 1575), London, British Museum, C 99, no. 114. (Courtauld Institute)

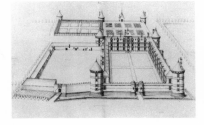

A3. Jacques Androuet du Cerceau: Bury, château (1514–1524). Ink on parchment (ca. 1575), London, British Museum, C 99, no. 116. (Courtauld Institute)

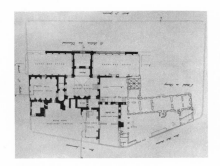

A4. Paris, Hôtel de Cluny (1456–1485) and The Roman Baths of Paris, Plan. Archives des Monuments Historiques. (Archives Photographiques)

■ = Roman baths of Paris
☐ = Hôtel de Cluny

A5. Paris, Hôtel de Cluny (1456–1485). Archives des Monuments Historiques. (Archives Photographiques)

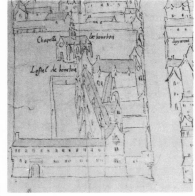

A6. Paris, Hôtel du Petit-Bourbon (1390–1418). Ink on parchment (ca. 1550), Archives Nationales, N III, Seine 63, no. 1. (Author)

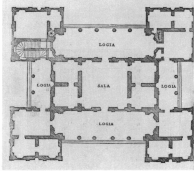

A7. Sebastiano Serlio: Poggioreale, variation. Book III (1540), folio CLII. (Avery Library)

II. VILLA TYPE II. VILLAS DERIVED FROM THE CASTLE PLAN

A. Projects

N 13 (Pls. IX, X), P 15 (Pls. XIV, XV), Q 16 (Pls. XVI–XVIII), R 17 (Pl. XIX), S 18 (Pls. XX, XXI), 22 (Pls. XXVIII, XXIX), Et 23 (Pl. XXX), Et 24 (Pl. XXXI), 30 (Pls. XLIII, XLIV) and 31 (Pls. XLV–XLVII).

B. Description

N 13, P 15, Q 16, R 17 and Et 23 have interior courtyards, 30 has a *donjon* or interior keep. 30 and 31 have an *enceinte* with dwellings for officials.

C. Examples

1) P 15. A fortified entrance and staircase (A) with guard rooms on the side (B). In the back are two apartments (K, I and H), on each side of the courtyard. The apartment on the left for the *Capitano* has thicker walls.[24]

2) Q 16, Château of Ancy-le-Franc. On the first floor (Pl. XVI) a vestibule and a staircase (A), protected by two guard rooms, lead to the courtyard. The kitchen wing (C–G) with a dining room (F) is on the right; the kitchen itself (G), vaulted. Outside, at the back, is a well with pipes to bring water to the kitchen (G) and baths (X, Y and V).[25] An oval staircase at the left gives the owner access

to the baths on the first floor. On the right is a guest staircase leading to the second-floor reception rooms. On the second floor (Pl. XVII), a third loggia replacing rooms T, Y and I[26] has been added in the nineteenth century. The owner's apartment at the left has a bedroom (G: *camera per il padrone*), library (K: *libraria*), study (I: *picolò studio*) and hallway (L: *galeria secreta*) for private access to the chapel (M). Bedrooms for family (T, X, Y) are in the left wing; here *loggia* means an open passageway (A and O), and *galeria* (L), a closed passageway.[27]

3) 30 Central building. The King and his family live in four apartments in the corners. Each apartment has two rooms (M and N). Two apartments share a living room (L).

4) 31 Central building. There are two chapels (I and L). The sunken courtyard (H) is for festivals and triumphs. K is a room for musicians (P). The royal apartment has two bedrooms (P, O: *camera*), and small (N: *anticamera*) and large (M: *sala*) reception rooms.[28]

D. Additional Sources

1) N 13, R 17, Et 23. Variations of the Villa Poggioreale, Naples.[29]

2) Q 16. The plumbing system is similar to the one in the kitchen and mezzanine of the Hôtel Jacques Coeur at Bourges (1443–1453).[30]

3) P 15. The terrace on interior courtyard is similar to Sansovino's Villa Garzone (1540).[31]

4) 22. A drawing of a house by Francesco di Giorgio.[32]

5) Et 24. The Palazzo Farnese at Caprarola (1520–1573).[33]

6) 30. Room K is similar to one in a palace project by Giuliano da Sangallo and to Villa M 12.[34]

7) 31. Central building. The differently shaped rooms with niches derive from Peruzzi's drawings.[35] Room L resembles the so-called Temple of Minerva Medica (400 A.D.) in Rome.[36]

III. VILLA TYPE III. PAVILIONS

A. Projects

T 19 (Pls. XXII, XXIII), V 20 (Pls. XXIV, XV), Y 25 (Pls. XXXII, XXXIII), Ro 26 (Pls. XXXIV, XXXV), 27 (Pls. XXXVI, XXXVII) and 28 (Pls. XXXVIII, XXXIX).

B. Description

Small dwellings with centralized plans. Usually a circular room or hallway divides them into two apartments. Ro 26 and 28 are variants of H 8 and M 12, and Y 25 and 27 are variants of 30.[37]

C. Examples

1) T 19 and V 20. V 20 has a small chapel (F) off its central room. The niches in the central reception room of T 19 were to be used as seats. Light from adjacent rooms (D) comes from small openings in the side walls. Each apartment has a living room (C: *salotto*), a front bedroom (D: *camera*), a back bedroom (E: *rietro camera*) and a study (F: *studio*).

2) Y 25. From a vestibule (B: *vestibulo*) one enters a round, niched living room (C: *sala*) with a fountain at the center. The octagonal room (E) is the main bedroom with two beds opposite each other: "This will be the room for pleasure before the baths *(stufa)*."[38]

A heated oval room (P) is the equivalent of a Roman *calidarium*, while the unheated room (G) with its series of round benches corresponds to the *frigidarium*. H, I and K are bedrooms.

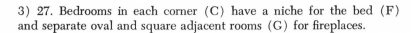

3) 27. Bedrooms in each corner (C) have a niche for the bed (F) and separate oval and square adjacent rooms (G) for fireplaces.

D. Additional Sources

1) Y 25. The plan of the central room depends on the niched vestibule of the peristyle of the Domus Flavia (81–92 A.D.).[41]

2) 27. The central room depends on the vestibule of the Esquiline Wing of the Domus Aurea (64–68 A.D.).[39] The colossal order of the façade is derived from Giulio Romano's Palazzo del Te in Mantua (1524) and the loggia of the Villa Madama.[40]

IV. VILLA TYPE IV. THE REVIVAL OF THE ROMAN *VILLA SUBURBANA*

A. Projects

X 21 (Pls. XXVI, XXVII), 29 (Pls. XL–XLII).

B. Description

Villas characterized by several inner courtyards.

C. Examples

X 21. The apartments (B, C and D; E, F, G and H; K, O, N, P, Q, R, S and T) are located around two courtyards, one surrounded by loggias, the other by galleries, which are fenestrated and on two levels.[42]

D. Additional Sources

1) X 21. Based on Francesco di Giorgio's plan of a house with two courtyards.[43] The galleries function like the double galleries connecting the east and west wings of the Château at Gaillon (1495–1507, figs. A 8–A 10).[44] The façade was designed "in the French style but accompanied with ornaments in the antique manner."[45] The frontispiece is similar to that of the Château of Azay-le-Rideau (1518–1527).[46]

A8. Alexandre Lenoir: Gaillon, château, East Gallery, Interior Courtyard (1495–1507). Pen and wash on paper (ca. 1799), Paris, Louvre, Cabinet des dessins RF-5279, no. 50. (Réunion des Musées Nationaux)

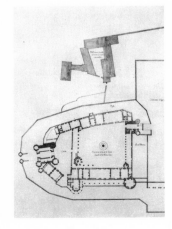

A9. Jacques Androuet du Cerceau: Gaillon, château (1495–1507), Plan. Ink on parchment (ca. 1575), London, British Museum, C 99, no. 50. (Courtauld Institute)

A10. Jacques Androuet du Cerceau: Gaillon, château. Ink on parchment (ca. 1575), London, British Museum, C 99, no. 56. (Courtauld Institute)

2) 29. Based on a drawing of a house with octagonal courtyards by Francesco di Giorgio.[47] Serlio compares the forecourt with apartments for visiting officials to a French *basse-cour*.[48] The original garden façade of the Palazzo del Te loggia is an Italian precedent for the columns on the façade.[49]

V. CITY DWELLING TYPE I

A. Projects

ʌ–O (Pls. XLVIII–LI).

B. Description

Houses with aligned rooms on a narrow lot.

C. Examples

1) A, C. House A has a bedroom (A) with alcove for the bed (C) and a passageway (B) to the garden (D), and well. The kitchen facilities are outside at the back. The richer owner of House C has a separate kitchen (C) behind the bedroom (A). He could also have a well and communal latrines in the courtyard (D), indicated by the smaller dots.

2) I, K. Shops (B, C), separate kitchens (H, F), on the courtyard. Privies are inside the kitchens.

3) Houses L–O. These houses have two wings on either side of a courtyard with connecting porticoes. The octagonal room in the back wing of house L could be either a chapel or study.[50]

D. Additional Sources

L–O. The symmetrical plans and varied number of porticoes recall Jacopo Sansovino's Palazzo Gaddi (ca. 1520), Antonio da Sangallo the Younger's Palazzo Baldassini (1516–1519), and Peruzzi's Palazzo Massimo (1532–1535) in Rome as well as Serlio's townhouse plans in the Polybius edition (figs. 34, 35).[51]

According to fifteenth-century French inventories, the first *corps de logis* usually contained the apartment of the owner and offices and shops, while the second housed the kitchen and stables.[52] Two French examples are the Hôtel Chambellan in Dijon (1488–1503, fig. A 11)[53] and the destroyed Hôtel Legendre in Paris (1504–1524,

A11. Dijon, Hôtel Chambellan (1488–1503). (Giraudon-Laurois)

figs. A 12–A 14),[54] where galleries connected a *corps de logis* on the street to the main *corps de logis* at the back.[55]

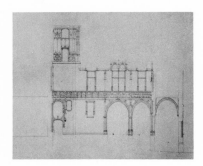

A12. Viollet-le-Duc: Hôtel Legendre (1504–1524), Main Wing and North Gallery. Ink on paper (1841), Paris, Centre de Recherches des Monuments Historiques, no. 1131. (Archives Photographiques)

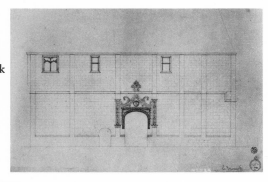

A13. Viollet-le-Duc: Hôtel Legendre (1504–1524), Main Façade. Ink on paper (1841), Paris, Centre de Recherches des Monuments Historiques, no. 1129. (Archives Photographiques)

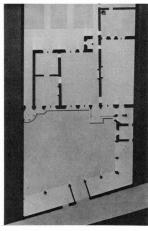

A14. Viollet-le-Duc: Hôtel Legendre (1504–1524), Plan. Ink on paper (1841), Paris, Centre de Recherches des Monuments Historiques, no. 1127. (Archives Photographiques)

VI. CITY DWELLING TYPE II. VENETIAN PALACE, P (PLS. LII, LIII; LVI, LVII)

A. Description

The central *salone* (P, Pl. LII) separates the building into two apartments, each with four bedrooms. Rooms (N) with their sleeping alcoves (H) are for the women of the house. They have their own hallway (A), so they can circulate unseen.[56] The small open courts on the sides of the hall (C) light the central hallway (P) and the bedrooms (M). The small, niched rooms at the back can be used as studies, oratories or baths. At the top of the folio are elevations of the screens (G, F) between the small courtyards and the central hall, and sleeping alcoves (H).

On plate LIII, at the left, is a cross section of the extremities of the building with the hallways (A), and the mezzanine above (M). Next is an elevation of the sides of the central *salone* (P). To the right, Serlio illustrates the cross section of the different levels around the central *salone* (P, Q, R; a loggia, S; and rooms N and M). The first two stories of the basement are vaulted. Room M has a painted wood hammerbeam roof. The attic is for the storage of grain.[57]

B. Additional Sources

Palace P is a reflection of two Venetian houses attributed to Mauro Codussi: Palazzo Corner Spinelli (1490) and the Palazzo Vendramin Calerghi (1502–1504).[58]

VII. CITY DWELLING TYPE III. THE CENTRAL ITALIAN PALACE AND FORTRESS

A. Projects

Variant of Palace P (Pls. LIV, LV), Q (Pls. LVIII, LIX), R (Pls. LX, LXI) and T (Pls. LXV–LXVIa).

B. Description

Rectangular plan with interior courtyard surrounded by loggias; similar to Villas N 13, P 15, Q 16, R 17, Et 23.

C. Examples

1) Q. Serlio states that this building type was used in cities in Italy outside Venice.[59] Apartments for guests are in the front near the entrance (A, B and C; E, F and G). The apartments of the owner's family are located at the back of the palace (K, L, M, O, P, Q and S). A bathroom (M) is heated.[60]

2) Palace for the Governor, T (Pls. LXV–LXVIa). The two front towers can be used as a place of refuge in case of attack. The Governor and his entourage are housed around the first courtyard and at the back in the wings along the garden (I). At the right side of the first courtyard is a large audience room (S); the corresponding room on the left is a chapel.[61] There is a staircase for horses at the front of the palace adjacent to the left tower (D and C). The second courtyard (H) contains lodgings for the soldiers (K); there are stables for horses (M).

D. Additional Sources

1) Variant of Palace P (Pls. LIV, LV). The interior elevation is similar to the courtyard of the Venetian Zecca, by Sansovino (1536–1547).[62] This palace reflects the Cà del Duca, built for Duke Francesco Sforza of Milan in Venice (1460–1461) according to a design by Filarete.[63]

2) Governor's Palace T (Pls. LXV–LXVIa). The lodgings for the soldiers (K) around the second courtyard (H) recall the plan of the Palace of *Questorio* [sic] in Serlio's version of Polybius (fig. A 15). The rusticated portal is similar to one of the gates in *On Roman Fortifications According to Polybius* (fig. A 16).

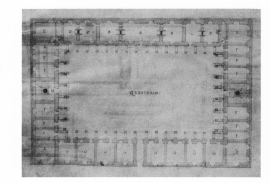

A15. Sebastiano Serlio: House of the *Questorio*. *On Roman Fortifications According to Polybius*, Munich, Bayerische Staatsbibliothek, Codex Icon. 190, folio 5r. (Staatsbibliothek)

A16. Sebastiano Serlio: Porta Decumana. *On Roman Fortifications According to Polybius,* Munich, Bayerische Staatsbibliothek, Codex Icon. 190, folio 17v. (Staatsbibliothek)

VIII. URBAN DWELLING TYPE IV. CIVIC PALACE OR PALAZZO DEL PODESTA, S (PLS. LXII–LXIV)

Description

There are shops (B) in the exterior porticoes, and offices for notaries (D) in the interior porticoes. The inner wing contains a large vaulted room for negotiations (G), two public law courts (H) and two private law courts (I). Below this wing are the prisons. The meeting room for the members of the city council is in the front wing of the building, as well as the apartments of the members of the Podestà's family.

IX. URBAN DWELLING TYPE V. THE REVIVAL OF THE ROMAN *VILLA SUBURBANA*

A. Projects

Palace of the Prince, V (Pls. LXVII–LXX); Palace of the King, W (Pls. LXXI–LXXIIIb).

B. Description

Palaces with several interior courtyards, similar to Villas X 21 and 29.

1) V. The apartments in the front wing are for guests and officials; those in the wings around the first and second courtyards are for the Prince and his family. There is a small chapel (G) and a corresponding tower (H). The third courtyard contains a garden, with apartments for officials on each side. Behind are two long stalls on horses and carriages (+). At the end of the third courtyard is a large room (K) *(capella),* for meetings of the Prince's council, triumphs and festivals.[64] Two tetrastyle atria beside K lead to another garden. Along this garden, there will be two narrow passageways so that the Prince can amuse himself privately; these are called galleries.[65] At the back of the garden are stables for the horses and lodgings for the grooms.

2) W. The wing along the street will be used for apartments for the King's guests and officials. The apartments for the King and his family are on the other courtyards. Each apartment contains a reception room *(sala),* a living room *(anticamera),* two bedrooms *(camera)* and a small room *(camerino).*[66] At the end of the third series of courtyards is a suite of rooms: R, for pleasure; S, a study; T, a bath; and V, a shaving room.[67] The hemicycle called a theater *(theatro)* is for the display of statues. On each side are two courtyards for the exercise of horses, with dwellings for the grooms.

C. Additional Sources

1) Prince's Palace, V (Pl. LXVIII). The interior space of Room K is derived from the loggia of the Villa Madama, and Bramante's Ninfeo at Genazzano.[68]

2) King's Palace, W (Pl. LXXI) depends on a palace planned by Francesco di Giorgio which contains a succession of octagonal, square and circular peristyles.[69]

NOTES TO CHAPTER I

1. William B. Dinsmoor, "The Literary Remains of Sebastiano Serlio: I," *Art Bulletin,* XXIV, 1942, 65–66, and James S. Ackerman, "Architectural Practice in the Italian Renaissance," *JSAH,* XIII, 1954, 4.

2. Serlio, Book IV, Venice, 1537, folio V cited in Dinsmoor, I, 66.

3. Serlio's Sixth Book, *On Domestic Architecture,* in the Avery Library of Columbia University, reproduced here in reduced 'facsimile', will be referred to throughout the present volume as *On Domestic Architecture,* Book VI or the Sixth Book; footnote references to Book VI give only plate and line numbers. References to the manuscript for Book VI in the Munich Bayerische Staatsbibliothek (*Il Sesto libro delle habitationi di tutti li gradi degli huomini*) are qualified as such.

4. Dinsmoor, I, 55–91; II, 113–154. Marco Rosci, I: *Il trattato di architettura di Sebastiano Serlio;* II: *Il sesto libro delle habitationi di tutti le gradi degli huomini,* Milan, 1967.

5. Dinsmoor, I, 55, note 4; 67–68, note 63; II, 128; 129, note 57. Stanislaw Wilinski, "Sebastiano Serlio ai lettori del III e IV libro sulla architettura," *BCISA,* I, 1961, 64–65. For the discovery of the portrait of Serlio, see Stanislaw Wilinski, "Z Treciej i Czwartej Ksieji o Architekturze Sebastiano Serlio," *Studiai Materialy do Teorii histori Architektury i Urbanistykii,* Warsaw, 1971, 195; 202, note 102. (I would like to thank André Liebich for the translation.)

6. Antonio Bolognini Amorini, *Elogio di Sebastiano Serlio architetto bolognese,* Bologna, 1823, 1–2. Léon Charvet, *Sebastiano Serlio,* Lyons, 1869, I. Dinsmoor, I, 56, note 2. The church is now destroyed, but the document is transcribed in Amorini.

7. Amorini, 3–4. Charvet, 7. Dinsmoor, II, 128, note 52.

8. Amorini, 5. Charvet, 7, 11. Dinsmoor, I, 62–64. Giorgio Vasari, *Le vite de' più eccellenti Architetti, Pittori, e Scultori,* Florence, 1550, ed. Ricci, Milan, 1927, III, 172, mentions Serlio only in the life of Peruzzi. In his revised edition of 1568, Vasari mentioned Serlio in connection with Marcantonio Raimondi, Jacopo Sansovino and Pieter Coecke. For the homage to Peruzzi, see Book VI, plate XXXVI, lines 7–10. All translations of the Serlio manuscripts and books and all italics in these quotations are the author's.

9. For a recent discussion of the Vatican workshop, see Ludwig Heydenreich and Wolfgang Lotz, *Architecture in Italy 1400–1600,* Harmondsworth, 1974, 152–162, 164–166, 173–177, 191, 194–196; Christoph L. Frommel, "Die Peterskirche unter Papst Julius II im Licht neuer Dokumente," *Römisches Jahrbuch für Kunstgeschichte,* 16, 1976, 57–137; Franz Graf Wolff Metternich, *Bramante und St. Peter,* Munich, 1971.

10. Dinsmoor, I, 64, note 49. Loredana Olivato, "Per il Serlio a Venezia, documenti nuovi e documenti rivisitati," *Arte veneta,* 25, 1971, 281: Venice, Archivio di Stato, Notario Avidio Branco, B99, folio 421.

11. Euclid's *Geometria* (1482), Francesco Colonna's *Hypnerotomachia Poliphili* (1499), Luca Pacioli's *De divina proportione* (1509) and Fra Giocondo's edition of Vitruvius's *De architectura* (1511). For general bibliography on Venice as a printing center, see Horatio F. Brown, *The Venetian Printing Press,* London, 1891; R. Brun, *Le livre imprimé hors de France des origines au XIXe siècle,* Paris, 1961, 24–25; M. Sander, *Le livre à figures italiens depuis 1467 jusqu'en 1530,* Milan, 1942–1969, 6 vols; Arthur M. Hind, *An Introduction to a History of the Woodcut,* New York, second edition, 1963, II, 415–422, 456–503.

12. Musi's engravings are now in the New York Metropolitan Museum of Art, Department of Prints and Drawings, illustrated in Dinsmoor, I, 64–65, figs. 1–4. A. Bartsch, *Le peintre graveur,* Vienna, XIV, 1813, nos. 382–383, 525–531, 1528–1536. Two more were issued by Serlio in France in 1544, 532–533 of Bartsch, figs. 5–6 in Dinsmoor. See Dinsmoor, I, 64, notes 52–53, for complete list.

13. This letter was discovered by Deborah Howard, "Serlio's Venetian Copyrights," *Burlington Magazine,* CXV, 1973, 512: Venice, Archivio di Stato, Senato Terra, reg. 25, 1528–1529, folios 70r–70v. See also her discussion of the engravings, 513, figs. 25–30.

14. Ackerman, 1954, 3–11. A discussion of Bramante's lack of knowledge of engineering is found in Ackerman, "Notes on Bramante's Bad Reputation," *Studi bramanteschi, atti del congresso internazionale,* Milan, Urbino, Rome, 1970, 339–349. See also Catherine Wilkinson, "The New Professionalism in the Renaissance," *The Architect, Chapters in the History of the Profession,* ed. Spiro Kostof, New York, 1977, 124–160.

15. Serlio, Book IV, Venice, 1537, folio LXXIv. See Olivato, 286.

16. Dinsmoor, I, 64, note 50. Marcantonio Michiel, *Notizie d'opere del disegno,* Venice, Biblioteca Marciana, Ital. Cl. XI Cod. LXVII (ap. Zen 346, folio 52), in T. Frimmel, *Der Anonimo Morelliano,* Vienna, 1888, 84. See also C. Gould, "Sebastiano Serlio and Venetian Painting," *JWCI,* XXV, 1962, 56ff.

17. Amorini, 5. Rudolf Wittkower, *Architectural Principles in the Age of Humanism,* New York, third edition, 1962, 102–113. D. Howard, *Jacopo Sansovino, Architecture and Patronage in Renaissance Venice,* New Haven, 1975, 64–74.

18. Amorini, 5. Wladimir Timofiewitsch, "Ein Gutachten Sebastiano Serlios für die Scuola di San Rocco," *Arte veneta,* 17, 1963, 158–160: Venice, Archivio di Stato, S. Rocco, N. 413.

19. Rosci, I, 1967, 24, fig. 28. Uffizi A5282.

20. Carolyn Kolb Lewis, "Portfolio for the Villa Priuli, Dates, Documents, and Designs," *BCISA,* XI, 1969, 353–370, figs. 209–218, and Lionello Puppi, "Un litterato in villa: Giangiorgio Trissino," *Arte veneta,* XXV, 1971, 72–91; 86, fig. 126; 89, fig. 128.

21. Dinsmoor, I, 55, note 2; II, 128. For the document, see F. Malaguzzi-Valeri, *Archivio storico dell'arte,* VI, 1893, 46.

22. Rosci, I, 1967, 34. Wittkower, 1962, 76–77. Serlio, Book IV, Venice, 1537, folio XXIV. Franco Barbieri, *La basilica palladiana,* Corpus Palladianum, II, Vicenza, 1968, 39; 36, Pl. IX.

23. Serlio, Book II, Paris, 1545, folio 64v. Olivato, 287. Amorini, 4. Rosci, I, 1967, 23–24. Lionello Puppi, *Scritti vicentini d'architettura del secolo XVI,* Vicenza, 1973, 15, note 16. G. G. Zorzi, *Contributo alla storia dell'arte vicentina dei secoli XV e XVI, il preclassicismo e prepalladiani,* Venice, 1937, 50–51.

24. For the career of Giovanni Caroto, the brother of Giovan Francesco Caroto, see Maria Teresa Franco Fiorio, *Giovan Francesco Caroto,* Verona, 1971, 67–76.

25. Rosci, I, 1967, 23, 27. Palazzo del Te (1524–1534): Serlio, Book IV, folio LXIXv; Book II, folio 25v. Villa Imperiale (1531–1533): Serlio, Book IV, folio III; Book II, folio 25v. Cornaro Odeon (after 1530): Serlio, Book VII, folios 218, 219, 223. See also Amedeo Belluzzi and Walter Capezzali, *Il Palazzo del Te a Mantova,* Mantua, Museo Civico, 1976; Bernhard Patzak, *Die Villa Imperiale in Pesaro,* Leipzig, 1908; Felton Gibbons, *Dosso and Battista Dossi,* Princeton, 1968, 77–84; Craig Hugh Smyth, "The Sunken Courts of the Villa Giulia and the Villa Imperiale," *Essays in Memory of Karl Lehmann, Marsyas,* Supplement, I, New York, 1964, 304–313; Giuseppe Fiocco, *Alvise Cornaro, il suo tempo e le sue opere,* Vicenza, 1965, 63–66, figs. 37, 39, 46–59; and Wolfgang Wolters, "Sebastiano Serlio e il suo contributo alla villa veneziana prima del Palladio," *BCISA,* XI, 1969, 89.

26. Munich, Bayerische Staatsbibliothek, Codex Icon., 190, folio lr, lines 1–2; folio lv, line 33.

27. Dinsmoor, I, 84–88; and Paolo Marconi, "Un progetto di città militare, l'VIII libro inedito di Sebastiano Serlio," *Controspazio,* I, 1969, Part I, no. 1: 51–59; Part II, no. 3: 53–59. For the watermarks of the French paper, see C. M. Briquet, *Les filigranes,* second edition, Amsterdam, 1968, nos. 13145, 13154.

28. Dinsmoor, I, 90. I agree with Marconi rather than with Dinsmoor that *Dacia* is Datia, or Hungary, not Dalmatia, or Yugoslavia. See Marconi, 1969, no. 1, 57. Munich, Staatsbibliothek, Codex Icon. 190, folio lv, flap: lines 8–12 and 24–27.

29. Pio Paschini, *Il Cardinal Marino Grimani e i prelati della sua familia,* Rome, 1960, 14, 21, 27–29, 40, 41, 46, 50, 59, 60, 62–64. See also Rodolfo Gallo, "Le donazioni alla Serenissima di Domenico e Giovanni Grimani," *Archivio veneto,* L–LII, 1952, 34–77, and Pio Paschini, "Le collezioni archaeologiche dei prelati Grimani del Cinquecento," *Rendiconti della pontificia accademia romana di archeologia,* V, 1926–1927, 149–190.

30. Rosci, I, 1967, 28. Dinsmoor, I, 66–67. Serlio, Book IV, folios III and XXXIII–XXXV, for Venetian palace façades. These reflect the Palazzo Corner Spinelli (1490) and the Palazzo Vendramin-Calerghi (1502–1504) by Mauro Codussi. L. Angelini, *Le opere in Venezia di Mauro Codussi,* Milan, 1945, 82–94, figs. 69, 100. See also G. C. Argan, "Sebastiano Serlio," *L'arte,* XXXV, 1932, 190–199, S. Wilinski, 1971, 191–193, and 1961, 57–69. Francesco Marcolini da Forlì's career is discussed by G. Cassini, *Le edizioni illustrate di Francesco Marcolini da Forlì,* tesi di laurea, Università degli Studi di Padova, Facoltà di lettere e filosofia, 1962–1963; and David Rosand, M. Muraro, *Titian and the Venetian Woodcut,* Washington, 1976–1977, 265–268, 270–273. Paul F. Grendler, *Critics of the Italian World, 1530–1560, Anton Francesco Doni, Nicolò Franco, and Ortensio Lando,* Madison, 1969, 6–7.

31. Olivato, 281. Venice, Archivio di Stato, Senato Terra, 1536–1537, Reg. 29, C 116r, v, October, 1537, transcribed in Howard, 1973, 316.

32. Avery Library, J5527, eight drawings. These were formerly in the Coghan Briscoe Collection, London, and were attributed to the Sienese painter, Domenico Beccafumi. According to Donato Sanminiatelli, "The Beginnings of Domenico Beccafumi," *Burlington Magazine,* 1957, 401–410, and Rinaldo de Liphart Rathshoff, "Un libro di schizzi di Domenico Beccafumi," *Rivista d'arte,* 17, 1935, 33–70, they are copies of lost drawings by Peruzzi and are dated 1512. See Briquet, for watermarks nos. 459, 461–463 and 466.

33. Jean Adhémar, "Aretino, Artistic Advisor to Francis I," *JWCI,* 17, 1954, 316. Dinsmoor, I, 67.

34. Dinsmoor, I, 67–68, 73, note 89, for the letter of Marguerite de Navarre. Serlio, Book III, Venice, 1540, folios III–IV.

35. For Giulio Camillo, see Frances Yates, *The Art of Memory,* 1974, third edition, 129–172. For the Este family, see John H. M. Salmon, *Society in Crisis: France in the Sixteenth Century,* London, 1975, 120–121; Vicenzo Pacifici, *Ippolito d'Este,* Tivoli, 1923; and C. Terasse, *François Ier,* Paris, II, 1948, 99.

36. Dinsmoor, I, 62–63. Rosci, I, 1967, 17–22. Wilinski, 1961, 57–59, "Sebastiano Serlio e Andrea Palladio," *BCISA,* VI, 1964, 131–136; 1971, 193. Christoph L. Frommel, *Die Farnesina und Peruzzis architektonisches Frühwerke,* Berlin, 1961, 90–92. Serlio, Book III, 1540, Poggioreale Variation, folios CLIIr–CLIIv; Villa of Poggioreale, folio CLIr; Belvedere Courtyard, folios CXLII, CXLV; The Loggia of the Villa Madama, folio CXLIX; The Tempietto, folios XLI–XLIV; The Dome of St. Peter's, folios XXXIX–XL. Hubertus Günter, "Bramante's Hofprojekt um den Tempietto und seine Darstellung in Serlios Drittem Buch," *Studi bramanteschi,* 1970, 483–501.

37. Dinsmoor, II, 128, note 53: Archivio di Stato, Venice, Sez.Not. Chiodo Giacomo, Ba. 201, no. 148.

38. Dinsmoor, I, 55, note 4; 73, note 89.

39. Louis Hautecoeur, *Histoire de l'architecture classique en France,* I, 2, 1965, Paris, 181. L. de Laborde, *Les comptes des bâtiments du roi (1528–1571),* Paris, 1877, I, 172–173, for the complete text.

40. Terasse, II, 327–344.

41. Vignola arrived in 1541, and Cellini in 1542. For the latest investigation of François I's court at Fontainebleau and the art produced there, see *L'école de Fontainebleau,* Paris, Grand Palais, 1972.

42. Dinsmoor, I, 70–72. Robert Brun, *Le livre français illustré de la Renaissance,* Paris, 1969, 33, 175, 387, 313. J. C. Oswald, *A History of Printing,* New York, 1918, 158.

43. Hautecoeur, I, 1, 1963, Paris, 237–245, Fontainebleau, 238, fig. 116; Blois, 193, fig. 101. For Chambord, see Pierre Marie Auzas, *Chambord,* Paris, n.d., ill. 7; and Ludwig Heydenreich, "Leonardo da Vinci Architect of François I," *Burlington Magazine,* XCIV, 1952, 277–278. François Gebelin, *Les châteaux de la Renaissance,* Paris, 1927, 61, 68–74, 97–107.

44. Carlo Pedretti, *Leonardo da Vinci, the Royal Palace at Romorantin,* Cambridge, 1972, fig. 136, Codex Atlanticus 217v–b.

45. Serlio, Book III, Venice, 1540, folio III. Dinsmoor, I, 68, 73.

46. Serlio, Book II, Paris, 1545, folios 65, 67r and v, 68r and v, 69r and v, 70r and v, the tragic, comic and satiric stage sets, cited in Dinsmoor, I, 73–74. For Serlio's dependence on Peruzzi, see F. Cruciani, *Il teatro del Campidoglio e le feste romane de 1513,* Milan, 1968, and Henri Zerner, Robert Klein, "Vitruve et le théâtre de la Renaissance italienne," *La forme et l'intelligible,* Paris, 1970, 294–309. M. Rosci, "Sebastiano Serlio e il teatro del cinquecento," *BCISA,* XVI, 1974, 235–243.

47. Serlio, Book V, Paris, 1547, folio 7v, oval church after Peruzzi; folio 30v, French longitudinal church, as cited in Dinsmoor, I, 74. See J. Müller, *Das Regulierte Oval,* Bremen, 1967, 2–25; W. Lotz, "Die ovalen Kirchenräume des Cinquecento," *Römisches Jahrbuch für Kunstgeschichte,* VII, 1955, 97–98; and R. Billig, "Die Kirchenpläne al modo antico von Sebastiano Serlio," *Opuscula Romana* XVIII, I, 1954, 21–38.

48. M. N. Rosenfeld, "Sebastiano Serlio's Drawings in the Nationalbibliothek in Vienna for his Seventh Book on Architecture," *Art Bulletin,* LVI, 1974, 400–409; 402, fig. 1, folio 83r. Ackerman suggests *On Incidentals* as a more appropriate title for Book VII.

49. Serlio, Book V, Paris, 1547, folio 73r.

50. Serlio, *Extraordinario libro,* Lyons, 1551, folio 92v: cited in Dinsmoor, I, 76–77: Ackerman proposes *Supplementary Book on Doors* for the title.

51. The letter is in the Archivio Estense di Stato in Modena, busta xxviii, and was published by Pacifici, 142, and reproduced in Dinsmoor, II, 142, note 98.

52. Dinsmoor, I, 84, note 131. Marconi, 1969, no. 3: 53–54.

53. Serlio, Book VII, Frankfurt, 1575, Introduction by Jacopo Strada, folio aiiiv, as cited in Dinsmoor, I, 75, and II, 136, note 75. See Hind, II, 597–617, and Brun, 67–85, for Lyons as a printing center. I would like to thank Janet Brooke for information on the entry of Henri II in 1548, about which she completed an M.A. thesis at the University of Toronto in 1975. The entry was published as *La magnificence de la superbe et triomphante entrée,* Lyons, G. Rouillé, 1549, B.N. Rés Lb 31.14, and reprinted by Georges Guigue, Lyons, 1927.

54. Serlio, *Extraordinario libro,* Lyons, 1551, folio A2r, as cited in Dinsmoor, I, 76.

55. Rosci, I, 1967, 58. Dinsmoor, II, 129–131.

56. Boris Lossky, "A propos du château de Fontainebleau, identifications et considérations nouvelles," *Bulletin de la société de l'histoire de l'art français,* Année 1971, Paris, 1972, 27–28.

Abbreviations used in the notes:

BCISA = *Bolletino del centro internazionale di studi di architettura Andrea Palladio*

JSAH = *Journal of the Society of Architectural Historians*
JWCI = *Journal of the Warburg and Courtauld Institutes*
RIBA = *Royal Institute of British Architects*

For the convenience of the reader, the accepted English title of works has been used wherever possible.

57. Lucile M. Golson, "Serlio, Primaticcio, and the Architectural Grotto," *Gazette des beaux-arts*, LXXV, 1971, 95–108; 98, fig. 5. Hautecoeur, I, 2, 225–226, fig. 49.

58. For the drawings of *Minerva* and *Juno*, see S. Béguin and R. Bacou, *L'école de Fontainebleau*, no. 149, Minerva, Louvre, Cabinet des dessins, Inv. no. 8552, p. 140. The *Juno* is also in the Louvre, Cabinet des dessins, Inv. no. 8551, see L. Dimier, *Le Primatice*, Paris, 1928, Pl. xxxii. Maria Walcher Casotti, *Vignola*, Trieste, 1960, I, 41, thinks that these drawings were planned by Vignola, not Serlio. For the *Minerva Visiting Jupiter and Juno*, see also Béguin, *L'école de Fontainebleau*, no. 181, p. 161, Uffizi, 1502 E., ill., Dimier, 1928, Pl. xvi.

59. Serlio, Book IV, Venice, 1537, folio LXXr.

60. Serlio, Book VII, Vienna, Nationalbibliothek, Codex S.N. 2649, folio 13v. Rosenfeld, 1974, 408, note 21.

61. Lossky, 29–32. Gebelin, 1927, 100–101. Laborde, I, 221, 241. L. Dimier, *Le Primatice*, Paris, 1900, 148, 284. Serlio, Book VII, Frankfurt, 1575, folio 96.

62. Lossky, 28. See Hautecoeur, I, 1, 239, fig. 117.

63. Dinsmoor, II, 136, letter of May 5, 1546; Dinsmoor, 142, note 98, reproduces the Italian text, from Pacifici, 141; the letter is in the Archivio Estense di Stato in Modena, Carteggio degli ambasciatori in Francia, busta xxciii. For the letter of October 16, see Dinsmoor, II, 143, note 103; for the Italian text, as published by Pacifici, 142. It is in the Archivio Estense di Stato, archivio ducale secreto. The letter was also published by Adolfo Venturi, "Sebastiano Serlio," *Storia dell'arte italiana*, Milan, XI, 1939, 442. Examination of the Cardinal's correspondence, written while he was in charge of the Inquisition in France, and now in the Bancroft Library of the University of California, Berkeley, revealed no mention of his house or relations with Serlio. See *Lettere d'Ippolito d'Este, Cardinale di Ferrara, Legato in Francia, scritte a Pio Papa IV e al Sr. Card. Borromeo hora Santo*, Hearst Collection, *Papers related to the Counter-Reformation in France*, 3Ms Dc 116.7E7.

64. François-Charles James, "L'hôtel du Cardinal de Ferrare à Fontainebleau d'après un document inédit," *Actes du Colloque International sur l'Art de Fontainebleau*, Paris, 1975, 35–37. The document is in the Minutier Centrale, Paris, Etude CXXII, P. Leroy, S. Legendre, liasse 1064. Serlio, Book VI, Pl. XI, lines 1–3, quoted in Dinsmoor, II, 142.

65. Dinsmoor, II, 146–150. A. Larcher, *Ancy-le-Franc*, Tonnerre, 1969, attributed the château to Primaticcio because some of the interior decorations had been given to him.

66. Pl. XVIII, lines 11–12.

67. M. N. Rosenfeld, "Review of Marco Rosci, Il Trattato di architettura de Sebastiano Serlio," *Art Bulletin*, LII, 1970, 319–320. Jean Guillaume, "Serlio, est-il l'architecte d'Ancy-le-Franc," *Revue de l'art*, 5, 1969, 9–18. See also Munich, Bayerische Staatsbibliothek, Codex Icon. 189, Book VI, folio 16v, for Serlio's comments.

68. Munich version of Book VI, folio 16v. Avery manuscript, Pl. XVIII, lines 16–18.

69. Because only one ensemble, the *Chambre des arts*, can be attributed to an artist of the sixteenth century, I cannot agree with André Corboz, "Serlio au carré, pour une lecture psycho-iconologique d'Ancy-le-Franc," *Psicon*, 1, 1974, 80–90, that Serlio and Giulio Camillo outlined the iconography of the painted decoration for the entire château. There is one drawing for the painting of Apollo and the Muses in the *Chambre des arts* which has been variously attributed to Niccolò dell'Abbate, Primaticcio and the Master of Flora. The painting seems closest to the oeuvre of the latter. See S. Béguin, *L'école de Fontainebleau*, 125, no. 133; ill. 124.

70. Marconi, I, 54. Vienna, Nationalbibliothek, Codex 10101, folio 2v: "Dua tabula novem pedum im quadratura . . . qua qui facta est ab ipso Serglio instante dicto francisque cum vellet duo castra ad eam formam et modum unum im Piedmontanis alterum contra Flandros extruere. Has ambas tabulas ego dum essen in Francia ab ipse autore emi nec im eius alterius manibus nunc similes habentur." There is a copy which was cited by Marconi, but this version is in Jacopo Strada's own handwriting. See F. Eheim, "Ein Beitrag zur biographie Jacopo Stradas," *Mitteilungen des Instituts für Österreichische Geschichtsforschung*, LXXI, 1963, 124–126, and A. Lhotsky, *Die Geschichte der Sammlungen*, Vienna, 1941–1945, I, 163. Strada offered his library for sale to Rudolf II on September 11, 1576.

71. Rosenfeld, 1974, 408; 407, figs. 17–19 (Bourse). Serlio, Book VII, folios 208–217 (Château at Rosmarino); folios 192–195 (Bourse); folios 184–185 (Place des Marchands). Vienna, Nationalbibliothek, Codex S.N. 2649, folio 122r (Bourse). See also Rosci, I, 1967, 16; and Charvet, 76–80. The Bourse resembles the one by Soufflot which is on the same site. See Hautecoeur, 1952, V, 173–186; 175, ill. It is dated 1747–1749, and we don't know if it replaced Serlio's.

72. Charvet, 79–80. Lyons, Archives Communales, Registre Consulaire BB66.

73. Charvet, 92–94. Strada, introduction to Book VII, Frankfurt, 1575, folio aiiiv.

74. Lhotsky, 16–63. Eheim, 124–127. F. Schulz, "Jacopo Strada," *Thieme-Becker Künstler-Lexicon*, Leipzig, XXXII, 1938, 145–147. J. F. Hayward, "Jacopo Strada XVIth-Century Art Dealer," *Art at Auction, 1971–1972*, New York, 1973, 68–74.

75. Strada, introduction to Book VII, Frankfurt, 1575, folio aiiiv. Rosenfeld, 1974, 401, note 5. See also, Dinsmoor, I, 77–78.

76. For the letter of Ottavio Strada to his father, see Vienna, Nationalbibliothek, Codex 9039, folio 112r, published by Rosenfeld, 1974, 409. A different chronology has been suggested by Tancredi Carunchio, "Dal VII Libro di S. Serlio: XXIII Case per edificar nella villa," *Quaderni dell'Istituto di Storia dell'Architettura*, XXII (1975), 127–132; (1976), 95–126.

77. Strada, introduction to Book VII, Frankfurt, 1575, folio aiiv. See Dinsmoor, I, 84.

78. Vienna, Nationalbibliothek, Codex 10101, folio 3v: "Liber de castrorum metatione veterum Romanorum, hactens nondum visus: qui meis impensis in Gallia Lugduni compositus est à Sebastiano Serglio celebri satis viro et artificioso, Regis Gallianum olim imbri Architetto: Huius formas typographicas apud me habeo estquè tam magnus fermè sicuti Sebastiano Sergli de Architectura liber quem ego typis excudi feci Francforti ad Manum meis impensis." Marconi, 1969, no. 1: 54. Rosenfeld, 1974, 408, note 25. Dinsmoor did not realize that the book had been printed.

79. Dinsmoor, I, 87–88. Briquet, nos. 13145, 13154.

80. Lhotsky, 161. Dinsmoor, I, 86. Rosci, I, 1967, 58. Although the manuscript was sold to Duke Albert V of Bavaria in 1571, and received book plates of the ducal family in 1618 and 1623, it had been bought by the Fuggers by 1558.

81. Konrad Oberhuber, *Albertina Studien*, 1961, 2–3. Vienna Nationalbibliothek, 72. P.20. I would like to thank Konrad Oberhuber for giving me his photographs of the manuscript as well as his notes on the watermarks. They are as follows: Briquet, no. 314: France, 1567; no. 336: Paris, 1664; no. 651: Paris, 1690; no. 702: Paris, 1696; nos. 854–855: Troyes, 1590. See pp. 82–83, below.

82. Vienna, Nationalbibliothek, Codex 8709, folio 2v, line 2. This is a copy of a will and is signed Jacobum Strada Rome 1584. Dinsmoor noted the existence of the will but did not analyze its contents.

NOTES TO CHAPTER II

1. Dinsmoor, II, 117. See also the correspondence of Dinsmoor, Archives, Avery Library, Columbia University, New York. No records of the sale are currently in the possession of B. Quaritch Ltd., London.

2. Dinsmoor, II, 117–118. For the watermarks, see W. A. Churchill, *Watermarks on Paper in the XVII and XVIII Centuries*, Amsterdam, 1935, nos. 514, 516.

3. Dinsmoor, II, 117, 121.

4. Dinsmoor, II, 125; I, 85. Julius Schlosser, *Die Kunstliteratur*, Vienna, 1924, 363, 374; *La letteratura artistica*, translated by Filippo Rossi, ed. Otto Kurz, Vienna, third edition, 1967, 408–409, 418–419. Serlio, *Tutte l'opere*, Venice, 1619, Ridgewood, 1964.

5. Schlosser, 1967, 408. Rosci, I, 1967, 58. Dinsmoor, II, 140.

6. See Chapter I, 26, note 75.

7. Dinsmoor, II, 124. Rosci, II, 58.

8. Lhotsky, 161–162.

9. Dinsmoor, II, 124; I, 86.

10. Vienna, Nationalbibliothek, Codex 10101. See Chapter I, 25, note 70.

11. See Chapter I, 27, note 81.

12. See Rosenfeld, 1974, for a complete discussion of the Vienna manuscript for Book VII.

13. Dinsmoor, II, 120–124.

14. Dinsmoor, II, 121, 126, 135.

15. Dinsmoor, II, 122–123, note 31.

16. Rosci, I, 1967, 58.

17. Dinsmoor, II, 123–124.

18. Lotz, 1955, 21, 97–98, note 4. Book VI, Pl. XXVII, lines 15–16. "Since the feet can be measured on the plan, I will not strain myself to give all the measurements of the apartments since these can be found with a compass."

19. Rosci, I, 1967, 14. Munich, Bayerische Staatsbibliothek, Codex Ital. 37.

20. Wolfgang Lotz, "Das Raumbild in der italienischen Architekturzeichnung der Renaissance," *Mitteilungen des Kunsthistorischen Instituts in Florenz*, VII, II, 1956, 195, note 8, L. B. Alberti: "Laonde io certo lodo sempre grandemente lo antico costume delli edificatori, che non solamente con disegno di linee e con dipintura, ma con modelli ancora ed esempi, fatti di assicelle o di qual altra cosa si voglia, si esamini e pensi e ripensi . . . tutta la opera e tutte le misure delle parti sue. . . ." The English translation of this book (Cambridge, Mass., 1977) does not include the Alberti quote. Serlio, Book VI, Pl. LIII, lines 8–9.

21. J. S. Ackerman, "Science and Art in the Work of Leonardo," *Leonardo's Legacy*, ed. C. D. O'Malley, Berkeley, 1969, 205–225, and Ackerman, 1954, 3–11.

22. Pl. XLIX, lines 16–17.

23. Dinsmoor, I, 83, 91.

24. Dinsmoor, II, 119. Serlio, Book VI, Pl. XL, lines 1–2.

25. Dinsmoor, II, 116–117. Serlio, Book II, folio 73v.

26. Dinsmoor, II, 116–117, noted there were also several references in Book VII, Frankfurt, 1575, folio 94, to Book VI, but these do not appear in the preparatory manuscript in Vienna. Serlio, Book V, Paris, 1547, folios 17v, 33r: ". . . hora quivi sara il fine del libro di li tempii sacrii accio dio possa sequitare gli altri due libri, uno di tutte le habitatione, l'altro di molti accidenti. . . ."

27. Dinsmoor, II, 116. Letter reproduced, 142, note 98. See also, Adolfo Venturi, "L'arte e li Estensi: Ippolito II di Ferrara in Francia," *Rivista europea, rivista internazionale*, N.S., XXIV, 1888, 23–27. See Chapter I, 23, note 51, for same letter.

28. Dinsmoor, II, 116. The letter is reproduced on 143, note 103.

29. Dinsmoor, II, 131–135; tables: 130, 135.

30. Dinsmoor, II, 136–139; table: 139.

31. Dinsmoor, II, 139.

32. Dinsmoor, II, 138. Type I: Briquet, II, 650, no. 13065, Bunch of Grapes, ill. IV.

33. Dinsmoor, II, 138. Type II: Briquet, II, 653, no. 13145, Bunch of Grapes with initials BM at bottom, cross at top, ill. IV.

34. Dinsmoor, II, 138. Type III: Briquet, II, 653, no. 13154, Bunch of Grapes with initials DR in center, ill. IV

35. Dinsmoor, II, 116, 136–137.

36. Dinsmoor, I, 87–88. See Chapter I, 19, note 26.

37. Dinsmoor, II, 133–134.
Type IV: Briquet, II, 506, no. 9666, Shield with initials PS.
Type V: Briquet, II, 636, no. 12718, Cross with Setting Sun.
Type VI: Briquet, II, 635, no. 12694, Pot with initials AE.
Type VII: Briquet, I, 124, no. 1573, Fleur de Lys surmounted by a Cross.
Type VIII: Briquet, II, 677, no. 13766, Snake with Crown.
Type IX: Briquet, II, 677, no. 13767, Snake with Crown.
Types IV–VI and VIII–IX are illustrated in IV of Briquet, Type VII in III of Briquet.

38. Pl. VIII, line 1.

39. Pl. LVII, line 1.

40. Pl. XXXII, lines 4, 10, 11–12.

41. Dinsmoor, III, 123.

42. For the Codussi façades see Chapter I, 20, note 30. These influences will be discussed in more detail in Chapter V.

NOTES TO CHAPTER III

1. Strada, introduction to Book VII by Serlio, Frankfurt, 1575, folio aiiiir.

2. Hind, II, 396–397.

3. Hind, II, 402–403. Wilfred Blunt, *The Art of Botanical Illustration*, London, 1950, 32; 35, fig. 14b.

4. Hind, II, 456–463. Harrison Horblit, *One Hundred Books Famous in Science*, New York, 1964, no. 27. J. C. Oswald, *A History of Printing*, New York, 1928, 117. Brown, 2–55. Rosand, 10–11.

5. Hind, II, 403.

6. Rosand, 15–19, no. 1, 37–54. The cutter and publisher of the *Triumph of Christ* are unknown. See also Terisio Pignatti, "Begegnungen: Italien," in *Albrecht Dürer 1471–1971*, Nürnberg, Germanischen Nationalmuseums, 1971, 103–116, and "The Relationship between German and Venetian Painting in the Late Quattrocento and Early Cinquecento," in John R. Hale, *Renaissance Venice*, London, 1973, 244–274.

7. The publisher was Bernardino Benalio of Bergamo who was active in Venice from the end of the fifteenth century. The cutter was Ugo da Capri who had come to Venice in 1510 from Rome. Rosand, 19–20, 32–33; no. 3A, 55–70.

8. Rosand, nos. 7–10, 94–104: Vision of the Seven Candlesticks, Four Horsemen of the Apocalypse, Opening of the Fifth and Sixth Seals, Apocalyptic Woman. See also note 15, below.

9. Dinsmoor, I, 65; Ackerman, 1954, 4; and Rosci, I, 1967, 13.

10. For the most recent literature on Dürer's book on fortifications, see Alexander von Reitzenstein, "Die Befestigungslehre, Das Fechtbuch," in *Albrecht Dürer 1471–1971*, 355–362; Martin Biddle, introduction, facsimile edition of Dürer, *Etliche Underricht zu Befestigung der Stett, Schloss und Flecken*, Zurich, 1971, 77–139; and Hans Rupprich, *Dürer, Schriftlicher Nachlass*, III, Berlin, 1969, 369–425. See also, W. Waetzoldt, *Dürer and his Times*, trans. R. H. Boothroyd, London, 1955, 220–224.

11. Maria Cionini Visani, "Un itinerario nel manierismo italiano, Giulio Clovio (1478–1578)," *Arte veneta*, XXV, 1971, 120, 124.

12. Sander, VI, no. 748, 1288. Hind, II, 410–412. Peruzzi, Codex 10935, folio 15r, Vienna Nationalbibliothek. These drawings by Peruzzi should be compared to those by Francesco di Giorgio, who also knew of Valturio's book. See Corrado Maltese, Livia Degrassi, *Francesco di Giorgio Martini: Trattati di architettura, ingegneria, e arte militare*, Milan, 1967, I, Turin, Codex Saluzziano 148, folio 62, Pl. 115.

13. Liliana Grassi, introduction, *Antonio Averlino detto Il Filarete, Trattato di architettura*, Milan, 1972, CVI–CXIII. Maltese, introduction, 1967, I, XXXII–LXIV, and II. Florence, Codex Magliabechiano II. I. 141, 505, folio 98v, lines 25–27.

14. Dinsmoor, I, 56–62. Paolo Fontana, "Osservazoni intorno ai rapporti di Vitruvio colla teorica dell'architettura del Rinascimento," *Miscellanea di storia dell'arte in onore di I. B. Supino*, Florence, 1933, 305–322. Schlosser, 1967, 126, 251–258.

15. H. Lehmann-Haupt, "The Heritage of the Manuscript," in P. Hofer, *A History of the Printed Book*, New York, 1938, 2–23. Sandra Hindman and James D. Farqhar, *Pen to Press, Illustrated Manuscripts and Printed Books in the First Century of Printing*, Baltimore, 1977.

16. Brun, 163. L. DeLisle, *Recherches sur la librairie de Charles V*, Paris, 1907, I, 115–116. For the manuscript in the Morgan Library by Mazerolles, see *Le siècle d'or de la miniature flamande: le mécénat de Philippe le Bon*, Brussels, Palais des Beaux-Arts, 1959, 112, no. 119.

17. This drawing: Vitruvian rooms from Book II, chapters 8–10. See Heinz Spielmann, *Andrea Palladio und die Antike*, Munich, 1966, no. 39, 142–143, fig. 17.

18. Dinsmoor, II, 125–126. Rosci, II, 58.

19. Erwin Panofsky, *The Life and Art of Albrecht Dürer*, Princeton, third edition, 1955, 51–52. Rupprich, III, 1969, 399. Other drawings for Dürer's treatise on fortifications are in the university library, Erlangen; The Ambrosiana, Milan; and in Dresden. See also F. Winkler, *Die Zeichnungen Albrecht Dürers*, Berlin, 1936, 34–35, Pl. XVII, and Rupprich, III, 1969, 390–423, Pls. 285–313.

20. Since Dürer corresponded with Raphael, it is possible that he was also aware of the contents of Raphael's letter to Leo X. See the Raphael drawing that was sent to Dürer discussed by Alice M. Kaplan, "Dürer's Raphael Drawing Reconstructed," *Art Bulletin*, LVI, 1974, 50–57.

21. For the basic biography of Pieter Coecke, see Max J. Friedländer, "Pieter Coecke van Aelst," *Jahrbuch der Königlichen Preussischen Kunstsammlungen*, Berlin, 1917, 78–94; and *Altniederländische Malerei*, 12, Leiden, 1935, 52–68. The most recent discussion of Coecke's career is found in Georges Marlier, *Pierre Coecke d'Alost*, Brussels, 1966, 27–46.

22. Fritz Grossmann, "Brueghels Verhältnis zu Rafael und zur Rafael-Nachfolge," *Festschrift Kurt Badt zum siebzigsten Geburtstage*, Berlin, 1961, 135, 142, fig. 10, for a drawing by Coecke in the Victoria and Albert Museum, the *Transfiguration of St. Paul*, which shows a knowledge of Michelangelo's Capella Paolina. See also Friedländer, 75, 78. Marlier, 26–27, 42, 61–70, also discusses these trips. Coecke's trip to Constantinople is recorded in his *Les moeurs et fachons de faire de Turcz avecq les regions y appartenantes ont esté au vif contrefaictz par Pierre Coecke d'Alost lui estant en Turquie, l'an de Jesus Christ MD33*, published posthumously in 1553 by his wife in Antwerp.

23. H. de la Fontaine Verwey, "Pieter Coecke van Aelst en de uitgeven van Serlios architectur boeck," *Bouwkundig Weekblad*, 73, 1955, 173–175; "Pieter Coecke van Aelst en de uitgeven van Serlios architectur boeck," *Het Boeck*, XXXI, 1952–1954, 251–271. Marlier, 379–388.

24. Friedländer, 74.

25. Sune Schéle, "Pieter Coecke and Cornelis Bos," *Oud Holland*, 1962, 238–239.

26. Verwey, 1952–1954, 259; 261, fig. 1; 1955, 175. Marlier, 379–380. Schéle, 1962, 238. For the influence of Dürer's *Large Canon* woodcut of 1518 on Coecke, see Julius Held, *Dürers Wirkung auf die niederländische Kunst seiner Zeit*, The Hague, 1931, 130, Pl. VIII, fig. 4.

27. See Chapter I, note 31.

28. Schéle, 236–237. Between 1542 and 1545 Coecke traded books in partnership with Cornelis Bos. In 1542 Bos received a consignment from Coecke of 300 copies of Serlio's Book IV and 650 copies of Coecke's *Die Inventie der Colomnen*.

29. Friedländer, 82. Verwey, 1952–1954, 258; 1955, 174. Marlier, 45, 379, 380, fig. 134.

30. Pieter Coecke, *Die Aldervermaerste Antique Edificen*, Antwerp, 1546, last folio before colophon.

31. Marlier, 386. Verwey, 1952–1954, 264; 1955, 176. See also A. Corbet, "L'entrée du Prince Philippe à Anvers en 1549," *Les fêtes de la Renaissance*, II, *Fêtes et cérémonies au temps de Charles V*, Paris, 1960, 307–310. *Le triomphe d'Anvers*, Antwerp, 1550, folio ai v: Verona, Porta San Zeno (Porte de la Barrière hors de la ville), folio ciiii v: Verona, Porta Nuova, Venice, Fortezza San Andrea at the Lido (Porte Césarienne), folios giiiv–giiiir: Palazzo Pompeii, Verona (Galerie des Florentins), folio Kiii v–Kiiii r: Capella Pellegrini (L'Arc de Triomphe des Espagnols). For the buildings of Sanmicheli, see Pietro Gazzola, *Michele Sanmicheli, mostra d'arte della città di Verona*, Venice, 1960, no. 6: 108–109, figs. 27–34, Palazzo Pompeii (1530); no. 7: 110–112, Capella Pellegrini (1527–1529); no. 14, 126–127, figs. 82–91, Porta Nuova (1540); no. 22, 130–134, figs. 98–103, Fortezza San Andrea, Lido (1534); no. 23, 141–143, figs. 110–118, Porta San Zeno, Verona (1542). Except for the Porta San Zeno, all the dates indicate when the building was begun.

32. I would like to thank J. S. Ackerman for this suggestion.

33. See Hind, I, 352–355; 355, fig. 183.

34. Hind, I, 348–352; Blunt, 1950, 31–59; 46, fig. 23; 52, fig. 26a; 58, fig. 29b. William M. Ivins, Jr., *Prints and Visual Communication*, Cambridge, 1953, 31–44.

35. C. O'Malley, *Andreas Vesalius of Brussels*, Berkeley, 1965, 74–90. Rosenfeld, *Sebastiano Serlio (1475–1555), An Exhibition . . .*, New York, Columbia University, 1975, 3, 6, no. 10.

36. O'Malley, 124–136. Rosenfeld, 1975, 3.

NOTES TO CHAPTER IV

1. Serlio, Book IV, Venice, 1537, folio V. Dinsmoor, I, 66; II, 120, 122, 126–127.

2. Rosci, I, 1967, 59–60; II, 82.

3. For the date of Alberti's treatise, see Joan Gadol, *Leon Battista Alberti*, Chicago, second edition, 1973, 93, and Cecil Grayson, "The Composition of L. B. Alberti's *Decem libri de re aedificatoria*," *Münchner Jahrbuch der bildenden Kunst*, ser. 3, 11, 1960, 152–161. For Alberti's description of private houses, see *L'architettura, De re aedificatoria*, trans. Giovanni Orlandi, Milan, 1966, Book V, chapter I, 336, chapter II, 338–340, 342, chapter III, 348, chapter VI, 356–358, chapter VII, 359–360, chapter XIV, 398–402, chapter XV, 402–406, chapter XVI, 406–414, chapter XVII, 414–426, chapter XVIII, 432–438; Book IX, chapter I, 780–784, chapter II, 788–790, chapter IV, 802–808. See also Giorgio Muratore, *La città rinascimentale*, Milan, 1972, 91–98, and Zygmut Wazbinski, "La maison idéale selon Alberti," *Acta historiae artium academiae scientiarum hungaricae*, XIII, 1967, 13–16.

4. Grassi, xiii, xxviii–xxxi, xlvi–xlvii, lxxvi. Filarete, *Treatise on Architecture*, intr. and trans. John R. Spencer, New Haven, 1965, xvii–xviii; Book II, Vol. I, 20–21, Vol. II, folios 10r–11r; Book II, I, 26, II, folios 14r–14v; Book VII, I, 93, II, 54r; Book XI, I, 146–147, II, folios 84r–84v; Book XI, I, 148, II, folio 85v; Book XII, I, 149–150, II, folios 86r–86v; Book X, I, 123, 125–126, II, folios 70v–71r, 72v–73r; Book VI, I, 74, II, folios 43r–43v; Book VIII, I, 99–100, II, folios 57v–59r; Book IX, I, 122, II, folio 70v; Book X, I, 128, II, folio 74r; Book XII, I, 157, II, folio 90v; Book XIV, I, 184, II, folio 105r; Book XVIII, I, 251, II, folio 146v; Book XVIII, I, 258, II, folios 150v–151r; Book XX, I, 278–279, II, folio 162v; Book XX, I, 280, II, 163v; Book XX, I, 181, II, folio 164r; Book XXI, I, 290, II, folios 169v–170r; Book XXI, I, 291–292, II, folios 170v–171v; Book IX, I, 114–115, II, folios 66v–67r. (All folio numbers refer to Florence, Bibliotheca Nazionale, Magliabechiano, II, IV, 140).

5. Maltese, Degrassi, Vol. I, xiii–xv. Second version: Florence, Bibliotheca Nazionale, Magliabechiano, II, I, 141, Vol. II, chapter II, 324, 337–348, Pls. 192–202, folios 16r–21v; chapter II, 350–359, Pls. 206–208, folios 23v–24v; chapter III, 364, Pl. 212, folio 28v. See also Muratore, 99–127.

6. Brian Pullan, *Rich and Poor in Renaissance Venice*, Cambridge, 1971, 25–26.

7. Pullan, 1971, 3–5, 19–24.

8. Filarete, in Spencer, I, Book II, 21, II, folio 11r.

9. Filarete, in Spencer, I, Book XVIII, 251, II, folio 146v.

10. Alberti, in Orlandi, Book V, chapter VII, 359–360. Filarete, in Spencer, I, Book IX, 114–115, II, folios 66v–67r.

11. Ferdinand Braudel, *The Mediterranean and the Mediterranean World in the Age of Philip II*, New York, second edition, trans. Siân Reynolds, 1972, I, 326–328; II, 734–736.

12. Pullan, 1971, 216–218, 219, 223, 241–247.

13. Pullan, 1971, 247–257, and William J. Bouwsma, *Venice and the Defense of Republican Liberty*, Berkeley, 1968, 123–130.

14. Pullan, 1971, 3–8, 224–240, 254–257, 276. Delio Cantimori, *Umanismo e religione nel rinascimento*, Turin, 1975, 31–59. Roland H. Bainton, *Erasmus of Christendom*, New York, 1969, 65–78.

15. Paschini, 1960, 41; Bainton, 87; Cantimori, 65.

16. Pullan, 219. Fiocco, 1965, 74–79, 162. Copies of both versions are in Milan, Bibliotheca Ambrosiana, A 71 and R 124.

17. Rosci, 1967, I, 26–27. Cornaro's Odeon is illustrated in Book VII, folios 218, 219, 223. Serlio mentioned Cornaro in Book IV, Venice, 1537, folio III.

18. Fiocco, 156. (Author's translation.) Vitruvius discussed private houses in Book II, chapter I, and Book VI, chapters 1–8. See Vitruvius, *Ten Books on Architecture*, trans. Morris Hickey Morgan, New York, 1960, 38–39, 167–192, 193–221.

19. Kurt Forster, "Sozialer Wohnbau, Geschichte und Gegenwart," *Archithese*, 8, 1973, 2–5, figs. 2, 9. E. Trincanato, "Residenze collective a Venezia," *Urbanistica*, 42–43, 1965, 7–15, and *Venezia Minore*, Milan, 1948, 158–169, ills.

20. Forster, 1973, 3, fig. 3. Norbert Lieb, *Die Fugger und die Kunst*, Munich, 1952, I, 250–268; II, 282–310.

21. Lieb, I, 253; II, 285.

22. Pullan, 1971, 5–8. Frederick G. Lane, *Venice, A Maritime Republic*, Baltimore, 1973, 242–244. Felix Gilbert, "Venice in the Crisis of the League of Cambrai," *Renaissance Venice*, 1973, 274–292.

23. Pl. LX, lines 1–3.

24. Bouwsma, 89–90. Myron Gilmore, "Myth and Reality in Venetian Political Theory," *Renaissance Venice*, 1973, 431–434.

25. Paschini, 1960, 28, 40. Bouwsma, 76.

26. Bouwsma, 76, 108, 123–133. Pullan, 1971, 5–8. Paolo Prodi, "The Structure and Organization of the Church in Renaissance Venice: Suggestions for Research," *Renaissance Venice*, 1973, 409–430.

27. M. Rosci, "Forme e funzione delle ville venete pre-palladiane," *L'arte*, I, 1968, 2, 27–55. Rosci, I, 1967, 60. Angelo Ventura, "Aspetti storico-economici della villa veneta," *BCISA*, XI, 1969, 65–78.

28. J. S. Ackerman, *Palladio*, Harmondsworth, 1966, 48–54. Pullan, 1971, 15–20, and Bouwsma, 105. S. J. Woolf, "Venice and the Terraferma, Problems of Change from Commercial to Landed Activities," in *Crisis and Change in the Venetian Economy in the Sixteenth and Seventeenth Centuries*, ed. Brian Pullan, London, 1968, 175–203.

29. Forster, 1973, 5–6, figs. 9, 10. See also Rosci, 1968, 39, and Filarete, in Spencer, I, 280, II, chapter XX, folio 163v.

30. Rosci, I, 1967, 59.

31. Luigi Firpo, "Political Philosophy: Renaissance Utopianism," in *The Late Italian Renaissance 1525–1630*, ed. E. Cochrane, New York, 1970, 150–167. E. H. Harbison, "Machiavelli's *Prince* and More's *Utopia*," in *Facets of the Renaissance*, ed. William H. Werkmeister, New York, 1963, 41–71. J. R. Hale, *Machiavelli and Renaissance Italy*, Harmondsworth, 1972, second edition, 107–137. Thomas More, *Utopia*, trans. Paul Turner, eighth edition, Harmondsworth, 1972.

32. Firpo, 1970, 160–161, "T. More e sua fortuna in Italia," *Occidente*, III, 1952, 22–241; *Il pensiero politico del rinascimento e della controriforma*, Milan, 1966, 573–574. G. Curcio, *Utopisti e riformatori sociali del cinquecento*, Bologna, 1944. Grendler, 49–65, 70–103, 127–135, 162–177.

33. Machiavelli, *The Prince*, trans. Luigi Ricci, intr. Max Lerner, New York, 1950, 94.

34. Machiavelli, *The Prince*, 69.

35. Marconi, 1969, I, 52–53; II, 54. J. H. Hexter, "Seyssel, Machiavelli, and Polybius VI, The Mystery of the Missing Translation," *Studies in the Renaissance*, III, 1956, 87, note 41; 90, note 36. The passage is in Niccolò Machiavelli, *L'arte della guerra*, Milan, 1961, ed. Sergio Bartelli, Book VI, 465–474. See also Hale, 1972, 116, 144–149.

36. Writing in the second century B.C. (205–125), Polybius found a combination of monarchy, aristocracy and democracy in the Roman constitution that provided for the voice of the Consuls, the Senate and the People. Hexter, 79–80.

37. Pier Nicola Pagliara, "Influenze sangallesche sulla manualistica di Sebastiano Serlio," *Controspazio*, IV, 7, 1972, 48–51.

38. Marconi, 1969, 56, and "La città come forma simbolica," in *La città come forma simbolica*, Rome, 1973, 37–38, figs. 38, 107. Francesco Paolo Fiore, "La città progressiva e il suo disegno," in above, 219–220, fig. 208. Muratore, 66, note 24; 71, note 29.

39. Pagliara, 48–51.

40. André Corboz, "Contributo all' urbanistica Palladiana: la pianta di Hochelaga 1556 quale progetto del club Barbaro," *Institut Suisse de Rome*, June, 1977, typescript, 10–11.

41. Teresa Zarebska, "Théories militaires et habitations collectives," *Archithèse*, 8, 1973, 9–14.

42. Waetzoldt, 221–224.

43. Helen Rosenau, "Zum Sozialproblem in der Architekturtheorie des 15 bis 19 Jahrhunderts," *Festschrift Martin Wackernagel*, Cologne, 1958, 188.

44. Rupprich, 1969, III, 369–376. Alexander von Reitzenstein, "Das Werk: die Befestigungslehre, das Fechtbuch," *Dürer, 1471–1971,* Munich, 1971, 355–357. Biddle, 93–99, text, folio 15.

45. British Museum, Manuscript Department, Codex Additional 5229, folio 167 is from a sketchbook in which there are other drawings for the book on fortifications by Dürer. See also Rupprich, III, 1969, 390–405. This drawing is similar to other drawings by Dürer of Venetian buildings in the Berlin Kupferstichkabinett. See Winkler, 1936, I, nos. 93, 88, ill. p. 68. Dürer's drawing in the British Museum is similar to a house in the Calle dei Furlani in Venice of the fifteenth century illustrated in Trincanato, 1948, 184–185.

46. Biddle, 133. Waetzoldt, 223.

47. Salmon, 25, 54–55, 62–72, 92–95.

48. Gaston Zeller, "Royal Administration before the Intendents, Parliaments, and Governors," *Government in Reformation Europe,* ed. Henry S. Cohn, New York, 1972, 225–236.

49. Pedretti, 87–101, figs. 136, 137. Fiore, fig. 220.

50. Hexter, 77–78, 81–83.

51. Salmon, 94–95.

52. Salmon, 47–52.

53. Salmon, 42–46.

54. Salmon, 31.

55. Natalie Zenon Davis, "Poor Relief, Humanism, and Heresy," *Society and Culture in Early Modern France,* Stanford, 1975, 17–64.

56. Salmon, 85–87, 120–121.

57. Salmon, 86–87.

58. Salmon, 79–84.

NOTES TO CHAPTER V

1. Pl. II, lines 1–2.

2. Pl. II, line 14.

3. Pl. IV, line 1.

4. See appendix for a more detailed list and discussion of these building types.

5. Ludwig H. Heydenreich, "Entstehung der villa und ländlichen Residenz im 15. Jahrhundert," *Acta historiae artium academiae scientiarum hungaricae,* XIII, 1967, 912; "La villa, genesi e svilluppo fino al Palladio," *BCISA,* XI, 1969, 11–23. J. S. Ackerman, "Sources of the Renaissance Villa," *Studies in Western Art, Acts of the XX International Congress of the History of Art,* II, Princeton, 1963, 6–18. Jürgen Paul, *Der Palazzo Vecchio in Florenz, Ursprung und Bedeutung seiner Form,* Florence, 1969. Stanislaus von Moos, *Turm und Bollwerk,* Zurich, 1974. Carolyn Kolb Lewis, *The Villa Giustinian at Roncade,* dissertation, Harvard University, 1973, Garland Press Reprint, New York, 1977, 98–108.

6. *Armorial d'Auvergne* (Paris, Bibliothèque Nationale, ms. fr. 22297, folio 449) is dated between 1456 and 1461. See G. Fournier, *Châteaux, villages, et villes d'Auvergne au XVe siècle d'après l'Armorial d'Auvergne,* Geneva, 1973, 1, 7, note 3. This illustration is unpublished.

7. Richard Goldthwaite, "The Florentine Palace as Domestic Architecture," *The American Historical Review,* LXXVII, 4, 1972, 977–1012.

8. Pl. XLIX, lines 47–50.

9. Pl. III, line 10.

10. Pl. IV, lines 2–4. See Lewis, 1977, 177, note 67: one Venetian foot equals .347735 meters.

11. Martin Kubelik, *Die Villa im Veneto: zur typologischen Entwicklung im Quattrocento,* Munich, 1977, I, 19–21; II, 325, Pl. 1 (Pietro Crescenzi); 328, Pls. 4–5 (Serlio, Avery Ms., Pl. I); 329, fig. 6. Rosci, 1968, 27–55; "Ville rustiche del Quattrocento," *BCISA,* XI, 1969, 78–83; I, 1967, 32–34, 61–63. Bernhard Rupprecht, "Ville venete del '400 et del primo '500, forme e sviluppo," *BCISA,* VI, 1964, 239–251. Wolfram Prinz, *Anfänge des oberitalienischen Villenbaues,* Frankfurt, 1973, 7–9. L. Puppi, "Rassegna degli studi sulle ville venete, 1952–1969," *L'Arte,* 9, 1969, 215–226.

12. Villa Giustinian, Roncade: Lewis, 1977, figs. 85–92, plans and elevations; figs. 4–72, views of the exterior; analysis, 1–98.

13. See Ackerman, 1963, 14–15, for the survival of the Roman villa in southern Europe. Ackerman did notice, however, that there were Roman villas in northern Europe, see figs. 11 and 12, Pl. III.

14. Ventura, 65–78.

15. Georges Fouet, *La villa gallo-romaine de Montmaurin,* Paris, 1969, 35, fig. 9, Pls. IV, VI. It is located near Toulouse and is dated in the third century A.D.

16. Folio 456, unpublished. See footnote 6, above. For other fifteenth-century manors in France, see J. Gauthier, *Manoirs et gentilhommières du pays de France,* Paris, no date, I–X. For English fourteenth- and fifteenth-century manors, see Margaret Wood, *The English Medieval House,* London, 1965, 99–109, W. A. Pantin, "Medieval Priests' Houses in Southwest England," *Medieval Archaeology,* I, 1957, 118–146, and Anthony Emery, "Dartington Hall, Devonshire," *Studies in Medieval Domestic Architecture,* ed. J. Swanton, London, 1975, 134–152.

17. For the Fondaco dei Turchi, see Ackerman, 1963, 12–13, Pl. III, fig. 10, and Pl. III, fig. 13, The Villa of Theodoric. K. Forster, "Back to the Farm," *Architectura,* 1974, no. 1, 5; 6, fig. 9. Lewis, 1977, 188–189, note 177. Villa Bertoldi Negrar, Kubelik, I, no. 67: 112; II, 530–533, figs. 389–395. Loggia dei Valmarana: Kubelik, I, no. 86: 126–127; II, 574–577, figs. 473–482. See also Kubelik for the discussion of the *enfilade* plan as a Venetian type, I, 40–41, 348, fig. 57.

18. Dinsmoor, II, 141–146, figs. 11–13. The villa is described by Père Dan, *Le trésor des merveilles de la maison royale de Fontainebleau,* Paris, 1642, 188. See also, L. Charvet, 33–35, 69.

19. Pl. VIII, lines 19–21.

20. Kubelik, I, 73; II, 415, figs. 185–186.

21. The literature on the subject is immense. See J. S. Ackerman, "The Belvedere as a Classical Villa," *JWCI,* XIV, 1957, 70–91; P. Foster, "Raphael on the Villa Madama," *Römisches Jahrbuch für Kunstgeschichte,* XII, 1968, 307–312; and Bernhard Rupprecht, "L'iconologia nella villa veneta," *BCISA,* X, 1968, 229–241, and "Villa: zur Geschichte eines Ideals," *Probleme der Kunstwissenschaft,* II, ed. H. Bauer, Berlin, 1966, 210–251.

22. Von Moos, 151–172, 182–191, fig. 141: Francesco di Giorgio, Turin Codex, folio 4v (Maltese, I, Pl. 4); fig. 146: Antonio da Sangallo, The Younger, Ground Plan of the Fortezza da Basso, UA 758; figs. 147, 150: Giuliano da Sangallo, Poggio Imperiale. For the general history of the bastion, see also John R. Hale, "The Early Development of the Bastion," *Europe in the Late Middle Ages,* Evanston, Illinois, 1965, 466–494.

23. Pl. XIV, line 3. For the influence of Machiavelli, see Rosci, I, 1967, 59–60; 73–75, 83. See Von Moos, 218–219. Machiavelli was talking about Francesco Sforza's additions to the Castello in Milan in *The Prince,* trans. L. Ricci, New York, 1950, 81: "The castle of Milan built by Francesco Sforza has given and will give more trouble to the house of Sforza than any other disorder in that state. Therefore, the best fortress is to be found in the love of the people, for although you may have fortresses, they will not save you if you are hated by the people."

24. Pl. XIV, lines 7–9.

25. Pl. XV, lines 1–3.

26. Pl. XV, lines 13–15.

27. Pl. XVIII, lines 11–12, 14, 16–19.

28. Pl. XVI, lines 2–4.

29. Pl. XVI, line 12; Pl. XVIII, line 16.

30. Rosci, I, 1967, 67–79; 21, figs. 31 and 32. Serlio's rendition is based on Uffizi A 363v and 363r of Peruzzi. For the latest discussion of Poggioreale, see G. L. Hersey, *Alfonso II and the Artistic Renewal of Naples,* 1455–1495, New Haven, 1969, 58–70; 63, fig. 80, and "Poggio Reale: Notes on a Reconstruction," *Architectura,* 1973, no. 1, 13–20; A. Blunt, "Letter to the Editor," *Architectura,* 1974, no. 1, 94–96; Von Moos, 120–123, fig. 11b; 129–130, figs. 106–107.

31. Lewis, 1977, 109–132, fig. 287: Palace of Diocletian, Split; fig. 301: Château of Najac, Aveyron, thirteenth century; fig. 309: Castello of Frederick II, Prato, 1250; figs. 313–314: Visconti Castello, Pavia, fourteenth century; figs. 320–321: Castello Sforzesco, fourteenth–fifteenth centuries; fig. 327: Villa alle Quattro Torri, Siena, fourteenth–fifteenth centuries. Von Moos, 31–42; 43–50, 55–68, 120–130. Axel Boëthius, J. B. Ward-Perkins, *Etruscan and Roman Architecture,* Harmondsworth, 1970, 524–529, fig. 200, and K. Swoboda, "Problems of Iconography of Late Antique and Early Medieval Palaces," *JSAH,* XX, 1961, 78–89.

32. F. Gebelin, *The Châteaux of France,* London, second edition, 1964, Dourdan: 55; 56, fig. 2; Villandraut: 66–68. F. Benoît, "La livrée de Pierre de Thury à Villeneuve-les-Avignon," *Congrès archéologique,* CXXI, 1963, 191–193; 194, plan. Jacques Gardelles, *Les châteaux du Moyen Age dans la France du sud-ouest,* Geneva, 1972, Villandraut, 234, figs. 154–157, Pls. LXIX–LXI. See also, for this type, a sixteenth-century example, Volker Hoffmann, *Das Schloss von Ecouen,* Berlin, 1970, figs. 9–10.

33. *Richesses de la France, Côte d'Or,* no. 59, 1964, 56.

34. For the tradition of the keep in France, see Gebelin, *The Châteaux of France,* London, second edition, 1964, 24–52, especially "Etampes and Provins of 1150," 41, fig. 1. For Italy, see Arnaldo Bruschi, Gaetano Mariani, *Architettura sveva nell'Italia meridionale,* Prato, 1975, 23–26, figs. 4–8: Termoli (1250); 38–42, figs. 2–10: Frosinone, Rocca Janula (1227–1239).

35. Rosci, I, 1967, 76–77; André Chastel, "La Demeure royale au XVIème siècle et le nouveau Louvre," *Studies in Renaissance and Baroque Art Presented to Anthony Blunt,* London, 1967, 80–81.

36. Jean Guillaume, "Leonard da Vinci et l'architecture française: I. Le problème de Chambord," *Revue de l'art,* 25, 1974, 75–77. Rosenfeld, "Sebastiano Serlio's Late Style in the Avery Library Version of Book VI On Domestic Architecture," *JSAH,* XXVIII, 1969, 160–161. This château can be related to Bramante's project for the courtyard around St. Peter's, Uffizi A 104. See Bruschi, *Bramante,* London, 1977, 149, fig. 152.

37. Heydenreich, 1952, 277–281. Guillaume, 1974, 71–84. Windsor, no. 12591v, 77, fig. 21.

38. Pl. XLIV, lines 7–8.

39. Pl. XLVI, lines 1–3. Rosenfeld, 1969, 161, fig. 13. Compare to Serlio's illustration of the Colosseum in his Book III, folios LXIV–LXV, LXVII, LXIX.

40. Vladimir Juren, "Le projet de Giuliano da Sangallo pour le palais du roi de Naples," *Revue de l'art,* 25, 1974, 66–70. See also Ackerman, 1957, and *The Cortile del Belvedere,* Vatican, 1954.

41. Pl. XXXIII, line 13.

42. Rosci, I, 1967, 27, figs. 52–53. Serlio, Book VII, 1575, folios 218, 219, 223. See Fiocco, 1965, 44–53, figs. 37–39; Heydenreich, Lotz, 211–212, fig. 66. Serlio's projects in the Avery manuscript are closest to Villa II on folio 5 of Book VII. See Carunchio, 98, figs. 2A, 2B.

43. Pl. XXII, lines 26–28.

44. Andrea Palladio, *Four Books on Architecture,* intr. Adolf K. Placzek, New York, 1965, 41.

45. Belluzzi, Capezzali, 16, fig. 14. Pedretti, 108–112, figs. 152–158, 165, Arundel ms. 770v.

46. Rosenfeld, 1969, 160; William MacDonald, *The Architecture of the Roman Empire I,* New Haven, 1965, Domus Aurea, 31–41, Pl. 24, nos. 25, 27, 28; Pls. 29–30; Domus Flavia, 47–74, especially 54, Pl. 40, no. 8; Pl. 46.

47. Rosci, I, 1967, 76–77. Rosenfeld, 1969, 160, fig. 9, Church plan from Book V. Pedretti, 106, fig. 150.

48. Rosci, I, 1967, 79. Guillaume, 1974, 74, and "Chenonceaux avant la construction de la galérie," *Gazette des beaux-arts,* 1969, 38–51. Hautecoeur, I, 1, 43–44, note 62; Challuau, 235–236, fig. 114; La Muette, Saint-Germain-en-Laye, 236, fig. 115; see also the garden pavilions at Amboise and Gaillon by Pacello da Mocenigo, 116–118, figs. 71, 72.

49. See footnotes 21, 40 above.

50. Rosci, I, 1967, 26, 75, 77–78, 82–83; 25, fig. 49; 82, fig. 90. Serlio House on Monte Cavallo, Book III, folio LXXX, ill. in Rosci, I, 1967, 19, fig. 20. See also, Rosci, I, 1967, 19, fig. 24, Giuliano da Sangallo, Codex Barberini, folio 65r. Heinz Spielmann, *Andrea Palladio und die Antike,* Munich, 1966, 36–37, figs. 30, 31, no. 58, RIBA, XI, 23r. Pagliara, 22–37; 22, fig. 9; 23, figs. 15–21; 25, figs. 22–29; 28, figs. 36–38. For Francesco di Giorgio's reconstruction of the "Palazzo Maggiore" on the Palatine, see Maltese, I, Pl. 152, Turin Codex, folio 82v.

51. M. N. Rosenfeld, *The Hôtel de Cluny and the Sources of the French Renaissance Urban Palace,* 1350–1500, unpublished dissertation, Harvard University, 1971, 120, 129–130. Paul Marie Duval, *Paris antique,* Paris, 1961, 126–127, fig. 49: Roman villa, Montmartre, 141–150, fig. 58. G. de Jode, Engraving of the Palatium Cesaris, Musée Carnavalet. See also Corrozet, folio 10v, "Palais des thermes."

52. Pl. XL, line 18.

53. Hoffmann, 103–104. See also Rosenfeld, 1971, 39, no. III, 212–221. Henri Sauval, *Histoire et recherches des antiquités de la ville de Paris,* 1724, II, 271–278. F. Bournon, *L'hôtel royal de St. Pol à Paris,* Paris, 1880.

54. Rosenfeld, 1969, 165–167. Hautecoeur, I, 1, 190–194, fig. 100.

55. Pl. XLVIII, line 1. See the Map of Paris of 1550 in the Bibliothèque Nationale, Cabinet des Estampes, Réserve, AA6, 1550. Maurice Dumolin, "La famille du plan de la tapisserie," *Etudes de topographie parisienne,* I, Paris, 1929, 71–75, figs. 33, 34.

56. Pl. XLVIII, lines 2–3.

57. Pl. XLIX, line 64.

58. Pl. XLIX, line 67.

59. Walter Paatz, "Ein antikischer Stadthaustypus im mittelalterlichen Italien," *Römisches Jahrbuch für Kunstgeschichte,* 1939, 129–140. Axel Boëthius, *The Golden House of Nero,* Ann Arbor, 1960, 129–185. Boëthius, Ward-Perkins, 284–286, 312–318, 334–336; 335, Pl. 148, fig. 130c, House of Diana; 288, fig. 111, Pl. 149, House of the Three Windows.

60. Livy, Paris, Bibliothèque Nationale, ms. fr. 20071–72, folio 5. Jean Porcher, *Les manuscrits à peintures en France du XIIIe siècle au XVIe siècle,* Paris, 1955, 125, no. 257. The map of Venice shows houses in front of storage sheds near SS. Giovanni e Paolo, ill. in Lewis, 1977, fig. 165.

61. Viollet-le-Duc, *Dictionnaire raisonné d'architecture,* Paris, V, 1863, 214–272, figs. 106–118. Camille Enlart, *Manuel d'archéologie française,* Paris, 1929, I, 56–80. François Verdier, Aymar Cattois, *Architecture civile et domestique au moyen age et à la renaissance,* 1855, I, 69–86, twelfth-century houses at Cluny. Margaret Wood, *Norman Domestic Architecture,* London, 1977, reprint, original edition, 1935, 13–14, 72–76, 94–95. W. Pantin, "Medieval Townhouse Plans," *Medieval Archaeology,* VI–VII, 1962–1963, 202–239. P. A. Faulkner, "Medieval Undercrofts and Townhouses," *Studies in Medieval Domestic Archi-*

tecture, London, 1975, 118–133. Wolfgang Braunfels, *Mittelalterliche Stadtbaukunst in der Toskana*, Berlin, 1953, 174–181. T. Magnuson, *Studies in Roman Quattrocento Architecture*, Stockholm, 1958, 41–51. Trincanato, 1948. P. Chiolini, *I caratteri distributivi degli antichi edifici*, Milan, 1959, 317–340; 329, ill. Francesco di Giorgio, Codex Magliabechiano, folios 16v, 14r, Maltese, II, Pls. 192, 191.

62. Marcel Aubert, "La maison dite de Nicolas Flanel rue Montmorency, Paris," *Société d'iconographie parisienne*, I, 1929, 13–18, figs. 9, 10. See also Rosci, I, 1967, 80.

63. Pierre du Columbier, Pierre d'Espézél, "L'Habitation au XVIème siècle d'après le sixième livre de Serlio," *Humanisme et Renaissance*, I, 1934, 31–49; "Le sixième livre retrouvé de Serlio et l'architecture française de la renaissance," *Gazette des beaux-arts*, 1934, 42–59. Martin R. Huber, "Sebastiano Serlio sur une architecture civile alla parisiana," *Information de l'histoire de l'art*, X, 1965, 9–17. For the Maison d'Adam at Angers, see Hautecoeur, I, 1, 37–49, fig. 28.

64. Trincanato, 1948, 184, 185, ill. The drawing represents a fifteenth-century house in the Calle dei Furlani, discussed in Chapter IV.

65. Trincanato, 1948, 127–128; 129, ill. Wood, 1977, 40–42, fig. 8, Pl. VA–B, Pl. VIII.

66. Rosci, I, 1967, 26, 29–30. See G. Fiocco, "La casa veneziana antica," *Atti della reale accademia dei lincei, rendiconti*, VIII, 1949, no. 4, 38–52. Chiolini, 1959, 336–337. Trincanato, 1948, 60, ill.

67. Rosci, I, 1967, 81. See Serlio, Book IV, folio XXXV.

68. Pl. LII, lines 1–2.

69. Pl. LII, lines 5–9.

70. Pl. LIII, lines 24–28.

71. Pl. LIII, lines 31–32.

72. Pl. LX, lines 33–34.

73. Pl. LX, lines 5–9, 12–14, 17–18.

74. Pl. LX, lines 4–5; Pl. LXI, lines 9–10. See footnote 23, above.

75. Pl. LXV, lines 1–5.

76. Pedretti, see fig. 114 for the reconstruction.

77. Rosci, I, 1967, 81. Goldthwaite. Palazzo Farnese: C. Frommel, *Der Römische Palastbau der Hochrenaissance*, Tübingen, 1973, no. XI, vol. 2, 103–148; vol. 3, Pls. 38–61. Palazzo Strozzi: Heydenreich, Lotz, 137, fig. 44, Palazzo Medici: Heydenreich, Lotz, 22, fig. 11. For Giuliano da Sangallo's project for a new Medici palace in Florence, Uffizi A 282, see Pagliara, 1972, 42, fig. 82.

78. Paul, 80–81, fig. 18: Broletto, Novara, 1120; fig. 19: Broletto, Brescia, 1150; fig. 29: Castle of Frederick II, Augusta, 1250. Von Moos, 21–48, fig. 25.

79. J. Girard, *Avignon, ses monuments, ses hôtels, ses trésors d'art*, Marseilles, 1930, 76–80; 75, ill. J. Valléry-Radot, "Le Petit-Palais," *Congrès archéologique*, CXXI, 1963, 59–104; 67, plan. Sylvain Gagnière, *Le palais des papes d'Avignon*, Paris, 1965, 112, 9, plan.

80. Gagnière, 16–66; 132–133, plan.

81. R. Gauchery, "L'hôtel Jacques Coeur à Bourges," *Congrès archéologique*, XCVIII, 1931, 102; 61, 83, plans. See also, another French fifteenth-century palace with inner courtyard, Avignon, Hôtel Baroncelli (1485–1499): J. Girard, 76–80; 75, ill., and Besançon, Palais Graneville (1534–1540), Hautecoeur, I, 1, 491–492; 289, fig. 142.

82. Rosci, I, 1967, 81, proposed the model of Bramante's Palazzo dei Tribunali. See C. Frommel, 1973, no. XXX, vol. 2, 327–334; vol. 3, figs. 145–147, and "Il Palazzo dei Tribunali in via Giulia," *Studi bramanteschi*, Rome, 1970, 523–535, Pl. CXC, fig. 1, Pl. CXCIII, fig. 4. For the drawing by Francesco di Giorgio, see Codex Magliabechiano, folio 23v, Maltese, II, Pl. 206.

83. Paul, 36–44, figs. 18–20. Frommel, 1970, 535.

84. Inge Hager-Suk, "La Sainte Chapelle de Paris et les chapelles palatines au moyen âge en France," *Cahiers archéologiques*, XIII, 1962, 220–232, 243–257. See also Paul, 35–39, figs. 13–15.

85. J. Gérout, "Le Palais de l'Ile de la Cité de Paris des origines à 1417," *Paris et l'Ile de France*, II, 1950, 23–60, 78–204, Pl. IV, Androuet du Cerceau, view of the Grande Salle, Bibliothèque Nationale, Estampes, Topographie de Paris, Vx15, folio 269. For the influence of the vaulting of the wood roof of the Grande Salle on the Palazzo della Ragione in Padua (1306) by Fra Giovanni degli Eremitani, see H. Dellwing, "Zur Wölbung des paduaner Salone," *Mitteilungen des Kunsthistorischen Instituts in Florenz*, 14, III, 1969, 145–160. J. P. Babelon, *Le palais de justice*, Paris, 1966, fig. 30, Map of St. Victor, 1550.

86. Pl. LXVII, line 8: "atrio." Pl. LXVII, line 6: "vestibulo aperto."

87. Serlio had illustrated the hemicycle and concave-convex staircase and loggias of the Belvedere Courtyard in Book III (folios CXLVI–CXLVII; CXLII, CXLV). For the general configuration of the Belvedere Courtyard, see Bruschi, *Bramante*, Bari, 1969, 296, fig. 199. For the Ninfeo at Genazzano, see Bruschi, 1969, 865–882, figs. 203–205.

88. For the Hôtel de Nesle, see A. Berty, *Topographie*

historique du vieux Paris, Region occidentale de l'université, Paris, 1887, 25–31, 38–57, 582–586 (Inventory). See also, Pl. LXVII, line 32.

89. Rosci, I, 1967, 26, 82–83. Francesco di Giorgio, Reconstruction of the "Palazzo Maggiore," Turin Codex, folio 82v, Maltese, I, Pl. 152. Bates Lowry, "High Renaissance Architecture," *College Art Journal*, XVIII, 1958, 115–116, 120–121, fig. 3.

90. Bruschi, 1969, 297, 407–416. Serlio, Book III, folios CXLVI–CXLVII. Bruschi, 1969, figs. 269–271. Ackerman, 1957, 85–89; 72–76; Pls. 12a, 14abc, 16a, b. Dosio, Uffizi A 25559.

91. Rosenfeld, 1969, 163.

92. For the Louvre, see Lowry, 120–121; Rosci, I, 1967, 80–81; Chastel, 1967, 80–81.

NOTES TO CHAPTER VI

1. Munich, Codex Icon. folio 1r, 189, introduction, line 14.

2. Rosci, I, 1967, 58. Dinsmoor, I, 83, 91; II, 129–131.

3. Rosenfeld, 1974, 401, 409: transcription of the letter, Vienna, Nationalbibliothek, Codex 9039, folio 112r.

4. This may be true for the Polybius manuscript as well, Munich, Codex Icon. 190.

5. See Rosenfeld, 1970, 319–322.

6. Pl. XVIII, lines 11–12.

7. Rosci, I, 1967, 58. Dinsmoor, II, 122–123, note 31.

8. Elisabeth de Gramont, *La Famille de Clermont-Tonnerre depuis l'an 1070*, Paris, 1950, 36, 68.

9. Salmon, 87–92, 120–121, and Natalie Zenon Davis, "The Rites of Heresy," in *Society and Culture in Early Modern France*, 152–189.

10. The *Lettere d'Ippolito d'Este* are in the Bancroft Library, University of California, Berkeley.

11. See Chapter II, 31–32.

12. Munich manuscript, Codex Icon. 189, folio 14v, line 4.

13. Pl. XLI, lines 21–24.

14. Pl. LVI, lines 1–3.

15. Pl. LVI, lines 13–15.

16. Rudolf Wittkower, *Architectural Principles in the Age of Humanism*, New York, 1971, third edition, 18.

17. Wittkower, 1971, 18–19.

18. Wilinski, 1961, 57–69; "Miedzy Teoria a Praktyka W. Ksiegach O Architekturze Sebastiana Serlio," *Przeglad humanistyczny*, 10, 1975, 11–29.

19. Rosci, 1967, I, 25. Wilinski, 1961, 60, 63, 65. Serlio, Book IV, 1537, title page: "Regole generali di architettura sopra le cinque maniere de gli edifici . . . con gli essempi dell'antiquità che per la magior parte concordano con la dottrina di Vitruvio"; folio II: ". . . Io porro ne i principii de gli ordini i vocaboli di Vitruvio, accompagnati con li usitati moderni, commune a tuta Italia." Book III, 1540, folio CV, Arch of Titus: "Ben e vero che gli ornamenti de la maggior parte de gli archi di Roma si allontano molto da i scritti di Vitruvio"; folio XXIr, Doric order: "Ben che la presente projettura del capitello si alontano molto da i scritti di Vitruvio per esser perperpendicular al plintho de la base, non dimeno per haverne io veduto alcuni antiqui . . ."; folio XXIv, details of the Doric order; folios XLVII–XLIX, Theater of Marcellus; folio CLV: "Imitator del buon Vitruvio."

20. Rosci, 1967, I, 59–60.

21. Munich, Codex Icon. 189, introduction, folio 1r, lines 21–24: "Per cio che li sopra detto Marco Luccio Vitruvio ne ha parlato cosi difusamente nel primo libro al quarto capitolo et di poi Leonbattista delli Alberti anchor più amplamente che a me pare non si possi dire di vantaggio è pero come il dovero alli loro scritti al tutto io me riporto."

22. Munich, Codex Icon. 189, introduction, folio 1r, lines 17–18: "Ma quella fabriche che si fano nelle città nobili si deonno fare con più maturo giudiccio osservando in esse una certa maiestà decorata tutti piena di proportione e corrispondentia di membri a tutto il corpe. . . ."

23. Munich, Codex Icon. 189, introduction, folio 1r, line 33.

24. Munich, Codex Icon. 189, conclusion, folio 74r, lines 20–22.

25. Munich, Codex Icon. 189, folio 74r, lines 40–42. See also Ernst Gombrich, "Versuch einer Deutung zum Werke Giulio Romanos," *Jahrbuch der Kunsthistorischen Sammlungen in Wien*, VII, 1934, II, 142. *Extraordinario libro*, Lyons, 1551, folio A2v: "Ma o voi architetti fondati sopra la dottrina di Vitruvio . . . habbiate mei per iscusato di tanti ornamenti, di tante tabelle, di tanti cartocini, volute, et di tanti superflui, habbiate riguardo al paese dove io sono. . . ."

26. Pl. XXXVI, line 3. See also lines 5–6, about finding a good professor or mentor.

27. Pl. XVIII, lines 20–25.

28. Pl. LV, lines 6–8.

29. H 8, Pl. III, lines 17–18; Townhouse G, Pl. XLIX, lines 16–17; Townhouse P, Pl. LIII, lines 12–13.

30. Villa N 13, Pl. X, last line; Villa O 14, Pl. XII, lines 26–28.

31. Pl. XXIII, last line; Pl. XXIV, lines 19–20; Pl. XXV, lines 8–9.

32. Wittkower, 1971, 102–107, appendix I, 155–157.

33. Rosci, I, 1967, 61. For Palladio's system of harmonic proportions, see Wittkower, 1971, 102–142.

34. Munich, Codex Icon. 189, folio 74r, lines 22–23. See also, Avery manuscript, Pl. LIII, line 4.

35. Pl. LIX, lines 15–17. See also Munich, Codex Icon. 189, folio 74r, lines 13–14.

36. Munich, Codex Icon. 189, folio 74r, lines 7–9.

37. H 8, Pl. III; I 9, Pl. IV; Ro 26, Pls. XXXIV–XXXV; P 15, Pls. XIV–XV; A–K, Pls. XLVIII–XLIX; P, Pls. LII–LVII.

38. Wittkower, 1971, 126–127. Serlio, Book I, 1545, doorway, last folio.

39. Carunchio, 124; 126, note 27.

40. Richard Krautheimer, "Alberti and Vitruvius," *Acts of the XXth International Congress of the History of Art*, 1961, II, Princeton, 1963, 42–52.

41. Maltese, I, introduction, xvii–xix, xxix–xxx. Florence Codex Magliabechiano II. 1.141, folios 103–192. Maltese, II, 295.

42. *Vitruvio di Fabio Calvo*, Munich, Staatsbibliothek, Codex Ital. 37. Battista da Sangallo, Rome, Biblioteca Corsiana, 43G–43G8. See Rosci, I, 1967, 19–20, 25; and Paolo Fontana, "Osservanzi intorno ai rapporti di Vitruvio colla teorica dell'architettura del Rinascimento," *Miscellanea di storia dell'arte in onore di I. B. Supino*, Florence, 1933, 305–322, and Pagliara, 22. For the knowledge of Vitruvius in the Middle Ages and Renaissance, see Carole Herselle Krinsky, "Seventy-Eight Vitruvius Manuscripts," *JWCI*, XXX, 1967, 36–70.

43. Stefano Ray, "Bramante, Rafaello, e l'antico: 'gran luce Vitruvio, ma non tanto che basti,'" *Congresso internationale di studi Bramanteschi*, 1970, 405–411.

44. This section on pp. 66–68 is taken partly from my article, "Sebastiano Serlio's Late Style in the Avery Library Version of the Sixth Book on Domestic Architecture," 1969, 170–172. For an analysis of these components of French Renaissance Architecture and their influence on Serlio, see Anthony Blunt, *Art and Architecture in France: 1500–1700*, Harmondsworth, second edition, 1970, 1–17, 46–49.

45. Erwin Panofsky, "The First Page of Giorgio Vasari's Libro," *Meaning in the Visual Arts*, Garden City, 1955, 176–178. The entire *Libro di disegno* has been published by Licia Ragghianti Collobi, Florence, 1974. See also, Vasari, *Lives of the Painters, Sculptors, and Architects*, trans. A. B. Hinds, London, 1963, I, 12. Rudolf Wittkower, in *Gothic versus Classic*, New York, 1974, 83–84, discussed the fact that the term "barbarous" was applied to Gothic architecture by Filarete in Book VIII, folio 59r, but not by Alberti. Raphael, in his letter to Leo X, thought that Gothic architecture represented a decline of civilization, but admitted that it had its own rationale.

46. Pl. IV, line 6.

47. Vasari, 17: "Yet some rising spirits, aided by some quality in the air of certain places, so far purged themselves of this crude style that in 1250, Heaven took compassion on the fine minds that the Tuscan soil was producing every day, and directed them to the original forms."

48. Pl. LVII, lines 13–15.

49. See Panofsky, 196–202, and Richard Bernheimer, "Gothic Survival and Revival in Bologna," *Art Bulletin*, XXXVI, 1954, 262–285. Wittkower, 1974, 17–21, 25–26, 66–76. Frances D. Fergusson, "Leonardo and the Tiburio of Milan Cathedral," *Architectura*, 7, 1977, no. 2, 175–192.

50. Panofsky, 203–225, figs. 46–47, Vasari drawing. See fig. 55 for project by Vignola. For Peruzzi's drawing in the British Museum (Antiquarian 1898–3–28–1), see Philip Pouncey and J. A. Gere, *Italian Drawings in the Department of Prints and Drawings in the British Museum: Raphael and his Circle*, London, 1962, I, no. 246, 143–146; II, Pls. 220–227. For the project by Palladio, see J. S. Ackerman, "Palladio's Lost Portico Project for San Petronio in Bologna," *Essays in the History of Architecture Presented to Rudolf Wittkower*, London, 1967, 110–116, Pls. XI, 2, and XII, 3.

51. Ernst Gombrich, "Norm and Form, Stylistic Categories of Art History and their Origins in Renaissance Ideals," *Norm and Form*, London, 1966, 83–84, relates Vasari's condemnation of Gothic architecture to Vitruvius's criticism of grotesque wall decoration.

52. For this aspect of Alberti's theory see Wittkower, 1971, 3–13.

53. See Manfredo Tafuri, *Architettura del manierismo nel Cinquecento europeo*, Rome, 1966, 125–185, for the influence of this doctrine from Benedetto Varchi's *Lezione* of 1546 to Scamozzi.

54. See Anthony Blunt, *Artistic Theory in Italy 1450–1600*, Oxford, 1940, 7–9, 13, 21. Serlio revives only one Roman building type, the *villa suburbana*.

55. Rosci, I, 1967, 82–83. For a judgment of Serlio similar to mine, see also L. Puppi, *Andrea Palladio*, Lon-

don, second edition, 1973, 11.

NOTES TO CHAPTER VII

1. Kurt Forster, *Pontormo*, Munich, 1966, 29–38, 49–57, 61–67, 71–75: Stanza Borgherini, 1515; Visdomini Altar, 1519; Certosa di Galuzzo, 1521–1523; Capella Capponi, S. Felicità, 1525. John Shearman, *Andrea del Sarto*, Oxford, 1965, I, 66–67, II, 233–234, 300–304, especially the Chiostro dello Scalzo. S. J. Freedberg, *Painting in Italy, 1500–1600*, Harmondsworth, 1971, 121–122: Rosso: Assumption, S. Annunziata, 1517. See also Fritz Grossmann, "Notes on Some Sources of Brueghel's Art," *Album Amicorum J. G. Van Gelder*, The Hague, 1973, 151–152, for the interrelationship between Dürer, Andrea del Sarto and Brueghel in the Scalzo frescoes.

2. Franco Simone, *Il rinascimento francese*, Turin, 1961.

3. Munich manuscript, Codex Icon. 189, folio 35v, lines 3–4. Rosci, I, 1967, 32–35, 38, 77. Chastel, 1967, 80. See also, Wilinski, 1964, 131–144, for the influence of Serlio's Books III and IV on Palladio. Rosci, "I rapporti fra Serlio e Palladio e la più recente letteratura critica," *BCISA*, XV, 1975, 143–149. For the iconography of Palladio's Villa Rotonda, see W. Lotz, "The Rotonda, a Secular Building with a Dome," *Studies in Italian Renaissance Architecture*, Cambridge, 1977, reprint of an article published in 1962, 190–209.

4. Rosci, I, 1967, 32–33.

5. Howard Burns, *Andrea Palladio 1508–1580*, London, 1975, no. 270, 152. Corboz, 1977. G. G. Zorzi, "Progetti giovanili di Andrea Palladio per palazzi e case in Venezia e in terraferma," *Palladio*, I–II, no. iv, 1954, 119–120, figs. 20 (RIBA, Burlington Collection vol. XVI, folio 16r), 21 (RIBA, Burlington Collection, vol. XVI, folio 16v).

6. M. Rosci, "Schemi di ville nel VII libro del Serlio e ville Palladiane," *BCISA*, VIII, 1966, 130, fig. 137 (RIBA, vol. XVI, folio 7r). Burns, no. 329, 187.

7. Rosci, I, 1967, 28–32, 40, mixed up the chronology of Sansovino's buildings. See Howard, 1975, 38–47, fig. iii (Zecca, begun 1536); 126–132, fig. 92 (Palazzo Dolfin, begun 1538); 17–28, fig. 14, fig. ii (Library, begun 1537). B. Rupprecht, "Die Villa Garzoni des Jacopo Sansovino," *Mitteilungen des Kunsthistorischen Instituts in Florenz*, II, Heft, 1, 1963, 1–32. Lionello Puppi, "La villa Garzoni ora Carraretto a Pontecasale di Jacopo Sansovino," *BCISA*, IX, 1969, 95–113, dated 1536–1537. See also Howard, 1975, 47–61, figs. 44–48, fig. iv (Fabbriche Nuove di Rialto, begun 1554).

8. Howard, 1975, 132–146, figs. 97–105 (Palazzo Corner at San Maurizio). Camillo Semenzato, "Le ville del Sanmicheli," *BCISA*, XI, 1969, 113–130. Gazzola, Pls. 130–132. Rosci, I, 1967, 40, fig. 103. See also Howard, 146–154, figs. 106–110, fig. xix (Palazzo Moro); Gazzola, 172–175, Pls. 181–186 (Palazzo Grimani); 68–170, Pl. 135 (Palazzo Corner at San Paolo).

9. Anthony Blunt, *Philibert Delorme*, Paris, 1963, second edition, 41–69, Pls. 29–34, 36.

10. Naomi Miller, "Musings on Maulne, Problems and Parallels," *Art Bulletin*, LVIII, 1976, 196–215, figs. 1–5, 27.

11. Blunt, 1963, 127–156.

12. Hautecoeur, I, 2, 436–441, figs. 165–170; I, 3, 666–680, figs. 287–292.

13. Germain Brice and Claude Perrault claimed that Serlio's Royal Palace for a King was mentioned. See Chastel, 1967, 79–82, figs. 4 and 5.

14. Mary Whiteley and Allan Braham, "Louis Le Vau's Projects for the Louvre and the Colonnade," *Gazette des beaux-arts*, 1964, Part I, 285–296; Part II, 347–362. Wolfgang Hermann, *Claude Perrault*, London, 1973, 18–25. Claude Perrault published a translation of Vitruvius's *Ten Books* in 1673.

15. Wittkower, 1974, 89.

16. *Visionary Architects: Boullée, Ledoux, Lequeu*, intr. J. C. Lemagny, Houston, 1968, nos. 65–92, pp. 66–68. See Ledoux's treatise, *L'architecture considérée sous le rapport de l'art, des moeurs, et de la législation*, Paris, 1804. Helen Rosenau, *Social Purpose in Architecture, Paris and London Compared, 1760–1800*, London, 1970, 26.

17. Franco Barbieri, *Vincenzo Scamozzi*, Verona, 1952, and Vincenzo Scamozzi, *Taccuino di Viaggio da Parigi a Venezia*, ed. F. Barbieri, Venice, 1960.

18. Wittkower, 1974, 86–94.

NOTES TO APPENDIX

1. Pl. IV, lines 5–6.

2. Forster, 1974, 1, 3–4, figs. 4–7, pp. 4–5. Kubelik, I, 14, 21; II, figs. 7–8, p. 330 (Rovigo, Farm House); Villa Dal Zotto: I, no. 34, pp. 85–86; II, figs. 227–234, pp. 440–445.

3. For Francesco di Giorgio's illustration of this type of farm, see Forster, 1974, 10, and Maltese, I, Turin Codex Saluzzano 148, folio 24v, Pl. 24.

4. G. Doyon and R. Hubrecht, *L'architecture rurale et bourgeoise en France*, Paris, 1962, 205–214; 263, fig. 180; 207, fig. 141, Pl. XLIV (Maison Agricole près de St. Amour, Jura; Manoir de la Planche, Calvados; Maison de Vigneron, Mâconais).

5. Villa Dall'Aglio, Lughignano: Kubelik, I, 76–77, no. 25; II, 424, fig. 196. Villa Ca'Brusa: Kubelik, I, 123–125, no. 82; II, 565–569, figs. 455–464.

6. Kubelik, I, 202–205, no. 211; II, 782–792, figs. 839–860.

7. See Puppi, 1971, 86, fig. 126; 89 (plan), fig. 128.

8. Carolyn Kolb Lewis, 1977, 1–98, figs. 4–72 and 85–92, and *BCISA*, XI, 1969, 353–370, figs. 213–215, and Kubelik, I, 92, no. 43; II, 466–470, figs. 274–280.

9. Puppi, *Andrea Palladio*, London, 1973, 292–295; Burns, 194, no. 346. Palladio, 1965, 50, Pl. XXXVI (Book II, chapter XIV).

10. Frédéric Lesueur, *Le château d'Amboise*, Paris, 1955, 103, ill.

11. Rosci, I, 1967, 52–53. Wolfram Prinz, *Entstehung der Gallerie in Frankreich*, Berlin, 1970, 33. For Bury, see Hautecoeur, I, 1, 65; 66, fig. 50, and Martine Garczynska, "Le château de Bury en Blésois," *Information de l'histoire de l'art*, 10, 1965, 84–85.

12. For the Hôtel de Cluny, see Rosenfeld, 1971, 4; 120–156; 294–385, no. XIV. Prinz, 1970, 31. For the Hôtel de Bourbon, see Rosenfeld, 1971, 226–238, no. V; Adolphe Berty, *Topographie historique du vieux Paris: Région du Louvre et des Tuileries*, I, Paris, 1886, 1–39, 77–91, appendix iii–vi. See also Volker Hoffmann, "Review of W. Prinz, *Die Entstehung der Gallerie*," *Architectura*, 1971, no. 1, 103 (14th-century gallery in the Hôtel de Mahaut of the Comtesse d'Amboise, ca. 1315).

13. Rosenfeld, 1971, 138–140; 311–312, no. XIV.

14. Rosenfeld, 1971, 293, 320–323.

15. Rosenfeld, 1971, 300–302.

16. Rosenfeld, 1971, 228–229. Berty, 1866, I, 38–39. Censive du Chapitre de St. Germain l'Auxerrois, Archives Nationales, Paris, III, Seine 63, no. 1, ca. 1550: Berty, I, 1866, 135, ill. M. Hébert and J. Thiron, *Paris, Archives nationales, catalogue générale des cartes, plans, et dessins d'architecture*, Paris, 1958, no. 217: 31, Pl. I. Frank Buttner, "Zur Frage der Entstehung der Gallerie in Frankreich," *Architectura*, 1972, no. 1: 75, for the definition of the gallery as a passageway.

17. Rosci, I, 1967, 21–22, 41, 63–64; 22, fig. 34 (Peruzzi, drawing, Uffizi A 614).

18. Rosci, I, 1967, 23, fig. 37. See Pedretti, 41–52, figs. 50, 52 (Codex Atlanticus 271 v–a, 231r–b), fig. 53 (reconstruction), fig. 55 (Serlio, Book III, Poggioreale variation), fig. 60 (Codex on the Flight of Birds).

19. Ackerman, 1963, 12, related the Villa of Poggio a Caiano to the Venetian villa and town house. Stanislaus von Moos, 122–124, fig. 108, saw Poggio a Caiano as related to the castle. See also P. G. Hamberg, "The Villa of Lorenzo Il Magnifico at Poggio a Caiano and the Origins of Palladianism," *Figura*, Uppsala, I, 1959, 79–87, and P. Foster, *Lorenzo de Medici's Villa at Poggio a Caiano*, Dissertation, Yale University, 1965, New York, Garland reprint, 1978, and Hartmut Bierman, "Lo sviluppo della villa toscana sotto l'influenza della corte di Lorenzo Il Magnifico," *BCISA*, XI, 1969, 36–46.

20. Rosci, I, 1967, 44–45. For Madrid, see Hautecoeur, I, 1, 222–224; 223, fig. 112; 224, fig. 113. Monique Châtenet is preparing a dissertation on the Château de Madrid under the direction of Professor Jean Guillaume. See also Von Moos, 128–129, and Fritz Schreiber, *Die französische Renaissance-Architektur und die Poggio Reale-Variationen des Sebastiano Serlio*, Berlin, 1938, 6–9, 13–14, 52–53.

21. Lewis, 1969, 360.

22. Bruschi, 1969, 1048–1052, note 44; 713–717, figs. 476–483. C. Frommel, "Bramante's Ninfeo in Genazzano," *Römisches Jahrbuch für Kunstgeschichte*, XII, 1968, 137–160.

23. Pl. XXXIX, lines 18–23, and Patzak, 83–91; 68, fig. 35; 72, fig. 39; 92, fig. 59. See also Hugh Smyth, 304–313, figs. 3–7.

24. Pl. XIV, lines 31–32.

25. Pl. XVI, lines 19–23.

26. This gallery does not appear in 18th-century ground plans of the château. See Bibliothèque Nationale, Cabinet des Estampes, Topographie de la France, L'Yonne, Va 89, vol. I, 198, attributed to Robert de Cotte, about 1720. In the library of Ancy-le-Franc, there is also a drawing by Chevallot of this floor which shows no gallery (signed and dated 1769).

27. Pl. XVII, compare line 3 to line 11.

28. Pl. XLVI, line 15 for the description of the cortile; lines 20–21 for rooms K and L; lines 29–36 for description of the royal apartment.

29. See Chapter V for the discussion of projects P 15 and Q 16.

30. Gauchery, 104, mentioned in the inventory of the Hôtel des Archives Nationales, Paris, KK 328, cited by Gauchery. See also Rosenfeld, 1971, 281.

31. For the Villa Garzoni, see Puppi, *BCISA*, IX, 1969, and Rupprecht, 1963.

32. Rosci, I, 1967, 71. Maltese, II, Pl. 196: Francesco di Giorgio, Codex Magliabechiano, folio 18v.

33. Rosenfeld, 1969, 157–158. Rosci, I, 1967, 70–71; 75, fig. 176: Antonio da Sangallo, Uffizi A 775; 75, fig. 177: Peruzzi, Uffizi A 506. Von Moos, 131–135, fig. 119 (Caprarola, Villa Farnese); fig. 120 (Uffizi A 506); fig. 121 (Drawing by Vignola in Archivio di Stato, Parma); fig. 123 (Serlio, Book VI, Munich, folio 30r). For the latest discussion of the Villa Farnese, see Loren Partridge, "Vignola and the Villa Farnese at Caprarola," *Art Bulletin*, XL, 1970, 81–87. The ultimate source of this type of castle is the Castel del Monte of Frederick II (1250) in Sicily. See Cora Heckseper, "Castel del Monte Seine Voraussetzungen in der nordwest-europäischen Baukunst," *Zeitschrift für Kunstgeschichte*, 33, 1970, no. 3, 211–232.

34. Rosci, I, 1967, 36. R. Falb, *Il taccuino senese di Giuliano da Sangallo*, Siena, 1902, folio 17v, ill. in Rosci, 1967, I, 36, fig. 90.

35. Lotz, 1955, 97–98, note 4; 21, fig. 4, Peruzzi, Plan for the Garden of the Villa Trivulzio, Uffizi A 453; 21, fig. 5, Peruzzi, Plan for San Giovanni dei Fiorentini, Uffizi A 510.

36. Boëthius, Ward-Perkins, 509; 510, fig. 194. See also C. Huelsen, *Il libro di Giuliano da Sangallo, Codice Vaticano Barberiano, Latino 4424*, Liepzig, 1910, folio 6.

37. Chastel, 1967, 80–81. Rosci, I, 1967, 76–77. Rosenfeld, 1969, 160.

38. Pl. XXXII, line 22.

39. MacDonald, Pl. 24, nos. 25, 27, 28.

40. Heydenreich, Lotz, Pl. 231.

41. MacDonald, Pl. 40, no. 8.

42. Pl. XXVI, lines 15, 16.

43. Maltese, I, 30, Turin Codex, folio 7v, fifth plan down from the top.

44. Hautecoeur, I, 1, 150–155; 116, fig. 71. E. Chirol, *Le château de Gaillon*, Paris, 1952. René Crozet, "Un plan de château de la fin du moyen age," *Bulletin Monumental*, 1952, 120–124.

45. Pl. XXVII, lines 1–2.

46. Rosenfeld, 1969, 167. Hautecoeur, I, 1, 72–76; 68, fig. 52.

47. Codex Magliabechiano, folio 20v, Maltese, II, Pl. 200.

48. Pl. XLI, lines 4–5. See Bury (1514–1524), Le Verger (1499), Le Plessis-Bourré (1468–1473); Hautecoeur, I, 1, 55, fig. 49; 66, fig. 50; B. de Montgolfier, *Dictionnaire des châteaux de France*, Paris, 1969, 195, ill.

49. Drawing in the Düsseldorf Kunstmuseum. See Egon Verheyen, "Jacopo Strada's Mantuan Drawings of 1567–1568," *Art Bulletin*, XIX, 1967, 62–71, fig. 7.

50. Pl. L, line 15.

51. Manfredo Tafuri, *Jacopo Sansovino e l'architettura del cinquecento a Venezia*, Padua, 1969, 10, ill. Frommel, 1973, Palazzo Baldassini, no. III, vol. 2, 23–28, vol. 3, Pl. 13c, 14b; Casa del Pozzo or Palazzo Ferrari, no. XVII, vol. 2, 175–179, vol. 3, Pls. 72a–e; Palazzo Massimo, no. XX, vol. 2, 233–250, vol. 3, Pls. 92–104. Frommel, 1973, vol. I, 53–92, discusses the uses of the rooms in these Roman sixteenth-century palaces. See also, Pagliara, 48–51, figs. 72, 87, 122–124, for the influence of Antonio di Sangallo, the Younger, on Serlio.

52. Madeleine Jurgens, Pierre Couperie, "Le logement à Paris au XVe et XVIe siècles," *Annales, économies, sociétés, civilizations*, 1962, no. 3, 488–500.

53. E. Fyot, *Hôtel Chambellan*, Dijon, 1925, 22, ill., and "Hôtels et maisons à Dijon," *Congrès archéologique*, 1928, 128–138.

54. André Chastel, "Les vestiges de l'hôtel le Gendre et le véritable hôtel de la Trémoille," *Bulletin monumental*, CXXIV, 1966, 129–165.

55. Chastel, 1966, 157, ill. plan: Trocadero, Centre de Recherches des monuments historiques, Plan, no. 1127, signed 1841; façade along the rue de la Bourdonnais, no. 2511, unpublished; North side of the courtyard, no. 1131, unpublished.

56. Pl. LII, line 16.

57. Pl. LIII, lines 18–20.

58. Rosci, I, 1967, 80. See L. Angelini, *Le opere in Venezia di Mauro Codussi*, Milan, 1945, 82–85, figs. 65, 68; 92–100, fig. 100. For the latest discussion of these buildings, see Loredana Olivato Puppi and Lionello Puppi, *Mauro Codussi*, Milan, 1977, 203–206, 221–226.

59. Pl. LVIII, lines 6–11.

60. Pl. LVIII, line 25.

61. Pl. LXV.

62. Howard, 1975, 38–47, fig. 33.

63. John R. Spencer, "The Cà del Duca in Venice and Benedetto Ferrini," *JSAH*, XXIX, 1970, no. 1, 3–8, fig. 3. Filarete, folio 169v, in Spencer, 1965, vol. 2, ill.

64. Pl. LXVII, line 27.

65. Pl. LXVII, line 32.

66. Pl. LXXI, lines 9–10.

67. Pl. LXXI, lines 29–30.

68. Bruschi, 1969, figs. 203–205.

69. Codex Magliabechiano, folio 20, Maltese, II, Pl. 199.

PRINTER'S PROOFS FOR BOOK VI IN THE NATIONALBIBLIOTHEK, VIENNA

Unknown French artist after Serlio. Book VI, Vienna Nationalbibliothek,
72P.20, ca. 1700. Woodcuts. (Erich Lünemann, Albertina)

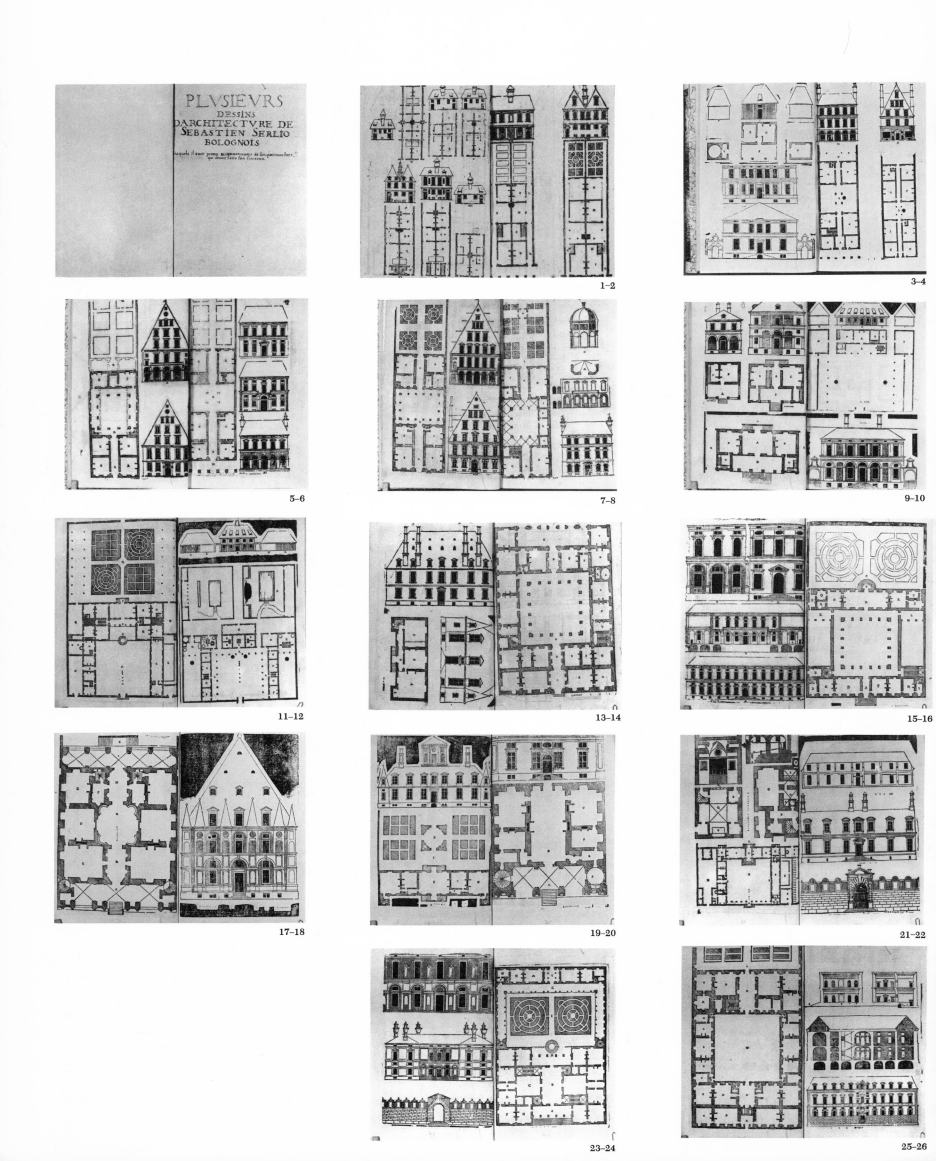

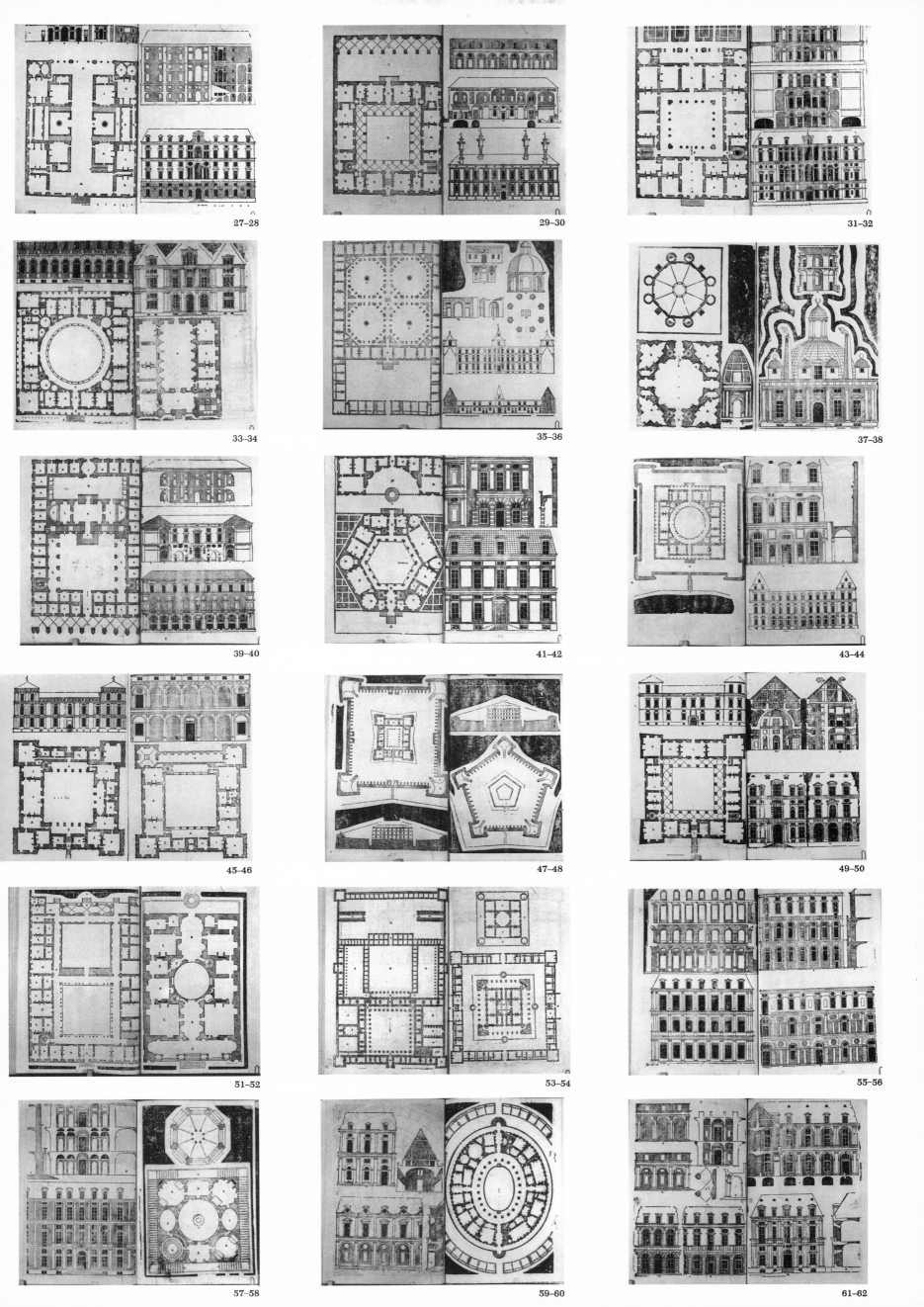

27–28

29–30

31–32

33–34

35–36

37–38

39–40

41–42

43–44

45–46

47–48

49–50

51–52

53–54

55–56

57–58

59–60

61–62

PAPER TYPES USED IN THE AVERY MANUSCRIPT

With Watermarks According to C. M. Briquet, *Les Filigranes*, Amsterdam, 2nd edition, 1968

Project Number	Lyons 1530–1533	Lyons 1545–1549	Lyons 1545–1574	Paris 1547–1550	Saint Germain-en-Laye 1561	Pontoise 1543	Orléans 1543	Valladolid 1550	Milan 1555	Paper types unknown
A1–C3	I									
D4–G7	II									text
H8	III									text
I9	IV									text
K10	V									text
L11	VI			variant text						text
M12		VII		variant text						
M12	VIII			text						
N13		IX						text		
N13		X						text		
N13a			XI					text		
O14		XII						text		
O14		XIII		XIII text						
P15	XIV			text						
P15	XV	XV			text					XV
Q16	XVI			text						
Q16	XVII	XVII		text						
Q16				XVIII text						XVIII
R17	XIX			text						
S18	XX			text						
S18	XXI			text						
T19		XXII		text						
T19	XXIII									variant text
V20	XXIV						text			
V20	XXV						text			
X21	XXVI			text						
X21	XXVII			text						
22	XXVIII									
22				XXIX						XXIX text
Et23	XXX									
Et24	XXXI			text						
Y25		XXXII		text						
Y25		XXXIII					text			
Ro26	XXXIV				XXXIV flap		text			
Ro26	XXXV						text			
27	XXXVI						text			
27	XXXVII						text			
28	XXXVIII						text			
28	XXXIX								text	
29	XL					text				
29		XLI				text				XLI
29	XLII					text				
30	XLIII					text				
30	XLIV					text				
31	XLV									
31	XLVI									text
31	XLVII									text
A–F		XLVIII								text
G–K		XLIX								text
L–M		L								text
N–O		LI								
P		LII								text
P	LIII									text
P	LIV									text
P	LV									text
P	LVI									text
P	LVII									text
Q	LVIII									text
Q	LIX						text			
R		LX								text
R		LXI								text
S	LXII					text				
S	LXIII									
S	LXIV					text				
T		LXV				text				
T		LXVI				text				LXVIa
V	LXVII									text
V	LXVIII									text
V	LXIX									text
V		LXX								
W	LXXI	LXXI								text
W		LXXII								
W	LXXIII	LXXIII								
W	LXXIIIa, b	LXXIIIa, b		LXXIIIa, b						

LIST OF ILLUSTRATIONS WITH CONCORDANCE BETWEEN THE DIFFERENT ORDERING OF THE MANUSCRIPT'S FOLIOS AND THE MUNICH VERSION

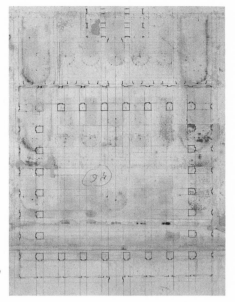

LV verso

Roman numerals have been used to number the folios of the present publication of the Avery Library manuscript of Serlio's Sixth Book in order to differentiate them from the Arabic numerals and letters used by Serlio to identify his projects. Text folios are reproduced on the left-hand pages facing their corresponding illustrations. When a text folio is missing, the left-hand page has been left blank. Variant texts for projects L 11 and M 12 (Pls. VI, VII) are on the verso and recto of a single folio; they have been reproduced separately. Project L 11 has in fact two texts, both reproduced here in their entirety on the same page (exceptionally, the complete folios on which these texts are written are not given here). The original text for project M 12 is missing. The text for project T 19 (Pl. XXIII) also seems to be a variant, since it does not correspond exactly to the illustration. Serlio's apparent error in placing the text for project V 20 (Pl. XXV) with project T 19 has been rectified in the present book. In the reordering of the drawing folios, Serlio's practice of placing the ground plan before the cross-section and façade elevation, unless otherwise indicated by Serlio himself, has been followed.

It was not possible to reproduce the flaps as they fold out from the original manuscript. The flap on plate XXXIV has been reproduced at the bottom of the page, the detail of the portal of project T (Pl. LXVIa) on the page following plate LXVI. The upper stories of the two wings of Palace W (Pl. LXXI) are included in the photograph of the whole plan. The cross section and plan of the vestibule of Palace W (Pl. LXXIII) are reproduced on the pages following the palace.

Of the plans drawn on the versos of three plates (LV, LVI, LXVII) only the first has been reproduced; it is felt that the plan on the verso of plate LXVII may not be by Serlio.

The illustration folios, with the exception of plates LXVII and LXXI are reproduced at 57% of their original size. The ground plans of Palaces V and W (Pls. LXVII, LXXI) are reduced to 37% of their actual size. All text folios are reproduced at 72% of their size. No attempt has been made to duplicate the variations of ink color in the manuscript.

By analyzing Serlio's handwriting in a letter to Pietro Aretino in the Pierpont Morgan Library, Dinsmoor concluded that, with the exception of three folios, all the Italian titles on the illustrations were written by Serlio. Titles by a second hand appear under elevations A and B (Pl. LXXII), above the roof of façade A (Pl. LXIX) and the descriptions of the rooms, except for the vestibule, on plate LXXI. Dinsmoor also identified a third hand for the French titles on plates I–VI, VIII, XIII and XIV. He felt that the script scrawled on the text of plate IX is the same that appears on the rooms illustrated on plates I–VII, XI–XII, XVII–XIX, XXI–XIV, XXVI–XXX, XXXII–XXXIII, XXXVI–XXXVII, XXXIX–XL, XLIII, L, LXII–LXIV, LXVIII–LXXII. He believed that these inscriptions represented Serlio's intention, at the end of his life, to make changes in the text of the manuscript. These notations on the room illustrations are not always accurate, and the reader is cautioned to look for the description of the rooms in the text.

The decorative motif is rendered from a detail in plate LXV.

Plate number	Project	TITLE	AVERY BOOK VI Folio Number in 1919 Binding	MUNICH BOOK VI Folio Number	MUNICH BOOK VI Project Number
		Country Dwellings	Missing	1r	Introduction
I	A 1	Farmhouse of the poor citizen for three levels of poverty	3	1v–3r	I III
	B 2	Farmhouse of the middle class citizen for two levels of poverty			
	C 3	Farmhouse of the rich citizen for two levels of wealth			
II	D 4	House of the poor artisan for three levels of poverty	4	3v–4r	IV–VII
	E 5	House of the poor artisan for two levels of poverty in the French manner			
	F 6	House of a citizen or merchant			
	G 7	House of a citizen or merchant or similar person in the French manner			
III	H 8	House for a richer citizen or merchant or similar person	5	4v–5r	VIII
IV	I 9	House for a richer citizen or merchant or similar person in the French manner	6	5v–6r	IX
V	K 10	House for a citizen or merchant different from the past project	7	6v–7r	X
VI	L 11	House for a citizen or merchant similar to the past project in the French manner	8	7v–8r	XI
VII	M 12	Villa for a noble gentleman	52	8v–9r	XII
VIII	M 12	Villa for a noble gentleman	53	9v–10r	XII

° Serlio's mistake

°° numbers added by author

Plate number	Project	TITLE	AVERY BOOK VI Folio Number in 1919 Binding	MUNICH BOOK VI Folio Number	MUNICH BOOK VI Project Number
IX	N 13	Dwelling for a noble gentleman	9	10v–11r	XIII
X	N 13	Dwelling for a noble gentleman	10	11v–12r	XIII
XI	N 13A**	Villa for a noble gentleman (La Grande Ferrare of Cardinal Ippolito d'Este)	11	14v–15r	XV
XII	O 14	House for a noble gentleman similar to the past project	12	15v–16r	XVI
XIII	O 14	House for a noble gentleman similar to the past project	13	15v–16r	XVI
XIV	P 15	House for a noble gentleman, the dwelling of the *Capitano*	14	12v–13r	XIV
XV	P 15	House for a noble gentleman, the dwelling of the *Capitano*	15	13v–14r	XIV
XVI	Q 16	Dwelling for a noble gentleman, the Château of Ancy-le-Franc	16	16v–17r	XVII
XVII	Q 16	Dwelling for a noble gentleman, the Château of Ancy-le-Franc	17	17v–18r	XVII
XVIII	Q 16	Dwelling for a noble gentleman, the Château of Ancy-le-Franc	18	17v–18r	XVII
XIX	R 17	Dwelling for a noble gentleman	19	18v–18a r	XVIII
XX	S 18	Dwelling for a Prince	20	18a v–19r	XIX
XXI	S 18	Dwelling for a Prince	21	18a v–19r	XIX
XXII	T 19	Small dwelling for a Prince	22	19v–20r	XX
XXIII	T 19	Small dwelling for a Prince	23	20v–21r	XXI
XXIV	V 20	Small dwelling for a Prince	24	21v–22r	XXII *
XXV	V 20	Small dwelling for a Prince	25	22v–23r	XXIII *
XXVI	X 21	Large dwelling for a Prince	26	23v–24r	XXIV *
XXVII	X 21	Large dwelling for a Prince	27	24v–25r	XXV *
XXVIII	22 **	Dwelling for a Prince	28	25v–26r	XXVI
XXIX	22 **	Dwelling for a Prince	29	26v–27r	XXVI
XXX	Et 23	Fortress for a Tyrant Prince	30	27v–29r	XXVII
XXXI	Et 24	Fortress for a Tyrant Prince	31	29v–31r	XXVIII
XXXII	Y 25	Pavilion for a King	32	31v–32r	XXIX
XXXIII	Y 25	Pavilion for a King	33	32v–33r	XXIX
XXXIV	Ro 26	Pavilion for a King on the same foundation as the past one	34	33v–34r	XXX *
XXXV	Ro 26	Pavilion for a King on the same foundation as the past one	35	34v–35r	XXXI *
XXXVI	27	House for a King	36	35v–36r	XXXII
XXXVII	27	House for a King	37	36v–37r	XXXII
XXXVIII	28	Small house for a King	38	37v–38r	XXXIII
XXXIX	28	Small house for a King	39	37v–38r	XXXIII
XL	29	Villa for a King	40	38v–39r	XXXIV
XLI	29	Villa for a King	41	39v–40r	XXXIV
XLII	29	Villa for a King	42	39v–40r	XXXIV
XLIII	30 **	Dwelling for a King	43	40v–41r	XXXIX *
XLIV	30 **	Dwelling for a King	44	41v–42r	XXXIX *
XLV	31	Dwelling for a King	46	missing	
XLVI	31	Dwelling for a King	45	42v–43r	XL
XLVII	31	Dwelling for a King	47	43v–44r	XL

Plate number	Project	TITLE	AVERY BOOK VI Folio Number in 1919 Binding	MUNICH BOOK VI Folio Number	MUNICH BOOK VI Project Number
		City Dwellings			
XLVIII	A	Hovel for a poor artisan	1	44v–45r	I–VI
	B	Hovel for a poor artisan			
	C	Dwelling for a poor artisan			
	D	Dwelling for a poor artisan			
	E	House of a better-off artisan			
	F	House of a better-off artisan in the French manner			
XLIX	G	House of a better-off artisan with an upper floor	2	45v–47r	VII–X
	H	House of a better-off artisan in the French manner			
	I	Dwelling of a rich artisan or good merchant or citizen			
	K	Dwelling of a rich artisan or good merchant or citizen in the French manner			
L	L	House for a citizen or merchant or similar person	48	47v–49r	XI–XII
	M	House for a citizen or merchant or similar person in the French manner			
LI	N	House for a rich citizen or good merchant	49	49v–51r	XIII–XIV
	O	House for a rich citizen or good merchant in the French manner			
LII	P	House for a noble Venetian gentleman	50	51v–52r	XV
LIII	P	House for a noble Venetian gentleman	55	52v–53r	XV
LIV	P	Variant of a House for a noble Venetian gentleman	51	53v–54r	XVI
LV	P	Variant of a House for a noble Venetian gentleman	56	54v–55r	XVI
LVI	P	House for a noble Venetian gentleman	54	52v–53r	XV
LVII	P	House for a noble Venetian gentleman	57	54v–55r	XVI
LVIII	Q	House for a noble gentleman	58	55v–56r	XVII
LIX	Q	House for a noble gentleman	59	56v–57r	XVII
LX	R	Palace of the *Capitano*	60	57v–58r	XVIII
LXI	R	Palace of the *Capitano*	61	58v–59r	XVIII
LXII	S	Palace of the *Podestà*	62	59v–60r	XIX
LXIII	S	Palace of the *Podestà*	71	missing	
LXIV	S	Palace of the *Podestà*	63	60v–61r	XIX
LXV	T	Palace of the Governor	64	61v–62r	XX
LXVI	T	Palace of the Governor	65, 65a	62v–63a r	XX
LXVIa	T	Palace of the Governor			
LXVII	V	House of the Prince	66	63a v–64a r	XXI
LXVIII	V	House of the Prince	70	missing	
LXIX	V	House of the Prince	67	64a v–66r	XXI
LXX	V	House of the Prince	68	missing	
LXXI	W	House of the King	69, 69a, 69b	66v–68r	XXII
LXXII	W	House of the King	73	68v–73r	XXII
LXXIII	W	House of the King	72	missing	
LXXIIIa	W	House of the King	72a	missing	
LXXIIIb	W	House of the King	72b	missing	
			missing	74r–74v	Conclusion

SEBASTIANO SERLIO
ON
DOMESTIC
ARCHITECTURE

The Sixteenth-Century Manuscript of Book VI
in the Avery Library of Columbia University

VIII ~~LIVRE~~ D

VIII LIBRO DI SERLIO
m: S:
Architettura

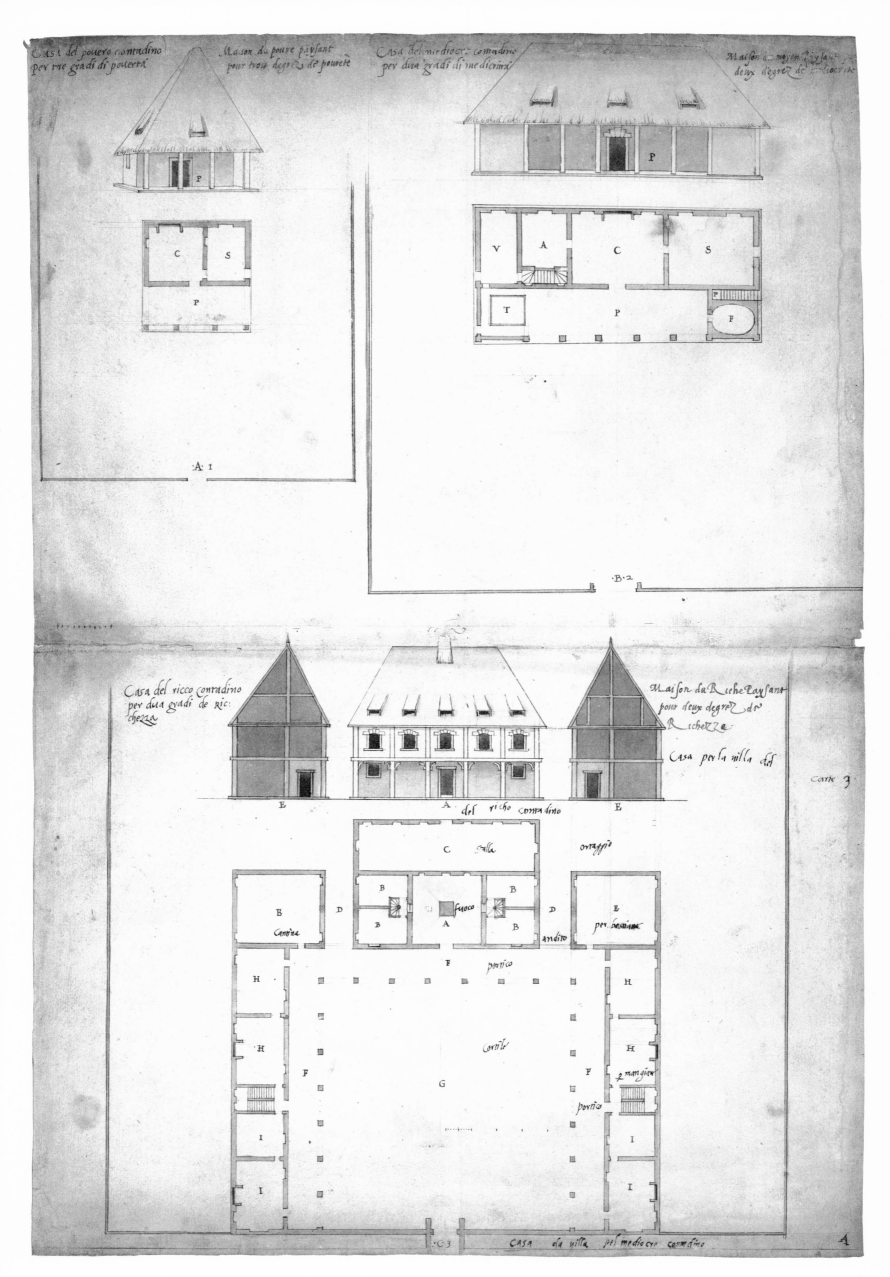

Casa del pouero contadino per tre gradi di pouertà

Maison du poure paysant pour trois degrez de poureté

Casa del mediocre contadino per dua gradi di mediocrità

Maison a moyen paysant deux degrez de mediocrité

A·1

B·2

Casa del ricco contadino per dua gradi de ric: chezza

Maison du Riche Paysant pour deux degrez de Richezza

Casa per la villa del

Carte 3

A del richo contadino

Casa da villa pel mediocre contadino

A

I

Circa alle habitationi de contadini ho trattato quanto mie è parso esser necessario: per che l'architetto prudente con questa poca luce ne potra fare assai: et in questo modo seruira a tutti li paesi. Hora io trattaro delle habitationi de cittadini: fuori delle citta sopra li suoi poderi: et possessioni, e cosi cominceno dal pouero artefice il quale habbia un poco di terreno sopra del quale sara necessari hauergli un poco de ridotto, il quale sara per lo manco piedi XIII di quadro doue si fara il fuoco et lo letto: et sara segnato B. et segli sara alquanto piu accommodato di beni: potra agiungerui una cucina che sia almen larga piedi VII et è segnata C. è ben che vi sia una scala per salire al suolo morto: non se diminuisce però la stanza: per esser detta scala uacua di sotto, E se anchora acadera maggiore habitatione e che l'huomo sia piu potente: essendo l'altezza delle prime stanze piedi XII: potra fare l'altro suolo piedi X et cosi hauera dua camere: una cucina: et un camerino, et anche la cucina si potra amezzare: per commodita de i serui e sel sito comportaua si caui sotto: potra leuarsi da terra II piedi e mezzo sotto IIII e mezzo è fare una cantina la quale sara di quella capacita che al bisogno del padrone sia basteuole, et a questa cantina si descendera per la cucina sotto la scala: ma di fuori sara una porte per mettervi le bone, et se anchora questo vora maggior casa: per esser piu ricco o piu animoso potra agiungerui una loggia: la latitudine della quale sia piedi IX. segnata A. doue cauando sotto tutta la casa, ella sara piu sana: et hauera maggior cantina: e sopra la loggia guadagnava una saletta alla quale si montaua per la scala della cucina: e cosi questa magione seruira non solamente a tre gradi di persone: ma a quatro agiuntoui la loggia: et chi vora contentarsi delle stanze da basso: atento che sono leuate dal altro piano e cauate sotto: potra mettere il tetto sopra la prima cornice l'essempio di questa si vedi qua dauanti segnata. D. +

Per che nel mio procedere io intendo di accompagnare le commodita francese col costume: et ornamento italiano io formaro una casa per il medesimo pouero e mediochre artefice alla francese, e prima la parte A. sara longa piedi XX. et larga XV entro la quale si faua il fuoco: et lo letto è questa sara per uno pouero artefice a suficientia: ma segli sara piu accomodato segli giungira una cucina: la sua larghezza sara piedi VIII e mezzo: entro la quale si mettera una vite el suo diametro sara piedi V. doue la cucina rimaua longa piedi XIII. è auanciaraui una picola saluaroba: la cucina sara segnata B. questa magione sara leuata da terra: et cauata sotto come la passata: et sel padrone sara anchora piu possente io: almen generoso leuara il suo coperto con le lucarne è faua disopra altre habitationi: e cosi questa casa seruira a tre gradi di persone: come l'altra: la qual si vedi qui auanti segnata. E. 5.

Sara dipoi un Cittadino: o un mercante: il quale per hauer piu terreno et altre faculta: vora una maggiore habitatione della passata. questa per piu magnificentia: et sanitade anchora si leuara dal piano di terra piedi V. cauando sotto piedi IIII si potra fare sotto terra la cantina: la cucina: et altre serui e cosi le stanze sopra terra sarano nette: e prima si montara alla loggia A. la sua larghezza sara piedi IX. et in longhezza piedi XXIIII. ne i capi della qua: lo sarandua camerini di piedi VII in larghezza: li quali si amezzarano, et in un di essi sara una scala per montare al suo mezzado: nel altro sara una vite per montare gl'al mezzado et disopra anchora: dipoi la loggia s'entra nel vestibulo segnato B. la larghezza sua è piedi VII. et in longhezza XIII. dal destro: et sinistro lato vi sono dua camere: quella segnata C. è di quadrato perfe di piedi XIII: l'altra segnata D. sara il medesimo: l'entrata della cantina sara sotto la scala che descende nel giardino: ma per gire coperto alla cucina: et anche alla cantina si descendera per la vite, l'altezza di queste prime habitationi sara piedi XIII. et quella delle seconde sara piedi X: et sara loggia sopra loggia: et anche la loggia disopra si potra fare fenestrata è seruira per saletta, et che si contentaua delle prime habitationi potra mettere il tetto sopra la prima cornice, e tutte queste case se intende che dauanti habbiano un couile et dalli lati della casa vi siani dua strade che si passi al giardino: doue il couile sara piu grande et la faccia della casa sara aricchita da quelle dua porte e questa sara segnata. F. 6

La medesima habitatione si potra fare al costume di Franza: ma di altra forma: la quale si leuaua da terra III. piedi e mezzo: et altro tanto si cauaua che saua VII. per le commodita che s'e detto qui adietro: e prima si troua uno andito D. dal qual si va alla camera principale. A. questa per ogni lato è piedi XXI: et nel rissetare di quel angolo di fuori che compagna la limaca vi è un spacio di piedi VII e mezzo in longhezza: e III e mezzo in larghezza: questo sara lo spacio di un picollo letto senza impedire la camera, è congiunto la guardaroba: che cosi segli dice di qua: la sua larghezza e piedi XV. et in longhezza XVI e mezzo, et è segnata B. nel capo del altro andito vie la limaca: per la quale si passa alla cucina. C. la sua longhezza e piedi XXI et in larghezza piedi XVI. per cagine del andito che toglie piedi V. con la grossezza del muro: e per la istessa limaca si descendera alla cantina et alli altri lochi simili: et per la quale si montara ad alto: e cosi questa limaca essendo fuori del muro: cosi dal altro lato vie quel rissalto per compagnamento della faccia della magione la quale e segnata G 7

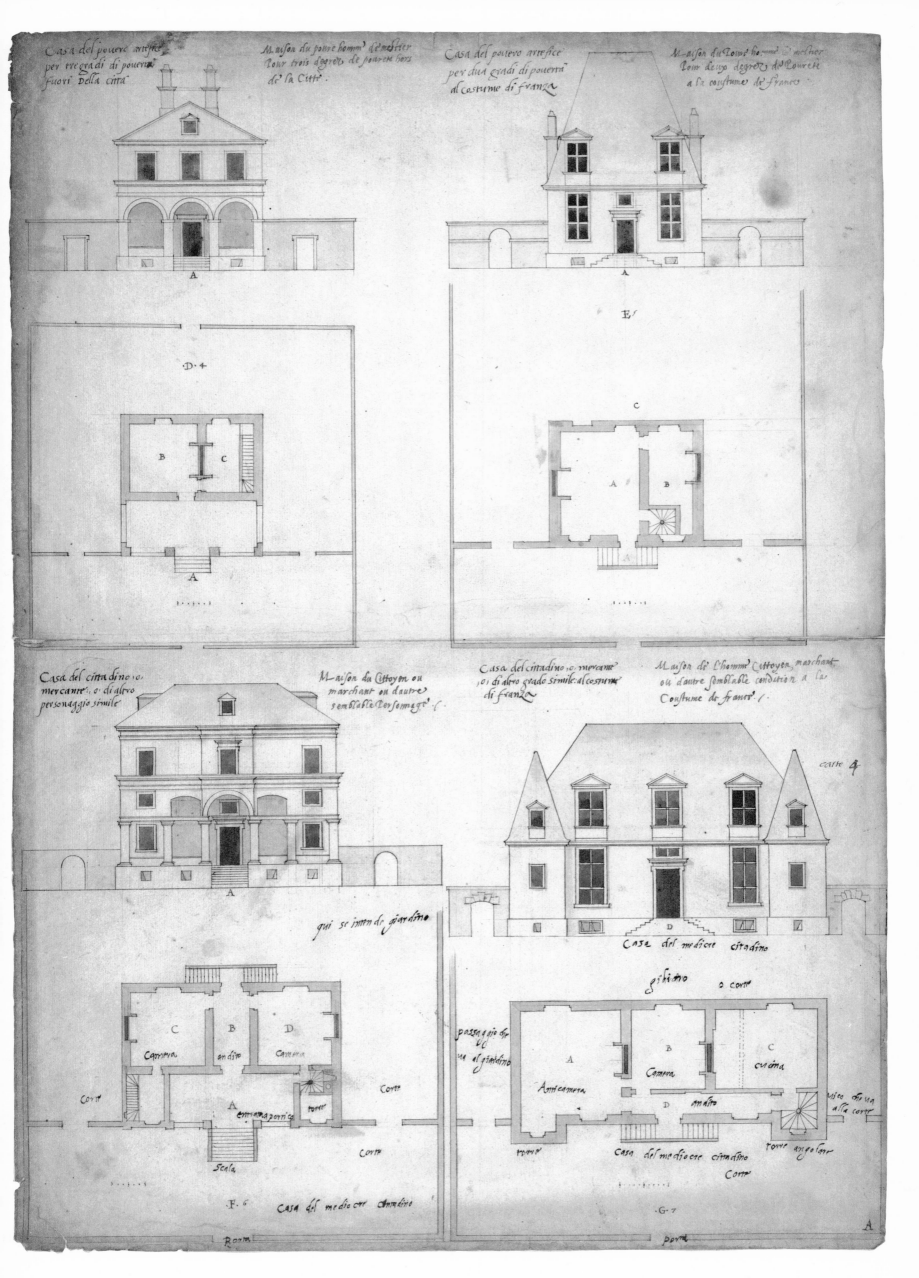

Casa del povere artefice
per tre gradi di povertà
fuori della città.

Maison du povre homme d'mestier
Pour trois degrez de poureté hors
de la Citté.

Casa del povero artefice
per dua gradi di povertà
al costume di franza.

Maison du povre homme d'mestier
Pour deuo degrez di poureté
a la costume de france

D.

E

A

C

B   C

A   B

A

A

Casa del citadino, o,
mercante, o, di altro
personaggio simile

Maison du Cittoyen ou
marchant ou d'autre
semblable personnage.

Casa del citadino, o, mercante
,o, di altro grado simile al costume
di franza

Maison de l'homme Cittoyen, marchant,
ou d'autre semblable condition a la
Coustume di france.

corte 4

qui se intende giardino

Casa del mediocre citadino

C   B   D
Camera   andito   Camera

gibidino   o corte

passagio che
va al giardino

A
Antecamera

B
Camera

C
cucina

Corte   Corte

D
andito

uiso chi va
alla corte

Corte

A
entramazorra

torre

franza

casa del mediocre citadino

torre angolare

Scala

Corte

F. 6   Casa del mediocre Citadino

G. 7

porta

porta

A

II

Si trouará taluolta un cittadino io mercante di più facultà è danari anchora et hauerà più grossa famiglia, onde gli conuerrà maggiore habitatione di quelle che più adrieto si sono dimostrate: onde qua dauanti ne dimostrarò una maggiore, nel mezzo di questa sarà uno andito o vogliamo dir sala: la latitudine del quale sarà piedi XX. et in longitudine piedi XXXVII e mezzo: che così uuole la proportione delle camere, e questo sarà segnato A. dalla destra et sinistra parte son dua anticamere: la sua larghezza è piedi XX. et la longhezza piedi XXIIII e son segnate B. dipoi queste son dua camere di quadratura perfetta segnate C. passando poi fuori del andito si troua una loggia D. la sua larghezza è piedi X. et in longhezza piedi XXI. ne i capi della quale son dua camerini inuno de quali si farà la scala: l'altro rimane piedi IX per quadro: ma vi sarà la scala: per montare al mezzado; et anche disopra: chi uora, et altro tanto habitationi sarà disopra, le stanze sotterrane: le qual sarano pel seruitio della casa: come saria: cucina: saluaroba: rinello: oltra la caniua hauerano dua entrate, una sarà sotto la scala dauanti: l'altra sotto la limaca, dalli lati della casa vi sarano dua giardini: o veramente andii la sua larghezza è piedi XIIII e mezzo e questo si fa accio chel couile venga a esser piedi C. et la faccia della casa si fa più ricca dale dua poue aresi andiri: li quali passano al gran giardino o veramente bruolo: et il gran couile dauanti seruirà di ara facendo poi dalli lati le habitationi de lauoratori: o in altra banda seppararti, la pianta di questa casa si vede qui dauanti segnata H-8 —

il diritto di questa pianta si vede sopra essa, il piano della quale sarà leuato dal pian di terra piedi V. l'altezza delle prime stanze sarà piedi XVI. l'altezza delle seconde sarà piedi XII. oltra il granaro. il quale sarà a beneplacito del padrone: ma il primo ordine di corniciamenti sarà piedi tre e mezo partito intre parti: una sarà l'architraue: una il fregio: l'altra la cornice: quelle disopra sotto il tetto sarano la quarta parte minco: partite come le altre: la larghezza delle fenestre sarà piedi V. l'altezza delle prime sarà piedi IX. quella delle seconde si farà piedi VIII. la porta sarà in larghezza piedi V. et in altezza X. la larghezza delle poue che passano al giardino sarà piedi VII. et l'altezza piedi XII. li ornamenti di esse si ueggono e porran esser fatte alla volontà del padrone: che questo importa poco

E' per che la parte di drieto di questa casa: verso il giardino, none men bella di quella dauanti: anci e tanto più bella per cagion della loggia la quale è molto lontana dalle altre ne suoi compartimenti: ho voluto dimostrare anchora questa parte: la quale si vede qua disopra questa loggia è leuata dal piano del giardino còme la parte dauanti: sopra la quale sotto le colonne vi è un parapetto che serue di piedestalo alle colonne: l'altezza del quale è piè di tre: l'altezza delle colonne è piedi XII. con le sue base: e capitelli, la sua grossezza è un piede e tre quarti et sarano poriche, la grossezza de i pilastri congiunti con esse colonne ronde sarà dua piedi e un quarto: da l'una e l'altra colonna ronda cioe la parte di mezzo sarà piedi VIII. li dua intercolunni acanto a essa parte di mezzo sarano larghi piedi III. quelli più verso li angoli sarano piedi IIII. et questo è fatto accio che le fenestre del andito: e quelle delle camere: scontrino ne i mezzi fra le colonne: la parte disopra sarà in tal modo che le colonne superiore poserano sopra le inferiori: ma disopra non vi è pilastri: ma vi sarano le colonne semplice et saran ioniche: l'altezza delle quali sarà piedi X. con le sue bassi et capitelli; la sua grossezza sarà un piede et un quarto: et se altre misure mancheuano li piedi sotto la pianta supplirano al tutto.

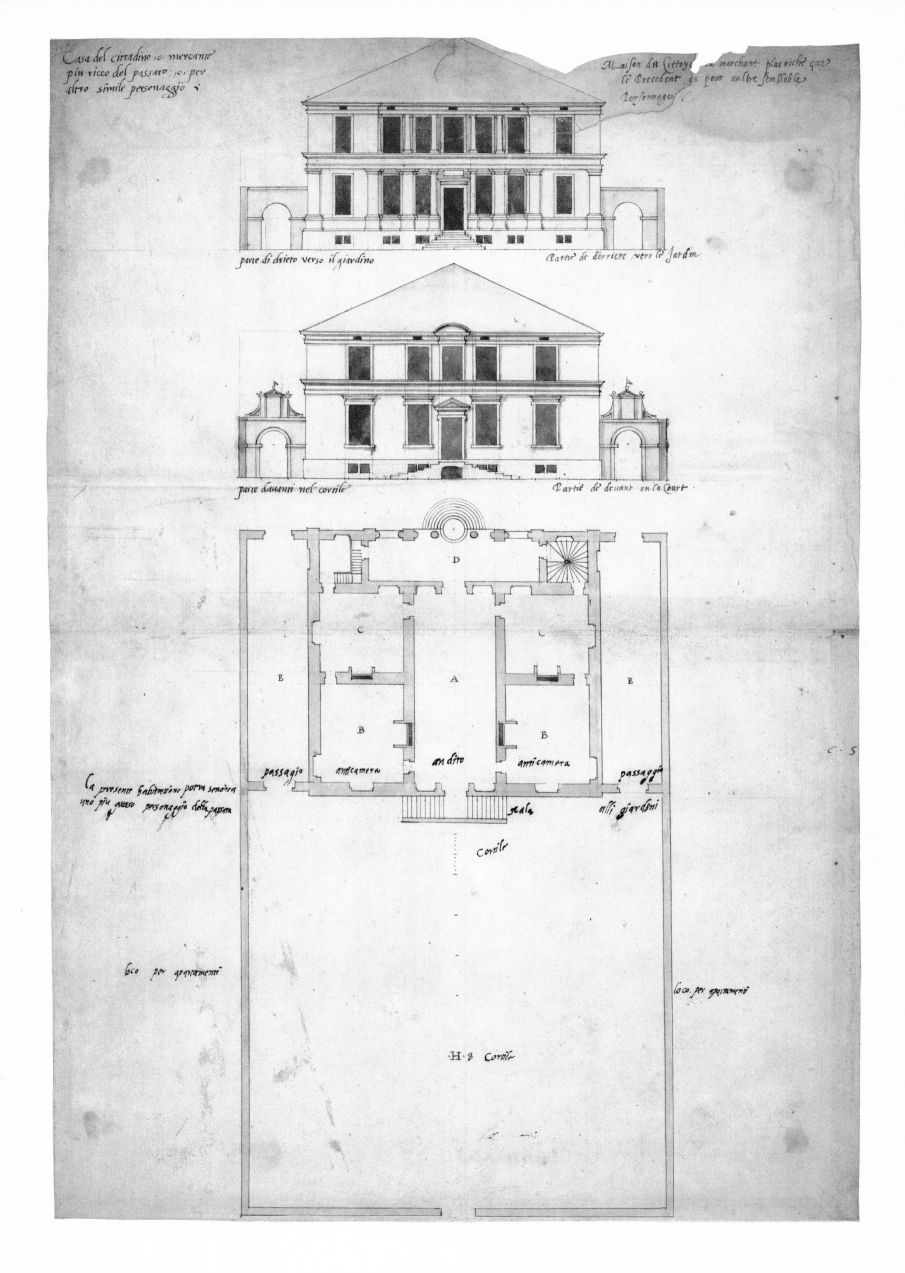

Casa del cittadino io mercante
piu ricco del passato, o, per
altro simile personaggio

Maison du Cittoyen, ou merchant, plus riche que
le precedent, ou pour aultre semblable
personnage

parte di drieto verso il giardino

Partie de derriere vers le Jardin

parte davanti nel covrile

Partie de devant en la Court

la presente habitazione potra servira
uno piu quesso personaggio delo passato

loco per appartamenti

D

C   C

E   A   E

B   B

passagio   anticamera   an dito   anticamera   passaggio

scala   alli giardini

covrile

loco per appartamenti

H 8 Covrile

C 5

III

Altro modo di habitationi costumano li francesi differenti dalli nostri, non di meno le medesime commodità, o, circa ch'io ho dimostrato nella
magione qui adietro: io le disponerò in altro modo, o, circa almeno, in questi paesi fuori delle città e massimamente in questi
circonuicini a fontanableo costumano una riuata di appartamenti in longitudine la larghezza de i quali per l'ordinario non passa xxiiii piedi
cio è lo netto fra li dua muri: et la grossezza de i muri non passa .ii. piedi: ma con gran coppia di legnami e ferramenti li sostengono
la presente habitatione adonca sarà leuata dal piano piedi .v. che sempre io leuarò dal piano tutti li edificij che sarano da me ordinati
per cio che a longo andar deglianni: la terra da sé partorisse et cresse come ne fan fede non solamente le cose antiche: ma le moderne di ccc
anni si trouano sotto terra: e questo si vede in ogni paese, è per cio montato piedi .v. al entrare della porta: si troua una limaca
sotto la quale si passa agiatamente da destra e sinistra: et in fronte questa e segnata .A. passando per uno andito da un lato si troua
una camera .B. la qual si dico guardaroba: il suo diametro è piedi .xv. et è quadrata, dipoi si troua la camera .C. di piedi xxi per tutti li
lati dal altro lato del andito vi è la camera .D. della grandezza del altra .B. passando più la vi e la camera .E. de la istessa grandezza della
compagna .C. nel mezzo poi vi e un camerino .F. la sua larghezza e piedi .vii. et in longhezza .xiii. et altre tanto habitationi sarà di
sopra: et chi vora una sala, o, da basso, o da alto prenderà una camera maggiore insieme con la menore et quella parte del andito: et
haueua una sala di larghezza piedi .xx. et in longhezza piedi xxxix. et come ho detto delle altre tutte le officine sarano sotto terra: et
rimarano le stanze di sopra: et da basso tutte libere, è per dua lochi si andarà alle stanze sotterranee: per sotto la scala che monta al piano
della casa: et per la limaca anchora, dauanti questa casa sarà un cortile di tanta larghezza: et longhezza quanto sarà tutta l'habitatione: che è
piedi Lxxxvii. Dalli lati del cortile sarano portichi, o, archati, o, a pilastri con li traui sopra: et sarano partiti in sette parti: nella parte di
mezzo si serrara tre spacij de iguali si farà habitationi e stalle: per cauallii et per altre bestie: e quatro lochi segnati .G. sarano portichi
tenerui diuerse cose: per cio che il cortile seruirà per ara da condure le entrate, drieto la casa sarà brulo e giardino il quale si passara
per li lochi .H. e questi porano essere, o, coperti e discoperti, e questa pianta qui dauanti e segnata .I.

La parte qua sopra dinota la facia della casa qua sopra discritta: et qui sono dimostrata, la quale come si è detto e leuata .v. piedi dal altro
piano si per la sanità delle stanze e sotterranee et anche per quelle sopra esse: come per la bellezza, la latitudine della porta e piedi .v. et in
altezza piedi .x. et serrandosi la porta il frontispicio darà luce al entrata, la latitudine delle fenestre sara piedi .iiii. e mezzo: et la sua altezza
sarà .x. e mezzo, il parapetto di quelle di sopra sarà alto .iii. piedi: et le fenestre sarano piedi .vi. è mezzo in altezza, le prime habitationi
sarano alte piedi .xv. cioè le dua gran camere, ma le dua picole camere: col camerino se amezzarano et cosi l'andito anchora il quale andito
seruiua alle dua camere: et se .xv. piedi aua poca altezza per amezzare si porra far .xvi. senza menda alcuna e le prime camere sarano
.viii. piedi in altezza: un piede sarà la grossezza del suolo: e .vii. piedi sarà quelle di sopra: l'altezza delle habitationi che prendeno la
luce dalle lucarne sarà quanto tornarà bene nel coperto della casa: quanto alli ornamenti in cosi picola casa non mi fancaro a discriuere
le misure: ma ne sono de simili da me discritti minutamente nel terzo et quarto libro.

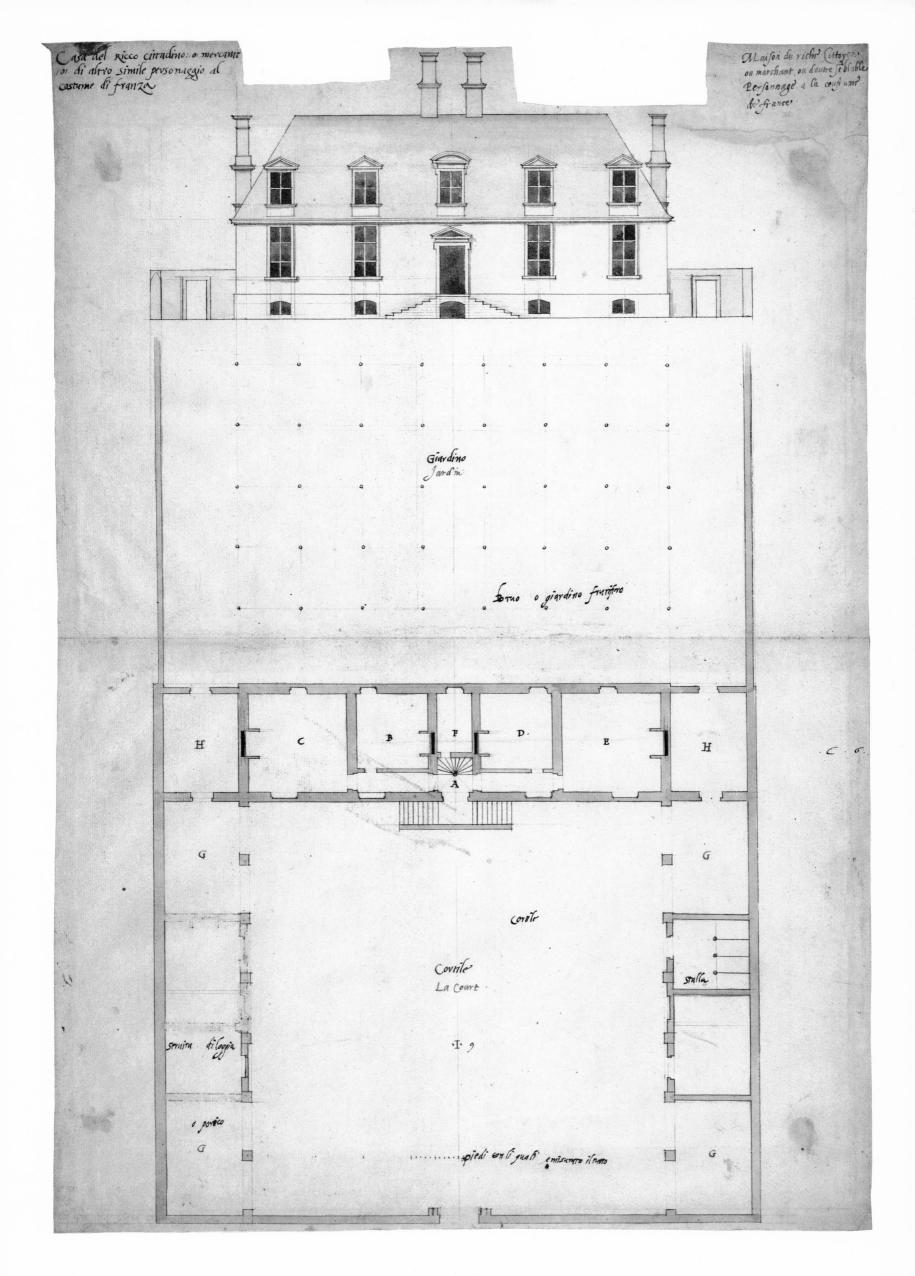

Casa del ricco cittadino: o mercante
o di altro simile personaggio al
costume di franza

Maison du riche Cittoyen:
ou marchant, ou d'autre semblable
Personnage a la coustume
de france

Giardino
Jardin

orto o giardino fruttifero

H   C   B   F   D   E   H   o
              A

G   G

                    cortile

             Cortile
             La Court

                    · I · 9

servitta di loggia   stalla

o portico
G   G

·········· piedi con li quali si è misurato il resto

IV

il variare è sempre bello è massimamente a satisfation di coloro li quali vorebbon veder piu cose per far poi eletione di quella: che piu le piace: et che piu commodo gli torna, è per cio la presente habitatione porra servire a' un cittadino io: un' mercante: come la passata: io a qualche altro perso naggio segondo le voglie: et insieme il potere deglihomini: questa è disposta in altro modo della passata: et ha gliappartamenti anche mag giori, Questa: è levata dal piano: come le altre per le ragioni antidette, montato adonca li .V. piedi si trova una loggia .D. la sua longhezza è piedi .LX. et in larghezza piedi .XIII. havendo dalli capi dua camerini .C. di quadratura perfetta quanto è larga la loggia: questi havevano le scale per salire alli mezzadi: et anche per montare ad alto: accio non sia: impedito ne la sala: ne le camere di questa loggia si trova la sala .A. la sua larghezza è piedi .XXXII. havendo dalli capi da camere .B. di perfeta quadratura quanto è larga la sala, e cosi della sala se dissende al giardino: chi trova sotto la qual scala sara la porta della cantina: et altri officij, è quantunque il giardino .E. paia picolo questo è per il poco spacio che è qui: ma s'intende di quella grandezza che al huomo pareva, o veramente chel sia un cortiletto che vicingha la casa: io un giardino delicato: e poi dalla colombara in la sia orto è bruolo, la qual colombara sara nella parte di fuori piedi .XXVIII. è nella parte di dentro piedi .XXII. per cio che la grossezza de i muri sara tre piedi .III. non dimeno accio vi sia luoco per la scala: l'andara di mezzo sara larga piedi .X. lassandovi dal altro lato altro tanto pei necessarij communi: ma nella parte di sopra prima che si trovi la colombara: vi sara una camera di piedi .XXII. e .XVI. l'altezza di questa colombara sara piedi .LXXX. fin alla summità

la faccia di questa casa: sara in latitudine piedi .LXXXII. è prima nel mezzo si fara tre archi et alli angoli dua: che saranno .VI. la grossezza de i pilastri sara .II. piedi e tre quarti: la latitudine fra l'uni pilastro al altro sara piedi .X. quei dua intercolunnij estremi saranno ciascuno piedi .V. è cosi li ottantadua piedi sarano distribuiti: l'altezza deglarchi sara piedi .XX. ma li dua angolari sarano chiusi per li dua camerini l'altezza della loggia sara piedi .XXI. e cosi sarano tutte le habitationi terrene: ma li camerini .C. et le camere .B. si porano amezzare: et se la loggia si fara in volta: sara bene a menervi le chiavi di ferro pel traverso: che per la longa non acadara per li dua angoli serrati chi sano bone spalle: quei dua intercolunnij sono fatti accio che li lumi della sala: e quei de camerini anchora venghino nel mezzo deglarchi: l'altezza del archirrave: fregio et cornice sara piedi .V. partita in parti .X. tre parti sara l'archirrave quatro parti lo fregio e tre parti la cornice: l'altezza delle colonne di sopra sara piedi .XIII. la sua grossezza un piede e tre quarti: l'archirrave: fregio: et cornice sopra esse colonne sara alta per la quarta parte mentore della prima partita nel medesimo modo, et nel fregio sarano le fenestre del granaro: la larghezza della porta: et anche delle fenestre sara piedi .V. l'altezza delle prime: et anche delle segonde sara piedi .X. le picole fenestre davan luce alli mezzadi le stanze sotterranee: servivano come ho detto per cantina: per cucina: et per altre cose simili alli quai lochi si dessendeva per le scale de i camerini: le qual dissese potvano anche esser sotto la loggia: anchora si dessendeva a questi lochi per una porta maggiore sotto la scale che va nel giardino, et anchora che la colombara paia esser sopra la casa a chi non vedesse la pianta ella e pero lontana da la casa: circa a piedi .XL. le dua porte: sono quelle che passano al picolo giardino per ampliare piu il cortile le dua parti piu fuori dinotano li dua portichi et habitationi dalli lati del cortile davanti la casa, il qual cortile è .C.X. piedi per ciascun lato e servira per ara: havendo dua portichi dalli lati: e quatro stanze da servirsene a diverse cose pertinente alla casa: e questa sara segnata .K. 10.

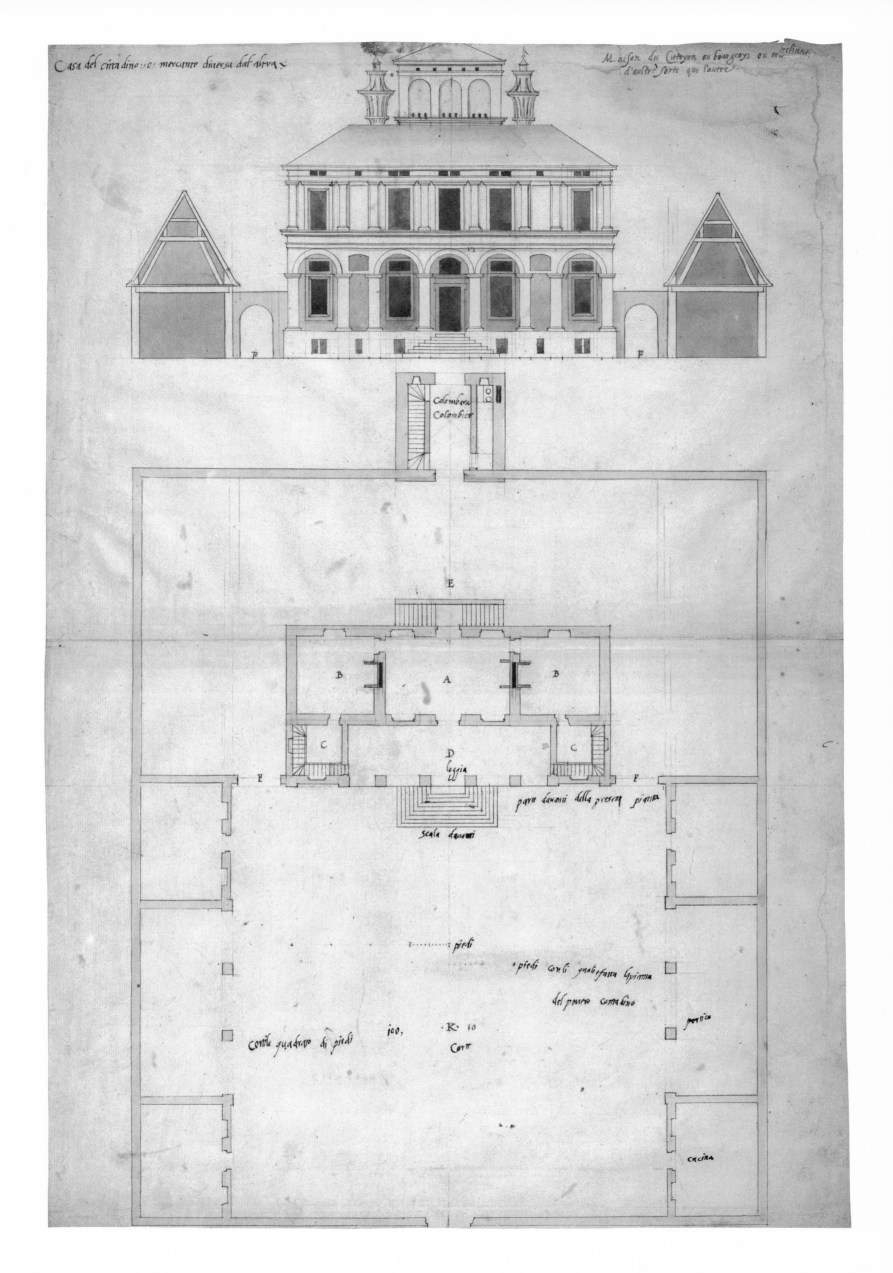

Casa del cittadino; o, mercante diuersa dal altra:

Maison du Citoyen ou bourgeoys ou marchant d'aultre sorte que l'autre.

Colombaia
Colombier

E

B   A   B

C   C

D
loggia

F   F

parti dauanti della presente pianta

scala dauanti

piedi

piedi con li quabefatta la pianta

del powro contadino

cortile quadrato di piedi   100,   K. 10
                                      Corti

portico

cucina

V

Vnaltra casa quasi simile alla passata si potra fare al costume di franza, prima si troua vna gran corte di quadrato perfeto: il suo diametro è piedi · C · IIII · che cosi è longa tutta la casa, questo ha dalli lati nella parte di mezzo dua portichi · B · con tre archi è dua colonne, la latitudine di questi è piedi · XV · et in longitudine piedi · XXXVI · dalli lati di questi sono quatro stanze · C · le quali potrani seruire a molte cose et in essi luochi accommodarci le scale per montare ad alto, li dua lochi segnati · D · io glintendo corticello le quali seruirano a molte cose: et massimamente sel padrone volesse di vna di quelle parti · C · farne la cucina: questo cortile saria molto al proposito, quei lochi · C · sono in longhezza piedi XXVIII · questo corpo di casa sara leuato da terra come ho detto gia deglialtri per diuerse cagioni, montato al detto piano si troua vna sala · E · la sua larghezza è piedi · XX · et la longhezza piedi XXX, negliangoli di questa, si troua dua antri · F · liquali passani sotto vna vite lassando da vno lato vna guardaroba segnata · G · la sua longhezza è piedi · XV · et in longhezza XIII · queste et glianditi si amezzarano et le limache non impidiscono da basso e montano alli mezzadi: et anche disopra: chi vora, passando l'anditto si troua vna camera · H · la sua grandezza è piedi · XX · per quadro alliangoli di queste son dua limache commune da montare disopra: per le quali anche si monta a queste camere; partendo della sala si monta nel giardino · I · il quale è pure di quadrato perfetto come il cortile lassando dalli lati dua piantate di fruti o veramente pergole, nel mezzo di questo ci è la colombara laquale nella parte di fuori è larga per tutti e lati piedi · XXII · et nella parte di drento è piedi · XIX · ma è di forma ottogona, si perche liangoli siani piu forti: come anche per loccarui vna limaca per montare ad alto: doue poi si troua vna camera prima che si monti alla colombara

Quanto alla faccia della casa: come s'è detto si monta · V · piedi l'altezza del primo suolo sara piedi · XIIII · che viene a essere sotto la cornice sotto il coperto, la latitudine della porta è piedi · V · et alta · IX · la larghezza delle fenestre è piedi · IIII · et in altezza · X · l'altezza de i parapetti delle lucarne è piedi · III · la luce delle lucarne è alta piedi · VII · le fenestre delle limache son larghe piedi · II · quanto agliornamenti si trouarano doue ho detto piu volte, l'altezza della colombara fin alla suppeviore cornice sara piedi · LX · quella parte che si scuopre sotto il tetto è piedi · XX · in altezza: quel poco basamento è piedi · IIII · l'altezza delle colonne è piedi · XIIII · l'architraue: fregio: et cornice è piedi · IIII · partito in tre parti vna sara l'architraue: vna per il fregio l'altra sara per la cornice, et si questi apartamenti cio è camere et la sala principalmente fussero picole alla voglia et bisogno del padrone: si potra cressere la misura de i piedi facendo che la sala sia XXIIII piedi in larghezza: e cosi tutti li altri membri cresserano proporzionatamente: si nelle larghezze è longhezze: come anche nelle altezze, et anchora che queste dua scale è dauanti: è di drieto vadino cosi auite in parte: e parte piano: si potrano nondimeno fare in qualunque modo si vora: essendoui gran spacio: è questa casa è segnata · L II ·

La maggior parte delle habitationi di questi luochi circonvicini a fontanableo: luoco bellissimo: et sopramodo grato al nostro Re Francesco: si fano cosi continuare in longhezza, è per il commune uso a piu sono in latitudine · XXIIII · piedi dico il netto fra li muri, e primieramente al presente edificio si monta piedi · V · dal piano è quatro sene caua sotto terra che sono piedi · IX · per le cantine: e cucine, et altri uficii, al'entrara si truoua vna sala la sua longhezza è piedi XXXVII · e mezzo: la larghezza XXIIII · et è segnata · A · dalla destra et sinistra banda vi sono dua anditi al'entrara dei quali sono dua limache · B · F · la parte · C · serue per guardaroba et è in larghezza piedi XVII · la sua longhezza piedi · XX · poi si passa alla camera · D · la quale è per tutti li lati piedi · XXIIII · et il medesimo dal altro lato · G · H · l'altezza della sala è delle dua camere maggiori sara piedi · XVIII · ma le guardarobe: et li anditi sarano amezzati alli quai luochi si montara per le dua picole limache, per salire disopra, che qua si dice galata le dua limache · E · F · seruirano è cosi come da basso sono dua anditi: sarano anchora da alto ma continuati fin alle dette limache, ma la parte di mezzo potra esser sala: o veramente continuare il partite: et il rimanente seruira per loggia: che qua si dice galeria, l'essempio di questo è qui sotto dimostrato in pianta: et in diritto

gui va la pianta: et il diritto

· L · II ·

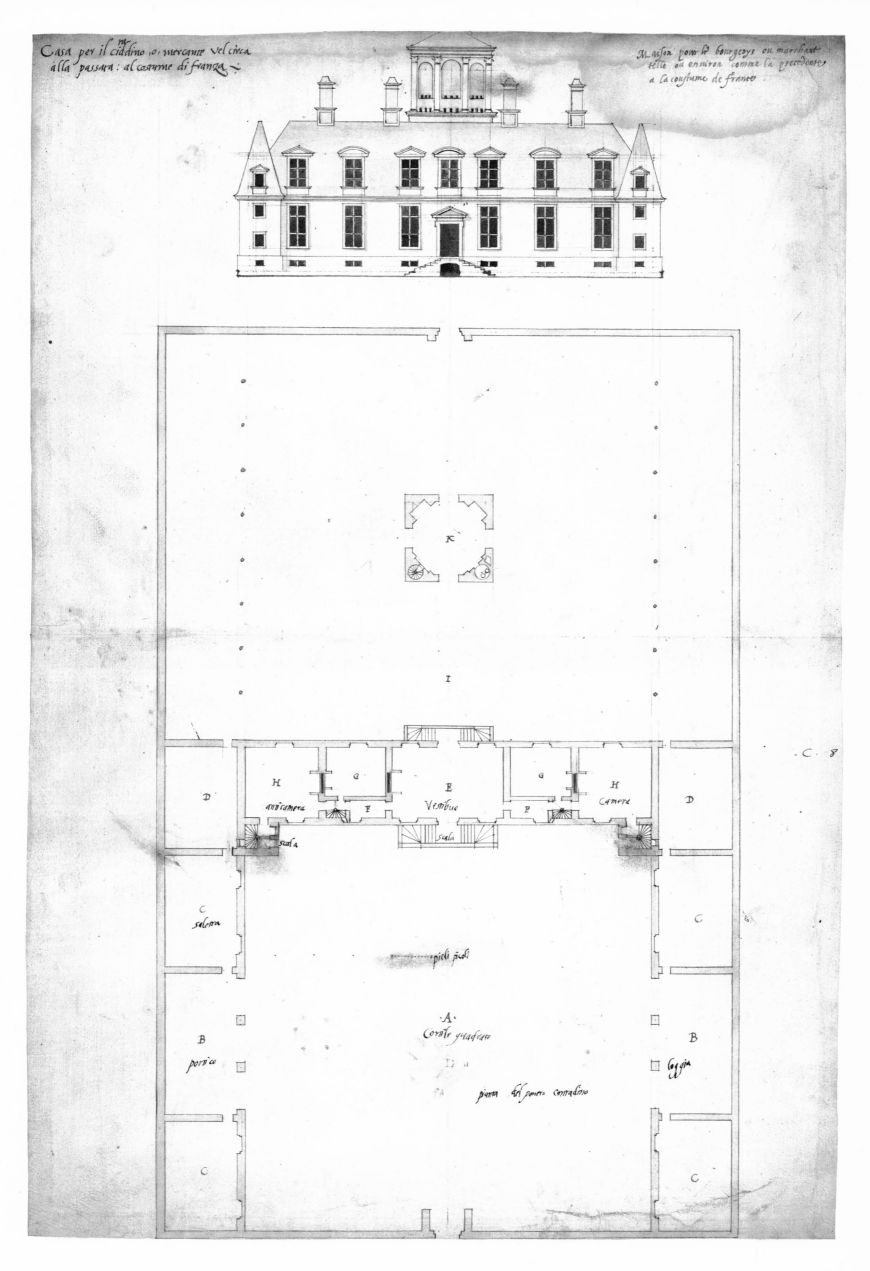

Casa per il ciddino o mercante vel circa
alla passara: al casume di franza

Maison pour le bourgeois ou marchant
telle ou enuiron comme la precedente
a la coustume de france

.C. 8

K

I

H   G   E   G   H
D   D
    antricamera   F Vestibue P Camera
    scala   scala

C   C
salotta

pieli picoli

.A.
B   Corale quadrato   B
portico   loggia

pianta del genere contadino

C   C

VI

Quanto alla Casa del gentil huomo per la uilla se ne trova molti hauere piu belle habitationi fuori delle
citta: che in esse citta: et per hauere il sito spacioso senza impedimento vicinale: se dilettano di fare le
lhor case di bella apparentia, e pero la presente pianta qui auanti dimostrata è molto differente dalle
case commune, questa primieramente hauera un cortile di quadrato perfetto con una porta di bona quan:
dezza la forma della quale si trouara nel quarto libro doue nhe di piu sorte, questa habitatione sara
leuata dal cortile piedi .V. doue si troua una loggia segnata .A. la sua larghezza e piedi .XV. et i lon:
ghezza piedi .LX. li suoi pilastri sarano piedi .III. per diametro al entrar di essa casa si troua un grande
vestibulo .B. la longhezza del quale sara piedi .LIIII. la sua larghezza piedi .XXVII. questo vestibulo saria vne:
broso prendendo solamente la luce dalle loggie: e pero vi è da ogni lato un cortiletto .C. la sua larghezza
sara piedi .XXX. et in longhezza piedi .XXXVI. e questi darau gran luce al vestibulo et anche alla sala che
sara sopra esso: di quella istessa misura, questa magione hauera quatro entrate chi vora, e pero li dua cortili
ciascun di esso hauera un picolo vestibulo segnato .D. la longhezza del quale sara piedi .XXIII. et la larghezza .XII.
et che si contentava di dua entrate la qual cosa io lodo: si potra di esso vestibulo et della camera .E.
fare una saletta: la quale sara in longhezza piedi .XXX. nel capo della quale sara una camera di piedi .XXIIII.
per ogni lato: dietro la quale sara una rietro camera segnata .G. la sua larghezza sara piedi .XX. et ha:
ueva la sua uscita nel capo della loggia e questa si potra amezzare et al mezzo della scala sara il suo mez:
zado, e cosi questo angolo hauera una saletta: e camerieui: et camerieue potrano aloggiarui commodamete:
e cosi vi sarano quatro habitationi seppavate luna dallaltra: et negli luochi sotterranei: che sarano parte
sotto terra sarano giustichi al seruitio di essi appartamenti: e quello che sara dabasso: sara di sopra,
alli quatro angoli del vestibulo .B. vi sarano quatro scale: dua che salgoono: et uitornano: et dua
alimaca: quelle da i uitorni sotto il riposo di mezzo: si guadagna un camerino segnato .X. la sua
latitudine sara piedi .X. ma la longhezza potra esser piedi .XV. andando sotto la scala: e prendera
la luce dal cortile: e seruira alla camera .G. e per la medesima scala discenderassi alle stanze sot:
terranee, dal canto delle limache, vi sarano dua camerini l'uni de quali seruira alla camera .G. et
l'altro alla camera .E. e questi prenderan la luce dal cortile: e per che questi sarano amezzadi quel:
lo congiunto alla limaca: essa seruira a salire a esso detto mezzado: ma nel altro camerino, sara necessario
faruii una scala per salire al suo mezzado: la larghezza di essa scala sara dua piedi ma entrando un pie:
nel muro il camerino vera a esse piedi .IX. per un lato: e .X. per l'altro. la grossezza di questi muri si
fava segondo la materia: come dispova lo experto muratore di quel paese: e tal grossezza vorano
se si hauera da uoltare: et altra grossezza se li suoli sarano di legname, si questo gentilhuomo si contentava
di questa habitatione facendola comsinare col semplice giardino lo potra fare: ma segli sara piu nobile
e di animo: et de ricchezza potra intorno questo giardino faruii loggie: et dalli lati ornare li parieti di
nichi e finestre morte per metterui statue: la latitudine di queste loggie sara piedi .X. et anchora chel giar:
dino segnato .I. sia di forma oblonga: sel sara di quadrato perfeto: sara meglio, et sel padrone
vora aumentare loggiamento potra dyieto la loggia .K. fare una tirata di loggiamenti che sarano piedi
.XVIII. e prima si trouera un vestibulo .L. di quadrato perfetto: il quale si potra fare senza le quatro
colonne chi vora: ma quantunque egli sia picolo le quatro colonne gli dariano e ricchezza: et forma, dal
destro: et sinistro lato: si troua una saletta .M. la sua longhezza sara piedi .XXIX. al seruitio della quale
vie una camera di quadrato perfeto: di dyieto essa sara un camerino. .O. la sua longhezza e pie:
di .XV. et in larghezza piedi .XI. e dietro questo sara uno studio la sua larghezza e piedi .VII. et la longhezza
.IX. congiunto col quale sara una limaca per salire: e alli mezzadi: et anche disopra: et in questi picoli lochi
si potra fare stua et bagno da un de lati .X.

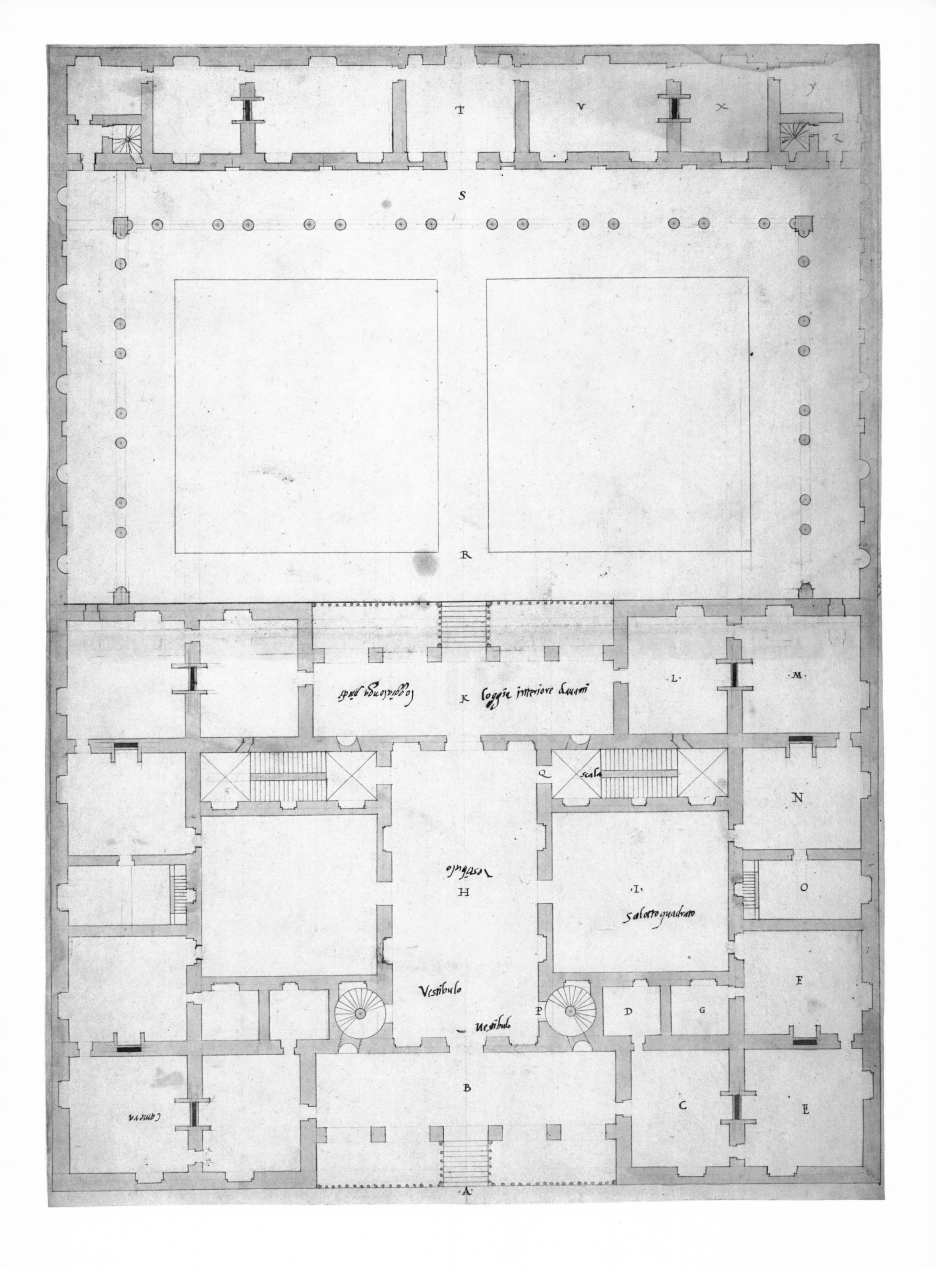

il disino qui auanti dimostrato nella parte di sopra rappresenta le loggie intorno del giardino della passata pianta
l'altezza di queste loggie sarà piedi xx. et sarano voltate per causa delli terrazzi che vi sarano sopra et
sarà necessario che pel trauerso delle loggie vi siano le chiaui di ferro sopra le colonne al nascimento della
forza degliarchi: che sarà sopra barchirraue almeno mezzo piede: e poste inopera queste chiaui nel modo
ch'io ho insegnato nel mio quarto libro a carte , ma per lo longo delle loggie non vi acadeua chiaui:
per cio che alli quattro angoli li archi trouerano buone spalle per contraforti: l'altezza delle colonne sarà
piedi xiiii. la sua grossezza piedi dua: il parapetto sarà di altezza piedi tre: et il terrazzo hauerà dipen-
dentia: et fatto di lastre ben congiunte accio non penetri le acque: l'altezza delle stanze superiori: sarà
piedi xviii: ornate poi nel modo che si uede:
La parte qui di mezzo dinota la faccia dauanti: et anchora quella di drieto, il piano delle prime stanze sarà
leuato dalla corte piedi v. l'altezza: si delle loggie: come dellaltre stanze sarà piedi xx. e sopra le loggie
sarà terrazzo: ma che sia pendente: et ben commesse le lastre con bonissimo cimento la larghezza delle
finestre sarà piedi v. l'altezza delle prime: sarà piedi ix. hauendo sopra esse le finestre bastarde per causa
de imezzadi; e doue non sarani mezzadi: sarano finite: l'altezza delle finestre disopra sarà piedi xii e
mezzo per causa della altezza e doue sarano mezzadi si prendeua la luce necessaria: et il rimanente
sarà chiuso nelle parti di dentro: ma di fuori sarà tutta apparente la finestra; l'altezza delle stanze di
sopra sarà piedi xx. perciò che li x. piedi del sopra terra dabasso leuati dal cortile fano ch'auere la parte
da basso di maggiore altezza: che quella da alto: l'altezza del granaro sarà almeno piedi vi. ma affin che la
sala habbia maggiore altezza: si potrà alciarla quei v. piedi che sarano xxv. e sopra essa il granaro
sia morto: e che prenda la luce sopra lo tetto. e per che la maggior parte di queste case in italia se di
pinggono di belle pitture: e di fabule: et de istorie in queste faccie vi sarano belli campi: et ben compartiti per ornarle di diuerse pitture:
la parte piu sotto rappresenta la muraglia del cortile, et la porta sarà piu magnifica se sarà leuata dalla strada tre gradi: o almeno uno: la latitudine di essa porta sarà piedi ix. et in altezza piedi xiiii. et sarà
rustica: seruando il decoro del loco: et se altre misure nella scrittura mancheuano li piedi che sono
li sotto suppliranno al rimanente

il diritto della loggia sopra il giardino della pianta passata.

Le droict de la galerie dessus le Jardin de la precedente Plate forme

il diritto della faccia della pianta passatax

Le droict de la face de la Plate forme precedente.

muraglia del cortile dauanti la casa della pianta passata ↘

No 12   Muraille de la court qui est deuant la maison de la precedente Plate forme.

VIII

La casa di un gentilhuomo: o di altro ricco personaggio si potra fare nel modo che si vede la pianta qui dauanti la entrata della quale
sara. A. hauendo da un lato una saletta. B. la sua larghezza è piedi ~~xxini~~ xxiiii: et in longhezza xxiiii. dipoi questa vie una camera. C.
di quadratura perfetta et il suo diametro è pie xxiiii. hauendo al suo seruitio dua camerini. D. E. ma il camerino .E. potra esser seppauato
et hauer la sua entrata per la lumaca passando lentrata: si troua una loggia ~~F~~. F. la longhezza della quale è piedi. Cini. questa circonda
un cortile. G. di quadrato perfetto: la prima loggia ha da un capo una lumaca, spaciosa per montare ad alto: nel altro capo al deuim
petto vi e una scala da dua vitorni, laltra loggia compagna a questa ha dalli capi dua logiette. H. sopra un cortiletto o giardino
Segnato I. è questi dua giardinetti con le sue loggie sono per fare la casa più aereata. et anche pernon ~~fare tanta spesa~~ in casamenti
dalle bande del cortile, passando più oltra si troua un vestibulo K. hauendo di un lato una camera L di piedi xxiiii per quadro
et ha alsuo seruitio la camera ~~M~~ dirieto a questa si troua una camera ~N. hauendo al suo seruitio un camerino. ,O,
et nivo delqual vie la porta di ulto: et questi dua membri potra esser seppauati: et hauer lentrata nel capo della loggia. passando il vestibulo
.K. se smonta al giardino per una scala .P. sotto la quale è la porta della cantina: et il giardino e segnato .Q. dal altro lato
della casa vi sono altra tanti loggiamenti: ne vi è altra defferentia che la sala a man sinistra: et la scala piana che ritorna
et questa casa essendo leuata da terra piedi V. sara tutta uuota sotto terra. doue io intendo non solamente la cantime: ma et tutte le
offfcine che accadeno al bisogno della casa: come saria cucine: saluarobe stanze per legne: Tinelli: et molte altre commoditta: eccetto
che per dormire, per che nel Vero anchora che dette habitationi siano la metta sopra terra: non dimeno io non le aprobo sane pel dor:
mire è certo se lle fussevo fodrate di legno intorno: et salegate di legno con carbone sotto: et in loco sciutto: per che di tale ne ho
fatto che sono sanissime: et habitabili ——— io non ci ho posto tutte le misure particulari per breuita ma li piedi sono qui sotto la
pianta dalli quali si prouera tutte le particulari misure

benigno et pio lettore io sono stato sempre di animo
di giouari alhuomo poi che iddio per sua benignita miha conceduto la
gratia chio possi giouari adlhuomini massime a quelli
che se dilettano di questa nobile arte per la qual cosa
io non voglio prezzar fatica nessuna chio non manifesti quello
che la benignita di Dio mi dono ne primi anni miei per laqual
cosa ho io voluto esser con se a tutti voi che delle mie
fatiche vi seruiter mettendoci li piedi poi disegni Valetini addonca
estati sani con animo lieto di questi mie fatiche

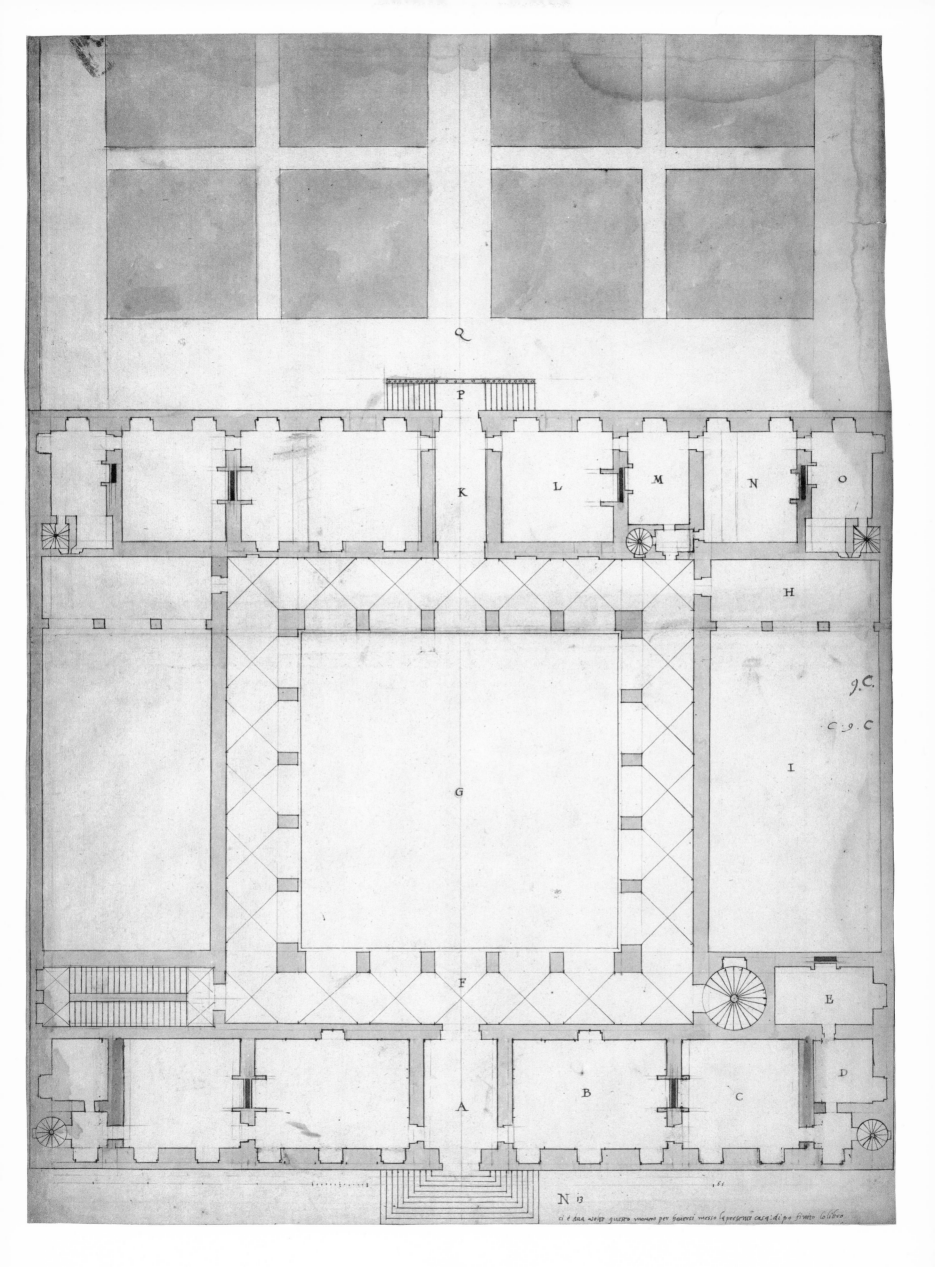

Q

P

K L M N O

H

ɡ.C.

C·ɡ·C

I

G

F

E

A B C D

N 13

ci è stra volta questo numero per haversi messo la presenti casa di p.o finito [libro]

IX

Della pianta qui adietro questi qui auanti sono li diritti: et primieramente questo di sotto rappresenta la faccia dauanti: et questa
habitatione per piu sanitta: et anche magnificenza sara leuata dal terreno piedi.v. le altezze delle prime habitationi sarano piedi
.xx. cioe dal pauimento fin sotto l'architraue: et per che visauano de luochi picoli che atale altezze parebbon torri sara bene
ad amezzarli et per questo ho fatto quelle fenestre sopra fenestre: per che alle stanze alte.piedi.xx. vna di queste fenestre
nella parte di drento se vidura in vna in apparenza aiutandosi con le spaladure: et cosi e di fuori: et di dentro risponderano
et seruirano al vna: et al altra parte — l'altezza del segondo ordine sara medesimamente.xx.piedi: ma quella da basso
rappresentaua la quarta parte piu alta per la leuatione sopra terra: et cosi medesimamente quelle forme ouali potrano
seruire alli mezzadi di sopra: et doue sauano le stanze grande: e camere: et sale le forme ouali dal canto di dentro sauano
quadre riducendosi in vna fenestra sola: li granari sauano nel mezzo di bona altezza ma nelle faccie non sauano piu
alti che il fregio: et la cornice: nel qual fregio si dauano le luce alli granari: l'architraue: fregio: et cornice del primo ordine sara
bassa.altezza.piedi.v. il supperiore ordine sara piedi quatro in altezza: et sara tutto ordine Thoscano: lesue proportional misure si
trouarano nel quarto libro al detto ordine

La parte di mezzo dinota il cortile di dentro: et cosi le dua loggiette dalli lati.H. significano le dua loggiette sopra li dua cortiletti
(o vero giardini: o giuochi di palla) sopra la loggia sara terrazzo: et della loggia si passaua sopra le loggette che sauano
pur terrazzi li muri dalli lati del cortile segnati.I. sauano al altezza degli altri muri del cortile per causa de venti: del sole
et delle pioggie: ma li muri dalli lati sauari fenestrati accio che dalli terrazzi si possi scoprire la campagna: per cio
che li muri segnati.O. che cingeno la casa non sauano piu alti che li parapetti delli terrazzi: et l'ordine del cortile sara
Dorico da basso ad alto: et le medesime altezze che son di fuori: sono di drento :.

La figura qua disopra rappresenta la parte interiore: come la detta casa fusse aperta: et primieramente la parte piu bassa
segnata.C. sono le stanze sotterranee per seruire a diuersi oficij et sauano la meta sopra terra: et la meta sotto terra la parte
habitabile sopra terra si potra voltare: et fare le muraglie e piu grosse: et piu sottile segondo la materia di che s'hauera a uoltare
ma sempre le mura grosse: et li buoni fondamenti sono da fare per piu sicurezza ma l'ordine segondo non si voltara
ma di buoni legnami si dauano li suoli: et la copertura, ma il vestibulo supperiore si potra per piu bellezza voltare di ma:
teria legiera hauendo per dottezza lo suolo sopra esso. quanto alle altezze si e detto quadisopra, del rimanente sempre se
rimette al buon giudicio del prudente architetto

Trattando delle case de gentilhuomini per fare alla villa, non par ame fuori di proposito di trattar di questa qua presente, la quale questi
anni passati mi ordinò chio facesse fare il Cardinal di ferrara qui a fontanableo la quale generalmente piace a tutte le sorte di persone
Questa magione nel vero e situata nel piu elevato luoco di fontanableo allentrata della quale si trova un cortile A di perfetta qua=
dratura, lo diametro del quale è piedi CXV vel circa, il corpo principal della casa è levato dal cortile piedi V dove si monta al
vestibulo B la longhezza del quale è piedi XXIIII et è largo piedi XV dal destro lato vi è una anticamera C di piedi XXIIII per ogni
lato, apresso vi è la camera D di piedi XXIIII per un lato, et di XXII per laltro dietro la quale passando per landito E si entra
nella rietro camera F per la quale si va segretamente nel giardino, et per landito E dalla limaca G si descende al giuco di
palla H dal altro lato si va al cortiletto segnato + lo qual sara coperto di una rete di fil di ferro dove saranno diversi augelli dalla
medesima limaca si va al bagno: et alle stuffe che sono sotto la rietro camera F ritornando dissopra dal a sinistro lato del vestibulo
vi è una sala I la sua longhezza è piedi XLVIII et larga XXIIII nel capo della quale ci è una camera M la sua longhe=
zza è piedi XX et è larga piedi XIX Dal andito E si va alla galeria, la sua larghezza è piedi XX et è longa piedi LXXV nel capo
della quale vi è una capella K per la qual si descende nel cortile: et altro la quale vi è una limaca che monta sopra la galeria, dove che
sopra la capella vi è una salva roba da mobili: et sotto la galeria vi è un rinello et altri officij et sotto li quali vi è una cantina
freschissima, dal sinistro lato del vestibulo B vi è una sala I la sua longhezza è piedi XLVIII et è larga piedi XXIIII nel capo
di essa ci è una camera M di piedi XX per quadro al servitio della quale vi è un camerino, ritornando nel cortile dal sinistro
lato nel mezzo vi è uno andito N dal qual si passa alla corte O altro della quale vi è la stalla, la sua porta è segnata
P et apresso la porta vi è la stanza del giardiniero, dal altro capo vi è un cortiletto segnato X per riporre le legna
da un lato del quale vi è uno andito per gire al giardino. dal altro lato vi è un medesimo andito per gire alle
camine, ritornando nel cortile dal lato sinistro vi è una limaca nel angolo segnata O la qual monta dissopra: et anchr
alla sala: et camera: et per la quale si va anchora alla camera R la qual serve per credenza, vedo piu qua si trova
una camera S questa serve per despensa piu qua si trova la camera T per despensare il vino, et anchr piu qua nel angolo
vi è la cucina V altro la quale vi è il salva vivande, et è congiunto con essa una cortcella col pozzo et il forno per la panizzaria
et per che li sopra detti officij sono al piano della corte: dal qual piano fin sotto il suolo della sala: et camere viene a essere XXII
piedi queste tal stanze sono amezzate sopra le quali sono di molte camere: et sopra la cucina vi è il rinello pei gentilhuomini
La pare qui sotto la pianta dimora la muraglia davanti lo cortile, ma è fatta con una misura maggiore come si vede
per li piedi li sotto, la larghezza della porta è piedi VIII et la sua altezza è piedi XIII et un terzo, la grossezza delle colonne
è un piede et mezzo, et la sua altezza è piedi XI et mezzo et sono di opera thoscana, del rimanente il tutto si trovera col compasso
in mano sopra li piedi che sono li sotto.

La figura sopra la pianta dimora la faccia davanti della sala: et camere la quale è fatta con la medesima misura che la
muraglia del cortile. il piano di essa casa è levato dal cortile piedi V il parapetto delle fenestre è piedi III in altezza: le fenestre
sono alte piedi XIII et larghe piedi V dal pavimento fin sotto lo suolo è piedi XVIII che viene a essere alla summità
della cornice sopra le fenestre da quella alla summità della cornice dissopra vi è piedi V del altre particolari misure
elle si trovarano col compasso

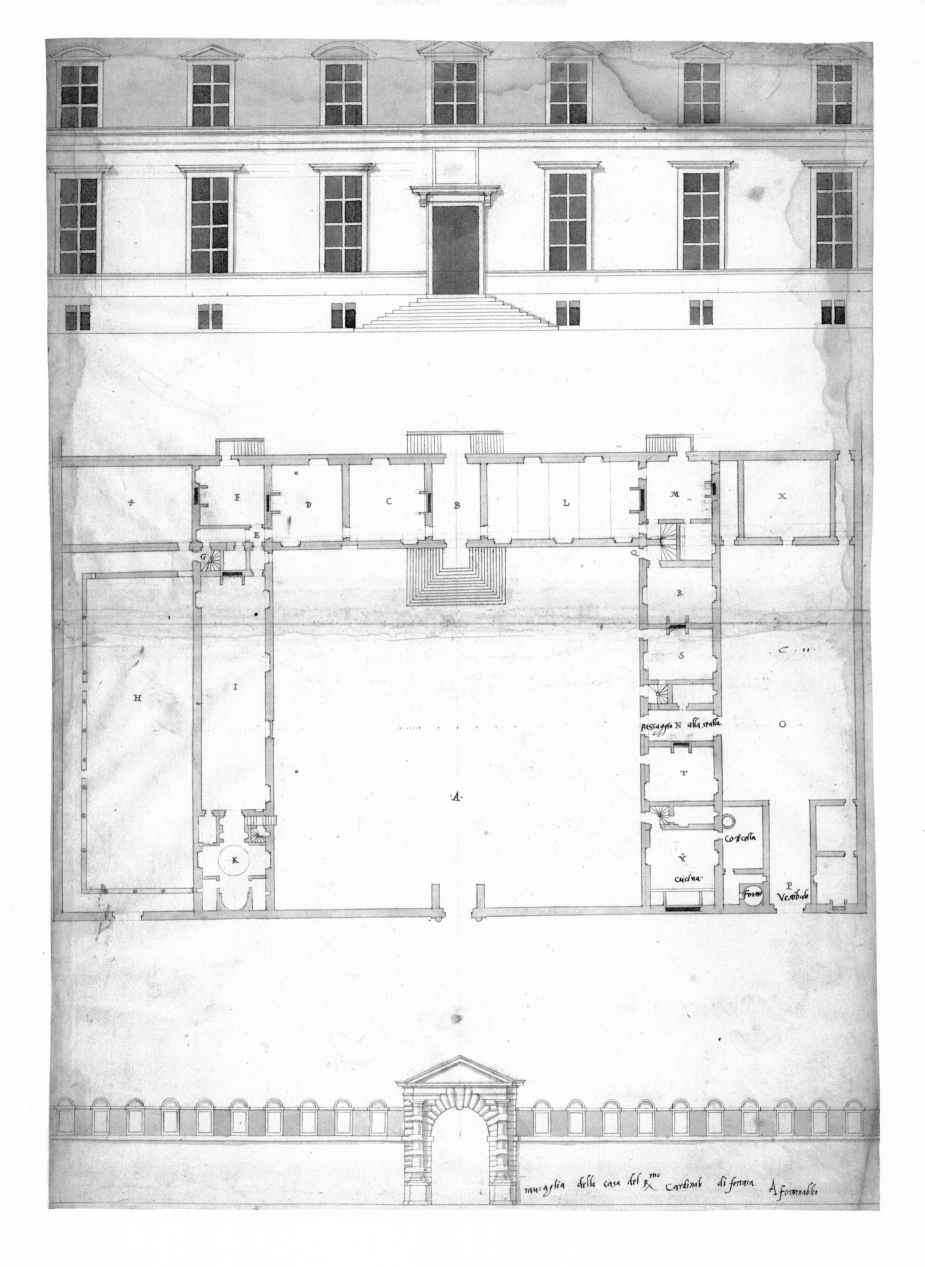

XI

il variare delle cose piace alla maggior parte delle persone et perciò io disporò una casa di un gentilhuomo nobile: la quale ad alcuno parerà forsi simile alla passata qui più adietro non dimeno ella è tutta diversa dall'altra: come si vede nella pianta à lato la prima entrata di questa sarà .A. et prima si trova un cortile .B. il diametro del quale è .c.III. piedi et è di quadrato perfeto, dal destro lato nel mezzo si trova un vestibulo segnato .C. dalli lati di esso sono diversi oficij pur segnati .C. ma dove è la cuoce: quella è la cucina: con la quale son congiunti il forno: et il guardamangiare et fra questi dua lochi si va alla corticella per servitio della cucina: et questi dua oficij sarano così bassi di copertura che non impedivano le fenestre della cucina sopra la bassacorte, sopra li oficij sarano camere à mezzate per esser quegli al pian di terra: et le altre habitationi levate da terra piedi .V. passando oltra il vestibulo si trova una corte .D. per la quale si entra anchora di fuori di un'altra porta: à lato della quale è la stanza del portinaio: che sarà anchor giardiniero et è segnata .E. la parte dentro la porta segnata .F. sarà coperta: ma bassa di tetto: sotto la qual copertura strano le carrette et questa parte si dice bassacorte in queste bande et con questa è congiunto la stalla .G. torniamo nel gran cortile in faccia del quale si trova una planicie levata da esso piedi .V. et è segnata .H. in favore à essa vi è una loggia .I. nel capo di essa si trova una scala .K. per la quale si monta ad alto: ma prima à basso si entra alla camera .L. et da questa: per uno andito si va al camerino .M. il qual sarà amezzato et si montarà per la limaca li acanto: et per essa si passa à una loggietta .N. della quale se smonta al cortile .O. et questo sarà un giardin segreto: chi vorà per il quale si va al gran giardino passando la loggia .I. S'entra alla sala .P. dal destro suo lato si trova una camera .Q. havendo al suo servitio un'altra camera .R. la quale accio sia di perfeta quadratura vi è una scala: un picol camerino: et un loco per il letto segnato .S. quel loco .T. sarà corticella per dar luce alle tre fenestre intorno à esso il muro verso la corte .O. sarà solamente alto piedi .VIII. sopra del quale sarà una rete di fil di ferro per tenervi diversi ucelli, et quel che è da questo lato se intende esser l'altro: eccetto la galeria segnata .V. et così la capella .X. li quai lochi sarà levati dal cortile .V. piedi come il rimanente della casa: et la capella haveva da un lato uno oratorio picolo: et dal altro una limaca per montare: et scendere: la qual limaca montarà fin sopra la galeria: et per che tutta la casa sarà cavata tanto sotto terra: quanto è sopra terra: sotto essa galeria sarà una sala per mangiare è la state et il verno à lato della quale sarano altri oficij al centro di questa galeria sarà un giuoco da palla che haveva una entrata dal corritoro .∂. che sarà segreta pel padrone: l'altra davanti per la porta di fuori pel commune questo sarà segnato .Y. et così tornando di sopra alla sala .P. per essa si descende nel giardino .Z. et per che come ho detto tutto questo corpo sarà voltato sotto terra: sotto il riposo di questa scala sarà la porta delle cantine per riporre il vino: ben che per tutte le altre scale si potrà scendere à dette cantine: et anche per altri lati si potrà fare la porta principale di esse cantine; in questa casa io non ho fatto mentione de bagni: et stue presuponendo che'l prudente Architetto si accommodava al sito et alle acque secondo il sito ma dove sono fontane vive et massimamente à tolle amorte quelle prestano gran commodità à tutta la casa, quanto al giardino esso sarà di quella grandezza che'l sito lo comportava: quanto alle particular misure li piedi picoli sono nel mezzo del cortile con li quali si trovaran tutte le misure: ma pel generale: la sala è larga XXIIII piedi et longa XXXXVIII: et le maggior camere son piedi .XXIIII.

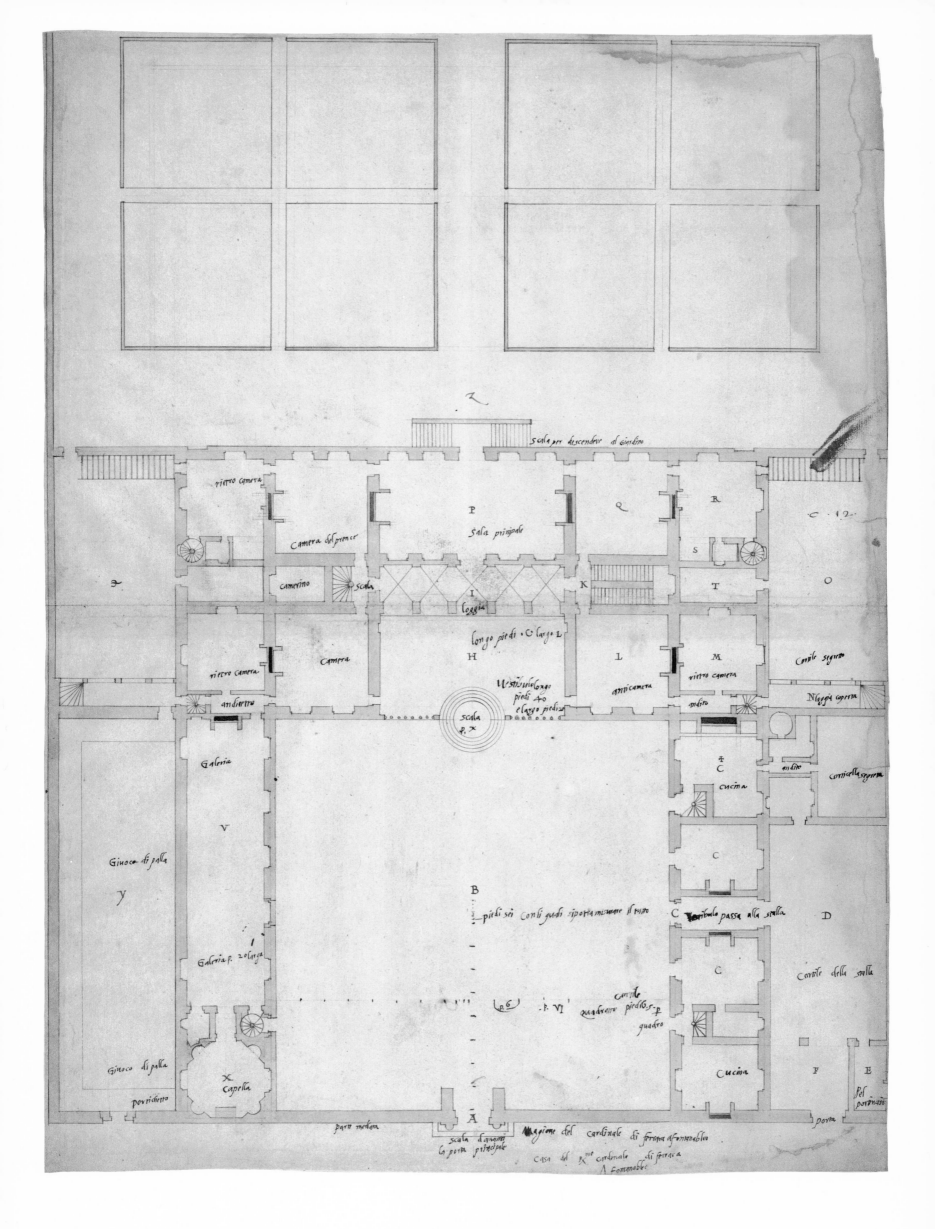

scala per descendere al giardino

rietro Camera

P

Sala prinipale

Camera del princr

Q

R

C 12

camerino

scala

S

T

O

I

K

leggia

longo piedi . C largo L

rietro Camera

Camera

H

L

M

Cortile segreto

andiretto

anticamera

rietro camera

Nleggia coperta

Galeria

Uestibulo longo
piedi 40
e largo piedi 20

scala
P. X

andito

Corticella segreta

cucina

V

C

Ginoco di palla

Y

B

piedi sei con li quali si porta a misurare il resto

Tribulo passa alla scala

D

Galeria p. 20 larga

VI

cortile
quadrino piedi 0.5.
quadro

C

Cortile della scala

cucina

Ginoco di palla

Capella

Cucina

F

E

del portinaio

portichetto

parte mediana

A

scala d'argenti
la porta principale

Magione del cardinale di ferrara a Fontanableo

porta

Casa del R.mo cardinale di ferrara
A Fontanableo

XII

il diritto della passata pianta si vedi qui auanti dimostrato: lo quale accio sia meglio inteso per
esser molto defferente daglialtri vsitati jo lho voluto dare alquanto in prospettiua: e massimamente
che pochi intendevebbon quella scala votonda chi non lhauesse reduta in fatti: la lettera A denota
la planicia del gran cortile: et il B rappresenta il pigno del picolo cortile: e cosi il C lo piano della
loggia laquale anchora sava leuata vn grado, laltezza di questa loggia: et cosi della sala: et camere sava
piedi XVIII sopra la quale sava vno terrazzo: per dare commoditta di andare alle camere et alle scale
senza entrare nella sala, si questa loggia sava voltata: quantumque ella sia stretta per piu sicurita sava
bene al nascer delle volte menerci le chiaui di ferro per trauerso della loggia: ma se in quel paese si trouauano
pietre di tal longhezza: la cosa sava piu sicura: et piu breue mettendo esse pietre sopra li archi et ben commesse
senza voltare altrimenti: facendo pendere il detto terrazzo accio le acque facilmente si scolino, laltezza
delle stanze seconde sava medesimamente piedi XVIII ma se le camere menori si vorano amezzare si
quelle da basso: come quelle da alto: sava necessario procacciare messe camere una picola scala: nel modo che in una di
esse ho dimostrato nella pianta, le tere habitationi che venggono ad essere al nascimento del coperto: doue son le finestre
sopra la cornice: che qui si dicono lucarne: queste si farano di quella altezza che comportava larmamenti de i legnami del
detto coperto, per cio che jo intendo questo coperto alla francese: et chi non haueva commoditta di hauere di
quelle scaglie di pietra sottile che di qua si costuma per li coperti nobili la quale se dice ardiosa et ha colore d'az:
zurro oscuro potra coprirli di pietra cotta sottile: et per piu nobilita potra vitriarla di varii colori: che sava
cosa bellissima. e durabile.

La figura li di sotto dimostra la faccia del cortile verso la strada. la latitudine del apertura de la
porta sava piedi VIII et in altezza piedi XVI ma bastava bene di aprire la porta di legno dalla fascia
in gin: che sava alta piedi XV e vn quarto: et il mezzo rondo stia sempre serrato, la grossezza de le colonne
sava piedi II le pilastrate dalli lati di I piede e cosi tutte, queste colonne pasarono sopra vn dado che seruiua
per sedile, laltezza delle colonne sava piedi XV e mezzo: che per esser legate nel muro et hauere le sue pilastrate
dalli lati posson essere alquanto piu gracili che le misure terminate, laltezza del architraue piede I il
fregio piede I la cornice piede I la summita del fruontispiecio sava piedi III e vn terzo: le tre acroterie
le quali sarano per metterui statue o vasi d'balle o altra cosa sarano infronte quanto e grossa la colonna
nella summa parte, li merli si vede laltezza sua come accompagna laltra opera

Parte dauanti della pianta passata

La faic de denant dela piare formt precedente.

C. 13.

Muvaglia del cortile dauanti della pianta passata

Muraille de la court deuant la Plateformr precedente. C.

XIII

il gentil huomo nobile: e pacefico: et amatore della giusticia facendo sempre il suo douero a cui deue la sua casa

potrebbe esser: quanto alla fortezza: di legno: di terra: di paglia: et di ogn'altra cosa debile et fragile: perciò

che tali huomini possono sempre dormir sicuri non essendo odiati da persona giustamente: anci la giusticia

di la su gli tiene il potentissimo suo scudo sopra il capo loro, MA il parciale che partecipa di tiranno hauendo

de molti inimici et odiando molti et sempre desideroso di vendetta: et sospettoso di esser offeso da tutto

l'hore: sara ben necessario che la sua casa sia forte per diffensarsi dalle insidie. e forze de suoi nemici,

la casa adonca del capo di parte fuori della città conueria esser forte si: ma di fianchi: torroni e larghi fossi

e ponti leuatori: li superiori suoi nonglel comportarebbono, ma potra bene sopra un suo terreno edificare

una casa con le mura grosse et bene asicurata per una battaglia da mano per difensarsi da suoi nemici

come è la pianta qui auanti dimestrata: la quale primieramente ha le mura che la circondano grosse

piedi N. e più se vora: et li muri di mezzo piedi III. et afargli più grossi sara sempre ben fatto accio pos-

sino meglio sostenere le volte, l'entrata sua A. sara stretta: accio che se per mala sorte la porta fusse. o

con foco, o con machine da guerra espugnata che gl'inimici impetuosamente nongli sia facile l'entrata, la

sua larghezza adonque sara piedi noui) e questa entrata hauera dalli lati dua camere segnate B. larghe

piedi XXII e longhe XXIIII. queste sarano al piano del cortile: perciò chio voglio sempre che la casa de villa

habbia il cortile dauanti: in queste dua camere B. dimorara sempre la guardia la quale se per mala sorte

fusse presa la porta da nemici: questi per fianco: e con armi e con moschetti et archibusi non lassarebbon

passar più oltra gl'inimici: li quali anchora trouarebbono un altro ostaculo perciò chio voglio chel rimanente

della casa sia leuato piedi VI e pero essendoui la scala da salire et hauendo contrasto per fianco e per

faccia: il padron di essa casa porria star sicuro: et si pure la scala et il cortile fusse preso dagl'inemeti: anchora

si troua loco da saluarsi come al suo loco ne diro, salito la scala di questa entrata si troua una loggia C.

la quale circonda un cortile il netto di questa e piedi X. li pilastri sono in fronte piedi III. per l'altro lato

piedi IIII. che così le volte sarai sicure senza le chiaui di ferro, alli capi di questa loggia sono dua scale: una

a lumaca: l'altra a ritorno: a canto le quali nei capi della loggia si troua inuna anticamera D. la qual sara amezzada,

e questa si troua una camera. E. di piedi XXIIII per ognilato o questa ha un camerino F. che sara mezzado

il mezzado se andara per la gran lumaca: o per la scala a ritorno, il cortile G. sara di quadrato perfetto et è

piedi LX. dalli lati di questo si troua una saletta. H. di piedi XXIIII in larghezza: e XXXIII in

longhezza: questa tiene al suo seruitio una camera. I. longa piedi XXIIII e larga XX. ma vie di più la posta

del letto: per cagione di una limaca priuata: che io intendo questa camera amezzada. drieto aguesta si troua

una camera K. di piedi XXIIII per quadro da l'altro capo della saletta vie un camerino. L. et quello che è da

uno lato se intende da l'altro. ma doue la H. sara circondata da quattro piani questa sara pel padron della casa: il quale

si saluara nel estremo: sentro la camera K la quale sara più forte dell'altre: per la grossezza de i muri: passando il cortile

si troua il vestibulo. M. della medesima grandezza del primo: et ha la medesima scala che dissende nel giardino circondato

di che e grosse mura: dal destro: et sinistro lato vie una camera. N. di piedi XXIIII per quadro hauendo un camerino. O. di

... di ... una loggia ... o questa sara amezzado: è questo basti quanto alle vicende

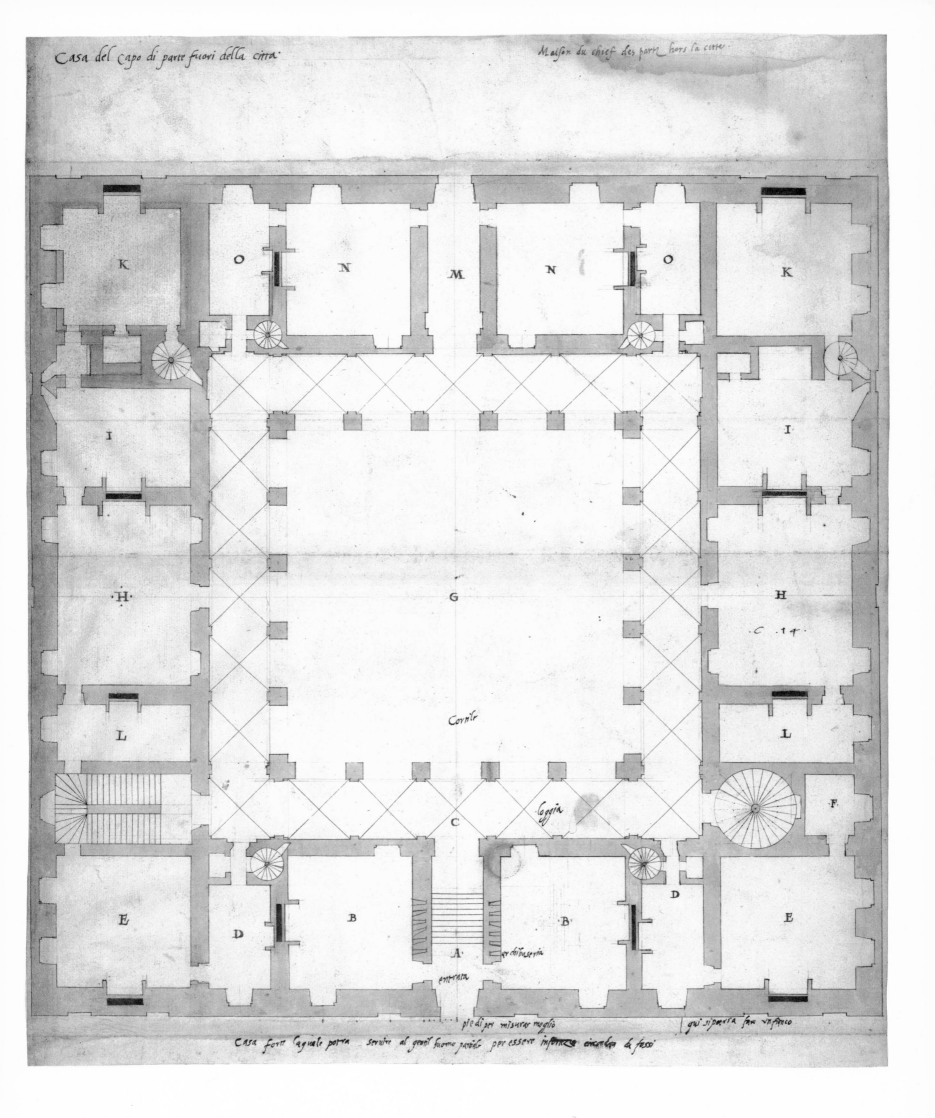

K   O   N   M   N   O   K

I   I

H   G   H

                                              C · 14

                    Cornir

L   L

                    Loggia   F

E   D   B   B   D   E

                    A   er chibuseria

                    entrata

la casa del partiale come ho detto deue esser forte di mura et che le finestre siano talmente
alte da terra che gli inimici non vi possino facilmente agiungere: et che siano ferrate: ma non a
gabiate per che la finestra agabiata serue per scala agli nemici. la parte di fuori de la passara
pianta: sara questa qua di sopra. la larintudine della porta sara piedi. VI. et. X. in altitudine;
la finestra di sopra essa è per aluminare il vestibulo: essendo serrato la porta. le prime finestre
sarano alte da terra piedi. XI. per la ragion sopra detta. la sua ~~alta~~ larghezza sara piedi. V. et
in altezza piedi. IX. l'altezza del primo suolo sara piedi. XXV. che viene à essere. la prima fascia, ma
questa altezza tale sara solamente dalla parte dauanti: e tutte le altre habitationi sarano piedi. XX.
in altezza: per causa della leuatione de i piedi. V. montando al cortile; l'altezza delle seconde habitationi
sara piedi. XVIII. et le finestre sarano alte piedi. XI. per dare maggior luce alle stanze. l'archittra:
ue fregio e cornice sara in altezza piedi. V. di tutta questa faccia sarano li suoi ornamenti di
basso rilieuo eccetto la cornice di sopra, & questo sara, che essendo gettaro à basso dalle finestre cosa
alcuna per offendere gli nemici che le proietture delle cornice: d'altri sporti: non diano impedimento,
quelli picoli fenestrini da basso voglio che siano oculi: ma a tempo di necessita si rompino et iui
sarano artelarie minute: per molestare li nemici)

la parte interiore di questa casa e' li piu abasso: questa sara piu ornata di quella di fuori per esser
piu sicura da nemici. la quale come ho detto è leuata dalla parte dauanti piedi. V. ma sara cauata
sotto per la commodita delle cantine et altre stanze pel bisogno della casa, e queste sarano sane
per esser parte di esse sopra terra: come si vede nel dissegno. la parte segnata K. dinota
l'habitationi del padrone: è cosi da alto anchora; & questa ha le mura piu grosse dell'altre. l'altezza
della prima è piedi. XX. et la seconda è altri piedi. XVIII. li granari poi nel mezzo si vano
alzando, et anche alle finestre del granaro si puote affacciare per essendi III piedi di altezza,
quanto alle loggie: et altri ornamenti si vede nel dissegno molto chiaro: et anchora vi e le sue
misure, sopra le loggie sara un terrazzo assai pendente: accio le acque facilmente si
scolino per le bocche di quelle teste di leoni)

Diritto della pianta passata: ciò è la faccia della casa

c·15·

Parte interiore della pianta passata

P. 15

XV

Qua nella Franza li gentil'huomini è massimamente i più nobili habitano fuori delle città: et quantunque
non sia in questo Regno partialità: ma tutti ubidientissimi al suo Re: Non dimeno egli se dilettano
che le lhoro habitationi siano in fortezza è circondate dalle aque sel loco lo comporta: et che al meno
possino resistere a battaglia da mano. E per ciò la presente pianta sarà di un palazzo accommodato alli
costumi di qua, quanto al abitare: ma osservato li accompagnamenti et il Decoro: quanto ho potuto X
questo edificio sarà circondato dal acque havendo li fossi di bona larghezza col suo ponto levatoro
allentrare della porta si trova lo suo vestibulo. A. et ha dal destro et sinistro lato duo lochi per le guardie
li quali con arvili da camera: et archibusaria molestarano per fianco glinemici se pure entravano drento la porta
oltra che haveran contrasto per faccia nel volere salir la scala: la quale monta piedi IIII e mezzo: et quivi sarà
la planitia di tutto l'edificio: e certo li dua primi lochi per le guardie, salito la scala si trova una loggia. B. la
sua larghezza è piedi XII. et in longhezza piedi LII, la fronte de i pilastri è piedi III. per l'altro lato è
piedi IIII e mezzo: onde saranno fovvi una camera. C. la sua longhezza è piedi XXVIII. et in larghezza XX.
si passa per una limaca e trovasi una camera. C. la sua longhezza è piedi XXVIII. et in larghezza XX.
di questa s'entra nella camera. D. la sua grandezza per ogni lato è piedi XXVI. è questa ha li suoi fianchi da andarla
minuta: drieto da essa si trova la vietro camera. E. la quale è piedi XX. per ogni lato: è questa: è l'altra camera K.
si porano amezzare. servendosi della limaca a montare alli mezzadi et anco salir piu su con essa limaca
passando avanti si trova un cortile di quadrato perfeto: il suo diametro è piedi LXXX. da un lato di questo
cortile: nel mezzo vi è una sala. F. la sua latitudine è piedi XXVIII. et in longhezza piedi LII. nel capo di
questa vi è un camerino in uno angolo: e dal altro angolo si entra in uno andito che va alla cucina. G. questa
ha dua picoli camerini pel suo servitio da uno angolo d'essa cucina vi è un andito lo quale va al vestibulo X per descendere nel fosso a suoi bisogni lassandosi da un lato dua lochi uno de iquali ha un pozzo è questi sono al servitio de
la cucina, de qual pozzo per un condotto nel muro si mette l'agua nella cucina: dal altro lato del vestibulo vi è un
loco V. questo sarà una camera per spogliarsi il loco. Y. sarà la stua: et lo X. sarà il bagno: se così piacerà al padrone
Allincontro della sala vi è una loggetta. M. della larghezza de l'altra: et in longhezza piedi LII. della qual si entra
al vestibulo N. et di quello alla camera O. della istessa grandezza de l'altra, al servitio della quale è la camera
P. e drieto a essa un camerino. Q. da questo lato anchora vi è una camera R. ma sarà apartata, da l'altre e tutti questi
lochi saranno amezzadi: et la limaca servirà a tutti: et anco per salire disopra, allincontro della porta sarà una altra
loggia S. della medema grandezza della prima. Da un capo di essa vi è la scala publica: da l'altro capo ve n'he
una privata nel altro capo della prima loggia B. si trova una camera I. della qual si va alla camera K. et driero a essa vi è la vietro camera L. questa è la camera I. si amezzarano: servendosi della limaca a esse congiunta. e questo basti quanto alla pianta terrena

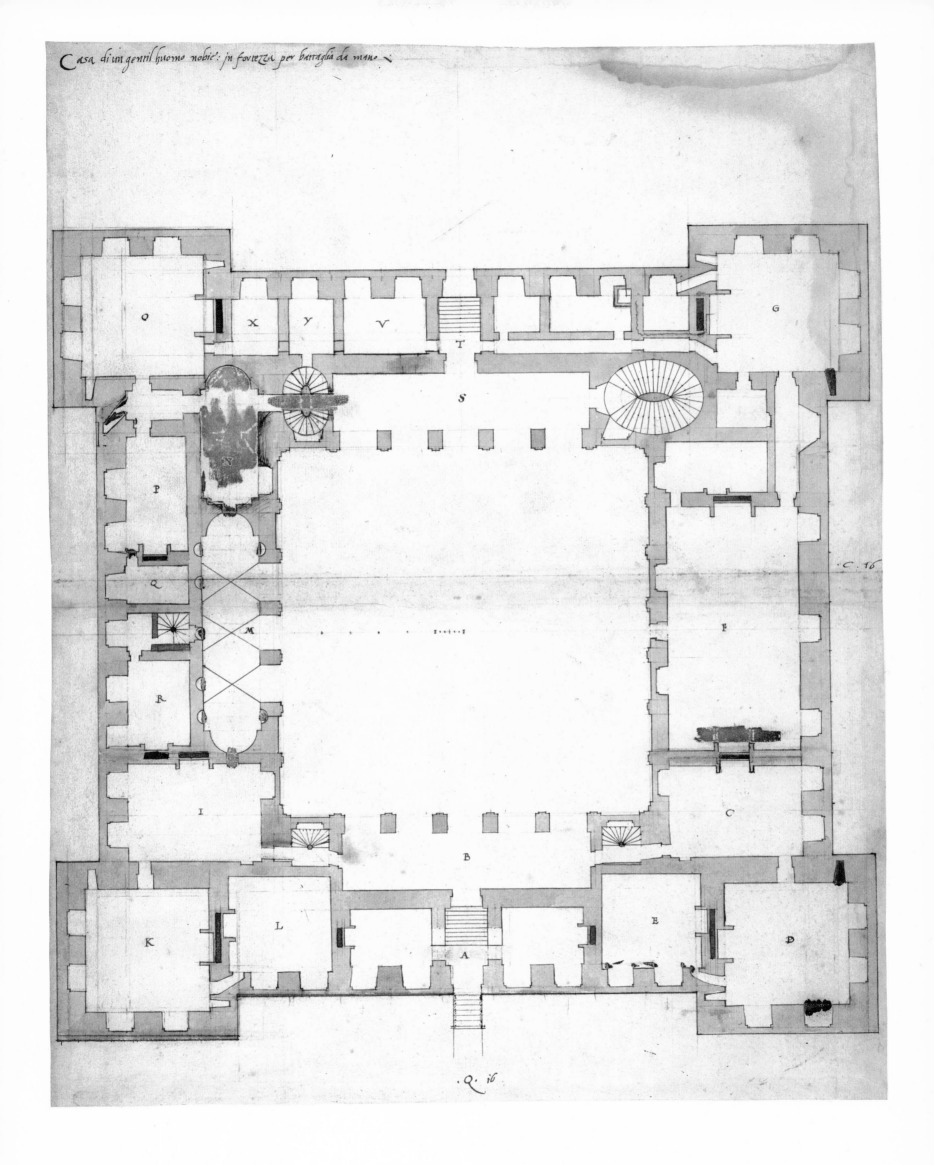

La pianta qui auanti uiene à essere la parte disopra e ben che li compartimenti paiano di altro modo: che quei
di sotto: non di meno li muri disopra venggono a posarsi sopra quei di sotto, Montato adonque la scala
principale si capita su la loggia .A. et cosi della medema scala si mene capo nel uestibulo .B. a questo
di qua si dice guardaroba, di questo se entra nella sala .C. la quale sara tanto maggiore di quella
di sotto: quanto li mura saran diminuite in grossezza: et cosi cresceranno alquanto tutte le altre stanze,
nel capo di questa sala si troua una camera .D. della quale s'entra alla camera angolare .E. drieto
la quale si è una camera .F. et questa sara amezzada: e cosi la camera .D. si potra amezzare, tornando
alla loggia .A. passando per la scala picola quale si troua: una camera .G. questa sara per il padrone
al seruitio della quale sara la guardaroba .H. et il camerino .I. et anco un picolo studio congiunto alla
limaca: la quale va da alto a basso; della camera .G. se entra alla camera .K. questa sara la libraria, dalla quale si va alla capella per la galeria segreta .L. la qual capella e segnata .M. enha
in uno angolo una picola sacristia .N. et ancho della capella si puo gire alla sala; torniamo alla
loggia .O. alla quale si sahisse per le dua limache ne i capi di essa: di questa loggia si trouaura
camera .P. col suo camerino .Q.: et unaltra .R. col camerino .S. questi quatro lochi saran amezzadi
seruendosi delle scale che sono in esse camere, da un capo di questa logia passando per la limaca
si troua una camera .T. della quale s'entra alla camera .V. e drieto a questa vi e una camera
.X. et dalla camera .T. si troua unaltra camera .y. queste tre camere cioe .T.X.y. si potrano
amezzare: doue in questo angolo vi saran sette camere tutte bone et humite insieme, o doue
qualche finestra: o porta impedivano la posta del letto si potra mutare: senza menda della faccia di
fuori per la commoditta delle finestre: che si posson e fingere: et fare aperte secondo acadera, in
questa parte io non ho narato le misure de i lochi et le grossezze de i muri per non esser prolisse,
ma col li piedi che sono nel mezzo del cortile si trouara il tutto puntalmente.

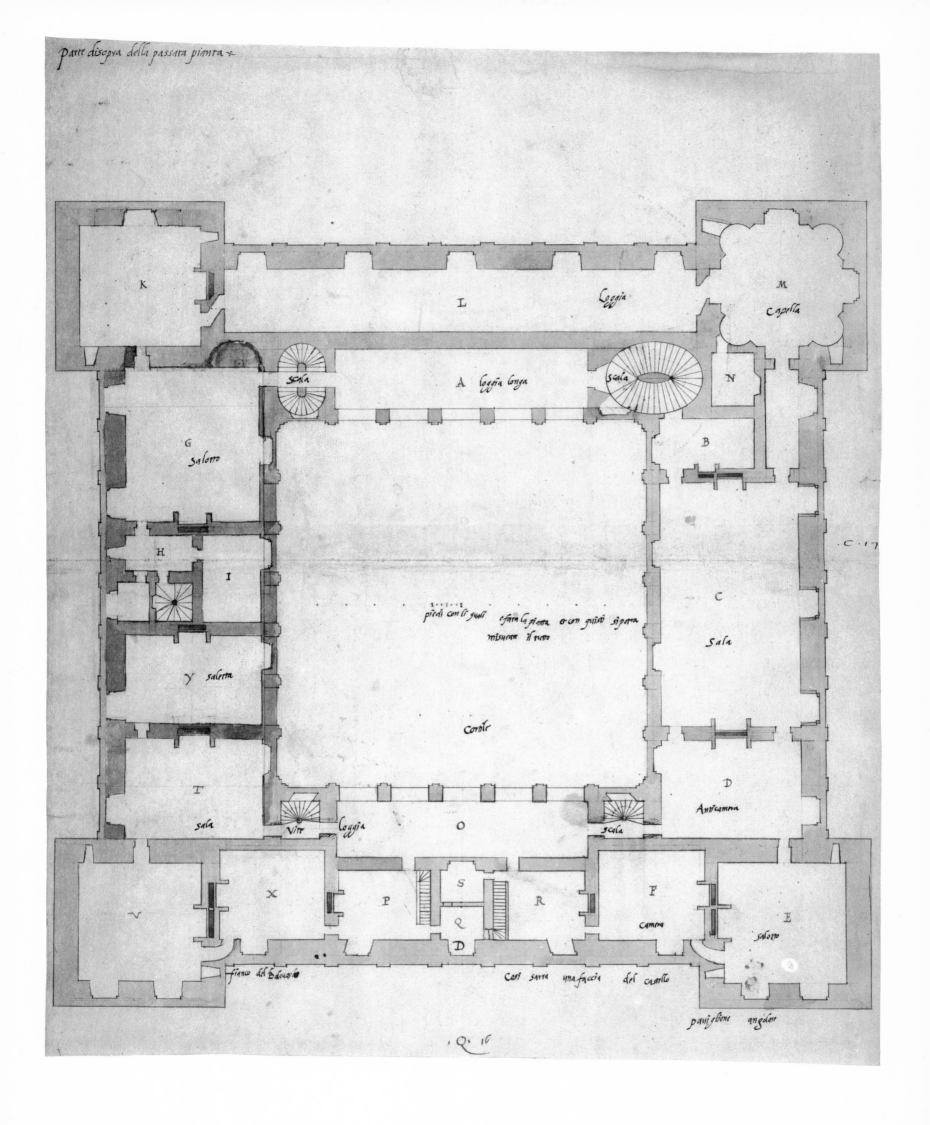

Parte disopra della passata pianta ~

K

L   Loggia   M
Capella

scala   A loggia longa   scala   N

G
Salotto   B

H
I
C
Sala

piedi con li quali
e fara la pianta et con questi si para
misuran il resto

Y saletta

Corile

T   D
sala   Anticamera

Vite Loggia   O   scala

X   S   R   F
V   P   Q   Camera
D   E
Scatto

fianco del Badouaro   Cosi sarra una faccia del castello

pauiglione angolare

. Q . 16

XVII

Delle piante qui adietro: le presente figure qui auanti sono li suoi diritti, quella piu basso dinota uno de i quatro lati: che tutti sono a un modo: eceto li dua lati che non ui si porta: Da un torrone al altro sono piedi LXXXXVII. la larghezza de i torroni è piedi XL. l'altezza delle prime stanze sara piedi XVIII. le se gonde sauano piedi XVII. che uiene a essere sotto l'architraue: sopra del quelli ui sara una altezza di VI. piedi doue son quelle finestrelle sopra la cornice è questa sara unt ambulatione: o coridore: ben terrazzato: questa cosa parra forsi licentiosa ad alcuno: non dimeno cosi piacque al padrone: et io non la biasmo essendo massimamente fuori della citta doue è concesso alcune cose che di lontano fan bella ueduta come è questa ma li torroni hano tre ordine: come è douero: e li dua ordini disopra son di una altezza medema: sopra li quali sara il medesimo ordine con quei coridori intorno è benche questa faccia habbia la scala di fuori fu poi deliberato chel ponte liuatoro battesse su la porta: et mettere la scala di drento: come è nella pianta delle altre misure: degli ornamenti non scriuo per che col compasso et li piedi si trouara il tutto: et benche questo edificio sia nella franza: ha uoluto il padrone chel tetto sia al costume italiano.

La parte di mezo sopra questa rappresenta quella di dentro: et ui sono le medesime altezze dette disopra: e be che nella pianta non si ueggono le loggie intorno: non dimeno questo medesimo ordine si uede intorno al cortile: ma parte serrato per le commoditra di alcune habitationi: le quai misure si trouerai sempre coi piedi che ui sono. le prime habitationi sauano uolute: et è tutto cauato sotto terra: Questo edificio al presente si uede sopra terra fin al nassimento degliarchi: cosi di fuori come di dentro tutto di pietra uiua, è bianca: et assai dura: et è edificato in un bellissimo sito: et abbondante di tutte le cose: è quantunque egli sia in una pianura doue non mancano le acque uiue ui colli e monti con selue possedute dal padrone il nome del quale jo non tacero per hauere inse queste tre parti che molto si conuengonno al gentilhuomo nobile, primieramente egli e ricchissimo: secondariamente: egli è letterato: et intende di tal arte quanto altro nobile jo conosca, terza egli ha il uolere et ha uoluto il consiglio di chi ha studiato: et praticato l'architettura gran tempo: ne si ha uoluto confidare nel suo ingegno: et sapere come molti altri fano che come hari quatro lettere è dua termini di architettura uogliono da lhoro istessi esser gliarchitetti: ma fatte le opere poi ui si uede quanto hano inteso tal arte Questo edificio è nella borgogna presso campagna di la da tonaua quatro leghe, il signore Anto nio di chiaramonte primo barone del delphinato conte di talardo, è padrone del presente edificio questa picola parte sopra l'alt dinota la parte interiore della capella percio che la sua altezza passa l'ordine segondo.

Parte interiore della capella
della passata pianta x

Parte interiore della passata pianta

C 18

Loggia di
sopra

luoghi amezzati

stanze sotterrance

Parte di fuori della passata pianta

Loggia   laspese comunciare: et finiti monsig. Antonio di claramon nella
Borgogna ad uno   suo luoco che si ches
Ansilafrane et lafrestrine

Q 10

ansi fu un corridore alsintorno della casa

alsintorno

plar   faccia della monastu

XVIII

Il palazzo che qui a dietro ho dimostrato et discritto è veramente molto commodo è coppioso di loggiamenti: et ricco di ornamenti: non di meno il vigoroso architetto porria dire che per non vi essere le loggie spaciose intorno: è ancho le cose no
si conuassero di una medesima forma: quanto alle parti di dentro: la qual cosa consiste nelle oppinioni, questo edificio
adonca non sara cosi coppioso di loggiamenti: ne cosi ricco di ornamenti: ma hauera dua parti principali piu osseruate, la prima sara
che si grandi spazzauano piu nettamente le faccie de i torroni: per vgni quegli fuori di squadro: come vuole il douero
della fortezza; laltra tutte le loggie sauano spaciose: et li membri tutti corrispondenti l'uno al altro, questo palazzo
sara circondato da fossi: e quanto sauano piu larghi gli nemici staran piu lontani, l'entrata di questo sara larga piedi xiiii
longa xxii et è segnata A. tutto l'edificio sara leuato dal piano piedi v. la qual montata per piu fortezza sara nel vestibulo, ma chi vorra montare a forza sara giandreggiato per le stanze sotterranee "dagli archibusi" et ancho all'inconto sopra la
scala troua ostaculo, salito la scala si troua vna loggia B. la quale circonda il cortile intorno: la sua larghezza e
piedi xii. con li contrapilastri: la fronte d'essi pilastri e piedi: et in grossezza iiii e mezzo, nel capo di essa loggia vi è
vna limaca grande: et ha vn vestibulo C. dal quale si va alla camera D. la sua latitudine per ogni lato è
piedi xxxi dipoi si troua vna camera E. la sua grandezza per tutti è lati è piedi xxiiii drieto la quale si troua
vna camera F. la sua larghezza e piedi xvi, et in longhezza e piedi xviii. e questa sara amezzeda da un lato
del cortile: nel mezzo si troua vna camera G. la sua longhezza e piedi xxiii. et in larghezza xxii. drieto a questa
si troua vna camera H. la sua longhezza e piedi xxii: et in larghezza xviii. hauendo al suo seruitio vn camerino
I. che x piedi e la sua latitudine: questi dua membri si possonno amezzare: alli quali si salira per la limaca
publia, dall'altro lato della camera G. sara vn camerino K. la sua larghezza e piedi xiii. et in longhezza xxii
e questo sara amezzado: e salirassi per la scala da vi torni d'esso mezzo, all'inconto della porta si troua vna sala
L. la sua longhezza è piedi xxxxiii et in larghezza piedi xxi. nel capo della quale si troua vna camera
M. la sua longhezza è piedi xxv. et in larghezza xxii. passando piu oltra vi e la camera N. la quale e piedi
xxx per ogni lato: e quel medesimo è dall'altro lato, li muri di fuori son grossi piedi v. e quei di dentro iii. e tanto piu
è meno si forno: secondo la materia commoda al paese:
il suo altezza si vede qua sopra: l'altezza delle stanze terrene sara piedi xxi. e cosi le seconde per ciò che le prime rap-
presentauano piu alte per cagione de i v piedi leuati dal piano, l'ordine terzo de i torroni sara alto piedi xvi; la causa
che vi sono le finestre bastarde: e cosi le quali sopra le altre io ho detto piu fiate: questo edificio sara tutto cauato
et le parti sotterranee seruiranno a molti seruicij della casa: è ben che in questo edificio: non vi sia stalle: ne molti
altri lochi pel bisogno di vna grossa famiglia: io intendo che fuori del edificio vi sia molte habitationi per
la famiglia: ma questo sia per la persona del gentil huomo et per la sua piu domestica famiglia
è questo è fatto al costume italiano: ma osseruato in esso alcune commoditta francese

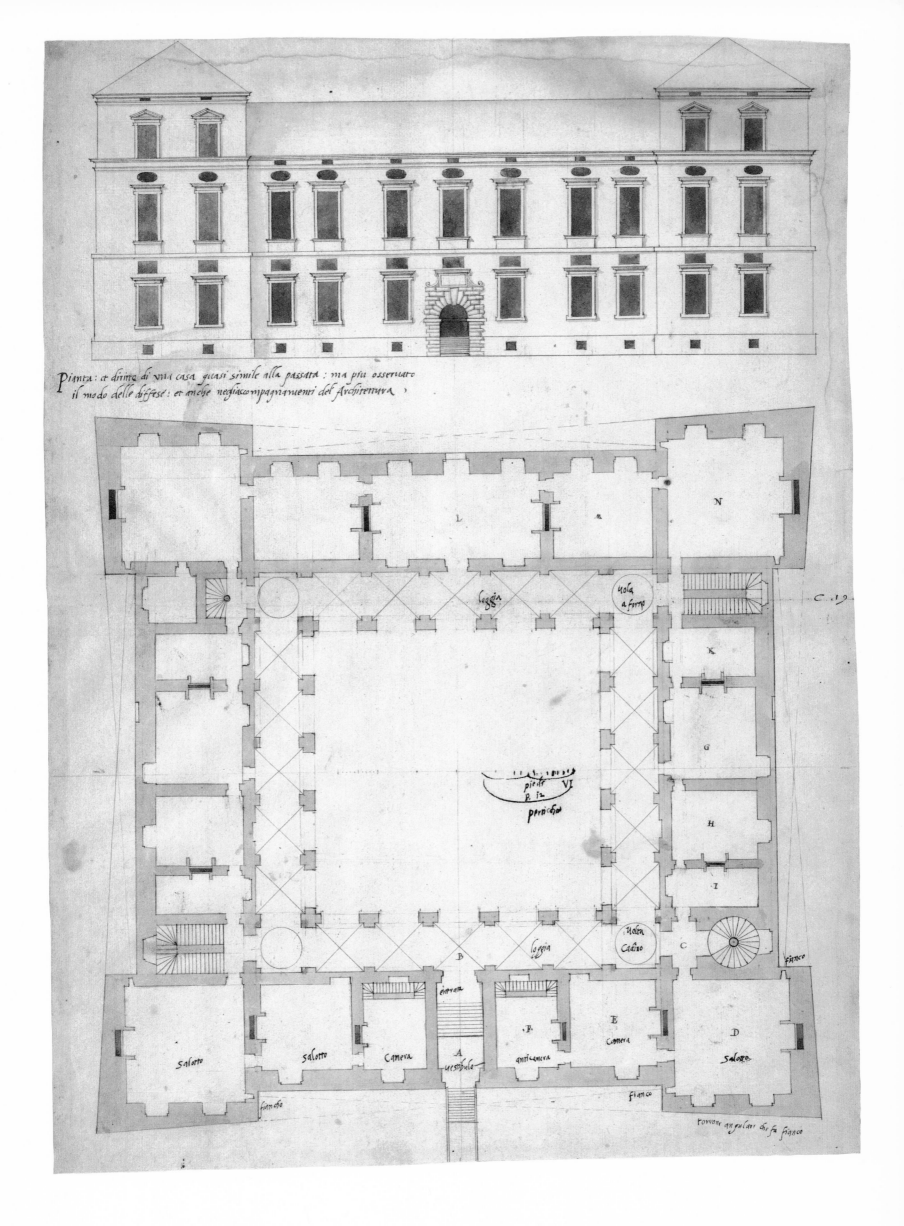

Pianta: et dritto di una casa quasi simile alla passata; ma piu osseruato
il modo delle diffese: et anche negliaccompagnamenti del Architettura

C. 19

L   M   N

loggia   uola
a forno

K

G

pied VI
p. 12
perticha

H

I

uolta
Cadino   C

B   loggia

entrata

salotto   salotto   camera   A
vestibule   anticamera   E
camera   D
salone

fianco   fianco

torioni angulari che fa fianco

XIX

Quanto alle habitationi de i gentilhuomini de tutti li gradi fuori delle città posso hauerne trattato abastanza

hora io comincerò alle habitationi de li principi: li quali tal volta si contentano di un picolo loggiamento per esser

piu liberi per qualchi suoi piaceri et se pure son seguitati da grossa famiglia vogliono starsi seppara[ta]mente,

La presente habitatione sarà di forma exagona: cioè di sei lati: cosi la corte come la parte di fuori, et si come

ho detto il principe non à gran loggiamenti per la sua famiglia: potra ordinare una strada prima che si gionga

alla sua casa di tanta larghezza: quanto sarà uno de sei lati, e questa sarà .A. et per piu commodità fargli li

portichi da ogni lato drieto alli quali siano loggiamenti ma bassi accio non tolghino la veduta di lontano della casa

principale, della forma: et misura di questi loggiamenti non parlaro altrimenti: ma della casa principale si

Questa sarà leuata piedi .V. dal terreno: doue si troua un vestibulo .B. la sua latitudine sarà piedi .XIII. et in lon

ghezza piedi .XXVIII. questo hauea da ogni lato una camera .C. longa piedi .XVI. e larga .X. dipoi si troua una camera

.D. di forma exagona el suo diametro è piedi .XXI. questo vestibulo ha da ogli lato le sue limache per salire ad alto

et alli mezzadi: per che tutti li lochi picoli si amezzavano, passando il vestibulo si troua una loggia .E. la quale

circonda il cortile: la sua larghezza non è che .V. piedi: per ciò che serue solamente di ambulatione per gire al coperto

il diametro del cortile è piedi .LXII. da un de lati si troua una sala .F. la sua longhezza è piedi .XXXI. et in larghez

za piedi .XXVIII. et ha in uno angolo una camera .G. di forma rotonda, el suo diametro è piedi .XXII. hauendo nel

altro igolo un camerino di piedi .VI. nel altra faccia si troua una camera .H. la sua larghezza è piedi .XXIII. et

in longhezza piedi .XXVIII. drieto la quale è una camera .I. et è per ogni lato piedi .XXI. hauendo al suo seruitio dua

camerini: nella faccia al rincontro della porta si troua uno andito .K. dalli lati del quale son scale da vitorni: et ha

da un de lati una camera .L. la sua larghezza è piedi .XVI. et in longhezza .XXIII. oltra che ha la pasta di un letto .M.

drieto del quale vi è un camerino, da l'altro lato si troua una camera .N. ch'è per ogni lato piedi .XVI. drieto

la quale è una camera .O. di forma penthagona: cioè di cinqui lati lo suo diametro è piedi .XVIII. nel altro

lato vi è una sala .P. la sua larghezza è piedi .XXVIII. et in longhezza piedi .XXXXVII. et ha in uno an

golo una camera .Q. questi tien forma di uouo naturale: la sua larghezza è piedi .XVI. et in longhezza piedi

.XXV. nell'altra faccia si troua una camera .R. la sua latitudine è piedi .XXII. et è longa piedi .XXIX. con:

giunto con questa son dua camere: una .S. larga piedi .XII. e longa .XVIII. l'altra .T. di piedi .XIIII. per ogni lato, la parte

.V. di la dal edificio: sarà una piazza di bona larghezza e quei pilastri dinotano una loggia da i lati della qua

le vi saranno habitationi: le quali sarano sopra li giardini quei muri li quali circondano l'edificio et lo mett

no in quadro facendo li quattro angoli .X. io intendo non siano piu leuati da terra che .V. piedi accio non tolghino la

veduta al edificio

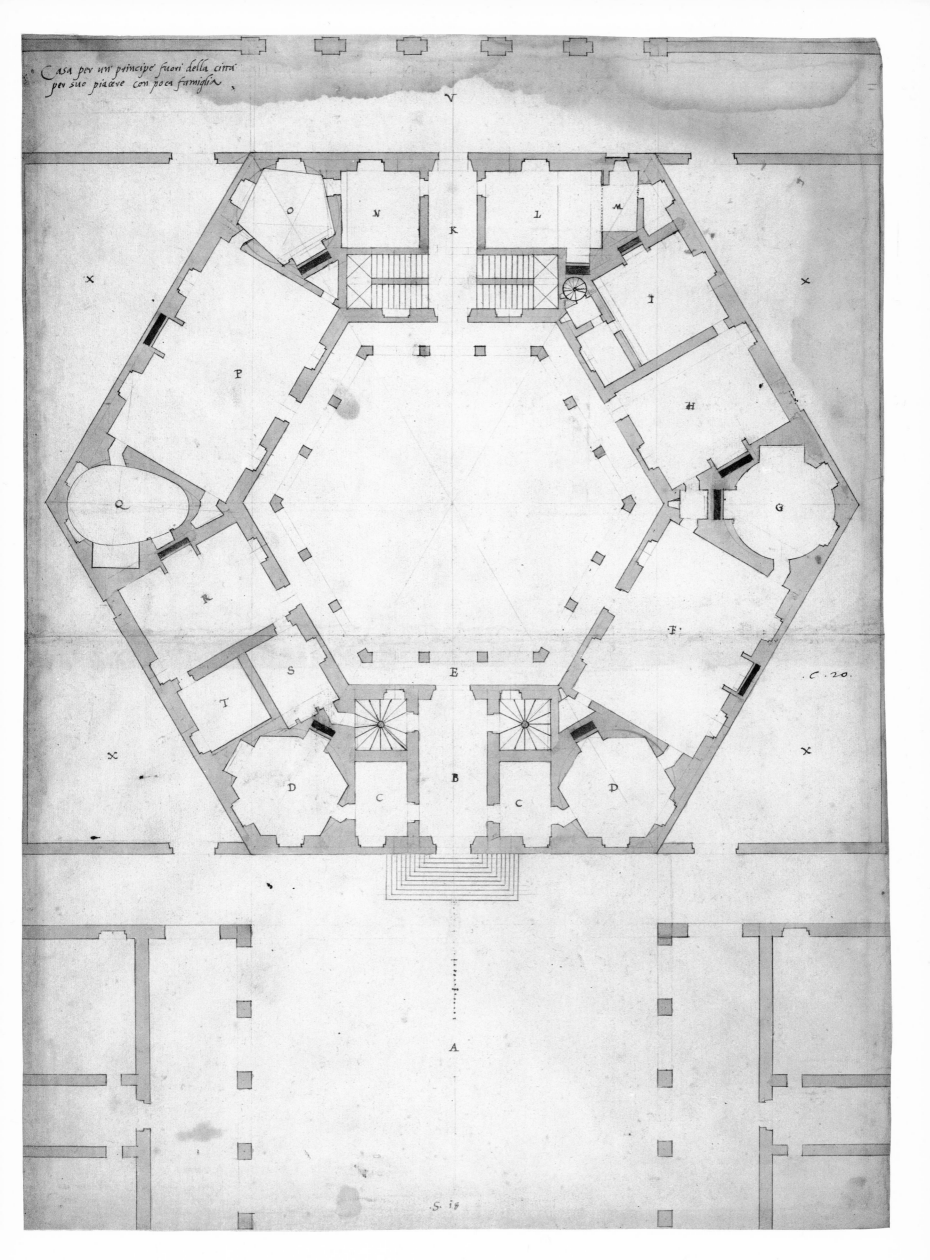

Casa per un principe fuori della citta
per suo piacere con poca famiglia

V

X   X

O   N   K   L   M

I

P

H

Q

G

F

.C.20.

R

E

S

B

X   T   X

D   C   B   C   P

A

S. i9

XX

L'edificio qui auanti dimostrato rapresenta la parte interiore della passata pianta; ma le altezze si faranno segondo li paesi che sel paese sara temperato e non molto ventoso: l'altezza delle stanze sara sempre lodata e massimamente le sale: et le camere grande: ma sel paese sara freddo et ventoso come sono questi doue al presente jo mi trouo sara necessario che le camere sieno di onesta bassezza: ma non pero manco di piedi xvi le maggiori: ma che l'altezza delle sale per esser grande non manco de XX piedi, nondi meno in queste presente altezze ho voluto acostarmi piu alla perfettione: ma non in tutto pero per che una stanza vorria essere al men tanto alta: quanto e la sua larghezza, L'altezza di queste prime stanze sara piedi xxiiii: amezzando tutte le stanze menori di piedi xviii in larghezza: et le segonde habitationi saran piedi xxviii in altezza cio e solamente le sale: ma tutti li altri lochi si amezzaruano: et alcuni de picoli camerini sarano tripplicati in una altezza: e doue le scale che vi sono non potra seruire adetti mezzadi vi e molti picoli lochi de iquali si faranno limache; le loggie che circondano il cortile non si voltarano: ma di pietre piane si copriruano: et ben comesse con bon cimento seruirano per terrazzo; e quancunque li ornamenti: e finestre: et altre cose sieno inparte al costume de italia: jo non dimeno ho voluto chel coperto sia al costume della frantia: per ciò che tre parti principali trouo in questi tetti la prima sono piu durabili de nostri: se sono ben gouernati et visti tan spesse volte: la segonda l'altezza di essi coperti di quella bella pietra che arduosa si nomina: torria quelle finestre sopra li tetti che si dicono lucarne fano grande ornamento a uno edificio: e massimamente alla campagna: et jo per me ne farei in alcuni luochi de italia doue fusse piu commoda la materia: o de arduosa: o di pietra cotta vitriata: e benche le stanze del segondo ordine saran piu alte delle prime: non

la parte qua piu basso dinota le parti di fuori del edificio: dimeno: l'altezza de iv piedi di piu: chi è la scala fa in apparentia la parte di sopra menore di quella di sotto come e il douero: quella del segondo ordine sara di iiii: le altre misure l'altezza del architraue: freggio: e cornice del primo ordine sara li sotto: e poi nel quarto libro difusamente tutti li membri si ro- di tutti li ornamenti si rouerano col compasso sopra li piedi li sotto: le stanze sotterranee potran seruire a molti ufficiij oltra le cantine uano: et essendo questo edificio cosi leuato dal piano per esser luminose: et in parte sopra terra: alli quai lochi si potra descendere per tutte le scale

S. 18

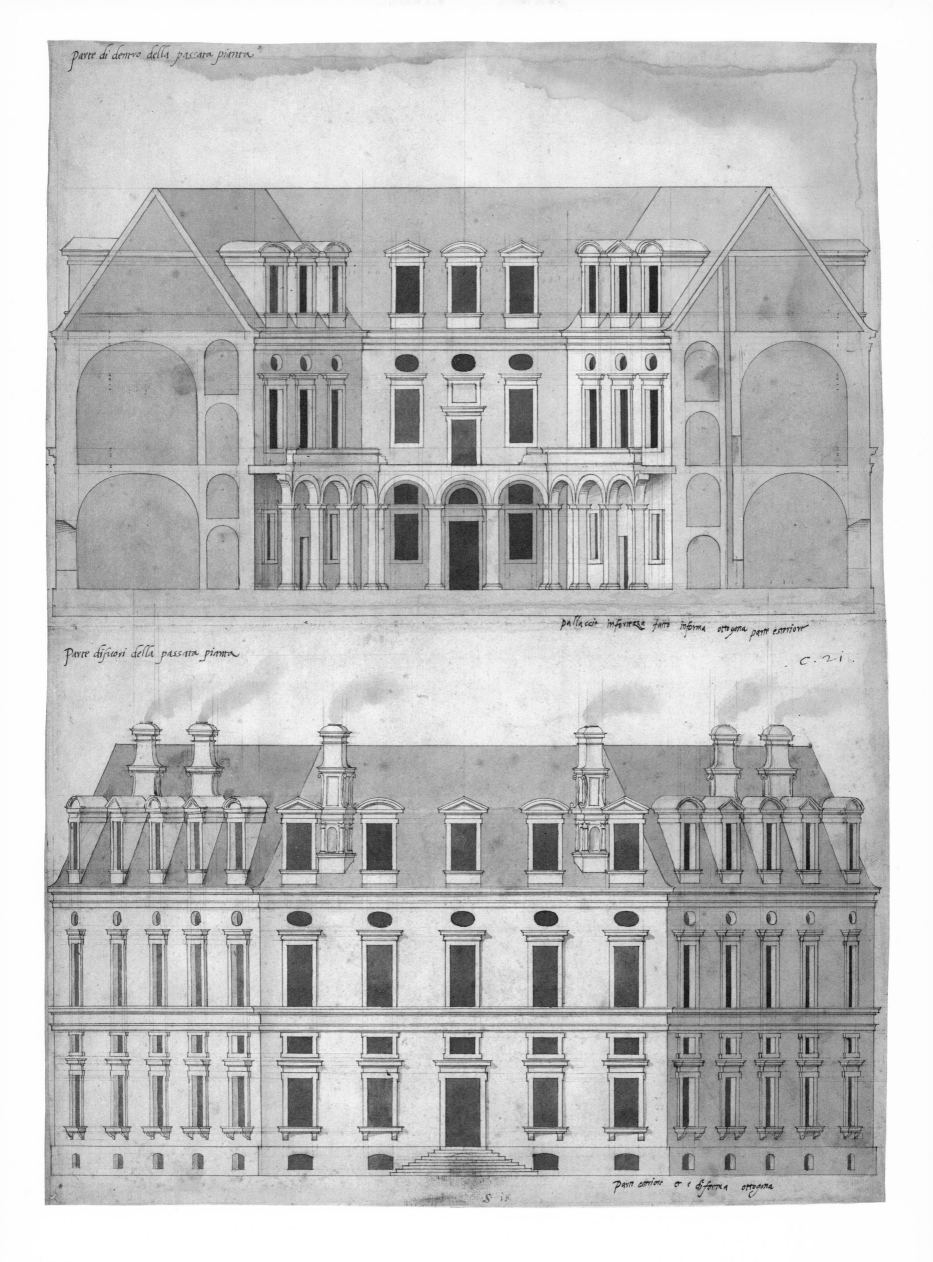

parte di denvo della passara pianta

pallaccia infortezza fatto informa ottogona parte esteriore

Parte difuori della passara pianta

C. 21.

S. 18

Parti entriore et e di forma ottogona

XXI

Li principi uogliono anchora qualche picola habitatione che à pena vi possino aloggiare conqualche sua compagnia, quanta
è per ciò la presente pianta porra servire ad ogni principe; la fronte di questa casa sara piedi· xc· gl'intercolunnii saranno
piedi· XIII è mezzo per ciascuno: li dua pilastroni, saranno piedi· XII· ciascuno et altro tanto quei dagliangoli agiungendo
tre quarti di piede· a ciascuno angulo per piu fortezza, la grossezza delle colonne sara· II· piedi· lo pilastrone che sostengon li archi
vn piede· è mezzo· ma quelle degliangoli dua· e cosi sara distribuito li piedi· xc· fra l'una è l'altra colonna per dar piu luce
alla loggia sara vna apertura di piedi· v· in larghezza, la grossezza de i pilastroni uerso la loggia sara piedi· v· la loggia
·A· sara larga piedi· XIII· il netto: la sua longhezza sara piedi· LXV· hauendo dalli lati negliangoli dua limache le quali salgano
alla sopra loggia· acanto le limache· nei pilastri· vi son dua lochi per li guardiani, di questa loggia si trova la porta la
sua larghezza è piedi· VII· dentro la quale è vn vestibulo· B· la sua larghezza è piedi· XIII· et in longhezza piedi
XXII· dal destro· et sinistro lato vie dua salette· C· la sua larghezza è piedi· XXIII· et in longhezza piedi· xxx·
di queste salette si entra alle camere· D· che son per ogni lato piedi· XXIII· di quelle si trova la rietrocamera
·E· la sua larghezza è piedi· XVIII· et la longhezza piedi· XXIII· dietro questa si trova vn caminino· F· largo piedi· x·
e longo· XV· col quale è congiunto vna limaca con vn picolo studio, laqual limaca andava da basso à alto· et anco alli
mezzidi· è quello che· da vn lato se intende dal altro, passando lo vestibulo· B· si trova vn cortiletto· G· di forma
ottogona· il diametre del quale sara piedi· XXVII· ma per li quatro nichi li quali saranno per sedere· et per temprare
che fan li dua finestroni dalli fianchi· et per le dua spaciose entrate: il detto cortile pareva maggiore, questo cortile e fatto
per illuminare l'andito che savia tenebroso· et anche da luce alle rietrocamere· E· che saranno tenebrose· ne vi è dubio
che rai cortili per l'altezza sua non siano lucidi: che i lumi perpendiculari hano gran forza, passando oltra questo
cortile si trova vn vestibulo· H· della medesima grandezza del primo· lo qual poi trova vna loggia· I· la sua
larghezza è piedi· XII· ma per essere impedita dalli contraforti: li passaggi non sono che otto· è questo è fatto
afin che la volta sia ben forte con quei sotto archi: la grossezza dei pilastri per fronte: è piedi· IIII· ma li contaforti
nali son piedi· VII· ciascuno l'apertura degliarchi è piedi dodici per ciascuna, è cosi vie a essere il tutto piedi· xc·
come d'auanti· ma la grossezza de i muri sara segondo la materia come altre volte ho detto, questo edificio sara
leuato dal piano al meno· IIII· piedi è mezzo· et anche piu· segondo lo sito· e sara tutto cauato sotto· et voluto
Si per la sanità come per la commodità di molti vfficii che vi saranno· chi questa casa sia circondata da mu-
ri· jo non lo lodo per cio che li muri di alcun cortile· o giardino ocuppareboono la veduta di essa casa· ma chi
con acque viua e ponti leuatoi la potesse serrare io lodarìa tal cosa· o veramente· questa fusse sopra vn
picolo colle· è quello circondato da muri non troppo alti questo sarìa bene·

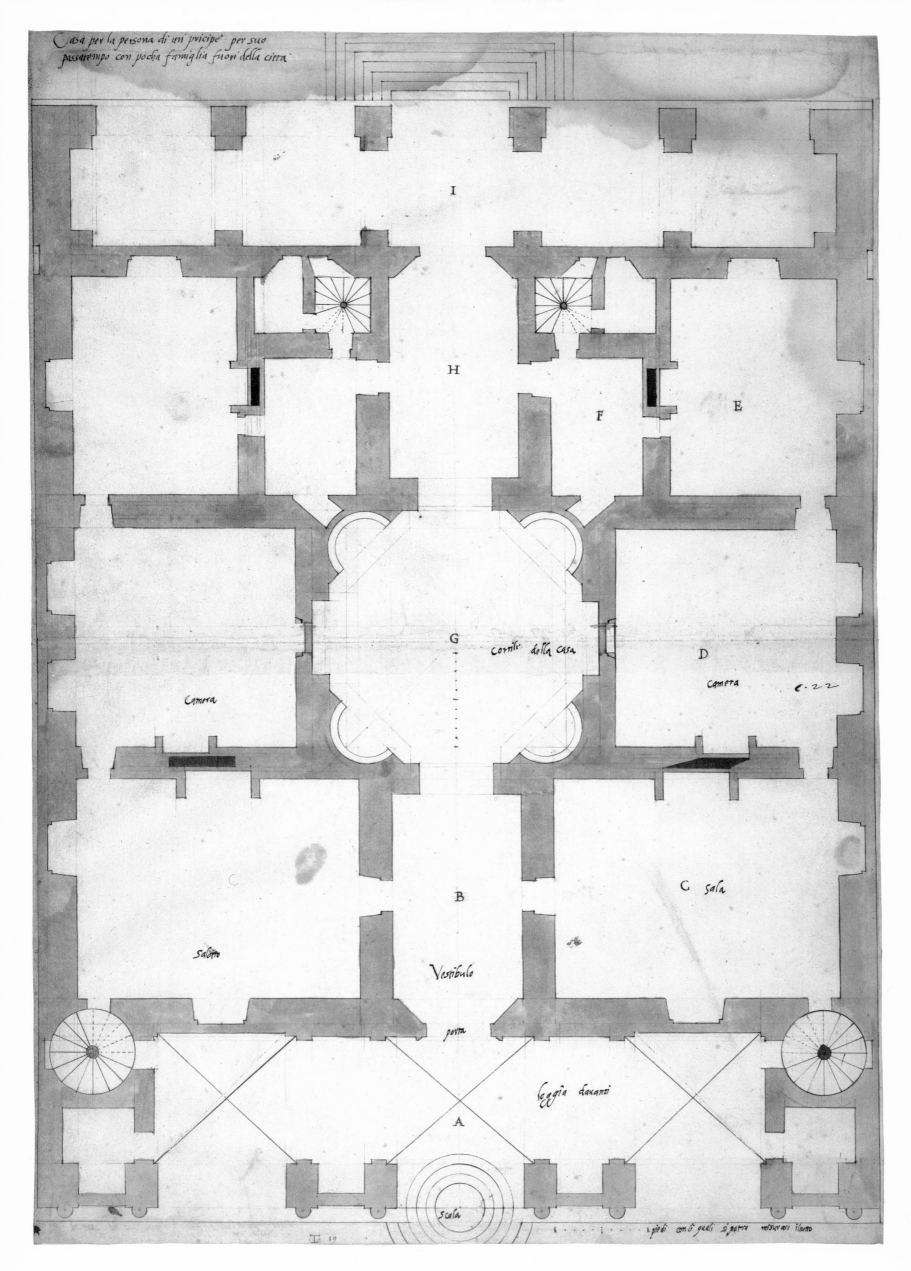

Casa per la persona di un principe per suo
passatempo con pocha famiglia fuori della citta

I

H

F   E

G   Cortil della casa   D

Camera   Camera   C. 22

Salotto   B   C sala

                              Vestibulo

                                porta

                                                loggia dauanti

                              A

                              scala

I piedi con li quali si potra misurare il tutto

XXII

Questi divini qui auanti seruono alla passata pianta: la loggia rustica sera per la parte di drieto: sopeua corinthia et
composita sara per la faccia dauanti: e prieramente parleremo di questa faccia: e quanto alla misura delle
colonne pilastri et intercolunni sopra la pianta s'è detto, ma parlando delle altezze: l'altezza della loggia sara:
piedi XXIIII. che viene a esser sotto l'architraue, l'altezza dei piedestali sara VI piedi: le colonne con le site basi e
capitelli son alte piedi XVIII. l'altezza degliarchi è piedi XXII. l'architraue: fregio: e cornice: è piedi IIII. l'altezza
della sopra loggia è piedi XXII. che comincia sopra lo primo architraue: e va fin sotto la cornice supperiore.
li piedestali delle prime colonne son alti piedi IIII. le colonne con basi e capitelli sono alte piedi XIIII. e mezzo, l'architraue fregio e cornice: è piedi IIII. e un quarto: e sopra la cornice è lo piano del terzo ordine, la grossezza
delle colonne e un piede e mezzo e questa è opera composita. dell'altre misure chi passo si trouerano li sotto
con li piedi segnati: e cosi le particular misure degli ordini si trouerano al quarto libro alli suoi lochi, la loggia
rustica qua sopra sara della istessa altezza de l'altra: e cosi la sopra loggia anchora, dell'altre misure non diro
per essersi già detto le grossezze et larghezze nella pianta, ma parliamo delle altezze di dento che tutte non si deono
fare ad una altezza: l'altezza del vestibulo et cosi quella de la saletta C. si farano come quella della loggia, ma quella della camera D. saria troppo bassa a amezzarla: e troppo alta alla medema altezza: ma di
piedi XVIII. facendogli un suolo morto: o veramente una volta morta sara bene; la camera E. si potra
amezzare quella di sotto sara alta piedi XV. quella di sopra VIII. et un piede di riempimento per la volta
o vero suolo che sarai ventiquatro piedi, il camerino F. sara cosi amezzado li primo sara XIII. piedi
il segondo X. et un piede di riempimento che son altri dodici: e cosi tutti li membri sarai proportionati inse-
ne iguali sara quella correspondentia che si puo dire armonia ultima ↘

Parte di drieto della passata pianta —

Parte dauanti della passata pianta

T . 19

faccia di un pallazze in fortezza cinto da fossi

XXIII

per non mancare de inuentioni jo dimostraro vna casa circa al sugetto della passata: ma alquanto maggiore
variata di ornamenti, la faccia di questa casa sara piedi LXXXXVII. e' prima si troua vna loggia. A chiusa
dalle teste: per piu fortezza: et anche sanitta, et ha tre archi la larghezza di ciascuno e piedi XIII. questi sono
sostenuti da quatro colonne: che venggono a fare vn pilastro ma traforato e cosi la loggia sara piu luminosa
et anche di piu bello aspetto, la grossezza di vna colonna sara un piede e treguarti: fra l'una e l'altra colonna
sara piedi V. e mezzo. li dua cantonali sara ciascuno piedi XI. e cosi sara distribuito li piedi nouantasetti
la latitudine della loggia sara piedi XIII come li archi accio le crociere siano perfete, la longhezza di essa loggia
con tutti li nichi sara piedi XC. la latitudine della porta sara piedi VIII. entrato dentro si troua un vestibulo
B. la sua larghezza e piedi XVII. et in longhezza XXX. dal destro et sinistro lato si troua un salotto C.
lo quale e piedi XXX. per ogni lato, dipoi se entra alla camera D. di XX. piedi di quadrato perfeto, dietro
la quale vi e vna rietrocamera. E. la sua larghezza e piedi XIII et in longhezza. XX. e nella camera. D.
vi e un camerino. F. il suo diametro e piedi. ix. passando il vestibulo si troua vna corte di forma rot=
tonda il diametro suo e piedi. XXXVII. in questa corte vi son dua limache: che mettono capo nei vestibuli
disopra, passando la corte si troua l'altro vestibulo. H. la sua larghezza e piedi XXIIII: et in longhezza
piedi XXXV. questo disopra seruira per sala: dal destro e sinistro lato vi e vna camera. I. la sua largez=
za e piedi XX et in longhezza piedi. XXVII. drieto la quale si troua un camerino K. la sua larghezza e
piedi. X. et in longhezza XVII. hauendo al suo seruitio un studio. L. lo quale e piedi. VIII. per quadro,
a lungo lo oposito al camerino votondo. F. vi e vna capeletta. P. la sua larghezza e piedi XIII ix: et in longhezza
piedi XIII, Hora parliamo delle altezze le quali uoglio esser proporzionate alle larghezze, la logia: li vestibuli et le
due camere. C. queste sauaro pedi. XXVII. in altezza, le camere. D. et. I. sauaro amezzate in questo modo
quelle dabasso sauaro piedi XV. in altezza: vn piede de viempimento del suolo che son. XV. e XII. piedi alta
la segonda: che sauaro li piedi ventotto, e medesimamente le camere. E. sauaro a questa altezza, ma li came=
rini. L. F. si potrano tripplicare per esse membri picoli, la grossezza de i muri maestri sara piedi
VI. e quei di mezzo. IIII. e li tramezti de i camerini piedi. III. in grossezza

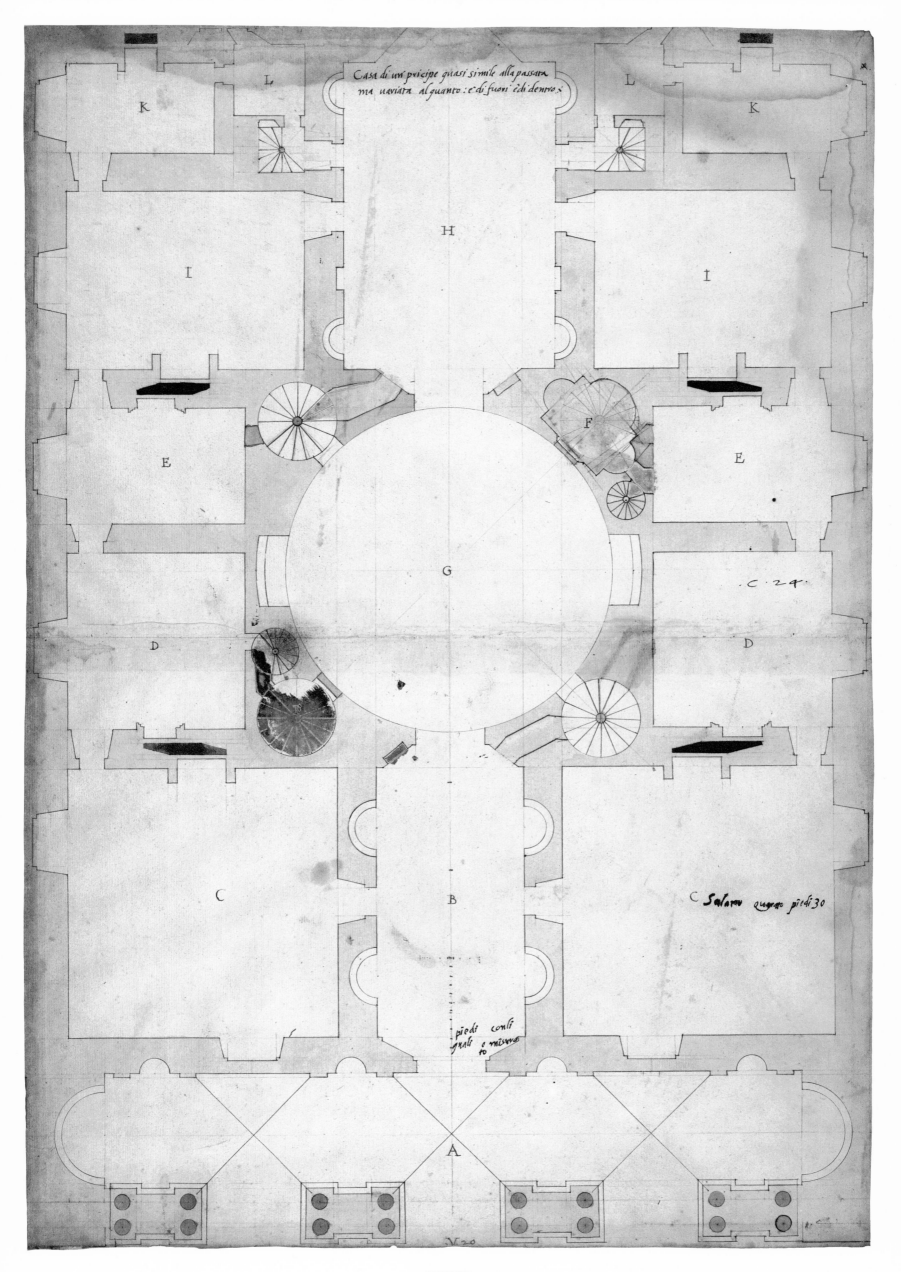

Casa di un principe quasi simile alla passata
ma variata alquanto: e di fuori e di dentro

K   L   L   K

H

I   I

E   E
                    F

G

C·24·

D   D

C   B   C Salotto quadro piedi 30

piedi consi
guali e misura
to

A

XXIV

Della pianta qui advieto dimostrata è discritta questa si è la faccia: è quanto alle larghezze et grossezze
delle colonne: si è detto nella pianta: hora se dirà delle altezze, prima tutto l'edificio sarà leuato da terra piedi .V.
et suso sarà lo primo piano di tutte le habitationi: l'altezza della loggia sarà piedi .XXVII. l'altezza de i piedestali
sarà piedi .V. e mezzo: et sarano huniti che vi posino sopra le quatro colonne: l'altezza delle colonne sarà piedi .VI. la
.XIII. è mezzo: l'architraue sarà di altezza vn piede è mezzo: dal dissotto del arco fin sopra il p.ro aperto sarà piedi .VI. la
larghezza delle finestre sarà piedi .VII. è la sua altezza piedi .XII. è questo se tutto per accordare le altezze delli
architraui: con le cornice delle finestre: et così de i piedestali, et similmente la porta viene vn piè più di dua quadri
per concordare la sua cornice: per che non è la più brutta cosa neglied ificij che la discordanza: la quale si vede nella
maggior parte degliedificij, merce' della presuntione: figliuola della ignorantia. l'altezza delle stanze di
sopra sarà piedi .XXII. è questo nonsarano volate di pietra: ma li suoli si farano di legnami con boi compassi:
menti: ne paia ad alcuno cosa falsa che le colonne superiori posino sopra li archi: per cio chio prendo tale uttorità
dal portico pompeiano in roma, opera veramente da tutti celebrata: l'apertura degliarchi superiori sarà larga piedi
.VI. la grossezza delle colonne sarà vn piede è mezzo: l'altezza dei piedestali sarà piedi .VII. l'altezza delle colonne
con le base è capitelli sarà piedi .X. è mezzo: hauendo sopra li capitelli vno architraue: la sua altezza sarà quanto è
grossa la colonna nella suma parte è sopra essi posavano li archi: sopra li quali archi sarà l'architraue: fregio: et cornice
l'altezza del tutto sarà piedi .II. è mezzo: sopra le cornice sarano le lucarne: la qual cornice viene à essere aliuel:
lo desuolo secondo, il parapetto delle lucarne sarà alto dalla cornice piedi .II. la lucarna di mezzo sarà larga piedi .V.
et in altezza piedi .IX. le altre misure si trouerano col compasso: ma torniamo a quello che importa molto, li architraui
sopra le colonne da basso: vogliono esser bene huniti et inchiauati insieme: talmente che posti sopra le quatro colonne
faccino vn sodo hunito come il piedestale: di maniera che voltandoui poi sopre li archi: trouerano talmente le quatro
colonne hunite coi piedestali: et li architraui: come se fusse vn sodo pilastrone: ma che li fianchi degliarchi: et delle
volte nonsiano ripieni di materia soda: ma di vasi di pietra cotta di più sotil: accio siano più leggieri: et sarà
fortissimo tal riempimento: Delli dua cantonali: è di altri ornamenti chio vo passando il tutto si trouava col
compasso a li piedi piccoli, e questo edificio anchora chel retto sia leuato al costume di frantia: potrà
non dimeno seruire a molti altri paesi.

C. 2.5.

XXV

il principe ha piacere de diuersi loggiamenti et ne uora de tali che vi possi commodamente aloggiare la sua corte: et di
vantaggio, come s'ara la presente pianta: la quale e molto coppiosa di apartamenti, questa primieramente sara
leuata da terra con tutta la sua planicie all'altezza del occhio di un huomo giusto: doue alentrare della porta che
sara larga piedi VII. e mezzo per lo meno: per cio che giuui non entra carri: ne cauagli, si roua un vestibulo A di
quadrato perfeto, il suo diametro e piedi XXIIII. da un delari si roua una saletta B. la sua longhezza e piedi XXX. di
poi e una camera. C. la sua larghezza e piedi XXII. drieto la quale ci è una vietro camera. la sua larghezza e piedi XVI.
hauendo al suo seruigio un camerino che in latitudine e piedi XIII. et in longhezza XVI. oltra che vie la porta p un letto
dal altro lato si roua il medesimo, passando questo si roua una loggia: la sua larghezza e piedi XII. la quale circonda un cortile di piedi XC. per ogni lato in capo di questa loggia vie una limaca: il suo diametro e piedi XX. drieto
la quale è una camera. larga piedi XVIII. e longa XX. passando piu oltra perdetta loggia si roua una saletta: la sua
larghezza e piedi XXVI. et in longhezza piedi XL. et e segnata E. et ha da un lato una camera F. che di larghezza
e piedi XX. et in longhezza XXIIII. drieto la quale è una camera. G. la sua larghezza e piedi XVII. da altro lato di
questa sala vie una camera H. di piedi XX. per ogni lato drieto da essa è la vietro camera I. la sua larghezza e piedi XVIII,
et il medesimo si roua da l'altro lato: ecceto che vie una scala piana dascalini piani, di questa loggia si passa
a una galeria fenestrata la quale circonda un cortile della larghezza de l'altro una piu stretto per l'altro verso: cio è
piedi LXXIIII per essere ocuppato dalla scala: della qual scala si monta alla sopra galeria. di questa galeria da
basso si roua una sala K. la sua larghezza e piedi XXIIII. et in longhezza come l'altra passatra: da un de lati
ha una camera L. che di larghezza e piedi XX. et in longhezza XXIIII. drieto la quale è una camera. M. la sua larghezza e piedi XVIII. et in longhezza XX. da l'altro lato di questa sala ci è una camera. N. drieto la quale è
la camera. O. della medesima grandezza delle altre dua. nel capo di questa loggia è una limaca: de la quale se
entra a uno andito p. del qual si roua una camera. Q. la sua larghezza e piedi XXIII. et in longhezza piedi
XXVIII. da questa: et per la limaca anchora si roua la camera. R. questa e piedi XXII per ogni lato: passando piu
la si roua una camera. S. la sua larghezza e piedi XX. dietro la quale è la vietro camera. T. che di larghezza e piedi XV. la galeria V. haueua tre porti le quali roua un cortiletto X. in faccia del quale vie una
loggia la quale e molto ornata drieto la quale si roua un gran giardino Z. nel capo del quale io farei
le stalle et habitationi pel mastro di stalla: e per paggi et altri simili ufficiali

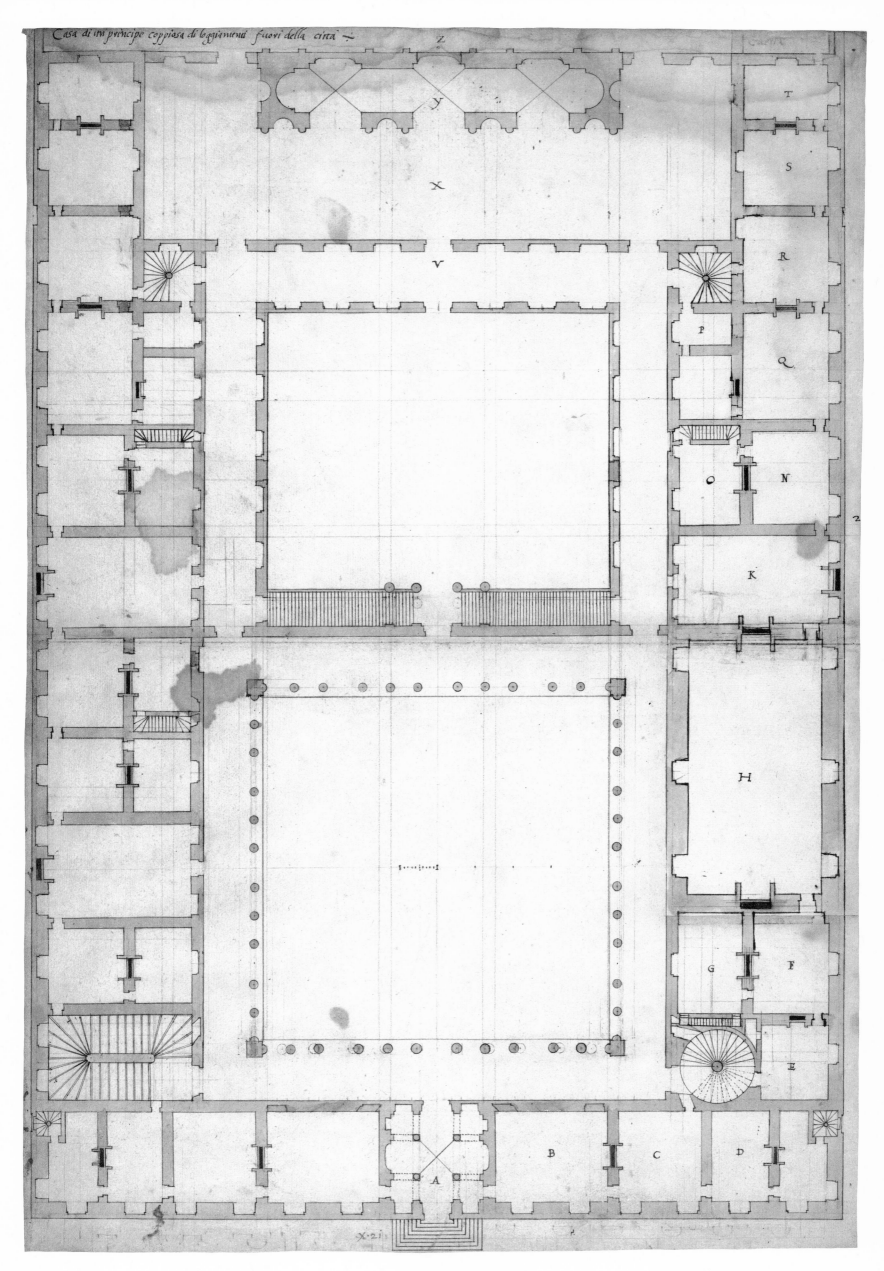

Casa di un principe coppiosa di habitamenti fuori della citta

X·21·

XXVI

Della pianta qui adrieto dimostrata: questi sono li suoi diritti: et sono come si vede al costume di franza ma acco=
pagnati con li ornamenti al modo antico, è prima parlaremo della parte interiore nella quale si veggono tutte le altezze,
quella linea doue sono le dua + dinota la superficie della terra: doue tutto l'edificio è leuato da essa piedi .v. et da li
in giu saranno le stanze sotterranee: entro le quali saranno di molti uffici, eccetto che per dormire: ben che alla corte
molti dormeno assai peggio, queste saranno .IIII. piedi alte sopra terra et .VI. sono terra è tanto piu: e meno secondo li lochi,
l'altezza delle stanze terrene sara piedi xxv. cioè le sale e qualche gran camera: le altre è mezzane: e picole saranno a
mezzade: come si vede nel disegno: è di tale altezza saranno le loggie sopra le quali sara un terrazzo: come dimostra
la parete di mezzo, l'altezza delle seconde stanze sara il medesimo per cio che nelle parti di fuori le altezze corrispondeno
bene, per cagione di quei .v. piedi di leuatione sopra la terra, lo primo ordine dalla summa cornice in su: la altezza sua sara
piedi xiiii. il secondo xii. il terzo ix. il quarto sara per granaro: che qua se dice galatta
La parte di fuori cioè la faccia si vede li sotto l'altezza della scala sara piedi .v. da li fin sotto l'architraue è piedi xxv. l'architraue:
l'architraue: freggio: e cornice sara piedi .IIII. e mezzo, dalla prima cornice fin sotto l'architraue secondo sara piedi xxi. l'architraue:
freggio et cornice sara in altezza piedi .III. e un terzo, le finestre delle prime stanze per piu fortezza: et anche per variare
li ornamenti ben che di fuori si mostrino ronde: non dimeno nelle parti di drento sarano quadrate, le finestre picole sopra
le grande seruiuano alli mezzadi: et alle sale è camere darano maggior luce: tutte le finestre sarano piedi .v. in lar
ghezza: ma de diuerse altezze: come con li piedi li sotto si potra misurare, no mi stendero in discriuer tutte le misure
deghornamenti: per che l'uniuersale si trouera col compasso: et il particulare: nel quarto libro si vede espresso
Questa parte qua sopra rappresenta quella loggia che è fra'l picolo cortile: et il giardino la quale io non intendo
che sia molto alta accio no oscurasse il picolo cortile: non dimeno il tutto sara piedi xxxvii. le altre misure si
potran trouare col compasso apresso poco

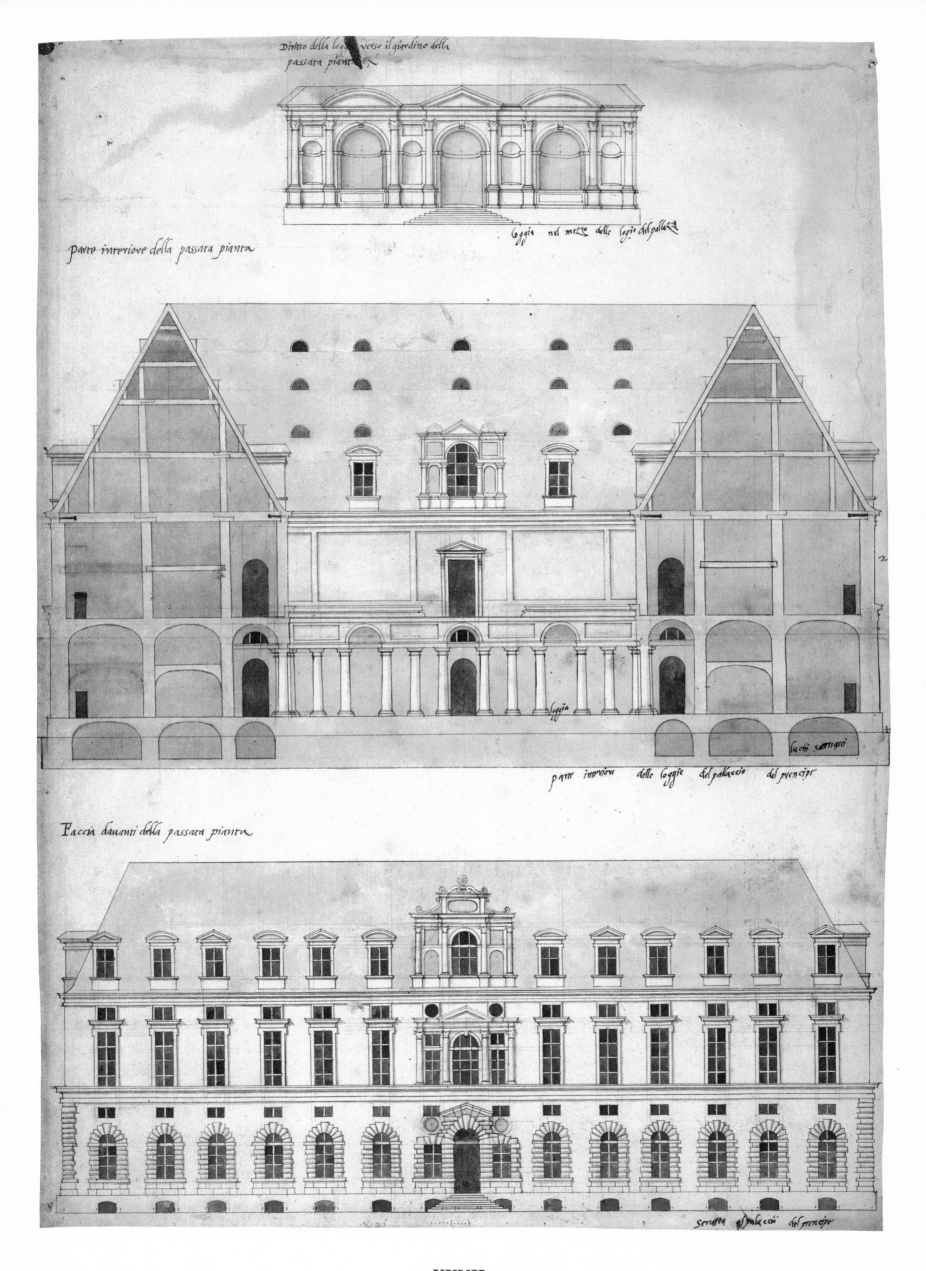

Diritto della legi verso il giardino della
passata pianta

loggia nel mezzo delle logie del pallazo

Parte interiore della passata pianta

parte interiore delle logie del palaccio del prencipe

Faccia dauanti della passata pianta

scritta al palaccio del prencipe

XXVII

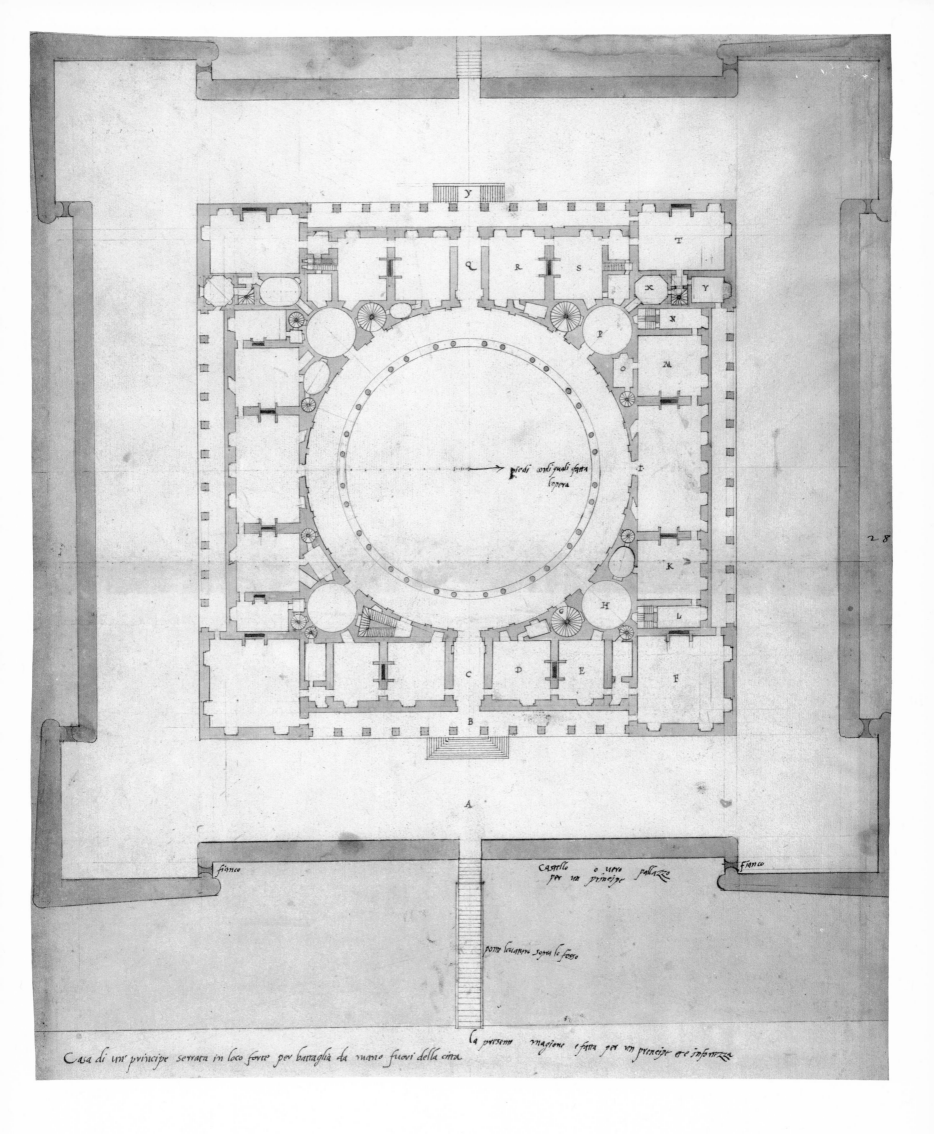

piedi 100 li quali sfatta
sopra

fianco   Castello o uero pallazzo   fianco
                          per un principe

                          ponti leuatori sopra le fosse

                          la presente magione e fatta per un principe o e infermezza

Casa di un principe serrata in loco forte per battaglia da nuouo fuori della citta.

28

XXVIII

Le dua figure che qui avanti si veggono sono li diritti della pianta passata: questo disopra rappresenta
la parte di dentro intorno il cortile: quello disotto dinota la parte disfuori: e tutte la quatro parti sono come questi
ma li piedi con li quali son fatte queste sono alquanto maggiori afin che meglio se discerna li ornamenti
Come s'è detto nella pianta: questo edificio sara levato da terra .v. piedi: si per la sanità come anche per
la presentia la latitudine degliarchi è piedi .x. et son alti .xx. la grossezza de i pilastri è piedi .v. ma la volta delle
loggie o veramente suolo di pietre piane sara piedi .xxi. per causa de i sotto archi e sopra sara terrazzo ben cimentato
la latitudine di tutte le finestre sara piedi .vi. l'altezza delle prime sara piedi .xi. quella delle seconde sara piedi .xii.
perciò che'l parapetto del terrazzo ne rubava assai: l'altezza delle lucarne sopra la cornice sara di piedi .viii. se intende
le luci: le finestre bastarde, è remenati: ovati e quadrangulo tutte son fatte per iluminare li mezzadi: l'altezza delle
stanze seconde sara piedi .xxii. e mezzo: l'altezza del ordine terzo nei torroni sara piedi .xx. ma le dua lucarne sopra essi
saranno più svelte un piede, è anchora che questi coperti siano alla francese: potriano non dimeno servire ad altri paesi,
la parte sua disopra: come io dissi viene à essere le loggie che circondano il cortile: et anco la parte disopra verso esso cortile,
l'altezza delle loggie è piedi .xxi. sopra le quali sara il terrazzo col suo parapetto, ma qua si disputava se queste sem:
plice colonne sosterano il peso delle volte: dira alcuno chi nò: per ciò che le volte sempre spingeno verso il suo nascimento:
et se non trovano buone spalle et contraforti si alargano le colonne et le volte si apreno: come s'è veduto in più luochi
et al presente si vede: io gli rispondo che ciò saria se la loggia fusse a linea vetta: ma per esser forma circolare
che rende al perfetto se li mura et i parapetti saranno ben murati e ben congiunte tutte le pietre delle volte: et fra le
commissure vi sia poca calcina: ma buona: sara impossibile che tal opera facci mutatione alcuna, e so pur l'huomo si
nova assicurare: potrà mettere le chiavi di ferro pel traverso della loggia sopra le colonne nella forza della volta,
le qual colonne son pero .ii. piedi grosse: e piedi .xv. in altezza: dove potrà ben sostenere tanto: e maggior peso anchora,
in questo edificio si troveranno molte cose assai dificile da intendere: dove sara forza à farne modello materiale per intenderle
et tal volta sara l'huomo astretto à mutare alcune cose è tal fiata si troverà meglio di quello ch'io non dimostro; et io dalle
case de poveri artefici sin qui non ho parlato de i necessarij: che anchora che siano necessariissimi: non mi è parso di
abbassarmi à cose così vile presuponendo che nelle grosse de i muri si habbino àfare: et massimamente che siano
nelle parti più alte con li suoi ? a fin che'l fettore si sparga nel aere ~

logietta   nel meggio per ogni lato del cortile

parte di fuovi della passata pianta

29

XXIX

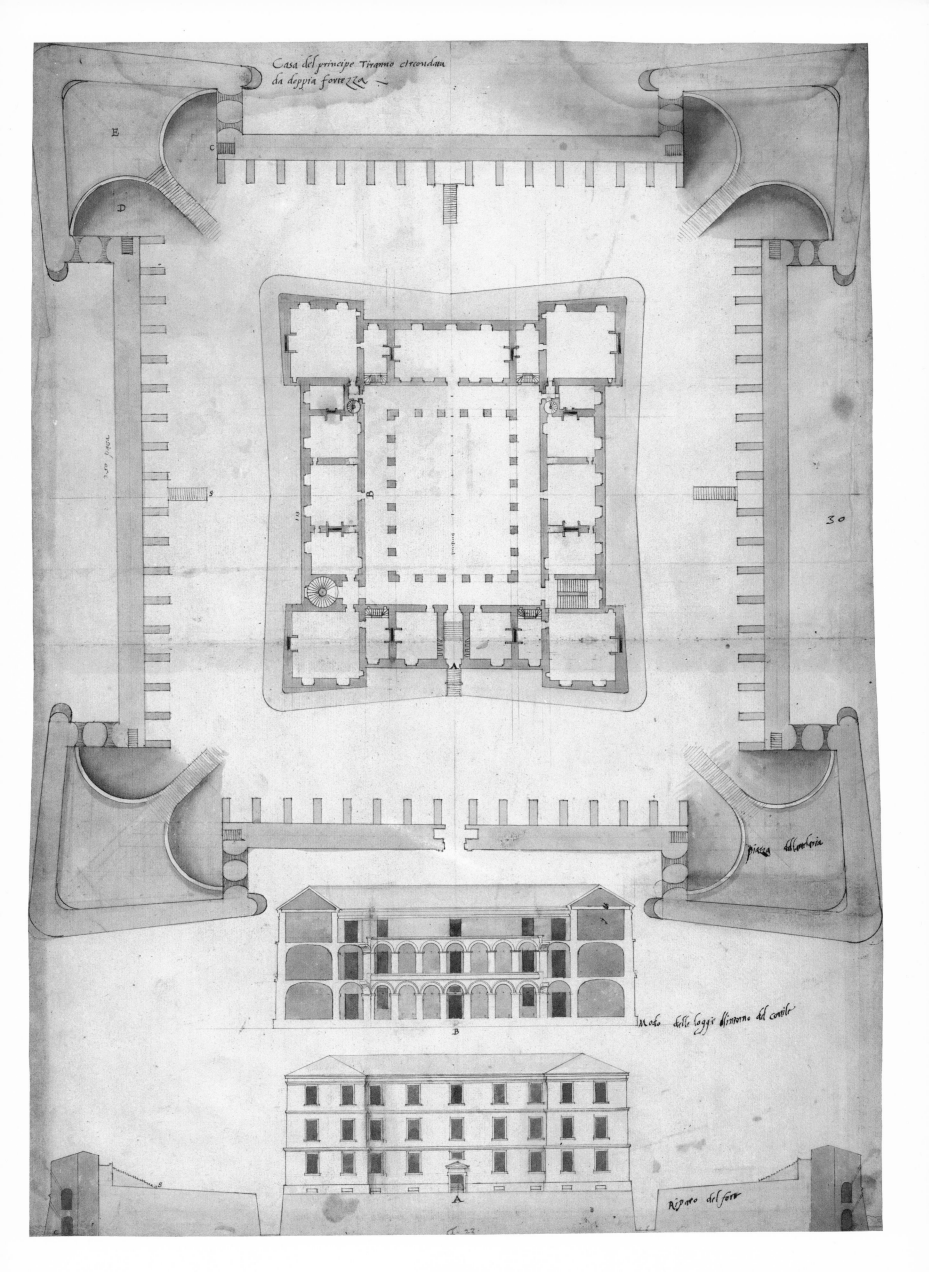

Casa del principe Tiranno circondata
da doppia fortezza

piazza della Caualleria

Modo delle loggie allintorno del cortile

Riparo del forte

XXX

Dopoi la forma quadrangulare la piu facile da mettere in difesa, lo triangolo: ma vorebbe gran spacio per cio che inuna forma picola come saria vna habitatione: li angoli acceti ne rubbarebbono vna gran parte: ma io trouo la forma del penthagono: cio è di cinqui lati apresso la quadrangola esser la piu facile, onde ho voluto anchora dimostre vnaltra habitatione pel Tiranno di questa forma, La circomferentia di questa forma si fara tanto grande che li fianchi de i balouardi non si offendino l'un l'altro, non hauendo riguardo al dissegno lo quale ho tenuto cosi picolo: accio possi capere nel foglio, questa fortezza sara circondata da larghissimi e profondi fossi et hauera vna entrata solamente pel ponte leuatuo è trouara la piazza .A. questa come ho detto sara di quella grandezza che al architetto bolio pareua, la grossezza della muraglia io la faria piedi .xv. li speroni per longhezza piedi .xviii. da l'uno al altro altro tanto: e questi si voltarano, e sarau tanti loggiamenti per soldati: ma a tempo di vna bateria se empirano di terra e questi son segnati .B. doue e il cauatei .C. si descende alle contramine: li acanto ouue è la .✠. si salisse alla diffesa delle cortine la parte .D. è per tartelaria de i fianchi, la scala .E. è per montare li cannoni e colobrine, alla piazza .F. la quale di loggia è spacia la campagna, e viene a supperare la tartelaria de i fianchi, passando auanti si trouà la casa per habitare, la quale tien la medesima forma del penthagono questa per piu sicurita sara cinta da vn fosso: almanco piedi .xv. in larghezza con la sua ponticella di piedi .v. in larghezza, dentro la porta si trouà vn vestibulo .G. il quale è diffeso per fianco dalli dua lochi .K. è per che l'edificio sara leuato dal piano della piazza .v. piedi quiui sara la scala per salire al cortile, apresso si trouà vna loggia .H. la sua larghezza e piedi .x. li pilastri son per fianco piedi .v. et in fronte piedi .iii. da i lati della loggia son le scale publiche per salire alle sopra loggie: in questo primo lato si trouà la camera .I. di piedi .xxiii. per lato, et ha vn cenerino .K. sotto del quale sara l'archibusaria che fiancheggia il vestibulo, nel segondo lato si trouà tre camere .L.M.N. di vna medesima grandezza cio è piedi .xxiiii. per quadro, nel terzo lato si trouà vna sala .O. la sua longhezza e piedi .xl. hauendo da vn lato vna camera .p. pur quadrata, dall'altro lato vn camerino. .Q. la sua larghezza e piedi .xiii. drieto del quale e vn studio di piedi .xii. per ogni lato, nel quarto lato si trouà vna sala .R. la sua longhezza e piedi .L. hauendo nei capi dua camere .S.T. di quadrato perfeto come le altre, nel quinto lato si trouà vna camera .V. la sua larghezza e piedi .xxiii. et in longhezza altro tanto: dal destro et sinistro lato vi e vna camera .X. e .y. le quali son di larghezza piedi .xx. hauendo ognuna d'esse vn camerino, nel primo lato a banda sinistra vi e vna camera .Z. di quadrato perfeto come le altre et ha vn camerino. .&. sotto del quale stara gli archibusieri come nel altro, quanto alle altezze io non e dirò altro per abreuiare ma qui sotto sonli piedi coi quali si misuera ogni casa e fa vn punto e l'altro son piedi .x. e come vno che è parrito in quarti di dua piedi e mezzo l'uno. la prima figura .A. qua disopra rappresenta la parte interiore verso il cortile quella segnata .B. dinota la parte di fuori, la porta .C. significa la porta della casa fatta in forma maggiore accio se intenda meglio, la porta .D. seruira per quella della fortezza, la parte .E. viene a essere il profilo della muraglia: come ben la intendera che di tal cose se diletta.

Casa del principe Tiranno circondata da fortezza
diuersa dalla passata fuori della citta

XXXI

Delle case de principi et altri gran personaggi per habitare in villa fuori delle citta a me pare di hauer detto abastanza

Hora delle case Reali: per quanto jo sapro comincero atrattare, e prima chio venga alle gran case jo dimos:
strarò alcuni membri particulari da fare in luochi appartati non congiunti con altri edificij: ma sepparati,

Nel bello, e ricchissimo castello di fontana bleo: oltra li ricchi cortili e belle fontane che fanno uno
stagno larghissimo e profondo: le belle loggie spaciose sale longhe galerie: camere: e camerini: et insfiniti
altri luochi: tutti adornati distucchi et de pitture fatte da bonissimi maestri: non senza grande abbon:
dantia di ovo avicchito: cose veramente degne di quel gran re che le ha ordinate: Vi e fra gli altri un gran
giardino nel meggio del quale e un stagno di acqua di fontane la larghezza del quale e piedi LXXV.
ma di longhezza una gran corsa di cauallo, Sopra di questo stagni vi e un ponto ben fondato et
di bonissima struttura fa una planicie di quadrato perfeto di tale larghezza: sopra del quale sono
stato fatti di molti dissegni: e modelli per farui sopra uno edificcio che qua si dice un pauiglione

Et hauendone jo fatto alcuni: per commissione di sua Cristianissima maesta: ho deliberato communicargli al
publico per che a diuerse cose poruebbono seruire, E primieramente la pianta qui acanto tutte sarano
Come grotte: ma però sopra terra et luminose doue per la grossezza de i muri saranno freschi la statte: e
calde il verno, prima si troua una piano auanti la porta largo piedi IX. questo sarai dua scale che circon:
dano l'edificcio et si comincia a salir al cauanti A. et d. L. si troua il piano sopra le grotte il quale supera le
mura del giardino: e questa sara scala pianissima da cavalli, a l'entrare della porta si troua un vestibulo: la sua
larghezza e piedi X: et in longhezza XVI. nel mezzo del loco vi e una sala di forma vottonda il suo dia:
metro e piedi XXX. nel mezzo della quale sara una fontana viua: per cio che la fonte del castello
si troua tanto alta da questo piano che questa sorgera abbondantemente, passando la sala si troua una
anticamera. D. della grandezza del vestibulo da un lato di questa vi e una camera di forma ottogona
E lo suo diametro e piedi XVI. et cui lo fuoco con la posta di dua letti, questa sara la camera di la
stua per spogliarsi, della quale si entra nella stua. P. di forma ouale la sua larghezza e piedi XII. e in
longhezza piedi XVII. di questa si troua lo bagno. G. di forma vottonda. lo suo diametro e piedi XVI.
questo ha li sedilli intorno: et un sedile porta dua gradi per descendere al fondo, cosi da l'altro lato vi
sono le medesime stanze cioe la camera. H. I. K. le scale che si veggono segnate. M. sono per
salire alli mezzadi delle dua forme ouali: che per esser membri piu picoli degli altri si amezzarano.

pauiglione al costume di franza

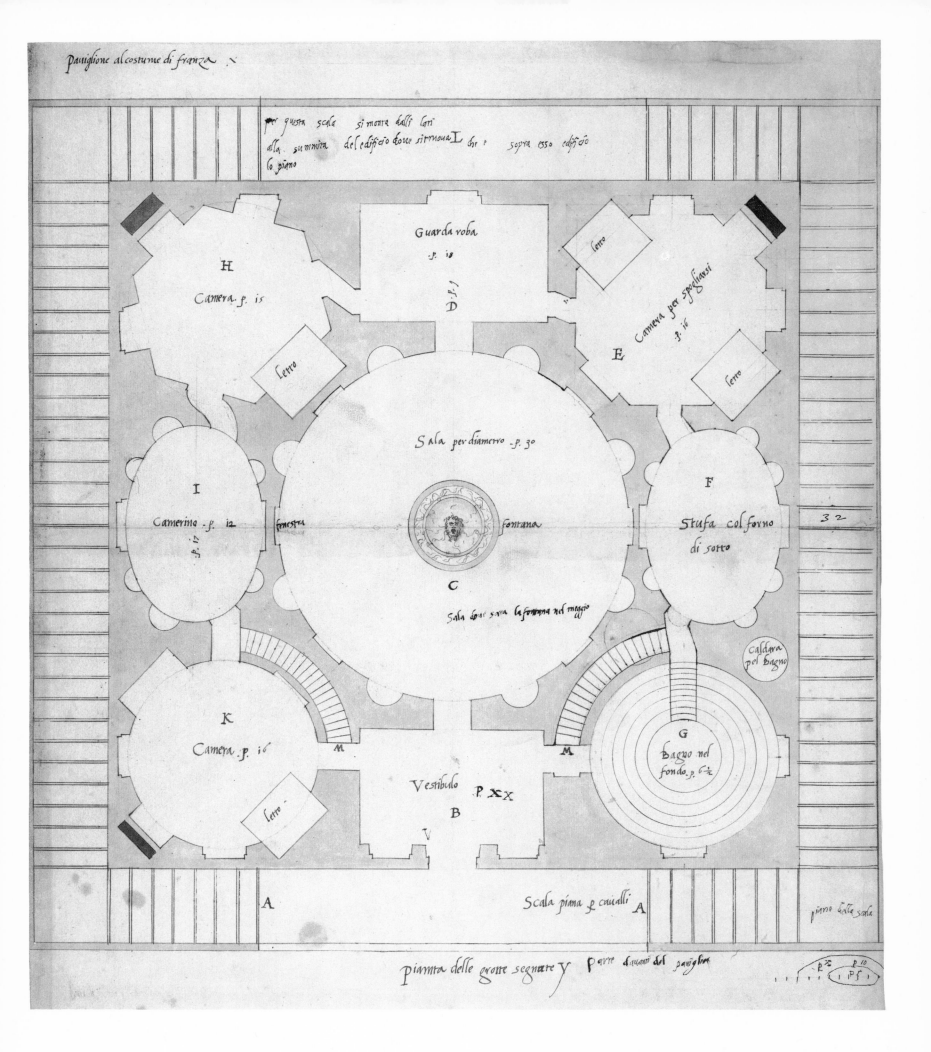

per questa scala si monta dalli lati
alla sumnita del edificio doue si trouua I che e sopra esso edificio
lo piano

Guarda roba
.p. 18
D S.I.

H
Camera. p. 15

letto

letto

Camera per spogliarsi
p. 16

E

Sala per diamerro .p. 30

fontana

letto

I
Camerino .p. 12
p. 12

fenestra

C

F
Stufa col forno
di sotto

32

Sala doue sara la fontana nel meggio

Caldara
pel bagno

K
Camera .p. 16

M

M

G
Bagno nel
fondo. p. 6½

letto

Vestibulo
B .P. XX

V

A

Scala piana p caualli

A

piano della scala

piamta delle grotte segnate Y parte dauanti del pauiglione

XXXII

La parte interiore della passata pianta: si vede # qua disopra et si conosse come lasala prendera li
lumi da alto li quali saranò a bastanza per esser quatro finestre, et anco dalli gradi per li quali
si salisse vn piede emezzo si potria guadagnare quatro altri lumi. l'altezza della sala sara piedi XVIII.
le altre camere saranno piedi XV. in altezza le forme quali per esser piu picole saranno piedi X. in
altezza: li suoi mezadi piedi VI. alli quali si montara per le scale. M. che si veggono nella
pianta. La parte difuori si vede qua sotto: la quale sara in latitudine senza le scale piedi. LVII.
la sua altezza senza la parte di mezzo: che è rregradi: sara piedi ~~XLIII~~ XX. la sua salita si
vede espresso. la quale sara scala: non solamente per cavalli: ma per carrette potra servire per cio che
partita in quatro parti: vna si monta, è questa altezza suppera di largo le mura del giardino: et
scuopre tutti li paesi intorno. l'apertura della porta sara in larghezza piedi: et in altezza X. le
altre saranò finte per ornamento della cosa: et cosi le finestre saranno finte doue non seruiuano
per luce' le colonne Thoscane su li angoli seruirano di camini, sopra di questo piano saranno
pauiglione ottogono il diametro del quale sara piedi XXX. cioe lo netto di dentro: et montarassi tre:
gradi della quale altezza si guadagnava li lumi per la sala dabasso prendendone vna parte sul piano
accio le boche delle finestre venghino maggiori, questa tribuna: o vero pauiglione per esser di otto lati:
parlaremo solamente di uno: l'apertura del arco sara piedi XI. et XVIII in altezza, la pilastrata sara vn pie' emezzo
et altro tanto il mezzo pilastro, l'altezza del architrave freggio: et cornice sara piedi quatro. partita in tre
parti eguali: circa alli altri membri il tutto col compasso si trouava: et poi piu minutamente' si vedera nel
quarto libro al ordini thoscano, quanto al coperto: chi uora lo potra fare di pietra per hauere bonissimo son-
damento: ma io lo fare' di legname è coperto di arduosa: et nella parte di drento di legnami con belli compartimenti è poi con la pittura et oro ornarlo: ela sua altezza dalle cornice insu le quali saran cosi drento
come difuori ma di manco sporto: sara di mezzo circolo: doue la sua altezza dal piano fin sotto la
volta sara piedi XXXI. che sara di tanta altezza: quanto è largo. e quel piede di piu per il sporto della
cornice di drento ⟍

Parte interiore a costume di Grotte
Della passata pianta.

Parte di fuori del passato pauiglione   A   Parte esteriore della pianta segnata Y·   A   diritto del pauiglione

La presente pianta fu fatta pel medesimo fondamento sopra lo stagno nel gran giardino la quale serviva per una habitatione,
davanti a questa casa si trova una loggia A. dalli lati della quale vi è la scala principale B. che viene a metter capo sopra
essa loggia: che sarà un terrazzo scoperto: da l'altro capo vi sarà una capella C. lo diametro suo sarà piedi XII: e così la scala
è questi capi servivano per pilastroni: e così la loggia sarà fortissima: la grossezza de i pilastri sarà piedi V. per ogni lato,
il netto della loggia sarà largo piedi XII. la sua longhezza sarà piedi L. la latitudine della porta sarà piedi VI. è piedi
tre sarà larghe le finestre in essa loggia ma quelle dalli lati e di dietro sarà larghe piedi V. fra l'uno è l'altro pilastro
sarà piedi XII. li dua cantonali: che servono di pilastroni ciascuno sarà sarà piedi XVI. e mezzo, al entrare della porta
si trova una sala D. la sua latitudine è piedi XXIIII et in longhezza piedi LI. havendo dalli lati una entrata E la
quale trova una anticamera F. la sua larghezza è piedi XII. et in longhezza XVIII. havendo un camerino di piedi X.
largo: e XII. longo, di questa si trova una camera G. la sua larghezza e piedi XVIII. et in longhezza piedi XXIIII.
et altro tanto si trova da l'altro lato: et vi e una scala privata di più: la quale va da basso ad alto, li medesimi
appartamenti sarano da alto: ma sopra la loggia sarà un terrazzo discoperto, dove la sala da basso non sarà troppo
luminosa per non havere che dua finestre nella parte di dietro et le porte quando sarano aperte, ma quella di
sopra sarà luminosissima per haver quattro finestre: et le dua porte, la grossezza delli muri maestri sarà
piedi V. et quelli di dentro sarano piedi IIII. e mezzo, le habitationi da basso sarano votate di pietra:
ma quelle di sopra sarano di legnami per più sicurezza: ma non sarano mancho belli li cieli di legnami
fatti a belli compartimenti è bene ornati: che sarebbono le volte di pietra

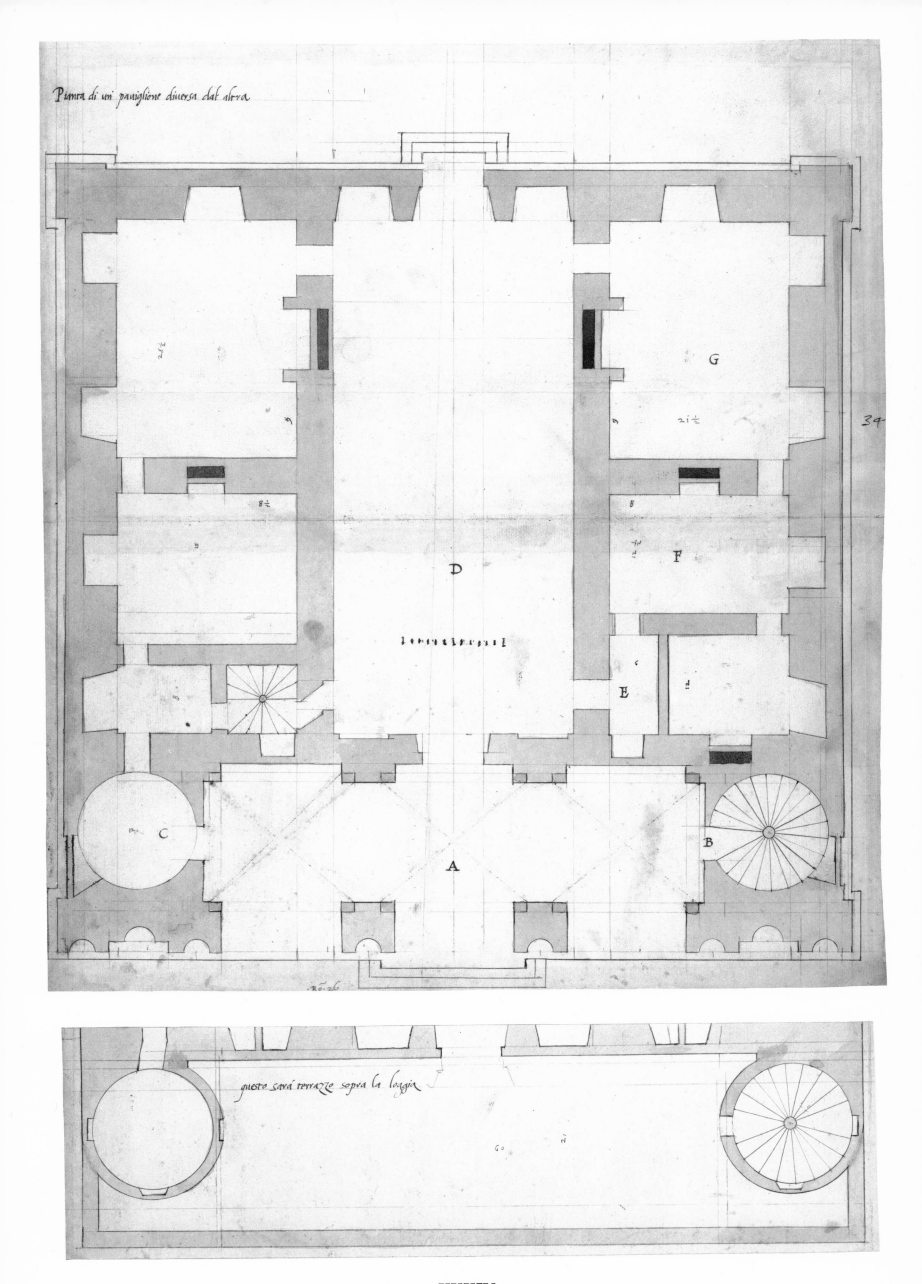

Pianta di un pauiglione diuersa dal altra

G

21½

D

F

E

B

C

A

questo sarà terrazzo sopra la loggia

A

XXXV

Ho io ueduto in piùluochi non solamente in italia: ma in diuerse parti del mondo qualche possente è ricco personaggio hauer gran desiderio di fare qualche bello edifici: et in effetto dar modo che si faccia: ma la sorte non hauuto chegli rincontri Architetto che ne di Theorica: ne per pratica: habbia possuto far cosa chi habbia da esseri lodata da coloro che di tal cosa hanno cognicione: è non di meno quel gran personaggio non ha mancato del suo bon volere: alargando sempre la sua liberale mano,

Io ho ueduto anchora de intendentissimi Architetti è di Theorica: è di pratica: studiare faticarsi et mostrare in milli modi, il saper suo: è non di meno egli non hano mai ritrouato alcuno gran personaggio chi habbia dato credenza altingegno: et saper suo, come fu agiorni miei lo intendentissimo precettore Baldessar peruzzi senesi il quale con honore di tutti gliatri non hebbe superiore: ne pari, onde io suo humile discepulo et impari herede di una minima particella del suo sapere: poi chio non ho mai prouato gran personaggio che mi dia carica di qualche impresa rara et degna di esser mirata: Ho intuto deliberato: se non per altro: almeno per mio piacere: è passatempo di esprimere in carte gli miei concetti a satisfation di coloro che dignerano seruirsene — è però non si admiri alcuno se io dimostro cose assai differente dalle altrui come he la presente pianta: la quale achiii la vedesse fatta se non ladmirasse come cosa rara è nuoua: forsi la lodaria, è per che io sono horamai agliedifici veggi: io disporò uno albergo come io lo farei nel mezo di un giardino del gran Re francesco mii hunico sig.r, Questo è difficio .Sara leuato da terra alcuni gradi: et allentrare della porta si troua un vesibule A. largo piedi VIII. è longo XVI. hauendo dua nicchi dalli lati di N. piedi ciascuno: et ha da un lato la scala segnata B. per la quale si passa d'una camera C. ne i capi d'essa son dua finestre D. et E. il netto di questa è piedi XII. in larghezza: e XVIII in longhezza: hauendo nella grossezza del muro la posta del letto. F. et allincontro il fuoco, per la quale si va d'uncamerino. G. è questo si troua alli quatro angoli: nel mezo si troua una gran sala di otto faccie: et piedi L. da quatro lati ha quatro entrate dalli altri quatro sono nicchi ornati di colonne: questo è quanto alla pianta da basso, Salito le limache B. si troua un terrazzo A. loquale copre tutto ledificio eccetto la sala, è per accompagnare le quatro limache vi sarano quatro camerini per ritirarsi è dal Sole: è dalla pioggia è questo terrazzo haueua li parapetti intorno, li quatro lochi I. son li camini sopra questo terrazzo nasceua la tribuna in cima della quale sara una lanterna per dar luce a essa tribuna: ben che vi sono in ogni faccia una finestra come meglio si vedeua nel dritto .

Casa per la persona
di vn Re fuori della citta
di forma inusitata

A

B

I

H

A

B

C

D

E

F

G

36

XXXVI

L'edificio che qui [sopra] si uede rappresenta tutta la massa della pianta che qui adietro s'è dimostrate e disegna, li tre membri che sono qua disopra .A.B.C. dinotano le parti interiore del edificio, e prima parlando de la parte difuori la quale e dorica: anchora che la porta sia rustica, La latitudine di tutta la faccia sara piedi LXXX. l'intercolumnio di mezzo doue è la porta è piedi xi in larghezza: li altri quatro son piedi x. e mezzo, la fronte de i pilastri che son piani sara tre piedi ciascuno, fra li dua pilastri angolari uie un piede e mezzo: e cosi son distribuiti li ottanta piedi, tutto l'edificio sara leuato dal piano v. gradi, l'altezza de li pilastri con le basi e capitelli sara piedi XXIIII. l'archit-raue: fregio et la cornice sara piedi v. e mezzo, partito poi nel modo: che nel ordine dorico nelle regole ho insegnato; e cosi anchora le basi e capitelli et altri or-namenti il tutto si trouaua nel detto libro, l'appoggio dele finestre sara alto dal piano iii piedi e mezzo: ma dentro ui sara un grado: accio lo prospetto sia commodo, la latitudine delle finestre sara piedi v. er in altezza x. le sopra finestre che seruirano alli mezzadi sarano altre piedi, tutte le finestre angolari non seruirano per lumi: ma si farano li suoi ornamenti per seguir l'ordine, nel mezzo del fregio uera a essere il liuello del terrazzo il quale si fara pendente alquanto accio meglio si scolino le acque, sopra questo terrazzo si leuara la tribuna, la quale si porra fare: e di pietra, e di legnami, sopra la quale si posara la lanterna: l'altezza dele colonne sara piedi x. l'archit-raue fregio e cornice sia fatta piedi iii. la cuppola di mezzo circolo le tribu-nette sopra il terrazzo: che son viii: quatro sarai le limache: et altre quatro saran camerini per ritirarssi dal sole: e dalla pioggia, li obelischi uoti nella cima: che saran quatro seruirano per li camini: et ogni lato della tribuna hauera una finestra per dar luce alla sala, La parte qua disopra .A. dinota un di quei lati che hano el nicchio: che son quatro, la sua larghezza è piedi vii. er in altezza piedi xiiii, l'altezza delle colonne che uolgon su la cornice che gira intorno sara piedi xx. la sua grossezza piedi ii. l'archit-raue: fregio: e cornice sara altro piedi iiii. sopra la quale si uoltaua la tribuna nel modo che si uede hauendo una finestra nella parte di mezzo, l'altra parte .B. ha il medesimo ordine: et misure: ma e forrato per che troua il vestibulo: et dessi concentara di due entrate alli uestibuli dalli lati si farai finestre ossia a cosi bene, la parte di mezzo .C. dimostra come sarai a mezzare le camere er le sue poste de i letti come ben chiaramente si comprende, ne e da du-bitar punto di quei lumi che uengono per angoli per li quali prende la luce quei camerini: et anchor le limache per che io ho per esperiencia: che reuscisseno benissimo: e se altre misure sarai rimaste entro la penna: li piedi picoli suppliraño al tutto.

parte di den
tro della cam
era disopra

parte di den
tro della ca:
mera da bas
so

C

parte interiore
della sala

parte interiore della
sala

A

B

parte di fuori della passata pianta

37

XXXVII

Il presente edificio quantunque egli non sia molto grande non dimeno alle commodita: et anche al decoro
de la persona di vn RE: con la sua banda piu grata: non si sdegnaria habitarui dvento, per alcuni giorni: e pero
jo lo voglio mettere nel numero delle habitationi Regali, presuponendo che intorno di esso vi siano diuersi
loggiamenti, si per gli uffici: come per altri principi e gentilhuomini, essendo questo di quadrato per fero:
per ciascun lato sara C v piedi, li cantonali che fan mostra di torroni ciascun dessi e piedi xxx in
latitudine, la colonna tonda con le dua mezze piane. e piedi v. fra luna e laltra colonna e piedi xx nel
mezzo di questi sara vna loggia di tre archi laperutra di ciascuno sara piedi x. ciascun pilastro con la
colonna tonda sara piedi v. li dua mezzi pilastri col quarto della colonna saran piedi v. e cosi li c v
piedi saranno distribuiti, questo edificio sileuara dal piano lalezza del occhio commune: et simonta alla
loggia A. la sua latitudine sara piedi xvII. er in longhezza piedi xxxxv. questa ha da vn de capi
la scala publica B. entro la quale vi e vna lumaca segreta: la qual menera capo nella camera principale. e la scala
commune ritornara sopra la loggia: che sara terrazo, nel mezzo della casa sara vna sala C. la sua latitudine per
ogni lato sara piedi xxxxv. questa prendera la luce dalle quatro loggie, da vn lato sara la loggia D. dallaltro sara
la medesima D. de la forma della prima di questi si troua le camere E. di quadrato perfetto quanto son
larghe le loggie nel capo di vna si troua vna capella F. hauendo acanto vna lumaca segreta le dua loggie dalli
lati saran serrate da vn parapetto alto trepiedi er anche si porra serrare di versi tutti larchi ine per cio la luce
della sala sara impedita: e seruiranno per dua sale... passando fuori de la sala si troua vna altra loggia G: questa
sara quella come quella dauanti: e questo loco sara tutto cauato sotto: si per li vini: come per altri vffici chi vora)
la scala da basso mette capo alla porta C la quale va sul terrazzo sopra la loggia er e segnato A. da questo si
entra alla sala B. la sua larghezza e piedi vL. er in longhezza piedi LXVIII. di questa si troua da vno lato
vna camera C. la sua larghezza e piedi xx: et in longhezza piedi xxvII. da vn capo ha la capella D. lo suo diametro
d' piedi xx. da laltro capo vie vnacamera E. la sua larghezza e piedi xv. dritto la quale si troua lacamera F. questa
sara di quadrato perfero: er altro tanto vi si troua da laltro lato cio e G. H. I. tutta la parte da basso si porrano far
di pietra: ma la sala non e dauoltare ma quatro colonne nel mezzo con li suoi piedestalli sotto per piu gracilita
fra: hauendo li traui armati sopra li quali sosternerano il suolo, la parte disopra non sara voltata ma tutta
legnami e sopra il tutto la sala hauera grossi traui armati: come san fare li fabri legnaui e massimamente
quei di franza

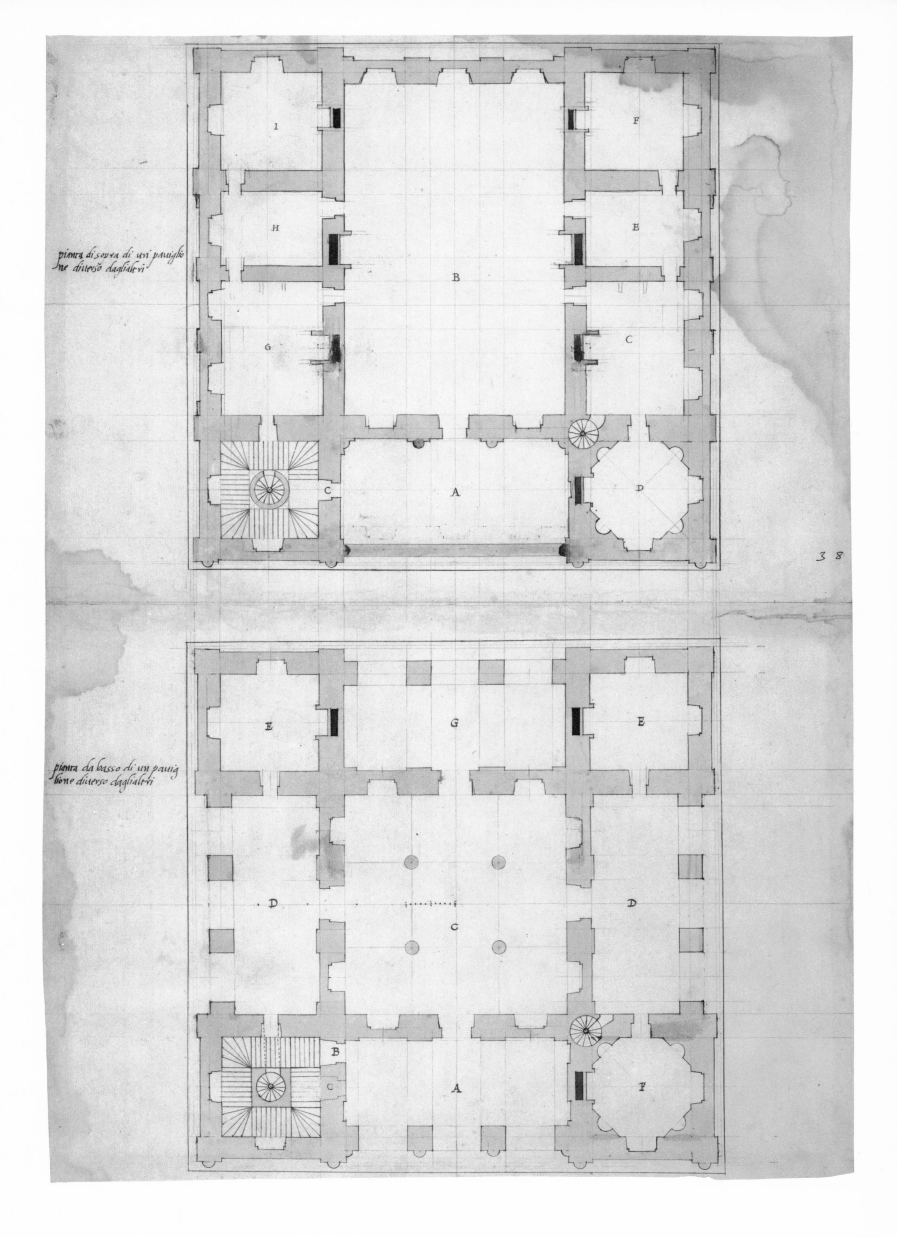

pianta di sopra di un paviglio
ne diverso dagliahri

pianta da basso di un pauig
lione diuerso dagliahri

38

XXXVIII

De la pianta passata questi sono li suoi diritti, ma parliamo di quel piu abasso il quale ce rappresenta la fac:
cia dauanti: delle larghezze e grossezze s'è detto nella pianta, hora parliamo delle altezze, tutto l'edificio
è leuato da terra IIII piedi e mezzo, l'altezza delle colonne con basi e capitelli è piedi XXII et cosi sara alta la
loggia: la sala e tutte le camere ma li membri piu picoli si amezzarano: facendo anchora qualchi suoli morti
chi non uora tanta altezza, l'archtraue: fregio e cornice sara piedi VIII in altezza l'altezza della sala sara piedi
XXV, ma pel grande interuallo da muro a muro bisognaua traui di piu pezzi bene in chiauati et di bona altezza
a fin che possino sostenere il peso: le camere poi si porrai tutte amezzare a tanta altezza, e far de suoli
morti segondo acadera, le colonne di sopra sarai leuate dalla cornice un piede e mezzo per piu gracilità d'esse
colonne, e questa leuatione seruira de plinto, l'altezza sua con le basi e capitelli sara piedi XIX l'archtraue, fregio,
e cornice sara piedi III e mezzo, quanto alle finestre da basso: di mezzo et da alto, e molte altre cose ch'io
non dico le misure, si porra col compasso trouare il tutto: et poi nel quarto libro sempre si trouaua difusa:
mente ogni cosa, io non parlo delle gran commodità delle camere: et camerini li quali si farano dalle
ultime cornice in su per che son cose che facendo si trouà

l'opera rustica che si vede qua sopra dinota la parte di drieto: et anche seruira per li lati, et le medesime
misure che sono nel opera dauanti: sono anchora in questa, cio è le aperture di gliarchi son piedi XX e
mezzo la grossezza de i pilastri V li dua mezzi pilastri altro V li dua torroni piedi XXX ciascuno
in larghezza li suoi pilastri V piedi di ciascuno, fra l'un pilastro al altro piedi XX e cosi e dispensato li
CV piedi delle altre misure come s'è detto tutte si trouauano e sopra l'ultima cornice si fara
le lucarne ma di opera piu soda per stare su questo ordine sodo. et anchora che questo edificio
sia fatto al costume di Franza porra pero seruire a diuersi paesi et segondo li siti et le commodità
delle acque et de fontane si porra fare nelle parti sotterranee molte cose e vtile, et diliziose come
saria conserue da acque stuo bagni grotte, e diuerse altre cose che facendo si vano trouando, come
puo far bontestimonio il bel palazzo imperiale fuor di pesaro mezzo miglio fatto la maggior parte
da girolamo genga ad instantia del Duca di Vrbino questi anni poco a dietro.

Parte didrieto della passata pianta :

Parte dauanti della passata pianta :

39

parte dauanti delpalla   ccio

XXXIX

li Re cristiani frequentano molto ~~alu...~~ il culto diuino: è massimamente il gran Re francesco: del quale jo
intendo sempre di parlare: si per esser il primo Re de' cristiani: si per esser mio hunico signore: et sostenta-
tore non solamente di me: ma di qualunque si fatica nelle belle arti liberale rimuneratore, jo disporò
adonca una habitatione regale per la villa nel mezzo della quale ui sara un cortile incrociato da loggie doue
che nel mezzo de la croce ui sara un tempio da celebrare i diuini uficij talmente disposto: che da tutte le parti
di esso loggiamento ui si potra andare; et non solamente andarui ma da ogni sala: camera: camerino: o altro loco
si potra vedere dentro da esso tempio, ma prima che uegnamo a questo cominciero al entrare della prima corti
primieramente allentrar della porta si troua un vestibulo.A. la sua larghezza e piedi.XVIII. et in longhezza ~~XVIII~~ dal lato destro et sinistro
vi si aueno dua camere.B. larga piedi.XVIII. e longa XXII diste le quali ui sara loco pei necessari et altri seruitij e questi sauano per le guardie; dipoi
si entra alla corte la quale ha intorno loggiamenti per ufficiali e da basso: et da alto: come si puo comprendere senza ch'io ui stia chi intorno
a questo. la latitudine di questo cortile sara piedi. LVII. et in longitudine piedi. CXIII. et chel uota di quadrato perfetto: si potra fare
passando la corte si troua un vestibulo.D. la sua larghezza e piedi.XVIII. e longo XXV. questo hauera dalli lati dua camere.E. per lo
guardie della porta. sopra questo vestibulo sara una sala prendendo le dua camere.E. la sua longhezza sara piedi.L. tornando da basso:
ou'è da ogni lato una riuata di camere la misura sua si prouara coi piedi nella coua, passando piu oltra, si troua le gallerie.R. le quali
facendo una croce formano nel mezzo di esse un tempio ottogono di otto pilastri tutto aperto col suo altare nel mezzo è piedi XXXIII.
questo e circondato da anditi: li quali anchora uan circuendo tutto il cortile afin che da tutti li lati si passi uenire al tempio e uengono a
formare quatro cortili.H. di forma ottogona: il diametro di ciascuno e piedi. LXXX. ma e pero un cortile solo quanto al aere
perciò che le loggie son tutte aperte e disopra sarai terrazzi: ma le ambulationi intorno il cortile: per la commodita del secondo suolo si potran fare galerie sopra galeria: et il terrazzo di sopra: per poter gire alle camere appartamente accio non siano senza una delle tre, quei dua triangoli
.G. sono per pilastri accio si possi commodemente uoltare li uolti da basso, questo cortile e circondato da loggiamenti: et alli quatro angoli
ui son le scale publiche et anche delle piuate: si per montar e descendere come anche per alcuni mezzati che ui sarano nei lochi picoli:
le dua forme di otto faccie dalli lati segnate.I. sarai sale di quella ~~forma~~ maniera: l'altra segnata.K. da basso sera vestibulo: et
da alto sara sala: e questo edifitio sara circondato da giardini: et da acque sel loco lo comporta: e sara leuato da terra piedi.
si per exaltarlo: come anchora per cauarlo sotto: al meno sotto le habitationi: e cosi tutto il reuerso delli fondamenti si mettera nel
cortile per alciarlo sparagnando la spesa: che non saria picola nel portar uia tanto terreno: e di molte misure ch'io passo tutte col
compasso si prouarano seruendosi delli piedi che ui son segnati

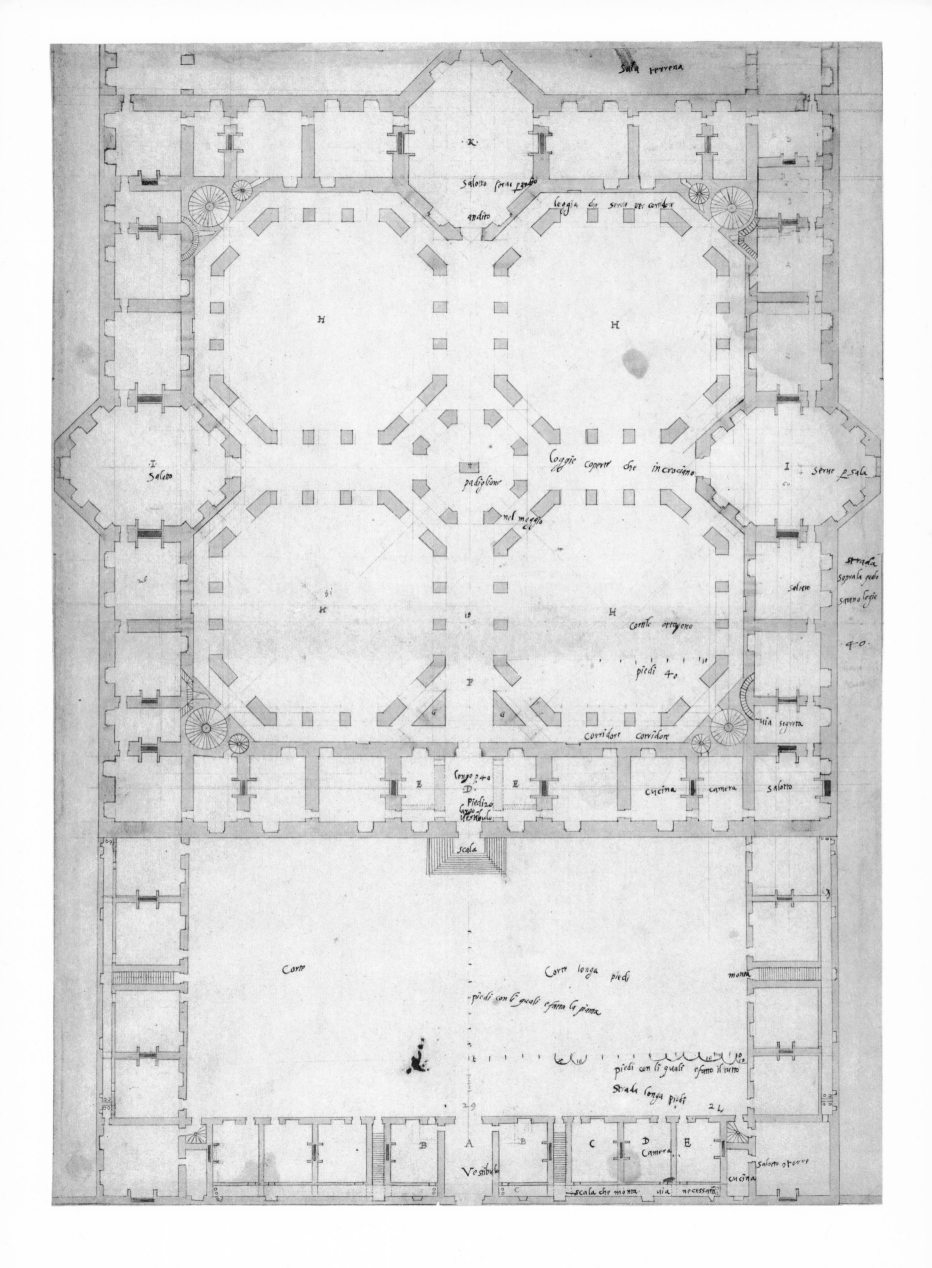

Sala terrena

Salotto serue p andito

andito

loggia che serue per corridor

K

H   H

Loggie coperti che incrociano

padiglione

I Salotto   I serue p sala

nel meggio   60

Cortile ottagono   strada
                                           sopra la pedi
Salotto   sanno loggie

H   19   H   40

piedi 40

F

G   G   uia segreta

Corridori corridore

longo p 40   Cucina camera Salotto
D   E
E   Piedi 20
Gymo o
Uestibulo

scala

Corte   Corte longa piedi   monta

piedi con li quali e fatta la pianta

piedi con li quali esento il tutto

Strada longa piedi

29   21

B   A   B   C   D   E

Vestibulo   Camera

scala che monta uia necessari   Salotto o torre

cucina

XL

La presente figura qua sopra segnata . A . Rappresenta la parte interiore che è nella entrata della corte dauanti la gran casa: et il medesimo ordine hauerano li dua lati di essa corte; è ben che nella pianta questa corte non sia di quadrato perfeto: non dimeno si procura fare tenendo tutti li tre lati di una medesima grandezza, e per che questi primi cortili si dicono in franza bassa corte: glie ben ragione che queste habitationi siano piu basse della principale: et reggia maggione, Queste sauano solamente leuate un piede dal piano della corte, l'altezza delle stanze terrene sara piedi XV. quelle disopra che venggono a essere nel tetto sauano di quella altezza che portarano li armamenti di esso tetto; Ma la entrata et li angoli sauano leuati sopra questi tetti come appare nella figura, l'altezza delle seconde stanze . E . sara piedi XIIII. l'altezza delle terze stanze D sara piedi XII. anchora la parte . C . porra seruire a qualche commodita, e questa parte anchora che sia piu bassa dell'altra non di meno essa piglia qualche concordanza nell'altra: come si vede scontrare le lettere . C . D . E . F . Questa parte maggiore segnata . B . dinota la faccia: et le altezze della casa reggia, la quale sara leuata dalla bassa corte piedi . V . e sara in qualche parte cauato sotto: si per la sanitra delle stanze: come per le cantine et altre commodita sotterranee, l'altezza delle prime habitationi sara piedi XX. et similmente le seconde sauano della medesima altezza: a tento che le prime in questa parte di fuori rappresentarano di maggiore altezza per la leuatione delli . v . piedi, l'altezza adonca delle terze habitationi sara piedi . XVIII e cosi li ordini verano a diminuire l'un sopra l'altro: come ne insegna natura in molte cose, li quali tre ordini di colonne son questi, il primo e dorico il secondo jonico: il terzo corinthio: et alli dua angoli vi è l'ordine composito che è il quarto; de i quali ordini in questo cosi picolo dissegno non e posso dare le particulare misure: et in scrittura jo sarei troppo longo in questa parte: ma nelle regole generali al quarto libro il tutto si ritroua, Questo compartimento de finestre parera forsi ad alcuno chegli discreti: ma si deue considerare alla commodita delle habitationi di dentro: et che le finestre seruino a quei bisogni che altre volte jo ho detto, e non dimeno in questa facciata si vedera armonia la quale sara discordia concordante: ma si questa sara oltra le colonne et altri ornamenti: ornata de piture Come in essa si vede que sei belli campi: sugeto apunto da dipingere li gesti di i passati et del presente Re: essa dimostrara gran bellezza: et richezza insieme

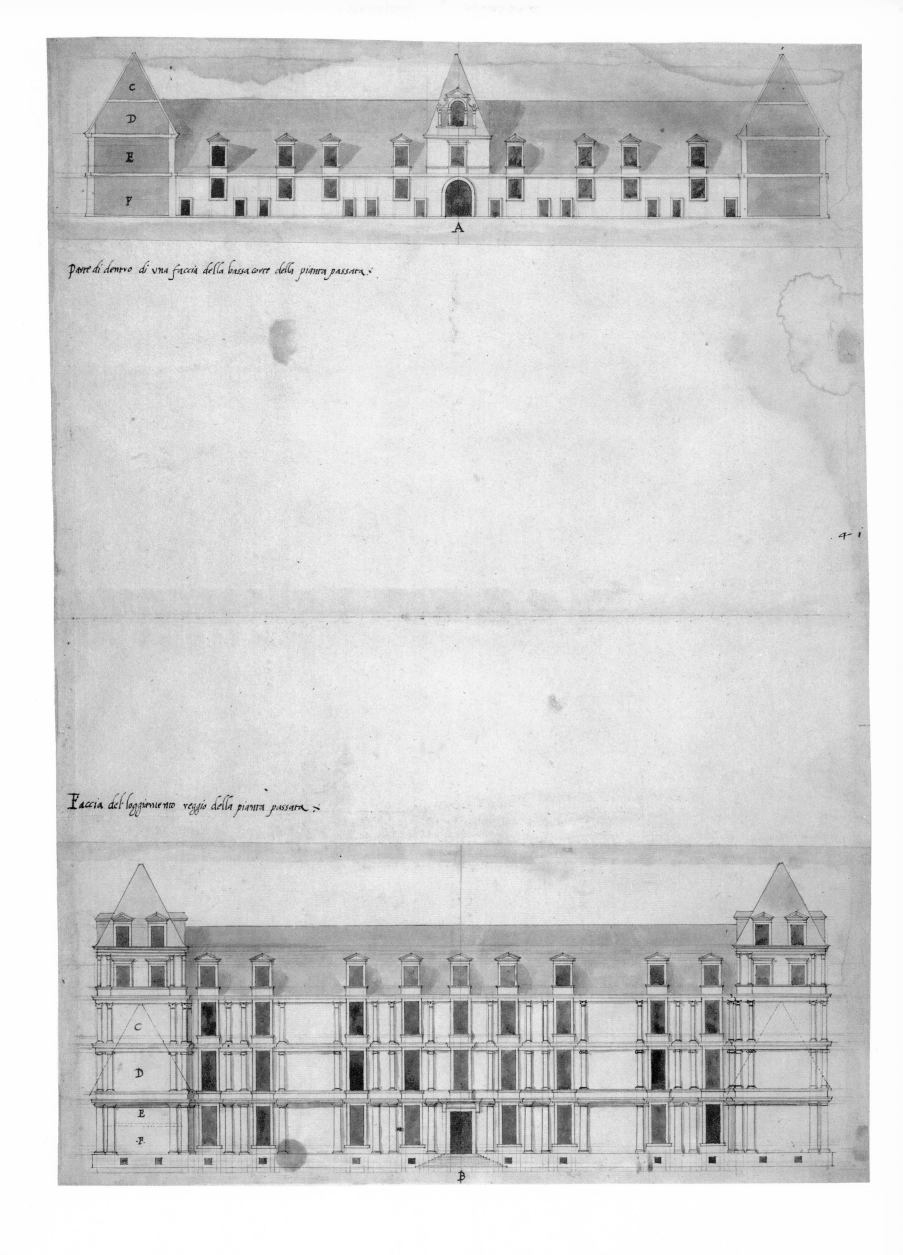

Parte di dentro di una faccia della bassa corte della pianta passata:

Faccia del loggiamento reggio della pianta passata:

XLI

Per che nella pianta qui adietro non ho potuto ben dimostrare la forma del tempio chi è nel mezzo del cortile su la crociera delle loggie: per esser cosa picola: hora nella presente carta qui auanti se dimostra in pianta: et in diritto, primieramente parliamo della pianta di esso tempio il diametro del quale sara piedi XXXIII. la grossezza de j pilastri è piedi V e mezzo. nella parte di dentro le dua faccie son piedi IIII e mezzo: et nella parte di fuori le dua faccie ~~~~~~~~~~ fra j pilastri son piedi XVIII. la grossezza ~~~~~~~~~~~~~~~~~~~~~~ delle loggie sara piedi XVIII. la grossezza de j pilastri ~~~~~~~~~~~~ misure se intende da basso. ma disopra perche sara terrazzo doue che vn parapetto di vn piede e mezzo bastara; di maniera, che il terrazzo sopra esse loggie sara largo piedi XXV. et li andii jntorno al tempio et anche quelli jntorno al cortile sarai larghi piedi X. e questa pianta serue per la parte da basso: et per quella da alto j et chi vora far tempio la parte da basso: si pora fare et questa seruira per le habitationi da basso: et il tempio disopra seruira per quella d altro j e questa pianta e segnata A B. la parte di mezzo qua sopra segnata B. dinota la parte interiore del tempio, l altezza degli archi e piedi XX. l architraue: fregio: et cornice sopra li archi à l altezza sua e piedi quatro: et e tutta opera dorica, dalla cornice fin sotto la lanterna della tribuna e piedi XVI. e mezzo, l altezza delle colonne della lanterna e piedi IX. et sono corinthie: la sua grossezza e piede I. il diametro di essa lanterna e piedi VII. l architraue freggio et cornice sara la quinta parte dell altezza de le colonne la tribunetta sara di mezzo circolo. questa parte A. dinota come si pora serrare il detto tempio ~~~~~~~~ dalli mali tempi: ma tutto pero di vetri transparenti j et sara opera corinthia, come si vede, questa parte rustica segnata C. rappresenta li archi delle loggie da basso: la lar: ghezza degli archi e piedi X. la sua altezza e piedi XX. la parte disopra dinota come si faraiu quelle loggie sopra loggie jntorno il cortile: per poter gire alle habitationi appartatamente e non far esse stanze seruir l una dell altra: et anchi chi non vora questa opera cosi soda: pora di colonne ronde: e quadre anchora compartite dua per pilastro: et vna sopra l archo roue j sopra vn architraue fregio et cornice col suo terrazzo il qual terrazzo sara à liuello del suolo secondo: sopra la qual cornice si faraiu parapeti di ferro, la parte di fuori di questo tempio si fara come la figura A. è quella di dentro si fara come quella di mezzo segnata B. è se qualche misure mancherano con li piedi picoli si trouara il tutto

Parti di dentro della pianta passata

'A'　　　　　　　　　'B'　　　　　　　　　'C'

'B'

'C'

'A'

XLII

Gliedificij alla campagna fuori delle citta è massimamente quei de gran' personagi ueglioni esser sepparati da cia
scuno altro edisicio et hauer bella apparenza, è però questa habitation Regale hauera forma assai diuersa
dalle altre la quale sara nel mezzo di una gran piazza circondata da loggiamenti: si per alcuni principi: come
per molti officiali et familiari del Re questa gran corte hauera tre entrate: e parlando della principale prima si troua
un vestibulo A la sua larghezza e piedi XIIII: et in longhezza XXIII enrrando dentro ha dalli lati un salotto B la sua larghez
za e piedi XXIIII et in longhezza XXVIII hauendo al suo seruitio una camera C di piedi XV larga: e XVII longa e questa sara mer
zada, et altro tanto sara disopra, e cosi vison dellaltre camere con le sue necessarie commodita, il modo di montare alle camere
di sopra: che son quatro: si vede alla scala D la quale mette capo al riposo E et afin che la scala sia piu agiata si montra V gradi da
agni lato e trouasi li andii per li quali sentra alle camere incapo de iquali vi sono li necessarij e cosi è da basso anchora, nelli quatro
angoli vie un salotto quadrato di piedi XXVII hauendo il suo seruitio una camera di piedi XV larga: et in longhezza XVII et sara a
mezzada, e similmente le altre habitationi vano per tal ordine le quali hano uno andito, leuato dalla corte un grado questa e segnata
F et e larga piedi XXXXV, da questa si mantra a una planicia sei piedi alta segnata G hauendo intorno li suoi parapetti
dipoi si troua una loggia H alli capi della quale son le scale per montare alli terrazzi: la larghezza di questa è piedi XII
et in longhezza piedi CX da questa si troua il vestibulo I la sua larghezza e piedi XIII e mezzo XXVIII dipoi si troua una
sala K di forma ottogona, il suo diametro è piedi XL hauendo alli quatro angole le scale per montare a tutti li lochi,
questa sala parebbe tenebrosa se la pianta superiore non si vedesse di questa si troua un salotto L la sua larghezza e
piedi XXVII et in longhezza XL hauendo da li lati una camera M di quadratura perfetra: quanto e largo il salotto, drieto
la quale si troua una camera N la sua larghezza e piedi XIII et in longhezza XXV, e questa sara amezzada: et diral-
maniera son tutte le quatro parti, e questo è quanto alla pianta terrena,
La pianta di sopra si vede qua disopra appartamente doue sopra le loggie son terrazzi e sopra le scale son quatro tribu:
mente, et cosi sopra il vestibulo I et le due camere N vi è terrazzo discoperto, e questo e per dar luce alla
sala ottogona la quale prende la luce da altro per le sei finestre per ciò che l'alteza di questa sala perderia l'altezza di dua salotti cioe se li salotti sarano alti piedi XX questa sara alta piedi XL e tanto di piu: quanto e grosso
il suolo come meglio si vedera nelli suoi diritti nella seguente carta, e questo edificio per esser leuato tanto da
terra si porra cauar sotto una gran parte, doue molte commodita si trouerano e questo deue bastare quanto alla
pianta: e di sotto et di sopra

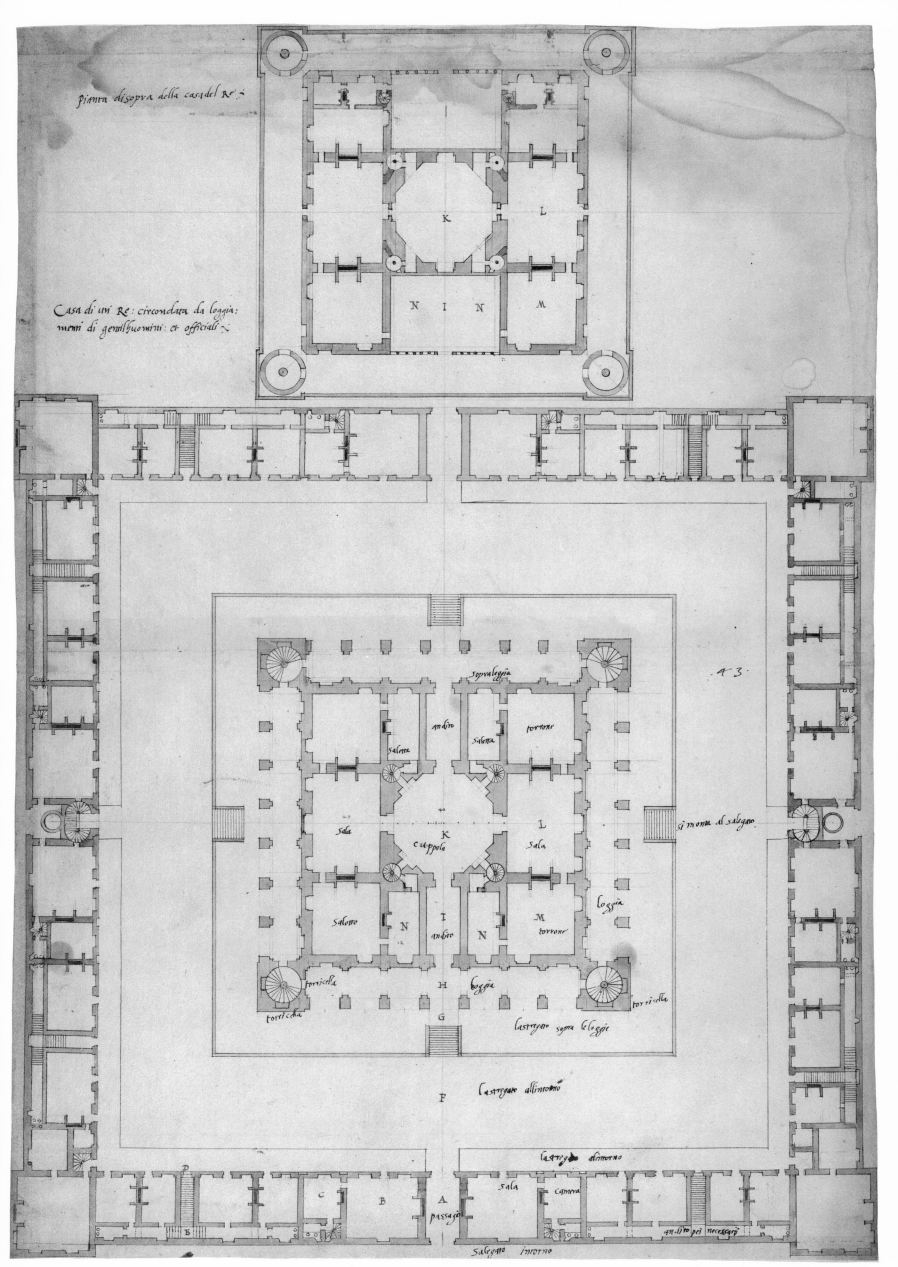

Pianta disopra della casa del Re.

Casa di un Re: circondata da loggia:
meni di gentilhuomini: et officiali.

.43.

sopra loggia

andito   Saletta   torrone

Saletta

sala

L
Sala

si monta al salegato

K
cuppola

loggia

Salotto   N   I   N   M
andito   torrone

torricella   torricella
H   loggia
torricella   torricella
G   lastregato sopra le loggie

F   lastregato allintorno

lastregato dintorno

D   sala   camera
C   B   A
passagio   andito pei necessarij

Salegato intorno

XLIII

De la pianta passata fatta per la magione Reggia questi sono li divisi, e primieramente parlaremo della parte inueriore laqualetumolto importa la forma della quale è qua disopra, doue si vede l'officio che fano le limache; si uede le altezze delle camere; e de i salotti; e come la sala da basso prende dua altezze e quella da alto ne prende tre che la sala da basso non habbia bona luce; non è da dubitare; quella di sopra è cosa certa che sara luddissima. l'altezza de la prima sara piedi XXXXIII per che il riempimento delli suoli delle camere la tezza delle quali una su l'altra e piedi XL; sara tre piedi almeno, questa prima sala non sara voltata accio receua maggior lume; ma di grossi traui armati di bona altezza per coxelle si porra fare il suolo; come si vede nel dissegno, la sala supperiore si uoltara; ma di legnami coperta poi di piombo; che non haueua arduosa l'altezza della quale sara piedi L senza la lanterna e tutta la lanterna sara piedi XX in altezza sopra la tribuna di maniera che tutto l'edificio sara in altezza sopra terra piedi CC XXV.

Questa parte che è nel mezzo rappresenta uno dei quatro lati de la parte inueriore della bassa corte; che cosi di qua si dice l'altezza delle habitationi terrene sara piedi X; ma quelle sarai levate un piede dalla corte quelle disopra; sara piedi XLIII in altezza, ma li quatro pauiglioni angolari per la sua magnitudine saranno piu alti; la prima altezza sara piedi XVIII la sego da piedi XVI; la terza piedi XII; di poi il galattas; e le medesime altezze hauerano le tre entrate nelli quali locchi potra a loggiare ogni honesto personaggio hauendo da basso ad alto ——→

la figura qua di sotto dimostra uno delli quatro lati; ne parlaro piu delle altezze per hauerne detto di sopra; ma basti solamente il vedere la dimostratione di tutta la massa; per mezzo della quale si puo comprendere come la cosa reuscira vegendo di lontano quelle cinque altezze sepparate l'una dall'altra; oltra le quatro tribunette piu basse; di poi la bassa corte con otto pauiglioni cinta di casamenti intorno, le quali tutte cose potrebbe fare la grandezza del re francesco in breue tempo pure che gli cadesse in pensiero

Parte interiore della casa del Re sopra la pianta passata

Vna delle quatro faccie della bassa corte la qual circonda la casa del Re

Parte difuori della casa del Re sopra la pianta passata

XLIV

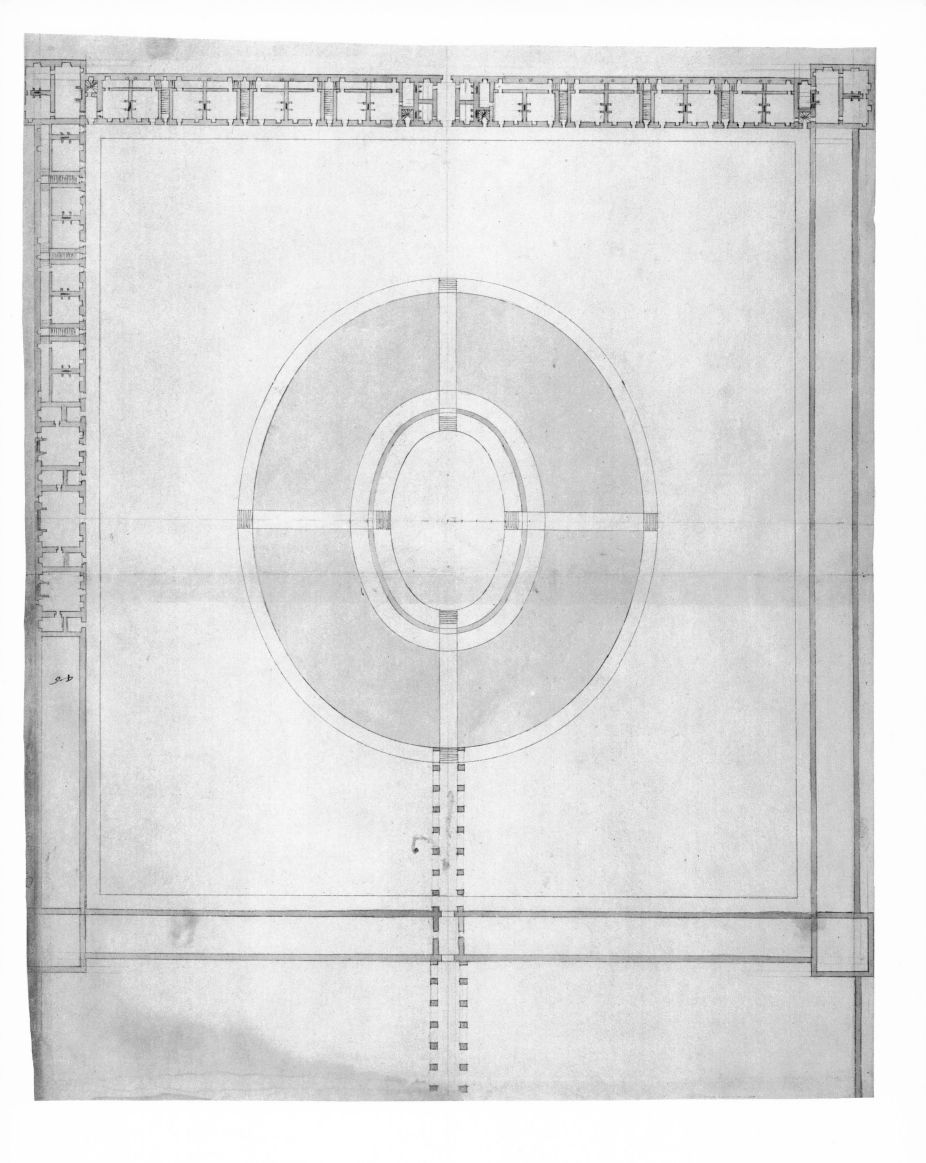

XLV

Li antiqui Romani fecero li amphitheatri per far giuochi publichi: triomphi e feste: ma tali edificij non erano habitati: eccetto forsi a qualchi guardiani per custodia del loco. Hora mi è caduto nel pensiero de disporre una habitationi reggia in forma di amphitheatro: come si dimostra nella presente pianta. Questo edificio primieramente sara leuato da terra piedi vi. e mezo: che sara la planicia A. la sua latitudine sara piedi xii. et hauera li suoi parapetti intorno per appoggiarsi nel entrare della porta si troua il vestibulo B. la sua latitudine è piedi xviii. et è in longhezza piedi xxx. questo ha da un lato una sala C. la sua larghezza e piedi xxxvi: et in longhezza piedi liiii. questa prende la luce maggiore nella parte di fuori et una luce menore dalla parte di dentro: ma è assai luminosa. dall'altro lato del vestibulo E. la sua larghezza e piedi xiiii. et in longhezza piedi xl. questo puo esser sepparato da uno antiporto: ma che la sua altezza non eccoda a piedi ix. però no impedire le luce che si scontrano. passando l'andito si troua una loggia F. la sua larghezza è piedi xii. et gira intorno la fronte delli pilastri e piedi v. et altrotanto per li fianchi. la apertura fra l'una pilastro al altro e piedi xi. fuori di essa loggia nella parte interiore vi è uno andito scoperto G. la sua larghezza e piedi x. questo ha li suoi podij a balaustri per appoggiarsi percio che tanto se descende quanto s'è salito et si troua un cortile H. di forma ouale: la sua latitudine e piedi lxxx. et in longitudine piedi cxii. in questo cortile si potrà fare di ogni sorte di feste e triomphi che da tutte le parti si potrà vedere et udire ogni cosa. io non descriuero: ne dato misura di tutti li appartamenti: che saria troppo longo: ma di alcuni membri principali fossi più difficili a capere io ne daro le misure: et il modo: come del tempio segnato I. lo diametro del quale sara piedi xxxvi. hauendo da quarto lati li nicchi: entro de quali vi sono li altari la larghezza di ciascuno e piedi x. dalli altri quatro lati vi sono capelle quadrate di piedi xii per lato. dua di queste recceueran la luce: una di fuori e l'altra di dentro: le altre dua seruiuano per anditi ad altre stanze: delle quali la misure si trouara con li piedi che sono nel mezzo del cortile. la sala K. con quella parte P. vengono a essere quanto alli lumi: et quanto alla vedura: tutto un membro: ma vi è quella sepparatione delle dua colonne: et le dua mezze le quali sostengono un palco: sopra del quale facendosi qualche festa in essa sala: li musici et altre persone vi staranno sopra: e cosi la sala uera a essere di perfeta quadratura: il suo diametro e piedi xxxvi: e cosi nella parte da basso fra le colonne sara sepparata da balaustri lassando di fuori la parte P. nel qual loco potran dimorare quelle persone alle quali non sara lecito entrare nella sala: e non di meno vederanno il tutto. la parte L. sara una capella di piedi xx. per quadro hauendo da dua lati li nicchi: la larghezza de quali sara piedi xv. la sala M. sara in latitudine piedi xxx. et in longitudine piedi l. passando questa si troua una anticamera N. la quale è di quadratura perfeta: il suo diametro e piedi xxv. ~~e dal sopra e sinistro lato del fuoco vi è le porte per dua lumi~~ hauendo da uno lato un camerino rotondo di piedi xiii per diametro il quale sara amezzato da l'altro lato vi è una scala del ~~medesimo diametro~~. la sua larghezza e piedi xxv. et in longhezza xxx. hauendo da un lato un camerino rotondo di piedi xiii per diametro dall'altro lato vi è una scala del medesimo diametro per la quale si passa alla camera O. questa è per tutti li lati piedi xxx. e fuori di questo quadro dalli dua lati del fuoco vi e la porta di dua lumi: larga piedi vii. queste saranno come dua archi uoltati a botte. da questa si va alla retrocamera P. la sua larghezza e piedi xx. et in longhezza xxviii. et ha nel mezzo la porta di un letro sepparato la quale e larga piedi x. hauendo dalli lati dua nichi per ornamento. et ha una uscita nel uestibulo per fianco hauendo al suo seruitio un camerino di forma ouale il quale sara amezzado. de l'altre misure che per breuita le passo tutte si trouerano come ho detto con li piedi. e questo basti quanto alla pianta.

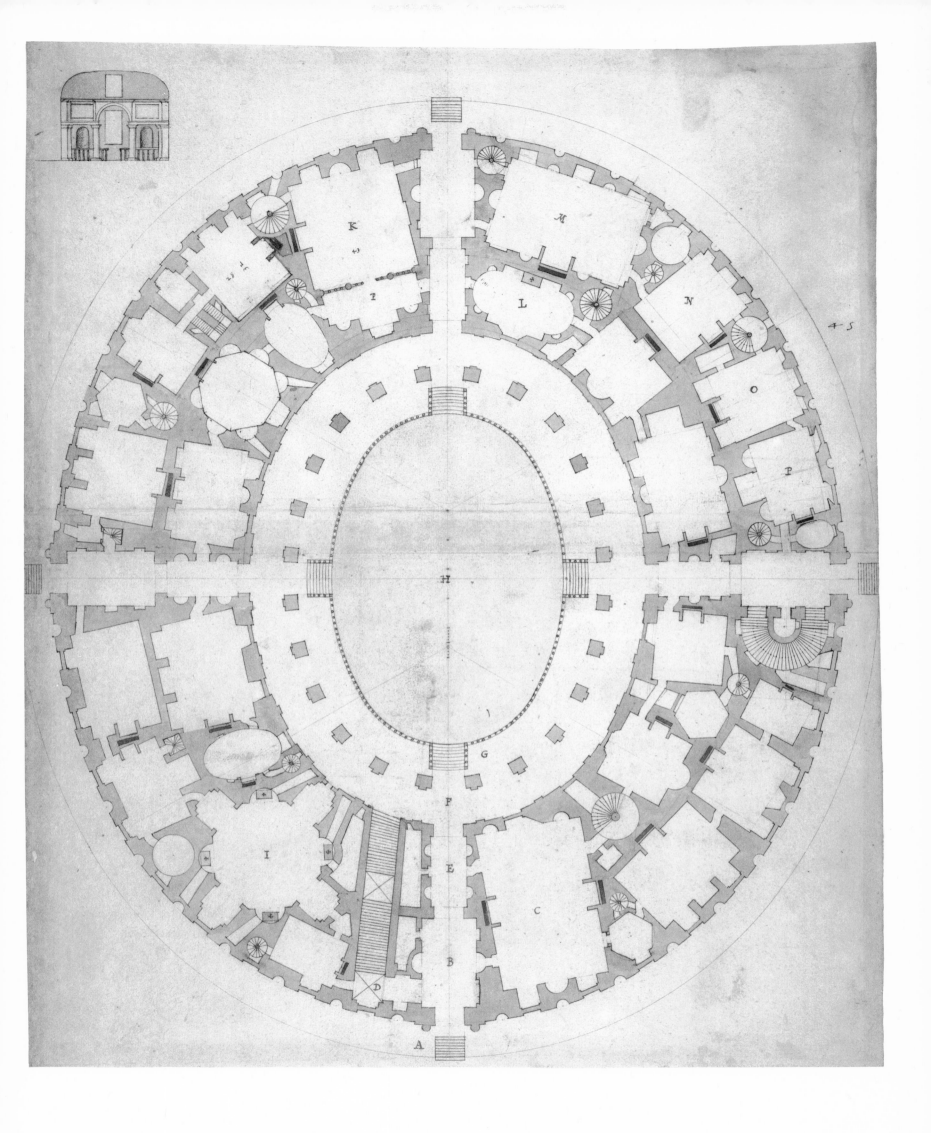

XLVI

La presente loggia qua di sopra segnata .A. dinota quella che circonda il cortile quale ma acio sia meglio intesa: che non
sara quella in forma picola: io lo transportata in forma maggiore: la fronte de ipilastri è piedi .V. la larghezza
degliarchi è piedi .XI. la sua altezza e piedi .XXV. ma laltezza di dentro e piedi .XXVII. laltezza delli basi è reguarti
di piede laltezza de icapitelli .Vn piede è mezzo: la latitudine delle finestre è piedi .VI. et in altezza son piedi .XII. e mezzo,
la cornice delle quali si accordara con li capitelli, le forme quali sopra esse serviranno ad alcuni mezzadi er nelle stanze grande
darano maggior luce; le finestre da basso darai luce alle stanze sotterranee,

la parte .B. rappresenta tutta la parte di fuori de le edificio la quale quanto alle luccarne per più ornamento del tetto ho fatta
alla francese: ma il tetto per non fare tenebroso il cortile di dentro io lho tenuto basso; tutte le finestre vano ornate: come
quelle acanto alla porta da basso ad alto, ma tutte non le ho ornate per non confondere le parti che scovriano, di quei nicchi che
sono fra le finestre: alcuni servirano per lumi segondo che acadeva nelle parti interiori; laltezza del primo piano sara piedi IIII è
mezzo laltezza della prima fascia sara piedi .XXX. dalla prima fascia fin sotto la segonda cornice sara altro tanto: ma laltez
za del primo piano: et larchitrave che sen trapone sotto la cornice fa parere lordine primo maggiore del segondo; dalla prima cor
nice: fin sotto lultimo architrave vie piedi .XX. di maniera che li tre ordini vano diminuendo come è il doveo segondo li
precetti del mastro degliarchitetti lucio vitruvio; le altezze delle finestre: et altri membri si potrai trovare con li piedi: et
poi quanto alle forme ricorrere al quarto libro alli suoi ordini segondo che accena le presente figura

la figura qui più dibasso segnata .C. dimostra la parte interiore del edificio, e primieramente le stanze sotterranee sarano
sopra terra piedi .V. e sotto terra piedi .VII. laltezza delle prime habitationi sara piedi .XXX. ma le minori savano a mezzade
e qualche vna delle picole se interzarano, laltezza delle segonde stanze sara piedi .XXX. medesima mente: er le menori
si amezzarano come si vede nel dissegno e prenderano la luce nel modo dimostrato nelle grossezze de imuri cosi di dentro
come di fuori: le terze habitationi sarano altri piedi .XVI. la parte .L. dinota la capella picola segnata L. nella pianta, la parte
.I. significa iltempio interiore che cosi è segnato nella pianta, laltezza del quale è piedi .L. e prende la luce da alto per trom
ba di fuori er di dentro: e cosi dabasso prende la luce di dentro è di fuori, alle quali luce, il prudente architetto gli trovava bo
modo, in questo cosi grande edificio vi sarano alcuni lochi tenebrosi, non dimeno tutti havevano vn poco di luce se:
gonda come si vede anchora in molti edifitij antiqui che di tani ve ne sono, ma chi sapra condure li lumi, e trasuer:
sali: e è diagonali tutti davano accommodata luce.

A

Parte difuori della passata pianta in forma di Amphitheatro

B

Parte interiore della passata pianta

.L.

A A

I

C

XLVII

Primieramente le habitationi de i piu poueri huomini sono ne borghi poco fuori delle città presso le porti, e questi sono artefici de diuerse arti basse, le quali habitationi: per quanto io ho ueduto in diuersi paesi sono strette di sito: ma assai longhe, per laqual cosa, io comincero àformare la casippola del piu pouero artefice dentro la città: et anche porra seruire pei borghi, questa non sara manco di piedi .x. in latitudine hauendo solamente nella parte dauanti una picola porta: et una fenestra, e questa prima stanza senza il loco del letto: sara in longhezza piedi xiiii. nel mezzo della quale sara il fuoco: lassanda dalli lati loco per una cassa o forciero, questa stanza pero sara longa .xx. piedi: ma vi sara una seppauatione di un pariete per il loco del letto: e cosi esso loco rimaua .vi. piedi. dalli piedi del letto sava un pariete lassandoui lo spacio per andar drieto al letto: e questa seppauatione fara un picolo andito, la stanza sara .A. et l'andito .B. et il letto .C. questa poca habitatione porria bastare à un pouero huomo: presuponendo che vi sia uno orticello: in capo del quale sava il necessario: et nella strada uno pozzo commune a molti vicini, e ben che quiui non sia cucina, ne cantina dico chel pouero huomo di cosi basso grado viue alla giornata: et si accomoda tutte le sue massaritie in un loco solo, ma se sel sava piu accommodato: er di maggior famiglia: si porra bene aggiungerui un'altra stanza di quadrato perfero: che sava .D. la qdale seruira per cucina: e per cantina anchora: et uisi porra fare uno letto prendendo la luce dal orto segnato .E. et di queste tal habitationi sava necessario d'farui ... ua: per cio che un pozzo vicinale seruiua a dua et cosi il cammino dal fuoco una canna seruira à dua, e taluolta una persona d'nauosa neporra fare una quantita per affittarle: e queste case io le intendo a terre no: salendoui con una scala senza solaio, ma se per piu bellezza: et sanità vi sava uno suolo morto: questo porra seruire a molte cose: salendoui con una scala damano, l'altezza del tetto dauanti: et di drieto basterà di piedi .viii. l'esempio di questa si vede gui dauanti: in pianta: et indirito segnata .A.

In altro modo si porra fare una simile casippola: ma di larghezza piedi xii. et la camera sava quadrata facendoui il fuoco nel mezzo: et se liluochi dalli lati del fuoco fossero picoli: si porra fare dettastanza piu longa: e questa e segnata .A. il loco del letto e segnato .C. longo piedi .viii. et largo .v. accio uisi possi andare intorno. et andando piu oltra si fava una cameretta di piedi .viii. per quadro, la quale seruira per cucina: et per cantina: et per altre commodita, e cosi vi rimava uno andito di piedi .iiii. in larghezza segnato .B. et la camera .D. et il giardino sava .E. in capo del quale sava il necessario, il pozzo sava nella strada cummune à piu persone, et di queste pocole case: come ho detto del'altra, sene porra fare una quantitta: le quali io le intendo a terreno, l'esempio di questa si vede qua dauanti segnata .B.

Sava tal uolta piu nel corpo della città qualche sito doue e piu caro il terreno: doue uno ricco vova piu presto una entrata di picole case: che una casa grande per suo habitare, queste habitationi haueuano la strada da dua lati, una di queste case sava larga piedi .ix. la prima stanza per dormire sava longa piedi .xii. accio che mettendo il fuoco ... acio mettendo il fuoco à canto il letto vie dal fuoco al muro dauanti vi sia loco per un forciero, ma in questo modo il fuoco none nel mezzo: non dimeno egli e ben commodo, questa stanza e segnata .A. et il loco del letto .B. apresso vi sara una cameretta: longa piedi .ix. et larga .vi. et e segnata .C. la quale seruira per cucina: per cantina: e taluolta per dormire: questa prendeva la luce dal cortile .D. la larghezza del quale sava piedi .vi. di maniera che una corte: con un pozzo nel mezzo incro ciata da quatro pariete: seruiua à quatro case: et cosi una fossa da necessarii seruiua a quatro medesi mamente: di maniera che una quantitta di queste casippole sauano tutte commode: et luminose: et furi vicino noui vedera l'altro l'altezza delle quali sava circa à piedi .viii. per cio che io le intendo a terreno, ma che le vova a solaio fava una scala nella camera .C. la quale prendera il lume dal cortile, l'esempio di questa si vede qua dauanti in pianta: et in dirito segnata .C.

Si rrouaua taluolta un terreno non tanto grande: come il passato: ma esempiogratia circa a .xl. piedi in latitudine: et in longitudine circa .c.lviii. nel qual sito si porra fare dua dugine di casette basse a terreno, la latitudine di una sava piedi .xii. et in longhezza piedi .xviii. la prima stanza sava piedi .xii. per ciascuni lato et e segnata .A. li sei piedi sauano per il letto: e facendo un pariete à piedi del letto: fara uno picol loco .B. il quale seruiua per piu seruicii: et il letto sava .C. e drieto lo letto sava il necessario: e cosi in .xii. et xviii piedi sava habitatione di un pouero huomo, et una fossa da necessario seruiua per quatro case: et dua pozzi uno per ruga seruirano a tutti, l'altezza di queste case dauanti bastera di piedi .viii. ma il colmo di esse sava di bona altezza, doue nel mezzo si porra fave un suolo morto il quale seruira à molte cose: ma salirassi con una scala damano per non impedire li lochi, l'esempio di questa e gui dauanti segnata .D.

Quanto alle humile habitationi à terreno uoglio hauer detto à bastanza, hora di quelle un poco maggiori: et à solai comincerò à trattare, sava uno artefice al quanto piu accommodato: et di maggior famiglia: non dimeno il suo sito non sava che piedi .xii. fra lidua muri vicinali, e questa casa si habitarà anchora disopra e porra seruire a dua famiglie: che una non sava impedita dal'altra, si fara uno andito .A. largo piedi .iiii. e mezzo, et in longhezza .x. il loco per la scala con li pariete: che sauano di poca grossezza: sava piedi .iiii. tal che la larghezza di essa scala sava dua piedi e mezzo, il rimanente: che sava .C. sava di larghezza piedi .iiii. e mezzo, e questo sava un camerino: taluolta una picola botega: sel loco lo comportaua, per salire à d' alto si comincieva al entrare della porta: l'entrata del camerino sava dal altro capo della scala sotto il riposo di essa scala, passando piu la si rroua una salena per dormire longa piedi .xx. hauendo il foco nel mezzo del pariete: et lo letto a canto il foco et e segnata .B. oltra di questa si rroua una couericella .D. di quadrato perfero: et vi e uno portichetto per gire al coperto il quale disopra seruiua per andito alla parte di drieto, passando questo si rroua una cucina .E. di piedi .xii. per ogni lato: col suo camino: et il necessario: ma quello che e fuori seruira per la parte disopra, passando piu oltra si rroua il giardino segnato .F. il quale sava di quella longhezza: chel sito lo comportaua: hauendo questa casa à seruire à dua famiglie: accio non se impediscono l'uni l'altro: colui che habitara à terreno godera l'orto: et colui che haueva la parte disopra godera tutto il granaro: et se la casa sava cauata sotto: si porra bene accommo dare dua entrate apartate per che colui disopra: haueva il camerino dabasso .C. et non si cauando sotto: questa sava cantina alui et l'altro haueva sotto lascala per cantina: e ben che quello da basso habbia tutto l'orto: colui disopra ha poi il granaro: et la cameretta da basso, doue si porran fare una gran ruga di case, e ben che le case gui adietro dimostrano in appauenza alla jtaliana: non dimeno elle porrano seruire in tutti li paesi: l'altezza del primo suolo sava piedi .x. et quella del segondo sava .viii. come si vede nella pianta e nel dirito segnato .E.

Si porrà anchora fave una casa quasi simile alla passara al costume di franza, la latitudine della quale sava piedr xii. hauendo nel'entrare di essa la sua limaca: il diametro della quale sava piedi .vi. lassando un picol vestibulo .A. di piedi .v. e mezzo, passando questo si rroua una camera .B. la sua longhezza e piedi .xx. hauendo il suo camino: et il loco del letto: come l'altra, et andando piu la vi e una corniciella .D. col suo pozzo: et uno portichetto per gir coperto alla cucina .E. la quale e di quadrato perfeto col suo camino: et il necessario: et in questa casa porra albergare dua famiglie: per cio che quello che haueva la parte disopra: nel entrave della porta salira alla sua parte: et ben chegli non godera del giardino: non dimeno haueva poi il granare per sua commodita: et passando sopra il portico della corniciella: andava alla cucina, fuori della quale vi sava il necessario, quanto al tenere il vino la caua sava sotto terra: la quale si accommodava à tutte dua le parti apparatamente, et cosi al costume francese si porra fave una gran ruga di case: tutte concordate: con ordine, l'altezza del primo suolo sava piedi .ix. et il segondo piedi .viii. le quai case porano seruire a tutti li paesi: seruendosi di quegli ornamenti che nei paesi si costumano: l'esempio di questa si vede qua dauanti in pianta: et in dirito segnata .F.

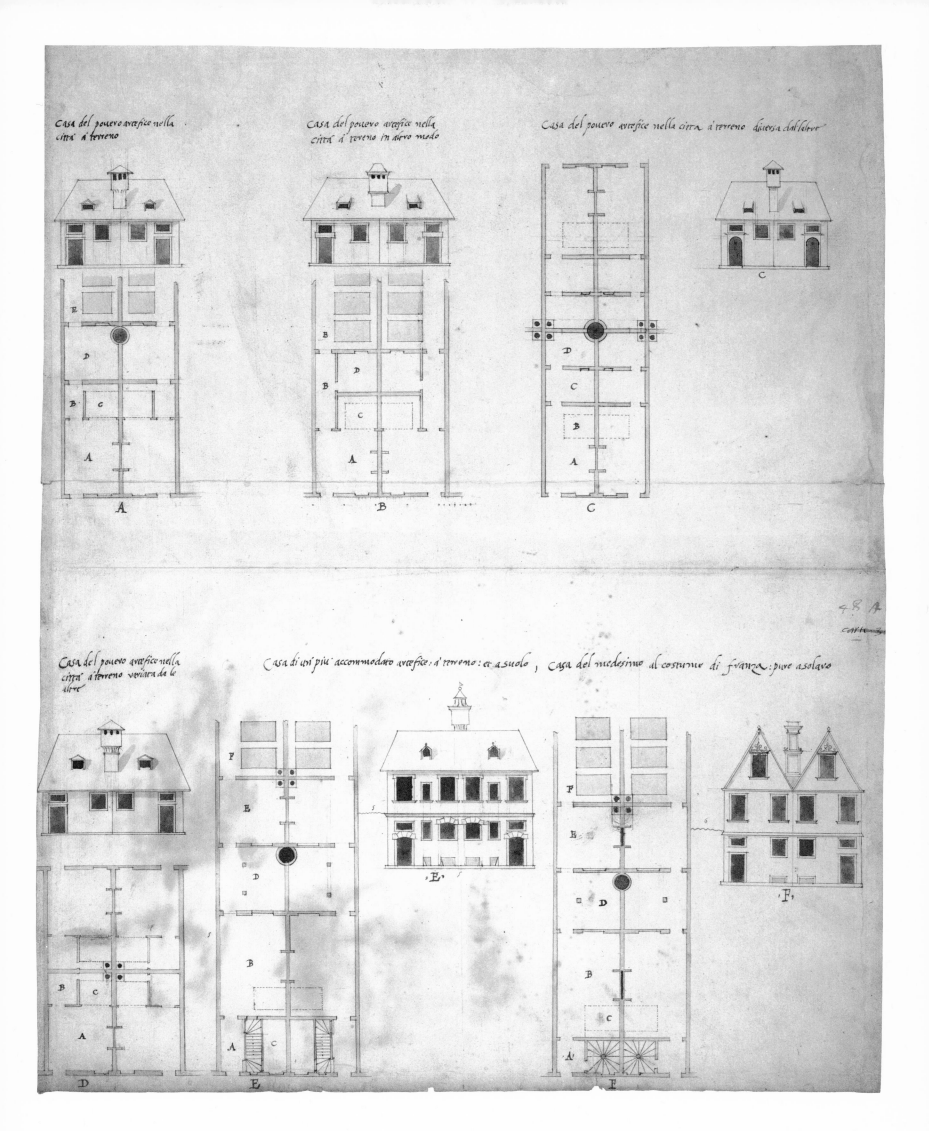

Casa del pouevo artefice nella
città à terreno

Casa del pouevo artefice nella
città à terreno in altro modo

Casa del pouevo artefice nella citrà à terreno diuersa dal libro

Casa del pouevo artefice nella
città à terreno variata da le
altre

Casa di un più accommodato artefice: à terreno: et a suolo,   Casa del medesimo al costume di franza: pure asolauo

XLVIII

In alcune città de italia sono de molti portichi: et massimamente in Bologna: et in padova: li quai portichi prestano grande
commodità, primieramente doue è l'aere sottile e penetrativo glihuomini si conseruano meglio, secondariamente per la pioggia
et per il sole questa è gran commodità: et apresso che le case guadagnano tanto di spacio sopra la strada: quanto è largo
il portico, et le habitationi son piu sane: perciò che doue batte la pioggia, conuiene che quelle muraglie tengano de l'humidità:
ben che alcuni diuano che quei lochi che prendon la luce sotto li portici non sono molto lucidi: et io gli rispondo che sono asuf-
ficientia: et piu sani deglialtri, hora senza piu disputare segnamo à questa casa la quale non sarà piu larga di piedi XVI
fra li dua muri vicinali: et la latitudine del portico sarà piedi VIII. et è segnato A. l'andito sarà largo piedi IIII. et è segnato B.
à lato di questo sarà una camera. C. la sua longhezza è piedi XVII. et in larghezza piedi X. et lassandoui la posta del letto
si metterà il camino nel mezzo: et lo letto è D. andando pel medesimo andito si troua una scala, di larghezza di piedi II. è mezzo,
à lato laquale vi è una camera. E. alla quale si va pel riposo della scala: è questa prende la luce dalla corte. F. la quale è per
un lato piedi XV. è per l'altro XII. et in questa sarà il pozzo. et un portico per girir coperto alla cucina. G. della medesima grandezza
del cortile: et in questa vi è il fuoco: et il necessario, il quale seruirà alla parte disopra anchora. di questa si va nel
orto. H. il quale sarà ò longo: et corto segondo il loco, questa parte dabasso godeua tutto il giardino: ma quella disopra hauerà
tutto il sopra portico: et anche il granaro: la cantina sarà commua: ma vi sarà ben modo di seppararla, l'altezza del primo solaro
sarà piedi IX: et cosi quello disopra oltra il granaro: et di queste case conuiin farne almen dui: le quali hauendo cinque colonne
la porta non può venire nel mezzo fra dua colonne, e però ho disegnato il portico li sopra con sei colonne: il quale sarà in
libertà del padrone à eleger qual sorà, l'esempio di questa si vede qua auanti segnata. G.

Anchora una casa simile a questa si porrà fare al costume di franza: et della medesima larghezza, questa haueua l'andito largo piedi III è mezzo
segnato A. hauendo da un lato una camera. B. longa piedi XV. senza la posta del letto. C. la sua larghezza sarà piedi XI. è mezzo
passando l'andito si troua una limaca di commoda grandezza: sotto la quale si passa al cortile D. questo è di quadrato perfetto:
col suo pozzo vicinale: et ha il portico da dua lati: dal lato per il longo per girir coperto alla cucina. E. dal lato per trauerso: questo
viene à fare dua seruitii: l'uno che si po girir apigliar l'acqua del pozzo sopra esso portico, l'altro che viene a coprire quella muraglia
a canto il letto et la defende dalla humidità, andando piu la si troua una cucina longa piedi XV. e larga quanto la camera da
uanti, questa ha il suo camino et il necessario, passando la cucina se l'huomo uola piu loggiamento, si trouerà una camera. F.
della grandezza della cucina: da questa in la vi è l'orto: e questo è quanto dabasso, la parte di sopra hauerà altro tanto loggiamento: ma
il granaro di piu nel quale, alcostume francese vi si fa di buone camere: la cantina si porrà poi diuidere in dua parti, dando a ciascuno
la sua parte. è di queste tal case sarà forza pel camino: et per il pozzo farne dua. l'esempio di questa sarà qui auanti segnata. H.

Delle casipole de i poueri artefici à terreno: et anche di quelle a solari piu accommodate: che nel uero sono mezze case: voglio hauer detto
abastanza. Hora io trattarò di quelle di maggior larghezza: et che hano piu del perfetto per la sua corrispondentia: et compagnamente:
sarà per accidente uno sito la latitudine del quale sarà piedi XLII. ma di buona longhezza, sel si hauerà da fare porticato: sia fatto
V. parti di questa faccia, facendo li pilastri piedi II. in grossezza: et la latitudine del portico: come gl'altri vicinali: et sia segnato A.
sel sarà in loco da far botteghe: le dua parti E. saranno per botteghe la sua longhezza sarà piedi XIII: et in larghezza X. il vestibulo
segnato B. sarà piedi X. per tutti e lati, la grossezza de i muri vicinali sarà II. piedi: e quei di mezzo piede I. è cosi sarà distribuito
li XLII. piedi, passando questo vestibulo si troua l'andito, la larghezza del quale è piedi V. et è segnato D. da un de lati sarà una
saletta: ò uero camera la sua larghezza sarà piedi XV. è mezzo: et in longhezza piedi XX. e sarà segnata E. il medesimo sarà dall'altro lato
ma tanto manco: quanto sarà la scala: che sarano piedi VII. è mezzo, è sotto essa scala vi sarà la posta del letto lassando la camera
netta: senza impedimento alcuno, per ciò che doue è la + si incomincia a montare: doue che tutta la parte sotto il riposo viene a essere
libera: et anche vi è loco da descendere alla cantina: andando piu oltra si troua una corte di quadrato perfetto: quanto è larga, tenebrosa
et è segnata. F. ma per piu commodità: si per gire al coperto nella parte dabasso: come anche per poter passare dalle parti auanti
a quelle di driero, ne per ciò la corte sarà tenebrosa: è darà tante commodità: andando piu oltra si troua una camera della
medesima grandezza di quella dauanti: et è segnata. G. all'incontro di questa vi è la medesima segnata. H. ma è impedita dalla limaca
et da i necessarii: ma questa sarà la cucina, passando queste dua camere uscendo fuori si troua una loggia. I. la sua larghezza
è piedi VIII. dipoi lo giardino: se vi sarà terreno: e questa casa io la presuppongo serrata dalli lati de mura vicinali: ma doue è la scala io
intendo vi sia, ò vico, ò qualche cortile il quale si possi sperare che non sarà fabricato: ò tal uolta per obligo di contratto. la pianta:
et il diritto di questa casa si vede qui auanti: e ben che nel disegno dimostri dua solari: non dimeno si porrà con l'ordine medesimo
farla a VI. solar solo, et hauerà conueniente aspetto, è questa tale habitatione porrà seruire à piu gradi di persone: tal uolta uno
buono artefice ne vora una tale, un buon cittadino per auentura se ne porrà contentare, ho veduto di grossi mercanti hauerne
di menori: et piu triste, per che tal fiata un huomo ricco: et auaro habita miseramente: et anche si vede tal uolta un mediocre
tanto genevoso di animo che la maggior parte del suo valore spenderà in una casa: per che nel uero dua cose transitorie fano
star l'huomo lieto: ciò è una bella et accommodata casa: et una moglieve bella: et dabene conforme alle sue voglie: ma
doue sono? è per ciò io non terminerò a chi grado io degia attribuire questa casa: la pianta: et il diritto è qua auanti segnata. I.

Una habitatione quasi simile alla passata si porrà fare al costume di franza: ma di minore larghezza, sarà per sorte questo terreno
fra li muri vicinali piedi XL: per la strettezza del loco si farà l'andito piedi V. largo: che sarà A. le dua botteghe sarano piedi
XIII. ciascuna et sarano di quadro perfetto, segnate. B. li muri dalli lati sarano grossi. II. piedi: è quei di mezzo di un piede: è cosi
sarano distribuiti li XL. piedi, dipoi le botteghe dalli lati del andito si troua dua camere segnate. C. della larghezza delle botteghe: et
in longhezza piedi XXI. ma una viene ocupata dalla limaca: questa non sarà molto lucida, per non hauere che una fenestra: per ciò
che l'altra mezza dà luce alla limaca, passando piu la si troua una corte di tanta longhezza: quanto la casa è larga: et è in longhez
za piedi XVIII. che viene à esser di dua quadri: e è segnata. D. nel mezzo di questa sarà una loggetta, sostenuta da quatro colonne accio
si possi passare alla parte di driero della casa: et anche disopra sarà il simile: è porrassi cauar l'acqua dalla parte disopra: ne per questo la corte
sarà impedita per esser detta loggia tutta aperta, passando la corte si troua dua camere segnate. E. la sua longhezza è piedi XX. et larghe
come l'altre: apresso queste son congiunte dua altre camere di quadrato perfetto segnate. F. ma una viene impedita dalla limaca: et da
li necessarii: e questa seruirà di cucina: è da basso: et da alto, andando piu la si troua un giardino: o veramente una corte: tal fiata
vi potrà essere una strada: porrà per accidente esservi uno orto. ò. un cortile vicinale dal quale le dua camere: et l'andito prenderano
la luce: e questo sarà. G. la faccia di questa casa io l'ho fatta coppiosa di lumi perciò che in molti lochi della franza ne ho veduto di simili: et
massimamente in Parigi: ma sono di legnami: ma se di pietra si hauerà da fare: le tre fenestre principali sarano aperte: et li quatro
nette fenestre si chiuderano: è questa casa viene hauere quatro suoli: che fano cinque habitationi: la prima: et la seconda habitatione sono di
una altezza cioè alte piedi XI. la quarta di X. et cosi la quinta: dipoi vi è il granaro che quasi si dice galata: et anche in altri paesi
casa porrà seruire: e massimamente in enghilterra. doue si delettano di gran luce: la pianta et il diritto di questa è segnato. K.

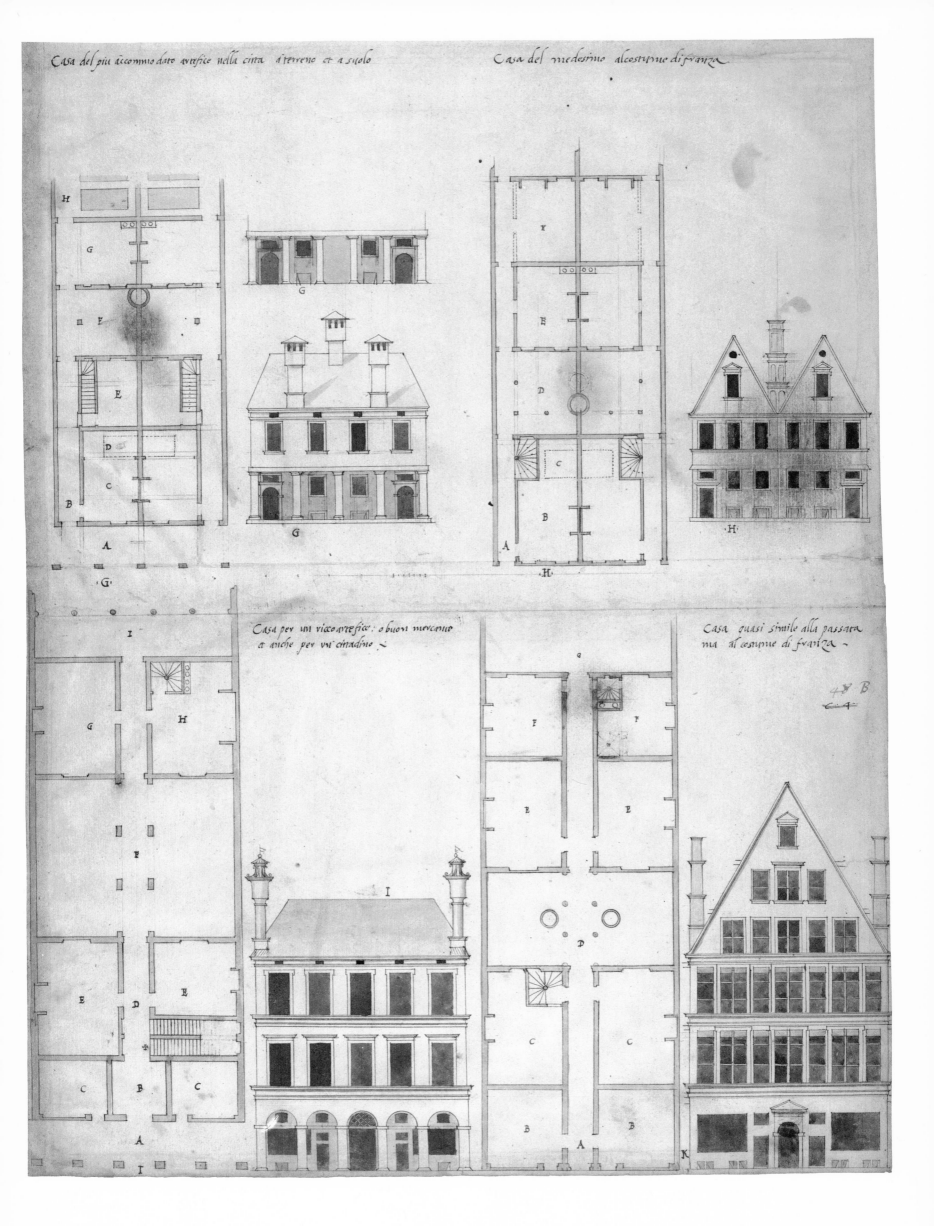

Casa del piu accommodato artefice nella cita d'terreno et a suolo

Casa del medesimo alcostume di franza

Casa per un ricco artefice: o buon mercante et anche per un citadino

Casa quasi simile alla passata ma al costume di franza

XLIX

Ben che piu adrieto io habbia dimostrato non solamente le case de piu poueri artefici et anche de i piu accommodati: in uarij modi: et poi di mercanti nobili
li quali per auentura habitano meglio: et uiueno piu suntuosamente di alcuni gentil huomini: per cagione de gran guadagni: che porta la mercantia
onde sara un mercante in una strada nobile: il quale haueua un terreno di piedi LX. in latitudine ouero fra dua uicini: et sara porticato li edifici
de i uicini: prima partira questa latitudine in parti V. facendo sei pilastri: la fronte de i quali sara dua piedi: ma per il fianco saranno piedi a. e mezzo
la qual grossezza sara basteuole: per hauere le spalle uicinali: ma se pel fianco fussero tre piedi et hauendosi a uoltare il portico la casa saria piu sicura
la latitudine del portico sara come i uicinali o piedi X. almeno et e segnato A. la grossezza de i muri uicinali sara piedi III. et quei di
mezzo piedi II. e tanto piu: e meno secondo la materia: per cio che la materia quadrata: et ben commessa e con poca calcina e assai piu forte: che
non e quella di scaglia: et di sassi de diuerse forme: e questi muri uogliono maggior grossezza di quegli di materia quadrata, L andito di questa
casa sara piedi X. in larghezza et e e segnato B. dal destro: et sinistro lato di questo sarano dua camere: le quali per ciascun lato sarano piedi XX: et cosi
li LX. piedi sarano distribuiti: passando piu auanti vi sarano dua altre camere della medesima larghezza: et in longhezza piedi XX. et sarano segnate
D. ma una di esse e impedita dalla limaca: et queste receueno la luce dalla corte: la quale e segnata E. et e di tanta longhezza: quanto e
larga la casa et la sua larghezza di essa corte sara piedi XXII. et chi uora gire al coperto per tutta la casa si porra nel mezzo a trauerso della corte
fare una loggia larga come il portico: e questa prestaria gran commodita alla parte disopra: per passare da uno appartamento a l altro, passando la corte
si troua una scala larga piedi IIII. sotto la quale nel primo riposo sara un camerino pel seruitio della camera d esso congiunta: all incontro di questa
vi e un camerino con la sua scala per che sara mezzato et di poi uno oratorio: o vero studio di forma ottogona: il Diametro del quale e piedi X. andando pi
auanti nel medesimo andito vi sono dua camere segnate F. la sua longhezza e piedi XXV. et prendon la luce dal giardino se vi sara, o, da uno cortile: tal
fiata da un altra strada: la parte dauanti sopra il portico guadagna quei X. piedi: doue si porria fare una sala: prendendo il portico: et le dua camere con l an
dito: et chi uora una menor sala prendera una camera: et l andito con una parte del portico: et sara congiunto con la sala una camera: quanto e la
camera C. aggiundendoui la parte del portico, Le habitationi terrene sarano alte piedi XX. et quelle disopra piedi XVIII: et sopra esse il granaro: et se
altre misure manchevano: li piedi picoli supplirano altro l esempio di questa casa si vede qui auanti in pianta: et in diritto segnata L.
sara per caso un sito la larghezza del quale sara piedi LXVIII: et sara la sua longhezza piedi CXLIIII. circondato da uicini: primieramente si fara l andito di
piedi XI in larghezza et sara A. il quale haueua dua camere dalli lati segnate B. queste sarano di quadrato perfetto: di piedi XXIII. li muri maestri
sarano grossi piedi III. e quei di mezzo II. e cosi sara dispensato il numero de piedi LXVIII. apresso le dua camere: er sarano dua altre camere
D. la sua euidenza sara come le altre dua, passando piu oltra si troua una loggia D. la sua larghezza e piedi VIII. da i capi della quale
son dua limache: per le quali si passa coperto alle altre loggie le quali circondano il cortile. E. il Diametro del quale e piedi XXXIII: di la dei
cortile ne i capi delle loggie si troua dua camere F. la sua larghezza e piedi XVIII: et in longhezza XXIIII. hauendo ciascuna un camerino. G. al suo
seruitio per cio che per essere amezzato: una haueua da basso: et l altra disopra, e cosi sara dispensato li cento e sessantaquatro piedi del terreno in longhez
za, questa casa e fatta al costume francese: et ha tre suoli, l altezza delle prime stanze a terreno sara piedi XVIII. ma leuate dalla strada uno
piede: e mezzo et il medesimo sara il primo suolo: l altezza del secondo suolo sara piedi XV. quella del terzo piedi XII. et anche uen
porra essere uno altro senza il galatta, la pianta: et il diritto di questa casa sara qua dauanti segnata M.

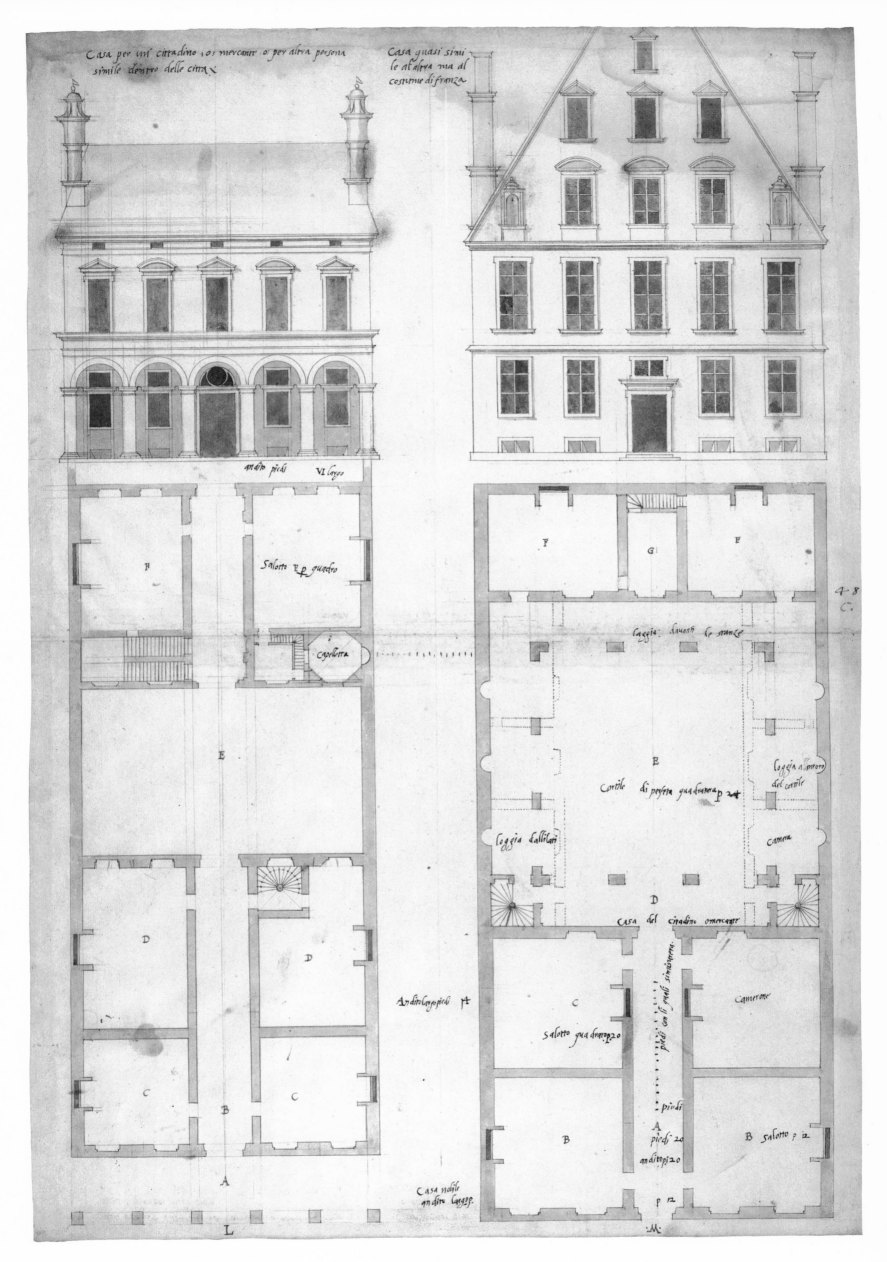

Casa per un cittadino, o mercante o per altra persona simile dentro delle citta

Casa quasi simile al altra ma al costume di franza

andito piedi VI largo

Salotto E p quadro

Capelletta

E

D

D

C

C

B

A

Anditro largo piedi 14

Casa nobile andito largo

L

F   G   F

loggia: davanti le stanze

E

loggia d'i pitoro del cortile

Cortile di perfeta quadratura p 24

loggia dalli lati

camera

D

Casa del cittadino o mercante

C   Camerone

Salotto quadro p 20

piedi con li scali sinistra

B   B salotto p 12

A piedi 20

andito p 20

p 12

M

L

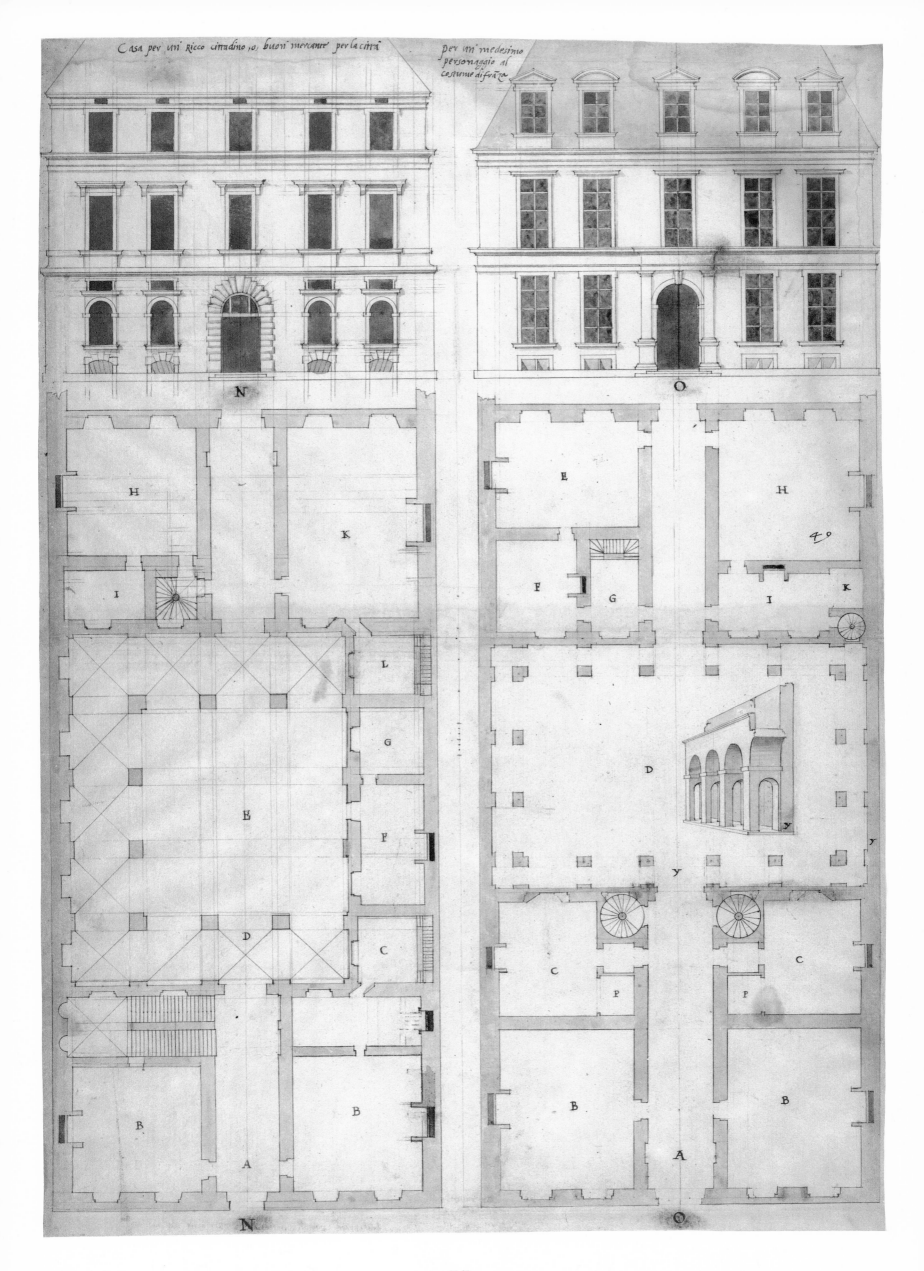

Casa per un Ricco cittadino, o, buoni mercante per la città

per un medesimo personaggio al costume di Fran.a

N

O

H

K

I

E

F

G

H

I

K

L

G

E

F

D

C

D

y

y

y

C

P

C

P

B

A

B

B

A

B

N

O

LI

La casa del gentilhuomo nobile et di buon grado deue essere sopra una piazza seglie possibile, o almeno su una strada nobile et isolata sopra il tutto. Ma hauendo jo da ratrare di una casa simile, glie ben ragione chio cominci dal costume del jnclita città di Vinetia veramente Madre: e parua di tutte le nationi: et massimamente di me: nella quale ho dispensato buona parte di miei anni: Tenendo di continuo comertio con quei nobilissimi jngegni dottati di tutte le buone arti e massimamente con quelli che nel mio quarto libro ho nominati: la qual degna Amicicia giamai si partira dalla memoria mia. Dico che per esser questa città nel acque: doue il terreno e molto caro: la maggior parte delle case non hano: ne giardini: ne cortili: ma le case prendeno la luce dauanti: et se sono longhe: la prendeno anche nella parte di drieto, onde per tal cagione hano un costume vniuersale di fare nel mezzo detta casa un portico di tanta longhezza quanto la casa et da quegli prendeno la luce: et se la casa sara troppo longa: farano nel mezzo di essa da un de lati una corticella per dar luce: al portico nel mezzo: et anche ad altri lochi; jo dispono adunque la casa di un gentilhuomo nobile di questa città, la latitudine di questo terreno sara circa a piedi. C. LXIIII. contute le grossezze de i muri li quali sarano piedi: cio è quei dalli lati è quei di mezzo piedi IIII. et a cio chel portico non venghi tanto longo jo gli faccio vna sala dauanti la casa la sua longhezza sara piedi XL la sua larghezza di piedi XXX. hauendo dalli capi dua camere della medesima longhezza: et in larghezza piedi XXIX. e questa sala è segnata. S. la quale viene a essere sopra il gran canale. da li angoli di questa sala si passa per vna limaca alla camera. N. la latitudine di questa è piedi XIX: et altro tanto in longhezza: ma vi e vn pariete lontano dal altro muro piedi IX. lassando nel mezzo loco per il letto longo piedi XII. da un lato vi e un camerino che prende la luce dalla strada: dal altro vi e il medesimo con vna scala che monta sopra il letto doue commodamente si fano tre letti et questo loco è per fanciulle è per nutrice: et a fin che le Donne possino segretamente passare di camera: in camera vie quel andito. A. al quale si va pel camerino: hora torniamo al portico. P. la sua larghezza e piedi XXX. et in longhezza piedi. C.XXIX. nel mezzo di questo portico vi son dua cortili. C. dalli lati de iguali vi sono le scale discoperte: che cosi si costuma: vna delle quali monta al piano. I. Questo piano sara per gire alli mezzadi per cio che in questa città per cagione delle acque: non si habita a terreno: ma è per magazini: per cantine et per altri luochi necessarii al bisogno della casa. e sopra questi lochi sono li mezzadi li quali si tengono con suma dilicatezza; l'altra parte della scala monta sul portico di sopra il quale come ho detto vi è jluminato nel mezzo da quel cortile cosi da basso come da alto dal destro: et sinistro lato del cortile vi sono dua camere. M. le quali recceueno la luce da esso cortile: et hano vna sola fenestra nel mezzo: la forma della quale è qua sopra segnata. G. e questa serue anchora per la fenestra del portico sopra il cortile: l'altra piu soda segnata. P. serue al entrare nel cortile da basso: la figura nel mezzo segnata. H. dinota la forma del pariete delle camere segnate. N. e tutte le quatro parti sono a un modo: nel capo del portico si troua vna loggia. L. della longhezza chi è la sala dauanti, ma di larghezza piedi XIIII. negliangoli di questa sono dua limache: il sua diametro e piedi XI. queste seruiuano per scale coperte all entrata di terra percio che ogni casa nobile ha la entrata per l'acqua: et anche per terra; questa loggia sara sopra un giardino: o cortile et se non vi sara terreno sara sopra la strada doue la parte da basso si seruira con fenestre: et la sua porta nel mezzo. ne i capi di questa loggia sono quelle forme diuerse le quali seruiuano per bagni è sue per ouatorij è sudij. et cose simili et sarano tutte mezzadi doue le limache seruiuano, li piedi qui sotto supliuano doue haueua mancato la scriptura. la dimostratione di questa pianta e qui alato segnata. P.

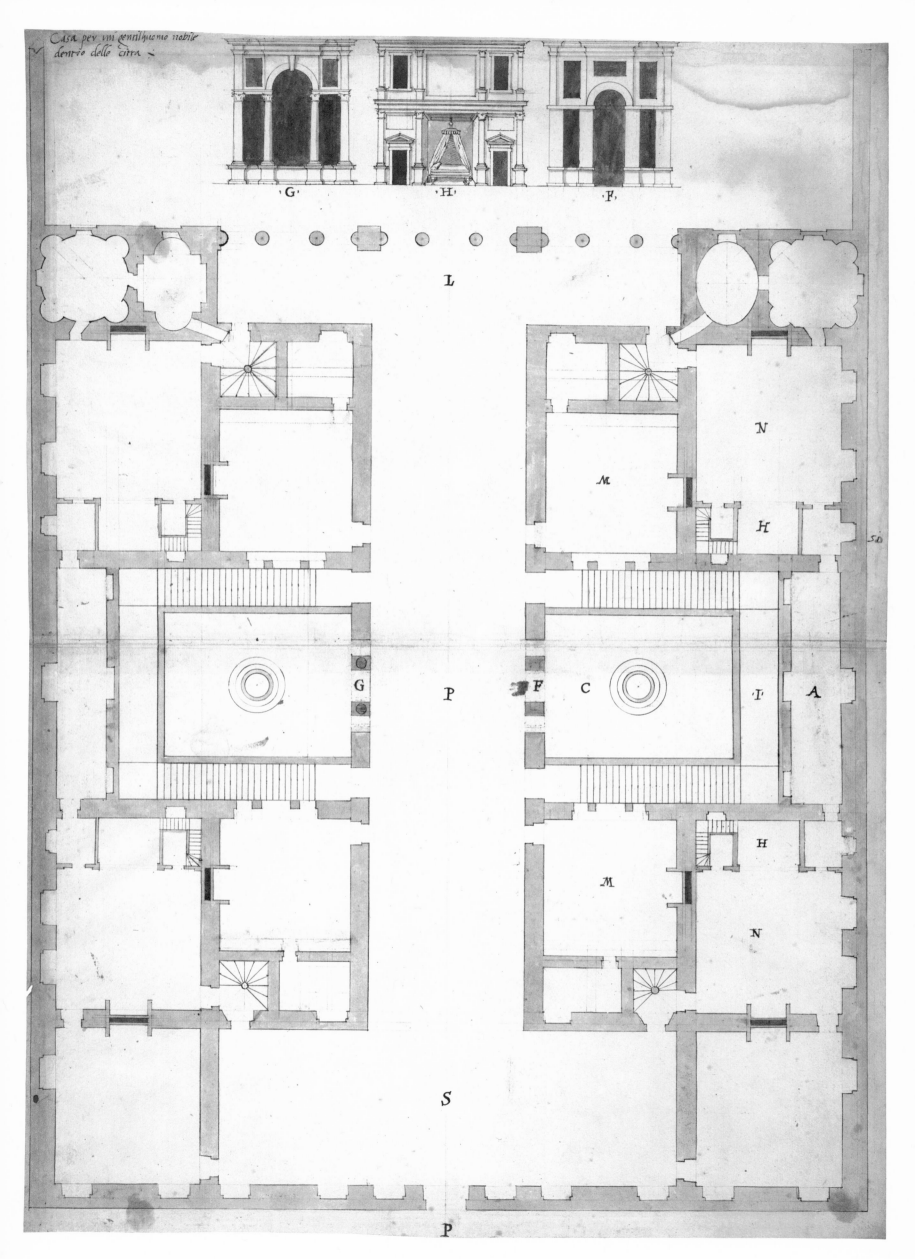

Casa per un gentilhuomo nobile
dentro delle citta

·G·   ·H·   ·F·

L

N

M

H

G   P   F   C   I   A

M

H

N

S

P

Questo diritto seruira per la parte interiore della prima pianta fatta al costume de vinetia: laquale ha il portico nel mezzo, il quale sara
di tanta altezza: quanto é la sua larghezza et e segnato P. l'altezza del portico segondo sara piedi xxix et e segnato Q. per esser questa la parte piu nobile la maggior parte delle camere sarano amezzade: et le camere principali che a tale altezza dimoravano: segli fava uno cielo
di legname tanto sfondrato all'insu che l'altezza della camera sara eguale alla larghezza. l'altezza del terzo portico segnato R sara piedi xvi.
ma chi uora alzarlo fin sotto il tetto entrando nel granaro guadagnara v piedi: che veria a essere piedi xxi e staua meglio: ma rompera
il granaro, Questa parte segnata C dinota il diritto del cortile da basso: ad alto: et la forma delle scale discoperte: et che parte delle fenestre viene offesa da dette scale; quanto alle prime scale li lumi venggono assai bene; ma le segonde scale le quali sono de punti si ornamenti di uno angolo: et anche alquanto di luce viene impedito, e per cio sono alcune cose che mal si possono dimostrare: senza il modello matevriale; col quale il prudente Architetto prende partito mutando tal fiata sugietto: e forma, Ma l'altro cortile se non ui sarano le
scale: et chel padrone della casa si contenti di una scala: il che si porra fare atento chi uisono altre limache: lo cortile sara spacioso ne sara
impedito cosa alcuna, la linea I doue mette capo la prima scala dinota il piano che va alli mezzadi: benche ad altri mezzadi si andava per
le limache: segondo le commodità, la parte segnata M la quale é voltata: è un loco longa da xl piedi e largo viii del quale si potra fare quatro
camerini per diuerse commodità della casa, sopra di questo al loco A sara quel andito segreto per le donne da passare di camera incamera,
l'altro disopra aquesto pur segnato M porra seruire ad altri camerini amezzadi: e sopra questo vi sara l'altro andito segnato A pel medesimo
seruitio alla parte del segondo suolo, l'altra parte segnata S dinota le altezze de iluochi, il primo luoco a terreno: chi e voltato dinota limagi-
ni et altri officij: lo segondo: rappresenta li mezzadi li quali anchova che dimostrino voltati: non dimeno egli si costumano piani di legnami et si ornano ricchissimamente de intagli: di ovo et de pittura. la terza parte dimostra l'altezza delle camere mezzane: con li suoi mezzadi
sopra: chi e la quarta: la quinta rappresenta le camere sotto il granaro, la camera maggiore segnata ✝ viene a essere del altezza del
portico: sopra la quale accio non sia tanto alta di cielo segli fara uno cielo nel modo che si vede nel profilo sopra essa, e cosi l'altadezza-
za sara moderata, Ma se queste tante altezze parevano ad alcuno fuori del commun uso et chei si voglia tenere piu basso: bene lo potra
fare: et il prudente architetto si seruira degliornamenti diminuendo alcune cose, et se questa casa sara lenata sopra lo piano delle altre casi vicinali: il che si puo fare essendo isolata: li magazini et altre stanze simili porrano essere al piano consueto: et hauerano maggiore altezza,
et per che inquesta citta per cagioni delle acque non si puo cauar sotto per fare camine da uini: onde non uisono uini freschi la state: si porria
bene nel fabricar una casa facendo elletione del loco della cantina: mentre le acque son piu basse hauendo cauato sotto quanti si puole:
e poi di terra creta fare un grosso suolo: et il medesime intorno alli muri et apresso un suolo di cemento di terrazzo grosso
e sopra quello un altro suolo de minuto benbattuto: et intorno le mura fare oltra la banca di creta ✝ un altro muro di pietra cotta
incrostata di terrazzo dua, os tre mano: et bene liunito intorno: sara inpossibile che le acque salse penetrino: eccetto che
disopra venendo qualche inondationi: che di rado venggono, porra forsi alcuni dire che per li gran sechi: la terra creta
se ritirava: facendo delle fissure: et che poi venendo il cressere delle acque penetrara per esse trouandola secca: qui vie rime-
dio anchora sia lassato intorno il muro di detta cantina al nassimento della volta una pietra col suo canale: per il quale mettendoci
del acqua: quella venga à dacquare tutta la banca intorno e tenerla morbida, e questo non sara gran cosa à un nobile gentilhuomo
per hauere li uini freschi la estate: che saria cosa vara in questa citta . ꓫ . il diritto qui auanti è segnato P.

Parte interiore della casa qui adriero: cioe della prima pianta,

LIII

La presente pianta potrà seruire medesimamente al gentilhuomo nobile vinetiano, et essendo in isola: come l'altra anchora, se questa casa si leuarà dal consueto piano fin a quattro piedi e mezo; farà tre buoni effetti: il primo la casa hauera piu magnifitientia: il segondo tutto il terreno de i fondamenti si metterà in alciare lo sito: che sarà gran spauagno: terzo la parte terrena si potrà habitare almeno la state, questa pianta è compartita sopra il medesimo sito della passata: et ha li medesimi lumi dauanti: et la medesima loggia nella parte di terra, ben che li altri compartimenti siano molto diuersi, prima al entrar della riua si monta al vestibulo A. la sua larghezza è piedi XXVIII. la sua longhezza è piedi XXXXVIII. hauendo dalli lati una saletta della medesima grandezza segnata B. dietro la quale è una camera C. di piedi XXVIII per tutti li lati dipoi quella si troua una camera di larghezza piedi XVI. et in longhezza XXVIII. questa hauera un camerino al suo seruitio sotto la scala la sua longhezza sarà piedi XVI. et in larghezza piedi VIII. et anche piu chi uoua, passando il vestibulo si troua una loggia. E. la sua larghezza è piedi XII questa circonda una corte F. il suo diametro è piedi LX. li pilastri di questa loggia son grossi III. piedi e mezzo, ne i capi di questa prima loggia sono dua scale principali: una in forma ouale: l'altra à ritorni: e parte a lumaca, la scala ouale hauera nel mezzo un pozzo molto commodo a tai lochi, al entrare della scala: si troua una camera G. la sua larghezza è piedi XXVIII. et in longhezza piedi XXXIII. dipoi questa vi è la camera H. la sua longhezza è come l'altra in larghezza: et è larga piedi piedi XXII. dietro di questa è un camerino I. la sua longhezza è piedi XXI. et in larghezza piedi XII. hauendo al suo seruitio un camerino di piedi VII. per quadro, passando il cortile si troua un vestibulo K. questo è per quadro piedi XXVIII. a canto del quale vi è una camera di quadrato perfetto della medesima misura et è segnata L. a presso quella ve nhe un'altra della medesima grandezza et è segnata M. passando il vestibulo si troua una loggia N. simile a quella della pianta passata, hauendo dalli capi quei quatro lochi li quali come io dissi seruirano astue: a bagni: ad ouatorij et a studij et a cose simili: questa casa hauera come ho detto dell'altra nella parte da terra: o cortile, o giardino, o veramente strada: ma sia chi esser si uoglia si salirà a quella altezza ch'io ho detto: o manche anchora segondo il voler del huomo: et le stanze mezzane: et picole tutte se a mezarano: e quello chi e da un lato se intende esserci dal altro: e questa casa non solamente seruira per la città di Vinetia: ma in gualunque paese potrà seruire: perche la gran copia de ilumi non sarà mai sprezzata: atento che pei gran venti et freddi grandi: se ne po sempre serrare una parte, e questa è segnata come l'altra P.

Casa per il medesimo gentil huomo come la passata

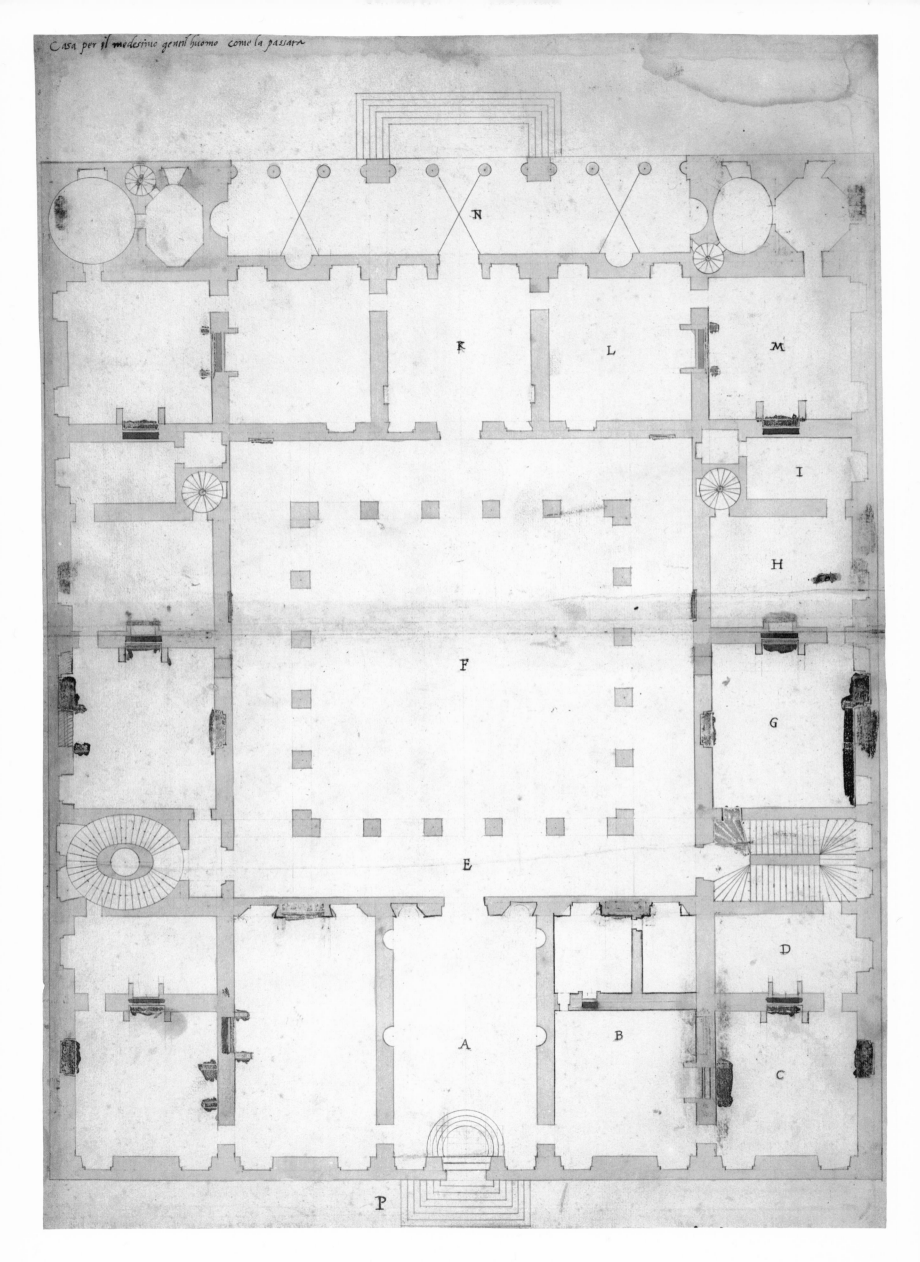

N

K L M

I

H

F

G

E

P A B D

C

LIV

il diritto qui davanti, servirà per la pianta passata, la quale ha nel mezzo un cortile con le sue loggie intorno: e parlando delle loggie, saranno in altezza piedi XXIIII.
et similmente saranno le sopra loggie: ma per che sopra esse sarà un terrazzo discoperto, se gli farà una volta morta, accio le humidità et le acque non
penetrino a basso cosi facilmente: l'altezza delle prime loggie, come ho detto, saranno piedi XXIIII. et cosi saranno alte le prime habitationi: ma alcune
saranno ammezzate: come sono le camere mezzane: et le menori: et li camerini anchora, la parte del primo suolo sarà in altezza piedi XXIX. ma
come ho detto la maggior parte saranno ammezzade salvando le salette: et le camere principali, il terzo suolo sarà in altezza piedi XV. salvando
un spacioso granaro: ma chi vora alciarsi fin sotto le catene del coperto, haveva le camere maggiori al altezza di piedi XX. ma il granaro sarà
impedito in questo caso, e però si avvertirà bene al uno: et al altro, et si farà quello che più sadisfarà al padrone: per che nel vero la casa è fatta
prima per la commodità: più che pel Decoro: ma si è l'uno: et l'altro in una casa si trovera, sarà quella più propinqua alla perfettione
Hor torniamo da basso parlando delle prime loggie, la grossezza de i pilastri è piedi III. fra l'un pilastro al altro è piedi VII. l'altezza degl'archi è piedi
XVII e mezzo. l'architrave: fregio: et cornice sarà piedi V. l'altezza del parapetto sarà piedi IIII. l'altezza degl'archi disopra sarà piedi XIX. acio che le
camere che prendeno la luce da essi archi siano luminose: et saranno della medesima larghezza di quei da basso, l'ordine primo si conosse rustico ma questo di mezzo è licentioso alquanto, la strettezza di questi archi alla sua altezza parerà ad alcuni cosa povera: ma avolerla regolare
quando le altezze si abassarano alquanto: li archi verano alla sua conveniente forma, la qual cosa si porrà facilmente fare senza
menda alcuna del edificio, e tornarà ancor bene, la latitudine della porta del vestibulo sarà piedi VII. et in altezza piedi XIIII. et il mezzo
circolo sopra essa sarà per dar luce al vestibulo essendo serrata la porta, la latitudine delle prime fenestre sarà piede V. et in altezza
piedi X. le fenestre del ordine segondo saranno larghe come le prime: et in altezza il medesimo. le picole fenestre sopra esse saranno
per dar lume alli mezzadi: et anche per aumentare il lume alle camere maggiori. l'altezza delle fenestre sopra il terrazzo sarà come
le altre: et le forme ovali per dar luce alli mezzadi si farano di quella altezza che comportarà il loco per cio che elle son fatte la
maggior parte per dar luce alli mezzadi, et quelli che daran luce alle gran camere, o sale: sarà bene che nella parte interiore siano
quadrate accio si accordino con le altre sotto esse: l'altezza del granaro in questo caso è tenuta molto bassa: per seguir l'ordine della
diminuitione delli tre ordini l'uno sopra l'altro: ma venendo il granaro più alto: qui è da avvertire che vi è qualche errore: per cio che in questo
granaro ci è discordanza: et sarà forza che le forme ovali daran luce al granaro et serrare quei fenestrini che sono nel fregio: et che le altezze delle stance: non passi XV. piedi, eccetto si come ho detto. l'altezza del portico havesse a rompere l'ordine del granaro accio che esso portico
havesse maggiore altezza: la qual cosa si porria fare, e questo sarà nel arbitrio del padrone: per cio che mai viene osservato un disegno
per bonissimo che'l sia. e questo diritto qui accanti sarà segnato . P.

Parte interiore della passata pianta, doue e' il cortile nel mezzo

P

LV

La faccia qui dauanti seruira à tutte dua le piante che qui adrieto ho dimostrato, è perche la maggior parte degl'ornamenti delle case di questa città sono licenciosi: et anche le cose disordinate; jo per ubidire alla gran coppia de i lumi: ho uoluto tenere uno ordine che forsi gli architetti vigorosi non lo loderano troppo, Ma jo son certo che la maggior parte degli'huomini ne rimarano satisfatti per la uarietà et uaghezza: et sugietto da ornare che iui si troua, Lo primo ordine si conosse da tutti esser Rustico l'altezza del quale dal pauimento fin sotto lo suolo è piedi .XXIIII. dal piano del primo suolo: fin sotto il secondo suolo sara piedi .XXVIII. è questa maggiore altezza del altra: non è senza cagione primieramente tutti li lochi mezzani è picoli sarano à mezzadi: et apresso alle sale et alle camere si farano soffittadi di tal fondo al insu: che con li fregi intorno occuppara sei piedi: onde le stanze non sarano di tanta altezza, Dal pauimento del secondo ordine fin sotto lo suolo del granaro sara piedi .XIX. torniamo à basso la latitudine della porta sara piedi .VII. et sara in altitudine piedi .XIII. Tutte le fenestre sarano in larghezza piedi .V. eccettuando quelle di mezzo, l'altezza delle prime: che son uoltate le quali seruirano à magazini sara piedi .IX. le fenestre sopra queste sono di quadrato perfetto: e seruirano alli mezzadi, l'altezza di quelle del segondo ordine sara .X. piedi le quadre sopra queste sarano alte .IIII. piedi: è parte di esse seruirano alli mezzadi et alcune aumentarano la luce alla sala: et alle gran camere, le fenestre del ordine terzo la sua altezza sara piedi .IX. le forme quali sopra queste sarano tre piedi in altezza, il segondo ordine si vede che è Dorico: et li ornamenti delle fenestre jonichi ma li Trigliphi son compartiti fuori de i precetti di Vitruuio: à fin che posino sopra ad alcuni uiui: et che anchora sostenghino alcri uiui, l'ordine terzo è jonico: ma si farano le fenestre ornate di opera corinthia: la qual opera non si conosce ad altro che alla gracilità: et ricchezza de lauori, l'architraue fregio et cornice viene à essere opera composita per cagione de i modiglioni che sono nel fregio: li quai modiglioni tornano molto al proposito per sostenere le cornice le quali recceueno le acque, l'ordione sopra l'ultima cornice è fatto per ornamento della casa: et è anche per commodità, per ciò che sopra à molti tetti anci sopra d'ogni tetto: Vi sono alcuni suoli di legnami sbauati intorno: per seruirsi del sole, Ma à questa casa così nobile non è onesto segli faccia tal cose, è per ciò uolendosi far questa: l'apertura di mezzo sara larga piedi .VII. et in altezza piedi .XIII. le aperture dalle bande sarano piedi .V. in larghezza, è piedi .VIII. la sua altezza: l'altezza delle colonne sara piedi .IX. et uno ingrossezza, l'architraue sara tre quarti di un piede: la cornice altro tanto, il frontispiccio sopra la cornice sara .III. piedi, l'apertura del arco sopra la porta sara piedi .VIII. in larghezza è piedi .XVII. l'altezza, l'altezza delle colonne è piedi .XIII. et ingrossezza uno è mezzo, l'altezza del architraue sara un piede e così la cornice sopra li occhi, l'apertura del arco del ordine segondo sara .VII. piedi in larghezza: et IIII e mezzo la sua altezza l'altezza delle colonne sara piedi .IX. et ingrossezza VII piede: et una onza, l'architraue sopra esse sara tre quarti di piede in altezza: et se altre misure mancarano il tutto si trouera coi piedi li sotto è questa faccia esegnata P

·54·

P

La presente figura qui dauanti seruira per ambidua le piante della casa del gentilhuomo di venetia per cio che le loggie di ciascuna prima
sono simili è di forma et anche de misura, è prima parlando degliuochi di mezzo la sua laritudine fra le dua colonne. è piedi. ix.
l'altezza di esse colonne è piedi. xvi. la sua grossezza piedi. ii. et un quarto: l'altezza del architraue è un piede è mezzo. l'altezza del
mezzo circolo è piedi. iiii. è mezzo: è cosi tutta l'altezza del arco viene à essere piedi. xxii. dal fondo del arco fin sopra la cornice sono. iiii.
piedi la quale si troua al piano del primo suolo: l'altezza del parapetto è piedi. iiii. l'altezza delle colonne è piedi. xiii con le basi et
capirelli: la sua grossezza è piede uno è tre quarti: l'altezza del architraue sopra esse colonne è un piede: et un quarto: onde tutta l'altezza del
arco sara piedi. xix è tre quarti. dal sotto arco alla summita della cornice sopra esso: vi sono piedi. vii. diuisi in tre parti: una sara
per l'architraue: una si dara al fregio è l'altra sara per la cornice: è questa sara à liuello del suolo segondo. l'altezza del poggio sopra
essa cornice sara piedi. iii. è mezzo: l'altezza delle colonne sara piedi. xvi. con le sue basi et capirelli la sua grossezza sara un piede
e tre quarti l'architraue: fregio et cornice sara in altezza piedi. iiii. diuisi in tre parti una sara l'architraue: una per il fregio con
li suoi modiglioni: l'altra si dara alla cornice: ma l'architraue non saria forte di un pezzo solo. da colonna à colonna. ma si fara
di pezzi ben comessi con buoni arpesi di bronzo bene impombati sopra esso prima che segli ponga il fregio sopra et li modiglioni
et di questi tai architraui ne ho veduto in piu luoche per gli edificij antichi: et massimamente in questa cita di venetia driero
santo eustachio in una ruuina non gia antica: ma ben vecchissima: che anchora vi sono alcuni architraui di pezzi sopra
colonne: ben che pero di opera barbara: ma per tanto egli sono stati forti nel opera: talqual è: a del ornamento qua disopra
nella parte di mezzo anchora cheglisia per ornamento: io ho pero detto la cagione nella scrittura della faccia dauanti: et perche
questo tale ornamento porria seruire a qualche altra cosa: io ne dato qualche particular misure: prima il suo basamento è piedi. iii.
in altezza: le colonne con le basi et capirelli sono alte piedi. ix. et in grossezza piede. ii. l'architraue: fregio et cornice sara la quarta parte
del altezza della colonna: diuiso in tre parti. una sara per l'architraue: l'altra pel fregio: la terza per la cornice: l'altezza della
tabella sopra essa con la sua cornice sara medesimamente per la quarta parte del altezza di una colonna l'altezza del fronti:
spiccio sopra essa sara dua piedi e mezzo l'intercolumnio di mezzo sara. iiii. piedi è mezzo glimercolumni dalli lati sarano
dua piedi et un quarto. tutte le fenestre sono piedi. v. in larghezza: l'altezza delle prime è piedi. viii. è mezzo: l'altezza delle
segonde è piedi. xii. è mezzo: che son dua quadri e mezzo: l'altezza delle terze sie piedi. xii. è porra anche esse dodici è mezzo.
quanto aglialtri ornamenti tutti si trouerano nel terzo et quarto libro. e questa parte è segnata. P.

P.

Parte di driero delle piante passate la quale serue à tutte dua le piante

Parte di driero delle piante passate la quale serue à tutte dua le piante

P

LVII

La maggior parte delle altre città de italia tenggono un altro modo di fabricare le sue case; et massimamente i gentil'huomini di buon grado: per cio che le parti dauanti hano le piu magne habitationi per trattenere li amici et forestieri, et come la parte dauanti è piu larga: et ornata di fenestre: et altri ornamenti: sempre si vede in essa maggiore magnificentia. La presente casa adonca qui auanti dimostrata in pianta: la sua faccia sara in latitudine piedi · C·XLVI · la grossezza de i muri maestri: sara piedi · V · et quei di mezzo sarani grossi piedi · III · et tanto piu: et meno segondo la materia di che sarani fatti: per cio che se di minuta pietra et non asquaro si farano li muri come saria di sassi di fiumi, o di scaglia di pietre vive: et anche di pietre di montagne: questi tai muri recercherano maggior grossezza, ma se di pietra viua tutta lauorata asquado: et ben colegata insieme: con poca calcina fra le commissure si farano: questi tali si porani fare di menore grossezza: ma di pietra cotta prima ben secca al sole: et dipoi ben cotta: senza auaritia di legne: questi sarano anchora piu durabili: come ne fano fede gliedificij antiqui di roma: et anche in altri lochi de italia, Hor tornando alli appartamenti di questa casa: prima si troua un Vestibulo · A · la sua larghezza sara piedi · XVIII · et la longhezza piedi XXII, hauendo dal destro: et sinistro lato una saletta · B · la longhezza della quale sara piedi XXXIIII · questa hauera al suo seruitio una camera · C · la sua larghezza sara piedi · XX · et in longhezza piedi XXII è cosi sara distribuito li cento quaranta sei piedi della faccia, et questo appartamento sara sepparato dal rimanento della casa mentre che sara serrato uno usciporto fra lo vestibulo: et l'andito: il quale andito: sara di larghezza piedi XII · et in longhezza XXIIII · et è segnato · D · dalli lati di questo vi è duecamere di quadratura perfetta: quanto è longo il vestibulo: et sono segnate · E · acanto a ciascuna si troua un camerino · F · la sua larghezza è piedi · XII · et in longhezza XXI, il quale sara amezzado, drieto di questo si troua una camera · G · la sua larghezza è piedi · XX · et in longhezza XXIIII, passando l'andito si troua una loggia · H · la quale circonda un cortile · I · la larghezza di essa loggia è piedi · X · la grossezza de i pilastri · è piedi · III · il netto del cortile è piedi · LXV · in longhezza: et in larghezza piedi · XXXIX; et anche si potra fare di quadrato perfetto, Dalli capi della loggia si troua dua scale: una diritta con li suoi ritorni di piedi · V · in larghezza: l'altra è alimaca et il suo diametro è piedi · XII · questa prende il suo lume di sotto la loggia: et anche prende lume segondo da un camerino drieto à essa, dal destro: et sinistro lato delle loggie vi è una camera · K · la sua longhezza è piedi · XXII · et in larghezza piedi · drieto la quale vi è un camerino · L · la larghezza del quale è piedi · XII · et in longhezza · XX · et questo sara amezzado, et sara il spogliaturo della stua: la qual stua è segnata · M · di questa si va nel bagno · N · questa stua si scalda di sotto al modo antico, passando fuori del cortile si troua uno andito: della medesima proportione del primo acanto del quale si troua una camera · O · la sua larghezza sara piedi XXII · et in longhezza XXIIII, al seruitio di questa vi è un camerino · P · la sua larghezza è piedi XII · et in longhezza XVIII: et sara amezzado, fuori del andito si troua una loggia · R · la sua larghezza è pie di · XXII · et in longhezza piedi · LXXXXI · ne i capi della quale vi son dua camere · S · la sua larghezza è piedi XXI · et in longhezza XXIII · drieto alle quali vi è una camera · Q · la sua larghezza è come l'altra: et in longhezza piedi XXIII · la sopra detta loggia sara sopra un giardino · T · la longhezza del quale sara segondo il sito: et in capo del quale si fara la stalla: hauendo un'altra uscita si sara possibile: facendoui anchora uno portico: per tener carri: et carrette: et cose simili: per cio che jo presupongo: che nella parte dauanti non vi entri caualli per esser leuata dalla strada cinquui gradi: è certo se talle leuatione non fusse pendente il che si porra fare: è questa pianta sara · Q ·

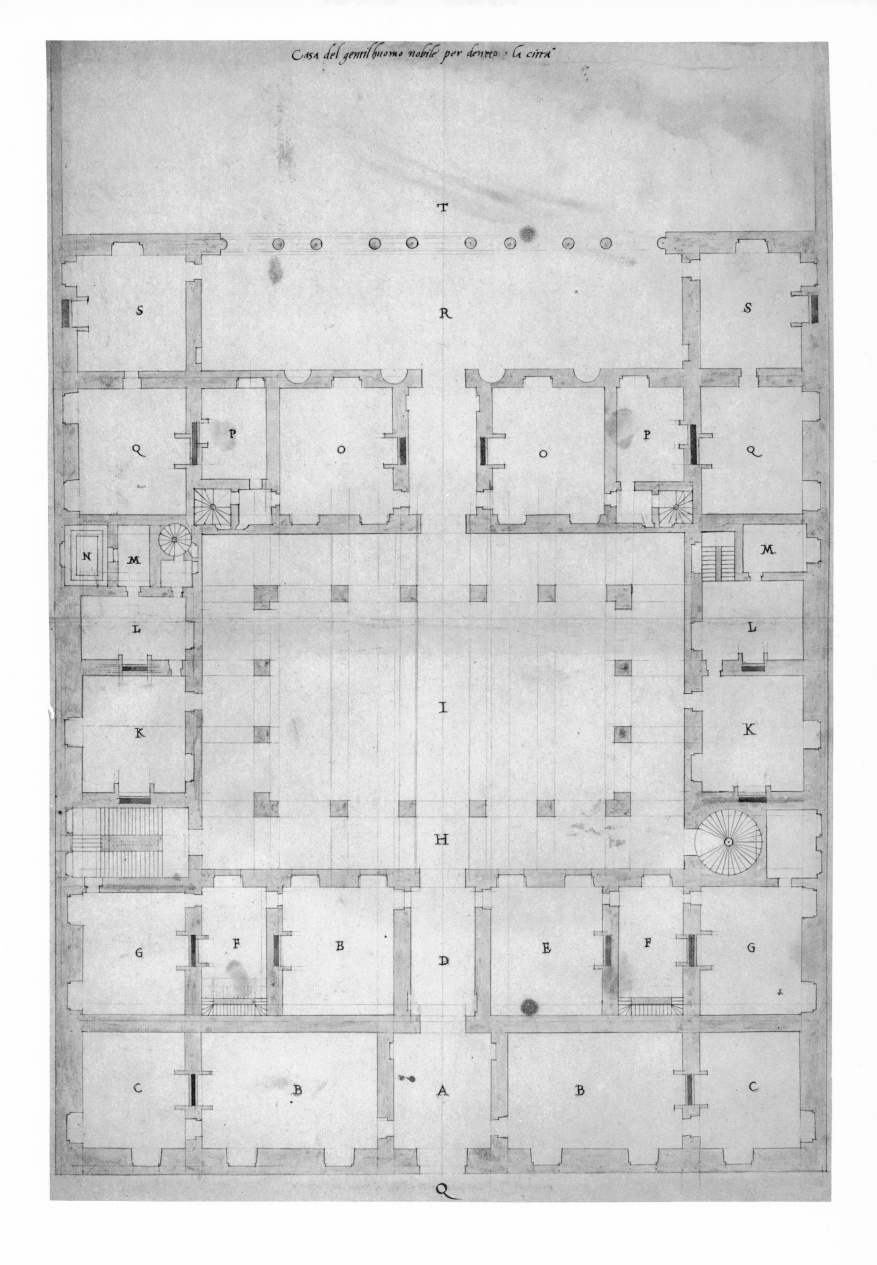

Casa del gentilhuomo nobile per dentro la città

LVIII

Della pianta qui adietro dimostrata: queste parti qui auanti sono i dirini e ben che
essa pianta potra seruire a tutti li paesi: per esser molto commoda. et per hauere
nella maggior parte delle camere quella commodita che altre volte ho discritto che
molto si costuma nella franza, mi e parso di fare li ornamenti al costume fran=
cese: ma pero misto con l'antico, La parte adonca qui piu basso rappresenta
la faccia dauanti: la quale per esseri isulata si potra leuare dalla strada quanto
si vorra: ma per lomanco dua piedi e mezzo: et sel sito lo comportaua sia tutta
Cauata sono: et iui sarano tutti li usficij pel seruitio della casa: e questa si potra
voltare chi vorra facendo le mura di quella grossezza che sara conueniente alla materia
di che sarano fatti: ma li grossi e' sodi fondamenti: et anche li muri sopra terra: nõ
sarano mai basmati percio che le habitationi che hano li muri grossi: sono calde
il verno: e fresche la state: calde il uerno per che li venti et le pioggie non hanno:
senza di penetrare cosi facilmente di dentro: fresche la state per cio che'l sole: et
l'aere caldo non vi ha possanza: le altezze delle stanze si farano secondo li
paesi: se li paesi sarano freddi e ventosi: no uoglion essere di grande altezia: se
sarano temperati sian di mediocre altezza: se sarano calidi la grande altezia sara
buona, ma l'altezza di queste prime stanze sara piedi: XVIII et altro tanto le sego=
de, e quelle terze si sarano piedi XVI: et anchor manco: chi vora sopra le quali
sarano li granari: hauendo li lumi sopra li tetti: tutte le finestre sarano larghe piedi
V. l'altezza delle prime sara piedi X: le segonde piedi XI: le terze piedi XIII=
e questo, e, che a mirar questa faccin alla sua debita distantia: tutte rappresentarano
vna altezza: La parte di mezzo dinota la interiore nella quale si uede le medeme
altezze et grossezze, e quanto alle loggie intorno il cortile: se la casa haueua tre ordini: sara
necessaria che sia loggia sopra loggia et il terrazzo disopra: ma che si contenta di dua
ordini: bastera una loggia: col suo terrasso sopra, La terza parte che e' disopra
dinota la parte di dietro verso il giardino: e quanti ordini haueua la casa: tanti
loggie vi sarano le quali per la larghezza sua non si comporta che si uolino di
pietra: ma di legnami si farano li suoli e cosi li segondi: e' perci architraui sarano
di legno sostenuti da colonne di che materia sara piu commoda al paese: ma bene il
primo ordine sara voltato di bona pietra: et cosi li architraui per essere di commo
longhezza sarano di pietra: e questi archi sarano fortissimi senza ferramenti
per hauere le sue spalle fortissime di quelle dua camere: le finestre di questa
parte da basso: sono di maggiore altezza di quelle dauanti per cio che e ben ragione
per la veduta del giardino: che li parapetti siano piu bassi al commodo appoggiare
del huomo: quanto alle particular misure: e' delle cornice et delle colonne: et altri
ornamenti: nel quarto libro si trouerano minutamente alli suoi lochi: et li sotto
anchora con li piedi che vi sono si potra trouar et e' segnata

Parte di dietro della passata pianta

Parte interiore della passata pianta

Parte davanti della pianta passata

LIX

Trattando jo alpresente delle case de gentilhuomini: non posso fare ch'io non raconti le miserie della bella: ma hair me divisa jtalia percio che in molte città di essa, vi sono discordie e guerre ciuili, et massimamente nelle terre et città sottoposte al papa: le quai discordie et guerre non sono senza crudelissime ocisioni: jncendij grandi: e ruuine di case: e dispersioni de famiglie. Per la qual cosa, quel gentilhuomo che sara jntricato in queste parcialita: sara jn effetto capo di parte: la magione del quale conuera sia forte si di sito: come di mura: ma di fianchi: ne di torroni: non gli sara comportata dalli supperiori. Bisogna adonca che questa casa primieramente sia jsolata accio ch'egli nemici suoi alongo andare non corompessero alcun vicino: et atempo di notte con qualche jnsidie nuocergli di mala maniera, et che questa casa non sia prossima al palazzo: Afin che per qualche disubidienza: facilmente il padrone di essa casa non sia offeso da esso palazzo: et che questa sia propinqua dal suo parentado per esser facilmente socorsa alli bisogni, che questa casa sia fra genti medio cre: et pouere: accia ch'el padron d'essa con la sua liberalita si faccia tutti amici donando sempre a piu poueri: et tratenendo i medio cbri con carezze et la maggior parte del tempo tenerli alla sua tauola: fauorirgli tutti ne suoi bisogni: come sono liti: quistioni et in alcune auuersita suuenirgli grossamente: che poi questi tali metterebon mile vite per lui: et gli altri che veggono questi belli atti: segli fano tal mente afetionati che ad ogni suo bisogno prenderebbero l'armi esponendosi a milli pericoli, jo non parlo ch'el sia racetatore di banditi: et dilinquenti percio che questa è la sua prima parte. Ma sopra il tutto ch'el capo di parte disaccia al tutto da se la brutta auaricia per cagioni della quale a giorni miei son stati morti miseramente molti capi di parte: per non hauere di continuo tenuto jncasa lhoro buone guardie et amici fedeli grauandogli la spesa del trattenergli: il nome: et il cognome de iguali jo saprei ben dire, ma jo voglio fare l'officio del Architetto e non de cronichista: per non offendere alcuno de i delinquenti: et anche de parienti: che anchora al di d'ogi sono viui, Ma venemo hora alla situatione et fondatione di vna tal casa, Questa primieramente sara jn jsola: ne mi curo ch'ella habbia piazza dauanti accio non si possi far massa grande de nemici ne conduruj artelarie coperta da machine di legnami: et che la porta non sia al dirimpetto di alcuna strada, per la medesima cagione ma vi sia bone qualche canoniera segreta et al bisogno discoprirla et con le artelarie spazare la strada, che li muri maestri siano grossi vi. piedi per lo meno: e quei di mezo almeno. iiii. la porta per piu fortezza non sara piu larga di. vi. piedi: al entrar della quale si troua vn vesti bulo. A. la sua larghezza è piedi xviii: e longo xxiiii. questo sara leuato dalla strada dua gradi: et hauera dal destro: et sinistro lato vna sala B. la sua longhezza sara piedi xxxvi: et al suo seruitio hauera vna camera. C. la sua larghezza piedi xxi: ma la longhezza sara piedi xxiiii: e cosi sara larga la sala: et queste sauano per li amici: et per guardia della casa: è quantunque la porta fusse espugnata: questi per fianco con armi d'asta et archibusi: batterano gli nemici aspramente: li quali trouarano vn altra dificulta che a mezo il vestibulo sara la scala che monta piedi. v. la quale atal bisogno sara coperta da dua ratto loni a costume di rebata: ne vi mancarano le sue diffese per li fianchi: et per faccia li dua vicchi sarani differa grande: sotto la scala vi sara vn pas saggio: accio che vna parte possi soccorrer l'altra: et anche abbandonando la parte dauanti ma ben serrate le dua porte de i fianchi con saua sinesche di fer ro le quai sarano nella grossezza del muro: potrano per via segretta andare al cortile: da uniressi con gli altri, montato questa scala tutto l'edificio si troua aquel piano: è prima si troua vno Atrio. D. chi è di quadrato perfeto di piedi xxiiii. questo ha le sue diffese per faccia: et anche per fianco: dalli dua lati son dua camere. E. della medesima grandezza del Atrio: è per cagion delle limache: per veguadrare le dette camere vi è la posta di vn letto. X. fra questa et la limaca sara sara l'entrata di essa camera. Drieto la quale sara vn altra camera: di piedi xxi et xxiiii: et e segnata. F. il montare delle limache comincera doue e. S. accio ch'el diffenssore disopra sia zoperto al disauantaggio del nemico: et il nemico che è disotto sia discoperto a suo disauantaggio e questo medesimo auuenimento si deue haue artine le scale che hano li vitorni, passando piu oltra si troua vn cortile segnato. G. la latitudine del quale è piedi. lxxxxii: et è quadro perfeto, questo non ha le loggie intorno come gli altri accio sia piu spacioso: si per esercitarsi di continuo ne i giuochi delle armi: si per star meglio in ordinanza alle diffese senza impedimento di colonne, dalla destra et sinistra banda vi è vna saletta. H. longa piedi xxx è larga xxiiii. et ha da ciascun lato vna camera. I. la sua larghezza è piedi xviii et ha vn camerino. K. longo piedi xv e largo ix: e questi si amezzarano, passando il cortile si troua un gran vestibulo segnato. L. la longhezza del quale e piedi lxxii è largo piedi xxiiii. questo ha da vn de lati la scala principale: et doue è. S. si comincia a salire: per la ragione aridenta da vn lato di questo ves tibulo vi è vn salotto segnato. M. la sua larghezza è piedi xxx: et jn longhezza piedi xxxiiii, questo sara pel padrone: hauendo vna camera N. di piedi xxiiii per ogni lato: ma nel andito piu comodo presso il fuoco sara vn camerino segnato. O. del quale si va a vna camera segnata. P. la quale sara la piu sicura parte della casa: perche calato vna saua sinesca bon forte nel entrare di essa: questa da basso: ad alto sara fortissima per battaglia di mano essendo ben fornita di viuere per alcuni giorni: et jn questo mezo gli nemici si strachano: o si piglia accordo: come piu uolte ho veduto fare à chi si troua in loco forte: e sicuro, Dal altro lato del vestibulo vi sono altre tante habitationi: ma in altra forma, la parte di drietro sara giardino con le mura grosse: et di buona altezza: et che la porta di drieto sia picola è forte: et quello ch'io dico da basso se intende da alto: et presupongo tutte le officine nelle stanze sotterranee, E s'io volesse scriuere tutte le auuertentie che atal casa bisognerebbe jo sarei troppo longo: doue faccio ogni cosa per esser breue, et questa pianta sara segnata R.

R

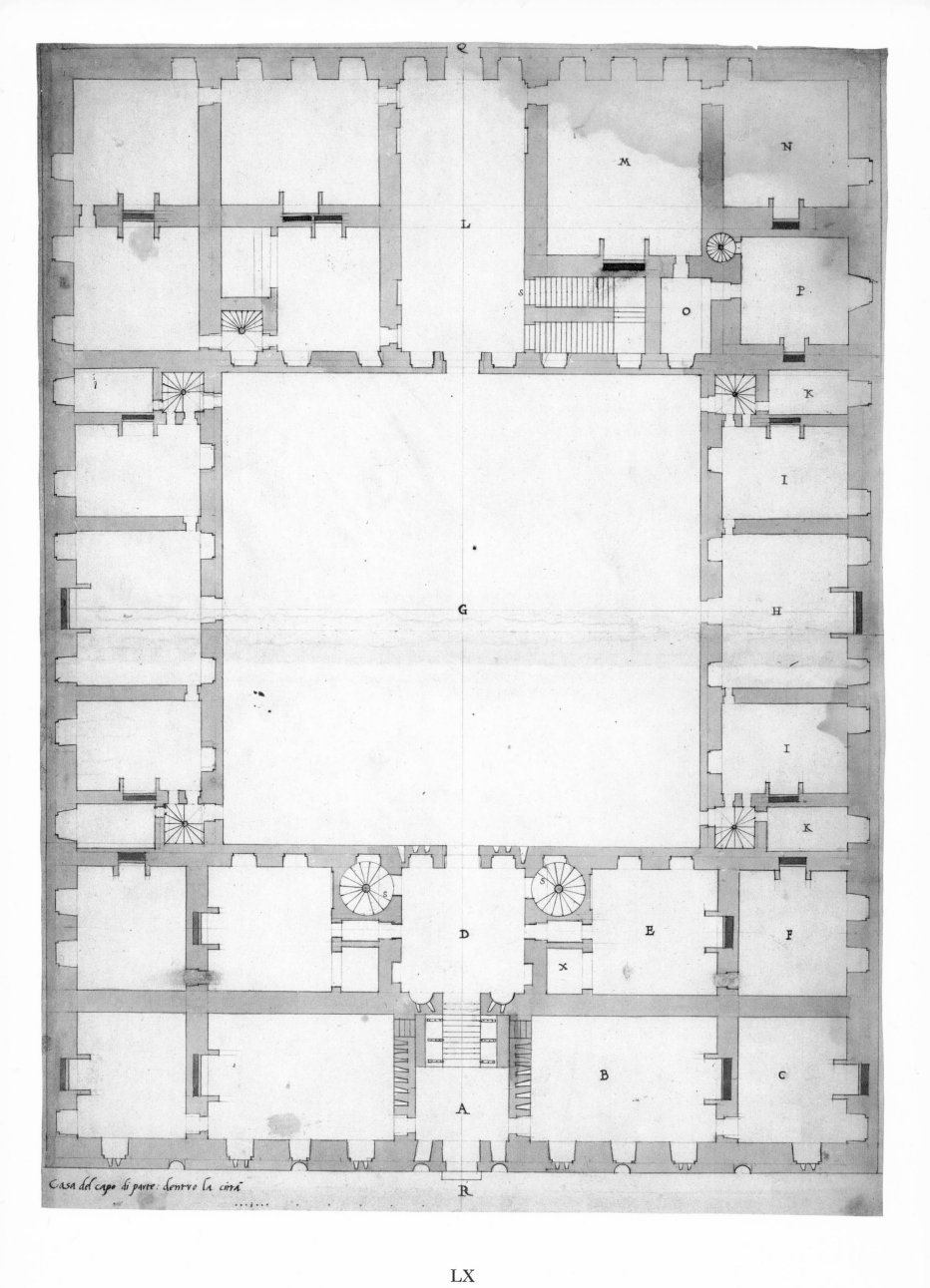

Casa del capo di parte: dentro la città

LX

La parte interiore si vedi qui dauanti dimostrata: la quale rappresenta la parte verso lo giardino: è quella linea di punti segnata T. dinota la planitie del cummun' piano vicinale: è tutta la casa eccetto le prime habitationi dauanti: viene à esser leuata da esso piano piedi v. è così le stanze sotterranee prenderano la luce viua sopra la terra: entro le quali sauano tutte le officine della casa: eccetto che per dormir ui imo in molti lochi ho fatto una stalla: et e tornata bene; et si questa casa fusse propinqua a qualchi ortaggi deserti: et in habitabili, o presso qualche torrente: o in luochi montuosi come in piu luochi drento le città ho veduto doue per qualche via secreta a qualche estre mo bisogno lhuomo si potesse saluare: saria bene; ma non poga qui lhuomo la sua speranza, ma di saluarsi per alcuni giorno nella sua parte segnata P. hauendo in essa da poter viuere et anche molestare gli nemici: per cio che sel sara combattuto dagli suoi particulari nemi ci: egli sara per diffensarsi et esser anchora soccorso dal suo pauentato, et segli anchora haueua il palazzo contrario: il pauentato suo: la sua parte ~~incuneata~~ trattauano accordo: et il palazzo pauoso del furore del populo: come saria quello di Bologna taribile in tal caso: si accordaua piu che volontieri: la parte sotterranea: come ho detto seruira per tutte le officine della casa: eccetto che per dormir ui la altezza delle stanze terrene saria piedi xx. le seconde piedi xviii. le terze xv. il granai poi saria di tanta altezza che commodamente si possi a faccire alle fenestre, queste altezze sono alquanto disubidienti da i scritti di Vitruuio: ma quanto al habitare sono assai: glie è ben vero, oglie bonuero che li vestibuli alla longhezza: e larghezza sua sono bassi: et chu gli facesse: alquanto piu alti come saria il primo vestibulo piedi xxv: et il segondo di xx: et poi il terze piedi xvi: et amezzare tutte le camere picole: la casa saria piu perte: et hauerebbe piu habitationi, e questi basti quanto alla parte interiore segnata. R.

La faccia della presente casa si vede qui auanti nella parte di sotto: et come ho detto, il vestibulo: le sale: et le camere dauanti sauano di piu altezza delle altre cio è per cagione della scala del vestibulo sauano piedi xxv. in altezza: le quali nel vero haueuari meglior forma de le altre: et massimamente le sale: ma le camere saria bene: a mezzare le camere et far le limache pei mezzadi nelle grossezze dei muri et se anche come ho detto nela parte di dentro si facesse le altezze maggiori li salotti dauanti per esser ridutto publico non sauano propo alti di piedi xxx: essendo in uolta: et l altezza del vestibulo saria perfetta. è come ho detto in piu di un loco non si admiri alcuno: se in questa faccia io fa fenestra sopra fenestra in uno ordine solo: conciosiacosa che una stanza di grande altezza ha bisogno di gran lume et facendo una fenestra della suo honesta proportione. la uolta di essa stanza saria tenebrosa: e pecio questi sopra fenestre verano nelle lumere della uolta. La causa per che son fatte quelle fenestre piu picole in forma di nicchi: è per dua cagioni: la prima è che le fenestre del vestibulo acanto la porta: non possono venire di tanta larghezza: come le altre: l altra si è che quei nicchi fra l altre fenestre non poteuano dar luce alle camere per essere incontro li muri, è vero: a tutte le altre fenestre ~~menori~~ che sono fra le maggiori ho uoluto dar forma di nicchi per compagnamento di tutta la faccia è questo fenestre prime sauan tutte ferrate per piu sicurezza della casa; le altre fenestre superiori per essere alte non acade ferri percio che: con sassi et altre materie grosse da gettare abasso sauano per diffesa della faccia, quanto alle altre misure del rimanente il tutto si prouaria ne i piedi li sotto segnati e queste dua parti sauano segnate R.

Parte di dentro della pianta qui adietro

L   O   P

R

61.

Parte di fuori della pianta qui a dietro.

R

il palazzo del pretore: cioe del potesta' doue si agitano le cause et si tiene giusticia conuiene esseve sul p[er]oro
cioe su la piazza: e per che la piazza deue esser coppiosa di boteghe; e necessavio che dauanti: et intorno
vi siano boteghe per la commoditta' del publico, questo palazzo dalla parte dauanti sava porticato
per ornamento della piazza: et anche per poter negotiare sotto esso portico, La latitudine del quale sava piedi
XXII cioe il netto: et e segnato ·A· fra l'uno et l'altro pilastro sava piedi· XVIII la grossezza de li
pilastri piedi· IX per quadrato, oltra la coloma di fuovi: et la bassa coloma dentro li quai dua membri
venggono a essere piedi· III et un terzo: cha fano lo pilastro per fianco piedi· XII e un terzo: lo quale sosteva benis=
simo la volta senza le chiaui di ferro, li cantonali savano dupplicati di colonne accio siano suficienti contra forti
è cosi la longhezza del portico sava piedi· CCLX· tutti li lochi segnati ·B· son boteghe e cosi intorno il palazzo
nella parte di fuori savano boteghe, nel mezzo di questo portico vi è la porta entro la quale si trova il vestibulo la sua
larghezza è piedi XXII et in longhezza· L· dal destro o sinistro lato vi sono officij segnati· D· li quai lochi savano per
notari: et altri scrivani, da questi si passa alle loggie· F· lassando nel mezzo un spacioso cortile di di perfeto quadrato
lo suo diametro e piedi· C· XXVIII· nel capo di questo si trova una scala la quale salisce piedi· VIII· e trova lo
riposo· F· dal lato destro et sinistro vi sono le scale per salire alle sopra loggie et alli altri tribunali, al medesimo piano
si trova la sala· G· la sua larghezza è piedi XL et in longhezza· LXVIII· questa sava per negotiare havendo dalli dua capi
dua gran camere di quadrato perfeto: quanto è larga la sala et savano segnare· H· nel capo delle quali vi savano li lochi per
li tribunali segnati· I· sotto questi lochi savano le prigioni per esser loco basso et forti, da questa sala si trova
la scala· K· la quale descende al cortile· L· la sua larghezza e piedi· LXVIII· et in longhezza piedi· CLVIII· pas=
sando alla altra porta si trova una torre· M· la parte di dentro e di otto lati per dar commoditta' alle dua limache
per salire ad alto il diametro di questa e piedi XXXII· la parte di fuori e piedi XL· ma li angoli son forti a
suficientia l'altra porta di drieto e segnata· N· nei capi di questo cortile savano boteghe, segnate· O· ma di poca
altezza accio non ocuppino le luce alle limache che sono negli angoli, le porti delle prigioni savano doue sono le
lettere· P· per che veglion esse dupplicate per piu sicurezza, doue è la torre· Q· se intende esser al piano della ca=
mera· H· dal quale si monta alle parti disopra per la limaca li acanto: sopra questa sala et li tribunali vi
savano altro tanto di lochi, ma piu spaciosi in altezza, sopra le boteghe dalli lati contenendo sei boteghe per
banda savano le habitationi del potesta' o cosi di drieto, sopra le loggie E· savano altre loggie: e sopra le boteghe
savano diversi officij, sopra li lochi· D· sava sopra loggia: e sopra le boteghe· B· savano altri tribunali,
sopra lo portico dauanti sava una gran sala la quale sava piedi XXV· in larghezza per cagion delli muri che
non sono cosi grossi: questa sava per il consiglio generale della citta: o per alcune feste publiche, segondo le
occasioni

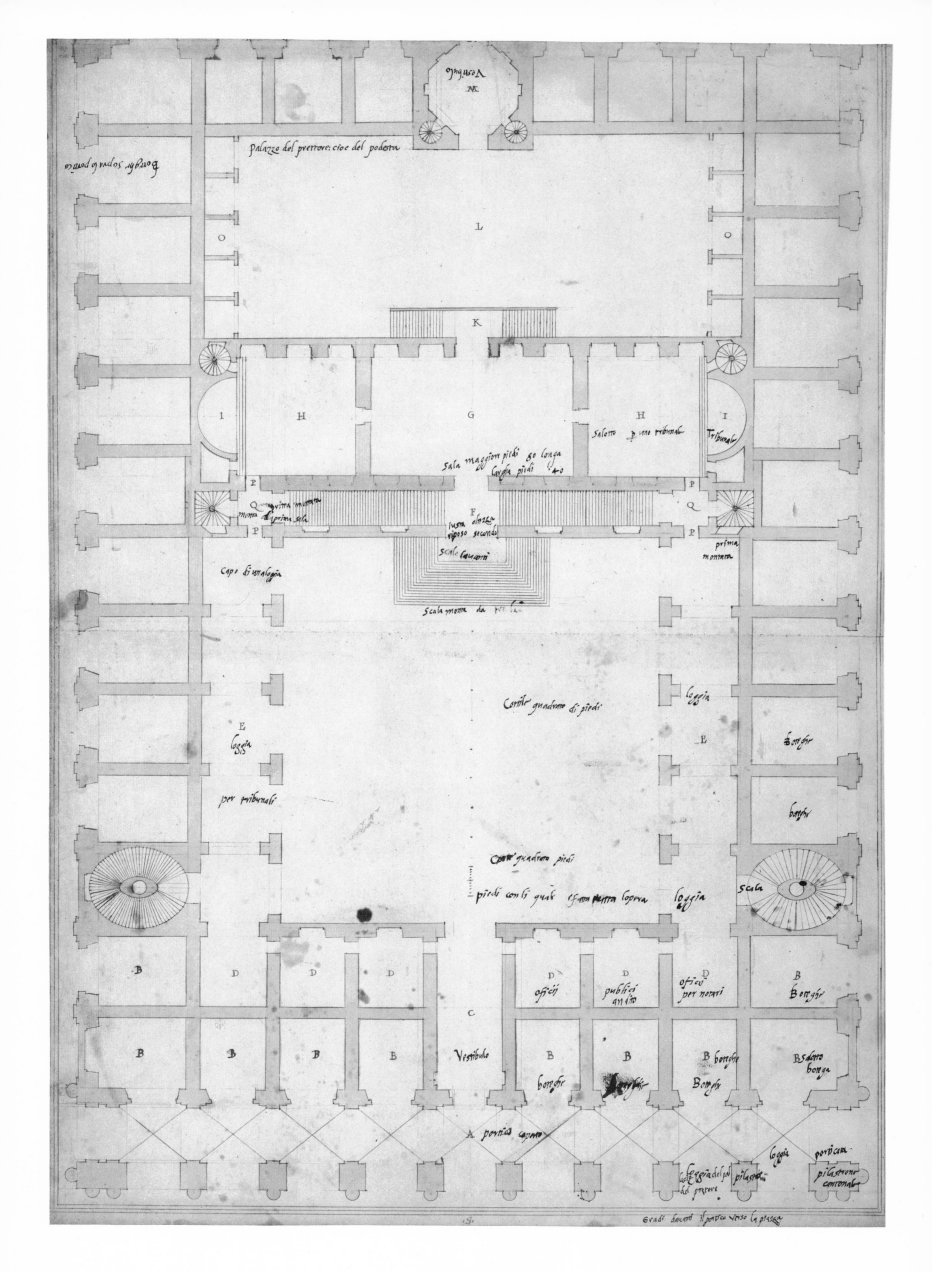

Palazzo del prettore: cioè del podestra

Sala maggior piedi 90 longa
Largia piedi 40

Salotto p uno tribunal

Tribunal

Cortile quadrino di piedi

loggia

loggia

boggh

boghi

oficii
publici
an tho
oficei
per notari

B

Botteghe

B

Vestibulo

borghi

Botteghe

Bottege

B botteghe

Bsotto
bottega

A portico caperto

loggia

porticu

pilastrone
coronal

Gradi davanti il portico verso la piazza

LXII

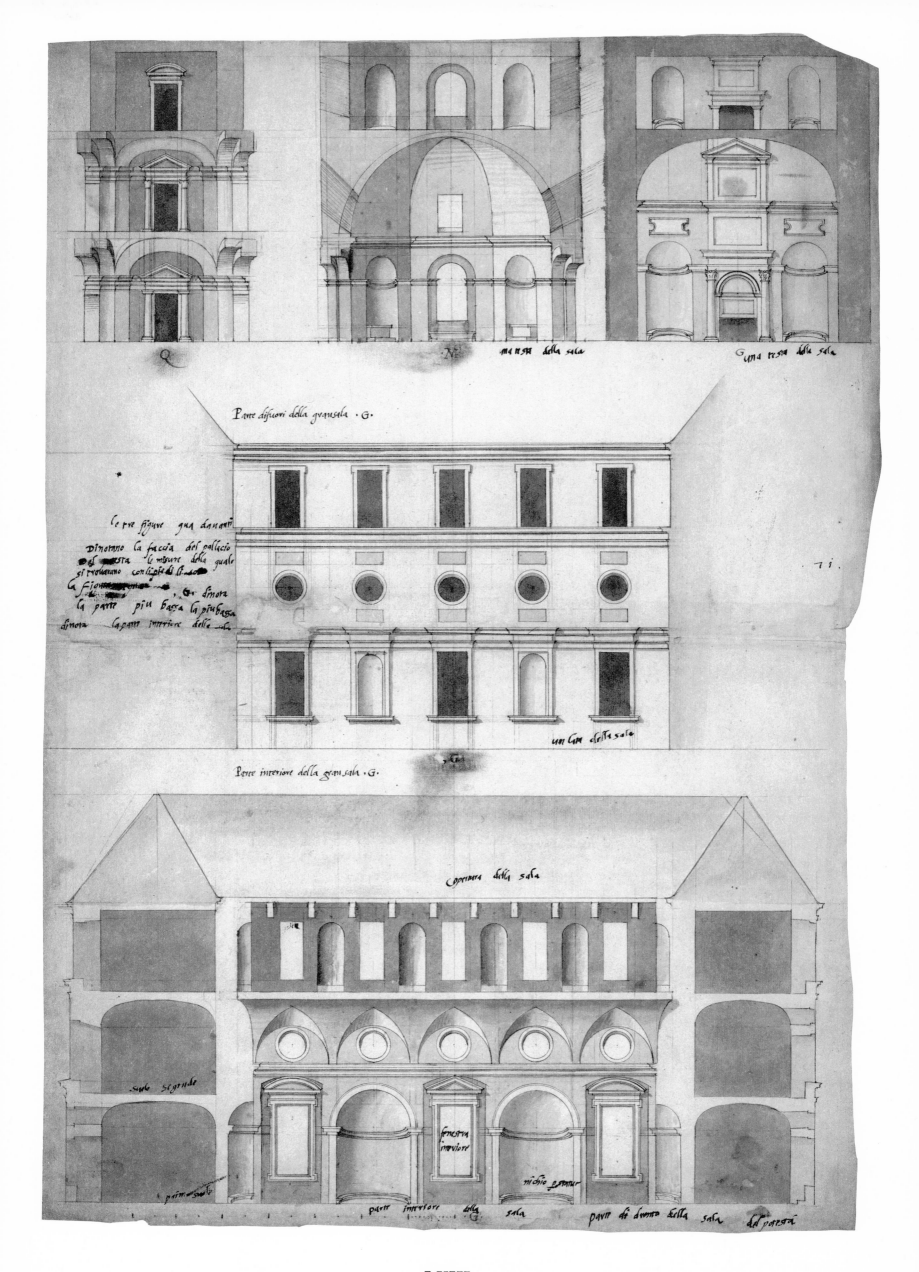

Q   N   mensa della sala   una testa della sala

Parte difuori della gransala · G.

le tre figure qua dananti
Dinotano la faccia del pallacio
et questa le misure della quale
si trouarano con li piedi di
la fiorentia   Et dinota
la parte piu bassa la piu bassa
dinota la parte interiore della sala

71

un fin della sala

Parte interiore della gransala · G.

Copertura della sala

sala seconda

fenestra
interiore

nichio p statue

pavn a terra   parte interiore della sala   pavn di dentro della sala
                                                                                              del portal

li diritti della passata pianta si veggono qui dauanti e prima parlaremo della parte dauanti che è qua piu basso, la latitudine degliarchi da l'un pilastro al altro sara piedi xviii la sua altezza sara piedi xxx. ma l'altezza delle volte del portico sara .iiii. piedi di piu che viea sotto l'archiraue et l'archiraue importara, il riempimento di essa volta, la grossezza de i pilastri sara piedi ix. e piedi .iiii. e mezzo sarano grosse le colonne et le dua pilastrate che rolgon su li archi sarano altro tanto e cosi le colonne sauan dupplicate su li angoli l'altezza del archiraue: fregio: et cornice sara piedi sei e tutta questa opera sara dorica: ma senza li trigliffi nel fregio per caua degli resalti che fan le cornice la latitudine della porta sara piedi xiii. et in altitudine xxviii. non dimeno il mezzo circolo non si aprira: ma dara luce al vestibulo: oltra la porta tutte le boteghe sarano a mezzade e di bona altezza; li archi supperiori e cosi li pilastri sarano come glialtri in latitudine ma in altitudine saran piedi xxxiii. ma lo suolo della sala sara sotto l'archiraue: et il parapetto di essa sara piedi .iiii. doue l'altezza di questa sala sara piedi xl. la grossezza delle colonne joniche sara la quarta parte menore di quelle da basso lo suo architraue: fregio et cornice sara altro piedi n., li muri di questa sala sarano tutti spaciosi accio li pretori vi possino mettere le loro memorie, ho voluto questo tetto farlo alla francese: per cagione delle lucarne che prestino piu presentia al edificio: per non esser che di dua ordini ~

La parte interiore si vede li nel mezzo, la lettera .F. dimora il piano della prima sala. le lettere .G. rappresenta la sala: cosi da basso come da altro, le lettere .H. sono le dua gran camere con li nichi pei tribunali e da basso et da altro, le lettere .P. son le porte delle prigioni che vengono ne i capi delle loggie .E. le lettere .Q. se intende il piano delli primi tribunali a canto del quale vi e vna limaca per andar di sopra: cosi alli tribunali: come sopra le loggie che savano terrazzo scopri et anche sopra loggie chi vora, le quali hauerano quella altezza: del portico dauanti, e dalli lati di esse loggie: sopra le boteghe sauanno officii: cio e dalli tribunali fin alla sala dauanti: ma cominciando drieto li tribunali fin alla parte di drieto sarano habitationi pel potesti et sua famiglia. le quali son segnate .R. e queste savano a mezzade per la grande altezza, li lochi segnati .B. son le boteghe con li suoi mezzadi, sotto li primi tribunali saran tutte prigioni le quali hauerano le sue finestre sul cortile di drieto: le misure del tutto si trouara con li piedi qua sotto, la parte qua sopra rappresenta la faccia di drieto la quale ha il medesimo ordine: et le medesime altezze di quella dauanti: et similmente seguira tal ordine all'intorno, la parte nel mezzo .N. viene a essere il torrone sotto del quale si passa alla parte di drieto: che sava pur strada nobile o vero piazzetta, la parte di questo torrone sopra il tetto sara corinthia: et sia diminuita dalla jonica la quarta parte: et cosi la parte di sopra che sara composita: ma senza capitelli per esser cosi alta: sava diminuita dalla corinthia la quartaparte: sopra la quale si mettera la tribuna di otto faccie, e questa torre sara per la campana dalla giusticia: et anche per dare al'armi alli bisogni e per gli incendij anchora, et di vora le particular misure di tutte le colonne et altri ornamenti le trouara nel quarto libra alli suoi lochi

Parte di driero della pianta passata

Faccia del pallaccio til piazza

Parte interiore della pianta passata

R
R
R

H

G

H

R
R

6.3

sopraleoger

B

Q B H

G G

F

parte sotteranei cioe camin

H

uolti sott sotto G

E Q

Capo di una loggia Botghi

P

P

parte interiori dalla corn   parte dauanti del pallaccio del pensa

Parte dauanti della passata pianta: sopra la piazza.

sala sopra   il portio   copra

Botte piedi con li quali e Botghe   dauanti   sopra la piazza   Botghi

LXIV

Oltra il palazzo, del potesta è necessario anchora quello del gouernatore: o presidente: o capitano: li quali aministrano
la giustitia piu violentemente: ne stano al sendicato come il potesta; onde tal fiata fano delle cose che prouocano
a una parte del populo a prender le armi: et afurore couere al palazzo: il quale se non e forte se impatronisseno
di esso: et anche de gouernatori a giorni miei sono stati uccisi: et chi fugiti, è però sel palazzo sara forte di
muua: et de difese: egli sicuramente si difensauano da glimpiti populari, questo palazzo adonca per mio auiso: sara
disposto nel modo che si vede qui dauanti, è primieramente la grossezza de i muri maestri non sara manco di piedi
.X. hauendo alli quatro angoli quei torroni con li suoi fianchi: oltra che sotto ciascuna fenestra vi sara una canoniera
per nettare la piazza, la porta sara nel mezzo e sporara in fuori piedi .XVI. sopra la quale sara una renghiera coperta
altri la dicono pogginole: et altri pergolo cosa molto necessaria à tal palazzo, questa porta non è molto leuata dal piano comu
le altre per cagione de i carri et uittuarie: et anche de i caualli: entro la quale si troua un vestibulo .A. hauendo dal destro: et
sinistro lato una tirata di loggiamenti, dipoi si troua un cortile circondato dalle loggie: lo diametro del quale è piedi .CC.X
nelli capi della prima loggia si trouano dua scale una da caualli segnata .C. è doue è .D. sara una porta che passando sotto essa
scala si va al torrone alle difese de i fianchi, dal altro capo di essa loggia si troua una scala alimaca: per la quale si passa allaltro
torrone, dalli lati del cortile sotto le loggie: nel mezzo si troua dua vestibuli: .E. .F. hauendo dalli lati: sala: camera: è rietro
camera, dal vestibulo .E. si monta piedi. a una sala .G. la quale ha dalli lati dua giardini, dal vestibulo .F. si monta à una
capella piedi .V. hauendo dalli lati dua giardini; ne i capi delle loggie sono dua scale da ritorni per montare ad alto, passando questo
primo cortile si troua una loggia ~~ne i capi~~ della quale ~~son dua guardi~~ nichi un vestibulo .G. dalli lati del quale sono dua
tirate di sale camere: e rietro camere: per ogni lato, andando piu auanti vi e una loggia .H. ne i capi della quale sono dua nic:
chi per li quali si passa a dua giardini alli lati de iquali son galerie segnate .I. le quali seruono à molti loggiamenti sopra li giardini;
andando piu auanti fuori della loggia .H. si troua una grancorte maggiore della prima. la quale è circondata da lioggiamenti
di soldati per la guardia del gouernatore: li quai loggiamenti haueuano da basso stalla per dua caualli: et di sopra loco per dua
soldati cioè dua per loggiamento: come si vede nelli dua primi segnati .K. oltra questa gran corte si troua un vestibulo .L.
da quale si va à una corte di tanta longitudine: quanto è largo il palazzo: interno la quale vi sono loggiamenti di soldati
dalli capi di questa corte sono dua gran stalle seppavate da tutti gli altri loggiamenti da i lati delle quali sono pozzi per beuerare
li caualli è queste sono segnate .M. jn questa pianta non vi ho discritte le particulari misure del tutto: per cio chio sarei stato
troppo prolisso, ma con li piedi che sono sotto la pianta, si trouera ogni cosa minutamente, è quantunque questo palazzo
jo habbia dedicato a gouernatori: egli potra non dimeno seruire agli principi tiranni: li quali di continuo viuono con spetto
mentre pero egli habbino una fortezza inespugnabile congiunta con le mura della citta: per poter fare risistenza contro
li suoi nemici piu potenti: doue che poi non mancano accordi honesti: non potendo risistere —

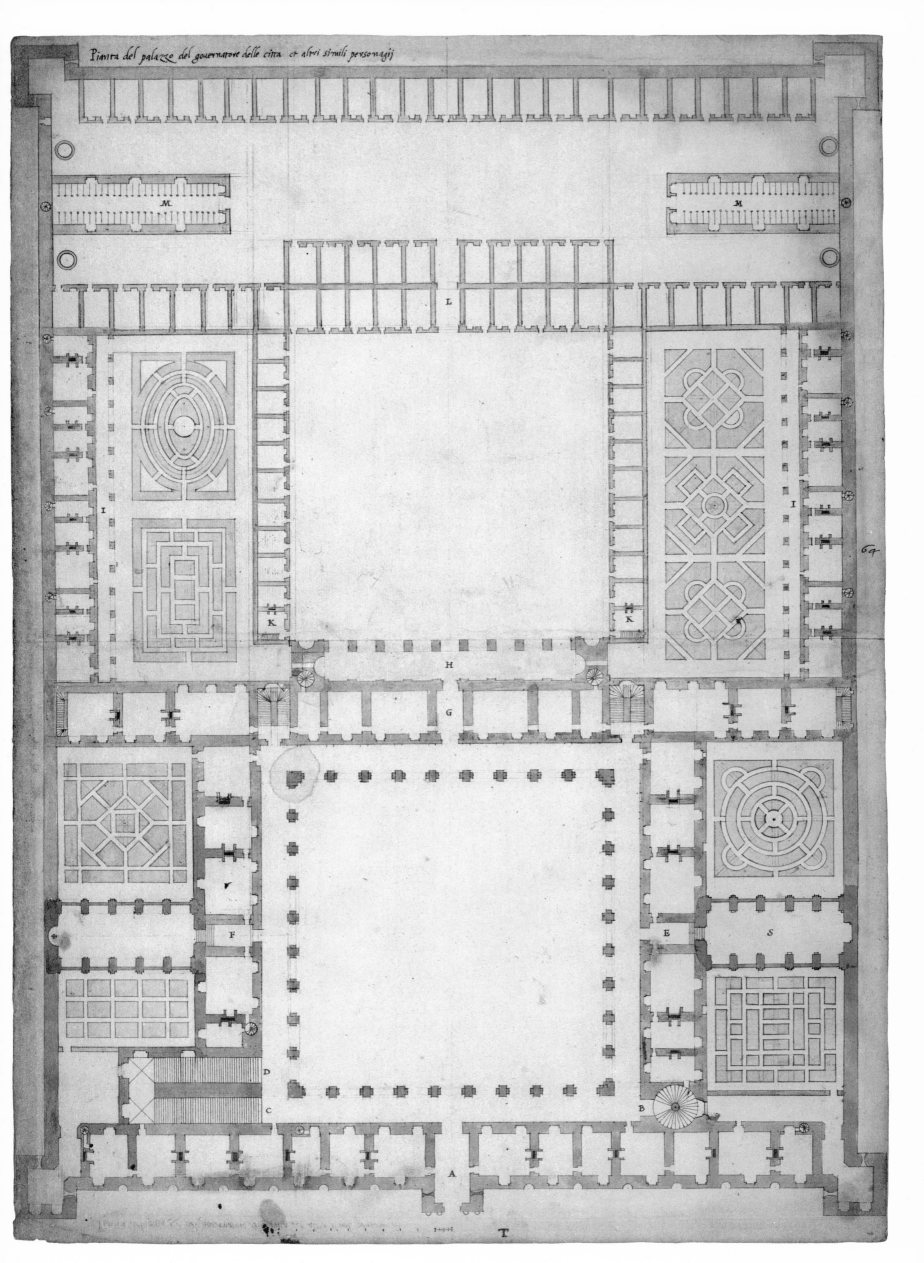

Pianta del palazzo del gouernatore delle citta et altri simili personagij

LXV

De la pianta passata questi qui auanti sono li diritti; la parte di sotto rappresenta vn pezzo della facciata da:
uanti. la parte di mezzo rustica la quale sporta in fuori piedi XVI. e' in latitudine piedi XXXXII l'apertura
della porta è piedi XII; et in altezza piedi XX. il rimanente da ciascun lato sara diuiso in parti X. dua parti sara cias:
cuna colonna: fra l'una et l'altra colonna sarai quarto parti la pilastrata della porta vna parte et l'angolo di fuori sara
l'altra parte, l'altezza delle colonne con le basi e capitelli sara piedi XXVI. e cosi sarano altri le habitationi terrene
cioè le sale: et le gran camere le camere picole et altri lochi si amezzano, e cosi la fascia sopra le colonne sara per il
riempimento del suolo. la latitudine delle fenestre sara piedi VII. e mezzo è la sua altezza piedi XV. il parapetto sopra la
fascia sara piedi IIII in altezza: ma nella grossezza del muro vi sarai dua gradi con li sedili per appoggirsi commodamente
l'altezza delle fenestre seconde sara piedi XVIII. et vn quarto: e dal pauimento fin sotto il suolo sara piedi XXIX.
che viene a essere sotto l'archirraue seconda. l'altezza del quale col fregio et la cornice sara VI piedi; la parte di mezzo
che è la renghiera le colonne posano sopra le inferior colonne: la sua grossezza è II piedi e mezzo: et la sua altezza è piedi
XVI. con le basi e capitelli; sopra le quali sara vno architraue: l'altezza sua sara vn piede e mezzo: il quale architraue
sosterà l'arco, e questi dua ordini sarano di opera Thoscana: il primo Thoscano rustico: il secondo Thoscano dilicato
le misure piu particulari di tutti li membri si trouarano nel principio del quarto libro, ma li ornamenti delle fenestre
a fronispitio sono di opera jonica la misura de iguali è nel medesimo libro al ordine jonico. l'altezza del terzo ordine nella
parte inferiore sara piedi XXIII. l'architraue fregio et cornice sara in altezza la quarta parte manco del secondo: e sopra
la prima renghiera sara vn'altra renghiera discoperta: come dimostra la cosa dissegnata e questa facciata hauera fra le
fenestre di spaciosi lochi per pittura la quale è grande ornamento agliedificii ma che sia fatta d'adotta mano et giudicioso huomo
la parte di mezzo di nota. le loggie intorno lo primo cortile; la grossezza di tutto vn pilastro è piedi X. partito in quatro parti, dua
sarano per la colonna di mezzo: et sara quadra: et vna parte sara ciascuna pilastrate: che sostiene l'arco l'apertura da vn pilastro
al altro sara piedi XIII. è la sua altezza piedi XXIII. l'altezza delle colonne sara piedi XXVI. e cosi sara alto la summitta
delle volte, sopra queste colonne non vi è architraue: ma vna fascia che serue di freggio: et di architraue: per mantenere
l'opera piu soda, la quale altezza è piedi VI. sopra di questa cornice vi sono colonne tonde, è ben che esse colonne dimostrano pos:
arsi sopra la proiettura della cornice elle posano sopra il sodo degliarchi: et le colonne quadre son tutte fuori del muro degliarchi sopra
le quali tornaria bone delle statue di bona grandezza. la grossezza delle colonne tonde è piedi dua e mezzo: et la sua altezza piedi
XIIII. sopra le quali sara vno architraue che sosterà l'arco: e questa sara vna loggia del'altezza che s'è detto del ordine
secondo, sopra li archi sara il medesimo architraue: fregio et cornice che s'è detto nel ordine di fuori, et medesimamente
la terza cornice, è questo ordine terzo sara pur loggia: ma fenestrata: nel modo che si vede, e degliornamenti delle fenestre
si trouarano le misure nel sopra detto libro: et anche nel terzo se ne trouarà in piu di vn loco
Le dua figure qua di sopra significano: la parte di fuori: et quella di dentro della sala segnata .S. questa segnata .A. è la parte
di fuori, la grossezza di pilastri è piedi VI. partiti in parti IIII. dua sarano per la colonna: et vna per lato delle pilastrate che sostien:
gono li archi, il piano di questa sala sara leuato piedi V. per piu magnificentia. l'altezza delle colonne che son ionice sara piedi XXIIII
l'altezza del apertura degliarchi è piedi XX. la sua larghezza sara piedi XIII. l'altezza de ipodii o parapetti che dir li vogliamo sara
piedi IIII. questi aperture sarano verriate accio che'l verno non sia fredda la sala: et l'state pe igran caldi si potrano
aprire, l'ordine secondo: et il terzo sono del altezza degli altri: et le medesime fenestre sarano intorno alli giardini per
dar luce alle stanze intorno a essi, l'altra parte segnata .B. è la parte interiore: con li medesimi ordini che sono di fuori.
ma questa sala per esser dedicata al negotiare, la quale sara sempre piena di persone è necessario che sia di bona altez:
za: e però in questo caso occuppara dua ordini et l'ordine terzo sara vna gran sala sopra essa: come si vede espresso
nel dissegno quelle fenestre quadrate sotto le lunette vengono a prendere il lume per tromba accordandosi con l'ordine di fuori
et il medesimo se intende della capella compagna a questa

T

Parte di fuori della sala . S.

Parte di dentro della sala . S.

·A·

·B·

Parte interiore del cortile principale

Vna parte della facciata dauanti del palazzo del gouernatore

T

LXVI

Faccia della porta

Fianco della porta

LXVIa

Ben che piu adietro jo habbia dimostrato alcune case le quali potrebbon servire a un principe: non dimeno jo ne dimostravo
vna la quale ogni gran principe sene poria contentare: et della quale qui davanti si vede la pianta, questa casa jo la intendo talmente situata: che la parte davanti sia levata dalla strada almeno piedi v. percio chio non intendo che per la porta davanti vi entrino cavalli ne carrette: ne altre cose simili; ma che dalli lati allincontro del ultimo cortile le entrate siano al piano
della strada: et quivi entrino carri: carrette: cavalli et altre simil cose. Parlando adonca della parte davanti la quale sara levata dalla strada piedi .v. primieramente si trovava vno vestibulo aperto: et assai spatioso: havendo dalla destra: et sinistra banda: sala:
anticamera: camera: rietro camera: e camerino) le quali habitationi savano per li forestieri nobili, depoi lo vestibulo si trova vno
atrio: o vogliam dire antiporta B questo si serva: ma nel vestibulo vi sta sempre la guardia: passando da ogni lato del atrio vi e saletta
et ne i capi della prima loggia sono dua ample scale: vna da cavalli: et laltra a scalini communi, quella da cavalli e segnara. C laquale
prende la sua luce dase stessa nel quadro in mezzo diessa: et li suoi parapetti sono abalausti accio sia piu luminosa: laltra scala D
prende il lume nel mezzo come laltra et e pur li suoi podij abalausti: ma dalla corte. X anchora prendera luce: ben che quella di mezzo sara
bastevole dalli lati del cortile alli cavalieri. E si trovano appartamenti dupplicati: vna parte prende la sua luce dal gran cortile: et laltra da
la picola corte: questi rai loggiamenti savano sanissimi: e di verno: et di state: per cio chel verno per cagion delle loggie savari diffensati dalle pioggie: et dalli venti: e la state il sole non vi penetrara: ne percio savano tenebrosi per laltezza delle volte: ne i capi di queste loggie dalle
bande vi sono dua scale a limaca: ma spatiose, passando il primo cortile si entra al vestibulo. F il quale ha dalli lati dua gran sale: dalle
quali si va a altri loggiamenti: ne i capi de quali da vno si trova vna capella. G da laltro si trova vna torre. H questa e per ritirarsi il principe per qualche suspetione: et avvertite che dove sono le. H. ivi e corte per dar luce, passando il vestibulo F si trova il segondo
cortile circondato da loggie: e ben chei non sia di perfetta quadratura: potra nondimeno esser ridotto atal perfetione, e questo ha dalli lati
loggiamenti dupplicati come il primo, passando questo si trova il vestibulo. I ma prima si trova nei capi delle loggie dua limache pu-
bbliche, dal destro: et sinistro lato del vestibulo: vi e sala: camera: et camerino: oltra che alargandosi piu si trovano dua corte vertonde con
quatro spatiose camere congiunte con esse. Sel principe si contentara di questi loggiamenti: facendo chel terzo cortile sia giardino: con loggiamenti
dalli lati: lo poria fare. Ma segli sara piu possente: et genevoso: passando il vestibulo. I si trovera il terzo cortile havendo dalli dua
lati le loggie con loggiamenti per officiali drieto alli quali savano dua cortili per li quali entrerano carri: carrette: et cavalli: et altre cose simili:
entro li quai cortili se ritirerano tutte le bagaglie accio chel terzo cortile sia sempre spatioso, nel capo di questo cortile si montara .vi. piedi
a vna capella. K la quale per essere il maggior membro di questo edificio potra servire a piu cose: prima per giesia: dove ogni grande esequi-
si poria fare: per vn consiglio grande: per conviti: triomphi e feste et cose simili: ben cheglie male honesto: non dimeno tutte le cose che
si fanno con honestate non dispezzando il loco: sono tolerabili al parer mio: dal destro: et sinistro lato di questa sala: vi sono dua transiti: cio e dua passagi segnati .L. per li quali si va al giardino, questi sono dua ridotti li quali peresser spatiosi savano per negotiare: vit-
tirandosi e dal sole: et dalla pioggia, alli lati di questi sono dua gransale: al servitio di ciascuna sono dua camere: ma essendo le sale di
bona grandezza: occuperano laltezza di dua camere: et cosi ogni sala haveva quatro camere al suo servitio, passando piu oltra si trovera
vn giardino: alli lati del quale savano dua andri serrati per spasseggiare il principe segretamente li quali digua si dicono galerie, questo
giardino sava di tanta longhezza: quanto al principe parera: in capo del quale jo ci farei la stalla con tutti li loggiamenti necessarii al mastro
di stalla: et alla sua famiglia, jo non ho parlato delle stue: de bagni: ne di fontane: et altre cose pertenente atanto edificio perche segondo
i lochi et commodita il prudente architetto vi trovara luoco: ne ho parlato delle misure: perche sarei stato troppo longo: ma li piedi sotto la pianta
davano tutte le misure minutamente: come anchora meglio si vedera nel diritto di alcune cose

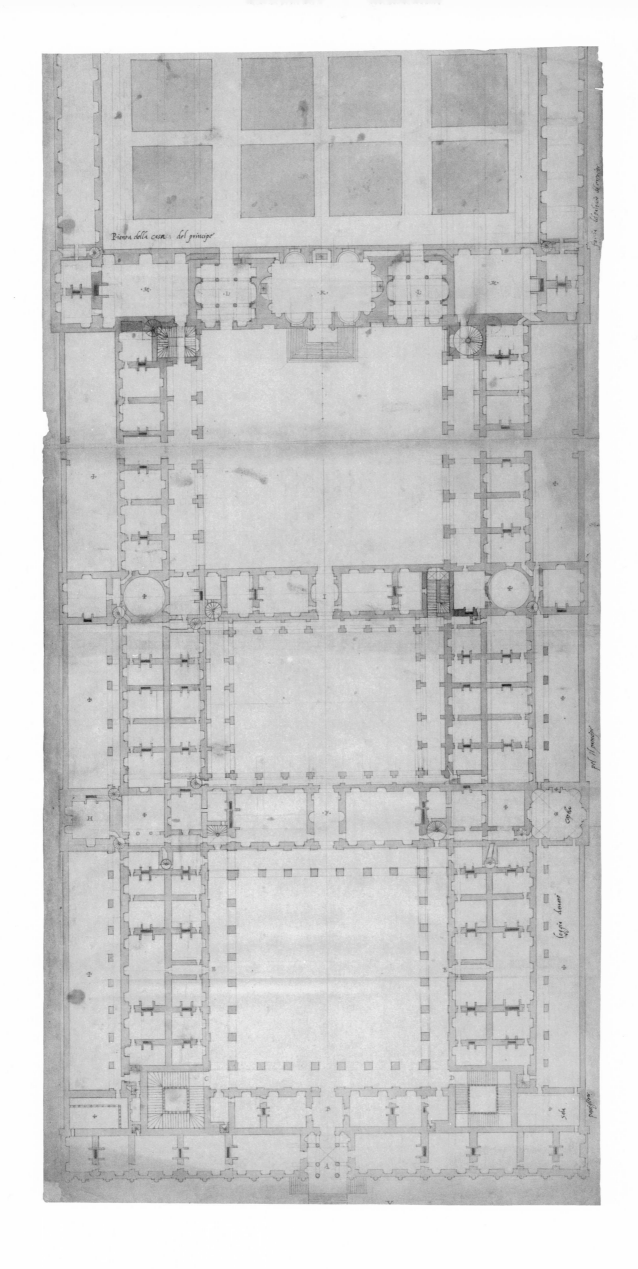

Pianta della casa del principe

LXVII

Di molte cose saria bene adimostrare idiritti: ma per esser cosa troppo longa: jo dimostrato quelle parti che ame pareva che siano piu dificile da intendere: e pero parendomi assai dificile in qualche parti et massimamente nei diritti quella gran sala: o giesia che dire lauogliamo. ho voluto dimostrarla in pianta: et di fuori: et di dentro insieme con li portici alei congiunti questa parte piu basso dimota la pianta traportata proportionalmente in misura maggiore della passata. la parte adonca segnata K. e in longitudine piedi LXXX. et in latitu-dine piedi XL. la grossezza de i muri e piedi XII. che cosi deue essere per sostenere la volta. a accio che detti muri non siano tanto materiali: vi sono li sei nicchi: e la porta et la fenestra. che leuano di molta materia: ne per cio si adebolisse la forza del muro: oltra li sei nicchi picoli, li portici o transiti che dir li vogliamo segnati L: sono di perfeto quadrato: il diametro de iguali e piedi XL. hauendo cias-cun di essi quatro finestre per dargli luce: oltra le porti, et anchora che li muri sono fortissimi a sostenere vna volta sola: senza altre colonne jo non dimeno ho voluto per piu ornamento metterci quatro colonne: atento che lloco e spatioso: ne sara impedito daquelle? sopra questi portici sarano dua saloti della medesima quadratura: dalli quali nella grossezza del muro per vna limaca si descendera alla detta sala: o capella: e questa sara via segreta per lo principe partendosi dalle sue habitationi: e questo e detto quanto alla pianta: hora segnamo alla parte di fuori:

la figura qui di mezo segnata K et L rappresenta la parte di fuori e della capella: et delli portici da runa croce al altra, la porta sopra la scala K. e l'entrata di essa capella: le dua fenestre dalli lati sono per dar luce a essa, et medesimamente la forma ouale sopra essa porta con lidua occhi sopra le finestre sono per la medesima luce; le porti segnate L. sono per li portici: et le fenestre dalli lati son per dar luce aquegli: la qual luce sara arronta per la concordantia di tutta lopera. la fenestra sopra la porta con le dua fenestre oblonghe: et lidua occhi con la forma ouale daranno la luce alla sala sopra esso portico: come si vedera nel di dentro qua di sopra, li dua nicchi tra le fenestre sono per ornamento: delli quali tutti ornamenti none do misura alcuna riportandomi al terzo et al quarto libro che di tal cose ne sono coppiosi: ben che pero delle misure sue si trauarano li termini con li piedi qui sotto

Questa parte di sopra dinota la interior parte: si della capella: come delli portici: ma parlando primieramente della capella: dico che per la latitudine: et longitudine sua: e ben ragione che la habbia la sua conueniente altezza: la quale con la summita della volta ua a si-mire sopra lultimo ordine ma non per cio impidisse cosa alcuna, hor diciamo di alcune misure piu necessarie: la larghezza de i nicchi sara piedi XV: et la sua altezza piedi XX: et cosi quei dalle teste: li nicchi picoli son larghi piedi VI. e in altezza piedi XV. le dua porticelle picole sotto essi: sono quelle che vengono dalla parte di sopra perla via segreta dalle stanze del principe, la latitudine della fenestra di mezo e piedi X. e in altezza piedi XXII e mezo, le fenestre dalli lati son larghe piedi VII e mezo: et altre XV. la forma ouale: li quatro occhi che son sopra la cornice: et anche li dua quadri sopra li nicchi sono tutti lumi: per dar luce alla capella: oueuo sala le dua figure dalli lati segnati L: sono la parte di dentro de i portici: le quali dimostrano come se hano auotrare sopra le quatro colonne la grossezza delle quali sara II piedi e tre quarti. et la sua altezza piedi XVI. e mezo. e queste per piu fortezza sarano Thoscane cioe di sei grossezze in altezza, e questo portico sara iluminato da quatro fenestre: ma la luce descendera perpendiculare: come si vede nella parte di fuori. sopra questi portichi sarano dua sale della medesima grandezza: iluminate nel modo che si dimostra: dalle quai sale si descendera per la grossezza del muro nella capella, quegli archi oscuri li quali sono nelle grossezze de i muri sono accio li detti muri non sien cosi materiali: et anche seruirano per qualche vie segrete: et per ocultarui molte cose alli tempi oportuni

Parte di dentro della gran sala del pricipe con li suoi povnchi d'canto

Parte di fuori della medesima sala: o capella: che si sia -

70.

Pianta de i diriti qua sopra dimostrati

K scala   Facciata del pallazzo Del prencipe

tribunale

L   sala del prencipe   locus tribundis

Vestibulo

sala davanti

Vestibulo

porta del pricipe   fenestra   porta   piedi conli quali e misurato iltutto   porta

fenestra   fenestra

per stafn

V

Le tre figure che si veggono qui dauanti son parte de i diritti della pianta passata, quella piu abasso segnata ·A· dinota vna parte della
faccia dauanti, e primieramente si monta al vestibulo da tre bande: vna per faccia: er dua per li lati; questo vestibulo come ho detto nel
la pianta non ha porta: ma è sostenuto da colonne ronde la grossezza delle quali e piedi ·III· et la sua altezza: con le basi: e' capitelli
è piedi ·XXV· è questa sara l'altezza de i primi appartamenti; lo intercolumnio di mezzo e piedi ·XII· e quei dalli lati son piedi ·VI· la latitudine
della porta è piedi ·X· et l'altitudine piedi ·XX· le altre colonne ronde sono li dua terzi fuori del muro, er son della grossezza delle altre
er le mezze colonne piane ciascuna è vn piede e mezzo er son di basso rilieuo fuori del muro, il spacio frà le colonne doue sono le fenestre, e
piedi ·XIX· la latitudine delle fenestre e piedi, et l'altitudine ·XII· le picole fenestre sopra esse tio detto altre volte la cagion per dir son fatte,
l'altezza del architraue: fregio: et cornice e piedi ·VI· dalla cornice fin sotto il secondo architraue sono piedi ·XIX· et cosi le colonne er le mezzecolonne
ioniche sarano diminuite la quarta parte in grossezza: et in altezza: et cosi sara diminuito l'architraue: fregio: et cornice; sopra la qual cornice sara
il piano del terzo suolo: sopra del quale sarano le fenestre: che di qua si dicono lucarne hauendo li suoi parapetti di ·III· piedi'in altezza, questi
terzi leggiamenti si guadagnano nel colmo del coperto al costume di franza il quale io non biasimo giamai si per la commodita come anchor
per la bellezza: che al parer mio quelle lucarne protano grande ornamento a gliedifici — ne mi fatichero molto in discriuere minutamente le
misure: per cio che li piedi li sono segnati supplitano al tutto) Questa parte segnata ·B· rappresenta lo profilo et la grossezza del muro: er come
si prendono li lumi, et massimamente le prime fenestre che anchora che siano dua nella parte di fuori: non dimeno nella parte di dentro sono
vna sola seruando il costume di qua: che le fenestre son fatte acroce: e pero si dicono croce

Questa parte disopra ·C· rappresenta vna parte del primo cortile, la grossezza de i pilastri e piedi ·VI· ma li angolari sono ·VII· e mezzo: fra l'un pilastro
al altro son piedi ·XV· l'altezza degli archi son piedi ·XXVI· e mezzo· l'architraue: fregio: et la cornice e' alto piedi ·IIII· è questa e opera rustica
accordata col Thoscano, l'altezza delle colonne ioniche e piedi ·XVIII· l'architraue: fregio: et cornice sara diminuito la quarta parte dal primo come quello della
facciata: et le lucarne sarano come quelle di fuori, et nella parte di sotto dinota come le habitationi sotterrane sono vna parte sopraterra
che è la ✠ al piano di terra: et da quella in giu sotto terra: le quali habitationi sarano buone: et habitabili: fuori che per dormire, ma per
molte commodita della casa seruirano, io ho voluto dimostrare queste fenestre alla franese per che nel vero io le truouo molto commode: a
rento che essendo cosi partite a croce si puo prendere e'piu luce: et men luce come l'huomo vole per cio che ogni quadro si serra appar
tacamente, non di meno si potra fare le dette fenestre a chi maniera si vora

La parte ·D· significa l'ordine del segondo cortile, e questo loggie da basso indubitamente sono fortissime: gli e il vero che non sono
molto spar…se per cagione di quei contraforti che vi sono nelli quali sono le porte che passano di l'una nell'altra, la fronte di tutto
il pilasto è piedi ·VI· et cosi la colonna piana è piedi ·III· et le pilastrate che sostengon li archi sono vn piede e mezzo, l'altezza: et larghez
za degli archi è come quella del primo cortile, et cosi le cornice anchora, si del primo ordine: come del segondo: et cosi le lucar
ne anchora: ben che piu larghe: et variate alquanto di ornamento, io non ho parlato delle misure particolari di tutti li ornamen
ti per cio che la scrittura saria troppo longa: et contro il mio costume che mi dispiace il ciançare ma di esser breue er ristretto
per cio che le figure et le misure notutare sotto esse parlano da sé con coloro che le sano guardare et considerare, e pero io lasso
molte cose per non esser prolisso a tento chel terzo: et il quarto libro publicato da me piu anni sono porra supplire a molti or
namenti li quali io non discriuo: ma accenno solamente alla inuentione ·~·   per chi l'intendera architetto intendera benissimo

Vna parte del primo cortile della casa del principe

Vna parte del segondo cortile della casa del principe

·D· faccia dela casa del prencipe

Vna parte della facciata della magiore del prencer
casa del principe

faccia del pallazo
del prencipe

B

A   faccia del palaccio   del prencipe   V

LXIX

faccia del pallazzo del prencipe

faccia del pallazzo del prencipe

LXX

La casa del Re deue essere sopra tutte le altre magnifica et grande: et richissima di ornamenti: et massimamente quella che hauesse aseruire al gran Re Francesco: l'ingegno: e l'animo: et il potere del quale si vedi in molti edificij da sua Ma.tà ordinati et in gran parte finiti: la casa adonca del Re dentro la citta deue hauere altra forma di quelle che fuori della citta: ho dimostrato: la quale deue essere su la piazza: et nel piu nobil loco della citta: la faccia della quale sara intorno a seicento piedi hauendo la sua entrata nel mezzo: et sopra il tutto sara leuata dalla planicie della piazza piedi v. doue si trouara vn vestibulo. A. questo sta sempre aperto: ne vi e porti che si serrino: ma vi sono le sbarre: et vi si tiene le guardie e di giorno: et di notte: questo vestibulo hauera da ciascun lato sala: camera et rietro camera: passando questo si troua l'atrio B. hauendo dal destro: et sinistro lato: anticamera: et camera: dipoi si troua la loggia C. dalli capi della quale sono due scale: vna da caualli: l'altra a scalini: et vi posi questa e segnata. D. la quale prende parte del lume dal cortile. + et sotto la quale si passa a vno appartamento il quale prende la luce dalla faccia dauanti: doue si troua sala: anticamera: camera: rietro camera: et camerino: et anchora: dal detto cortile si troua vna sala: dietro la quale sono due camere: et apresso: nel detto cortile in vno angolo per vna limaca si trouano due camere: et vn camerino: Dall'altro capo della loggia si troua la scale. E. commo da per caualli: et ha la sua luce da vn medesimo cortile: con le medesime habitationi del altro: Dalli lati delle loggie vi e vno vestibulo F. questo ha dalli lati camera: rietro camera et camerino: passando questo si troua vna loggia: che trauersando vno cortile si entra in vna sala. G. ne i capi della quale son due gran camere: et il medesimo e dall'altro lato: ne i capi di queste loggie sono dè sale. I. di forma ottogona: queste sono al proposito per le musiche: dal destro: et sinistro lato di queste loggie sono due medesimi cortili et auuertiti che doue sono le croci t'un sono cortili: nel mezzo della loggia in fronte: si troua il vestibulo. H. hauendo dal destro: et sinistro lato: vna camera: et vna rietro camera con vn camerino rotondo: passando piu auanti si troua vn cortile ottogono: con le loggie intorno: alli angoli del quale son quatro cortile exagoni per dar luce a alcuni luochi che altrimenti sarebbon tenebrosi: dalli lati di questo cortile si trouano due sale. K. hauendo dalle teste due camere: con due camerini: da queste sale si trauersa vn cortile sotto vna loggia nel capo della quale si troua vna sala. L. hauendo dalle teste camera: et rietro camera: da ciascun lato del cortile vi è vna saletta segnata. * la quale ha dalli lati camera: et camerino: ritornando alle loggie e passando piu auanti si troua li altri due cortili exagoni per li quali si passa a due capelle ottogone. M. queste prendeno la luce da due cortiletti: et anche dalli angoli di altri cortili maggiori per li angoli: passando il cortile ottogono: si troua il vestibulo. N. questo ha da ciascun lato camera: e rietro camera con due camerini: vno tondo: et l'altro in forma quale: da questo vestibulo si entra nel cortile rotondo: et ha le sue loggie intorno sostenute da colonne ronde: questo alli quatro angoli sono cortili rotondi: hauendo dalli lati le limache publiche: per che sono di bona grandezza: dal destro: et sinistro lato sono due vestiboli O. et hanno dalli lati camera: e rietro camera: dipoi si troua vn cortile: per la longhezza del quale sono loggie: et nella fronte sara il vestibulo. P. et ha dal destro: et sinistro lato saletta: camera: camerino: et contro: ritornando nel cortile: et passando piu oltra: si entra al vestibulo. Q. il quale ha dal destro et sinistro lato: saletta con camerino et studio et apresso: anticamera: camera et rietro camera: per li quai lochi si passa alli bagni cioè camera per spogliarsi. R. stua per sudare. S. bagno. T. e barberia. V. et questi lochi hanno vssita per cortile rei capi delle loggie: vscendo poi del vestibulo. Q. si entra nel giardino. X. et dalli lati sono due loggie. Y. dalli lati del giardino vi e vna tirata di appartamenti segnati. Z.: et all'incontro delle loggie. Y. viene sono due altre per compagnamento: nella fronte del giardino vi e vn mezzo circolo a modo di Theatro doue sono nichi per mettere statue: et cose simili: alli angoli di questo sono loggiamenti per li mastri di stalla: et dalli lati anchora sono due cortili per gouernare li caualli con altri loggiamenti per sopra detti et sua famiglia passando questo si troua due stalle di bonissima grandezza: dipoi le stalle vna gran praderia per maneggiar caualli: io non ho posto le misure in scrittura: ma col compasso misurando le cose coi piedi picoli sotto la pianta si trouera il tutto minutamente: —

Pianta del palazzo del Re

LXXI

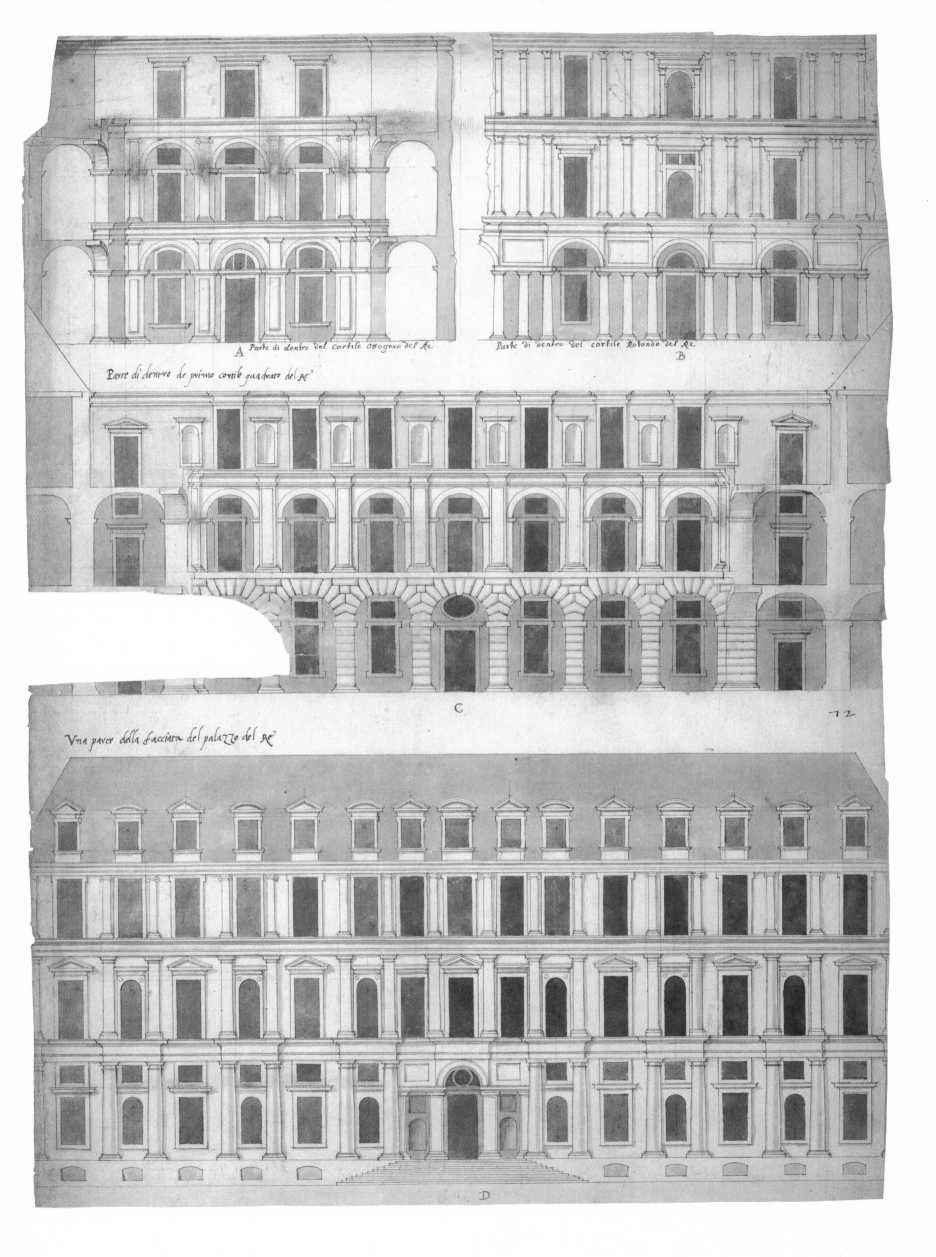

A Parte di dentro del Cortile Ottogono del Re

Parte di dentro del cortile Rotondo del Re B

Parte di dentro de primo cortile quadrato del Re

C

72

Vna parte della facciata del palazzo del Re

D

LXXII

LXXIII

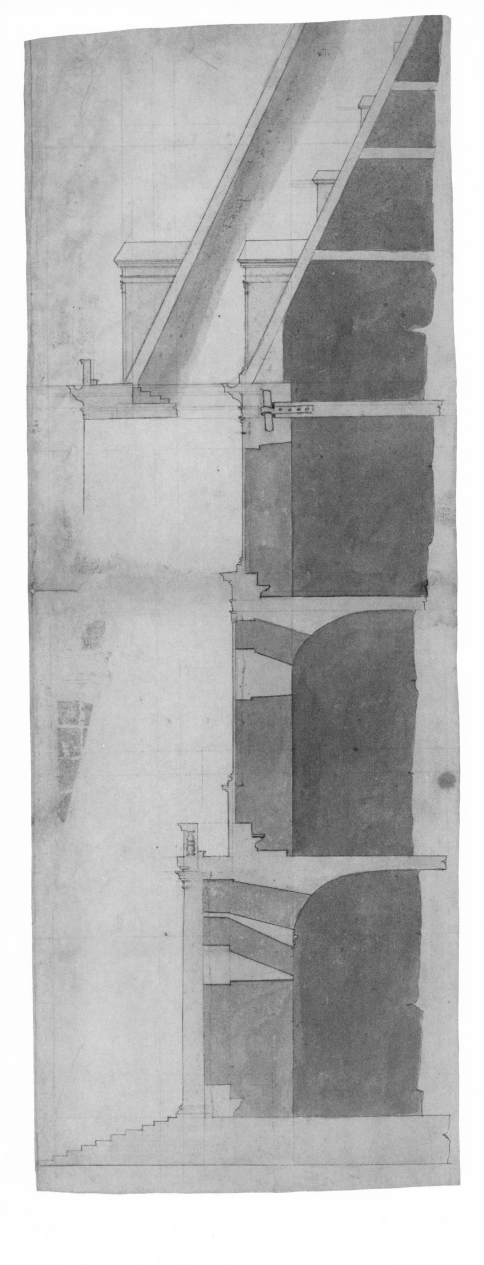

LXXIIIa

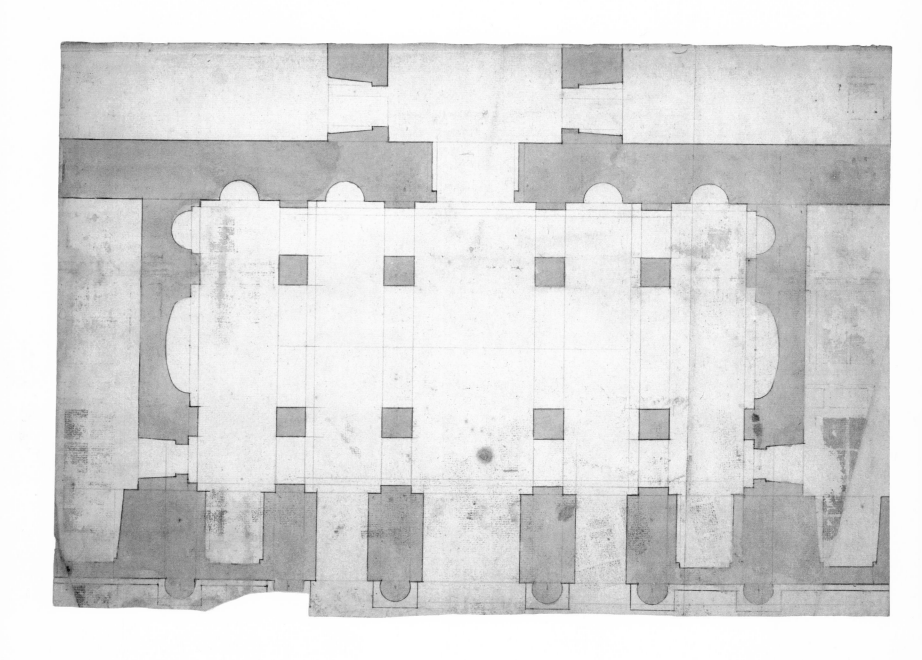

LXXIIIb